2009 | THE LITTLE GREEN DATA BOOK

THE WORLD BANK

ISBN: 978-0-8213-7849-6
E-ISBN: 978-0-8213-7851-9
DOI: 10.1596/978-0-8213-7849-6

The Little Green Data Book 2009 is a product of the
Development Data Group of the Development Economics Vice Presidency
and the Environment Department of the World Bank.

Editing, design, and layout by Communications Development Incorporated,
Washington, DC. Cover design by Peter Grundy Art & Design, London, U.K.

Contents

Acknowledgments

The Little Green Data Book 2009 is based on World Development Indicators 2009 and its accompanying CD-ROM. Defining, gathering, and disseminating international statistics is a collective effort of many people and organizations. The indicators presented in World Development Indicators are the fruit of decades of work at many levels, from the field workers who administer censuses and household surveys to the committees and working parties of the national and international statistical agencies that develop the nomenclature, classifications, and standards fundamental to the international statistical system. Nongovernmental organizations have also made important contributions. We are indebted to the World Development Indicators partners, as detailed in World Development Indicators 2009. The financial assistance of the Government of Sweden is also gratefully acknowledged.

The Little Green Data Book 2009 is the result of close collaboration between the staff of the Development Data Group of the Development Economics Vice Presidency and the Environment Department. Mehdi Akhlaghi, Perinaz Bhada, Kimberly Colopinto, Richard Fix, Kirk Hamilton, Jean-Jacques Helluin, Dan Hoornweg, Stephen Karam, Oceane Keou, Ali Louni, Saeed Ordoubadi, Beatriz Prieto-Oramas, Giovanni Ruta, and Alexandra Sears contributed to its preparation. Meta de Coquereaumont, Christopher Trott, and Elaine Wilson of Communications Development provided design, editing, and layout. Staff from External Affairs oversaw publication and distribution of the book.

Foreword

Welcome to *The Little Green Data Book 2009*. As in the 2008 edition, this year's edition includes a *Focus* section, four introductory pages that focus on a specific issue related to development and the environment. This year the focus is on urban areas and the environment, exploring how cities and climate change are affecting the way we live and how good public policies can improve prospects for future generations.

One of every two people in the world today lives in an urban area. By 2050 that number is expected to rise to 70 percent of the world's population, with urban areas home to some 7 billion people. These figures underscore how urbanization is increasingly shaping the world we live in, particularly in developing countries, where 90 percent of growth in urban areas is projected to take place over the next 20 years.

Urbanization and economic growth move in tandem. As emerging market economies develop, they increase their contribution to greenhouse gas emissions. The emissions of developed and developing country economies together increase the vulnerability of cities to climate change. Cities are particularly vulnerable to climate change impacts because they concentrate people, infrastructure, and economic activity. But good public policies can reduce greenhouse gas emissions and other pollutants while minimizing the impacts from climate change.

The Little Green Data Book 2009 is a collaboration between the Development Data Group of the Development Economics Vice Presidency and the Environment Department of the World Bank. We welcome your suggestions on how to improve future editions and make them more useful.

Shaida Badiee   James Warren Evans
Director   Director
Development Data Group   Environment Department

Focus: urbanization

Economic growth, urbanization, and greenhouse gas emissions

Economic growth and urbanization move in tandem. Because most economic activity is concentrated in urban areas, cities have a key role in climate change. Affluence and lifestyle choices determine greenhouse gases emissions, and historically, developed countries have had greater greenhouse gas emissions than developing countries. The world is urbanizing fast; 70 percent of the world's population will live in cities by 2050. Under the business-as-usual scenario greenhouse gas emissions will also increase significantly.

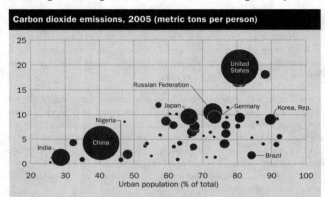

Carbon dioxide emissions, 2005 (metric tons per person)

Note: Bubble size corresponds to total carbon dioxide emissions (kilotons).
Source: *World Development Indicators* data files.

Cities consume the vast majority of the world's energy

Cities meet approximately 72 percent of their energy demand from coal, oil, and natural gas, the main contributors to greenhouse gas emissions. Cities also use about 70 percent of the energy from renewable sources; however, these sources still make up just a small share of total energy consumed. National governments and cities have choices regarding their energy mix, and public policies can play an important role in improving energy efficiency and reducing carbon dioxide emissions.

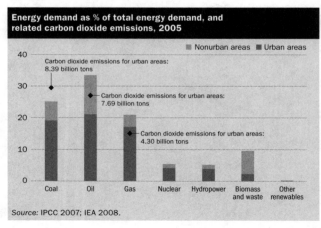

Energy demand as % of total energy demand, and related carbon dioxide emissions, 2005

Source: IPCC 2007; IEA 2008.

Coastal cities are vulnerable to sea level rise

Cities are vulnerable to the impacts of climate change. Some 360 million urban inhabitants live in low-elevation coastal zones, exposing them to sea level rise and storm surges. The Intergovernmental Panel on Climate Change estimates that average sea level rose 0.17 meter in the 20th century and predicts a 1 meter rise over the next 100 years linked to climate change.

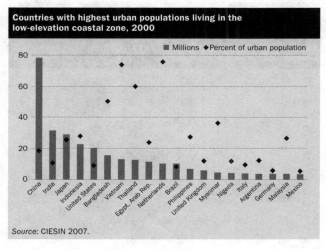

Countries with highest urban populations living in the low-elevation coastal zone, 2000

■ Millions ◆ Percent of urban population

Source: CIESIN 2007.

Infrastructure investments in urban areas

Urban areas, because of their density, offer mass-targeting options that provide access to water, sanitation, and solid waste management more cost-efficiently than rural areas can. Infrastructure investments can thus be cost effective in targeting beneficiaries. Latin America and the Caribbean and Eastern and Central Asia, with the highest urbanization rates, have greater access to sanitation services; South Asia and Sub-Saharan Africa, with the lowest urbanization rates, have the least access.

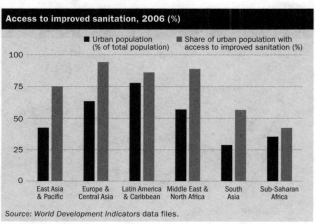

Access to improved sanitation, 2006 (%)

■ Urban population (% of total population)   ■ Share of urban population with access to improved sanitation (%)

Source: World Development Indicators data files.

Focus: urbanization

Policies matter

Policies to reduce greenhouse gas emissions can have a major impact. During the last 40 years Germany and Sweden adopted policies that have dramatically decreased per capita carbon dioxide emissions. As China and India urbanize and absorb an increasing share of global manufacturing, their carbon dioxide emissions will increase. Though their per capita carbon dioxide emission levels will be lower than those in developed countries, going forward, China and India will benefit from the experience of countries like Germany and Sweden.

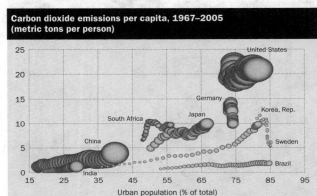

Carbon dioxide emissions per capita, 1967–2005 (metric tons per person)

Note: Bubble size corresponds to total carbon dioxide emissions (kilotons).
Source: *World Development Indicators* data files.

Compact cities tend to use less energy

Compact cities tend to be more sustainable than sprawling cities. Urban form can be important in determining land and energy use and the cost of infrastructure and municipal services. Denser cities use less energy for transportation, which lowers transport-related emissions, can provide access to services at lower cost, and implement more energy efficiency measures.

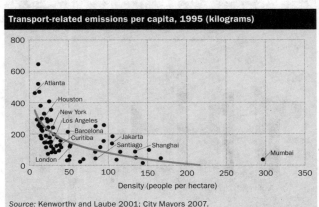

Transport-related emissions per capita, 1995 (kilograms)

Source: Kenworthy and Laube 2001; City Mayors 2007.

Choice of transport modes affects energy use

Countries favoring private transport use more energy per passenger kilometer than countries with high levels of public and nonmotorized transport modes. As density increases, people tend to use more public transportation and nonmotorized forms of transport, lowering transportation energy use per capita. High energy use per capita in the United States and Western Europe can be explained by high incomes; in Middle Eastern countries, by fuel subsidies.

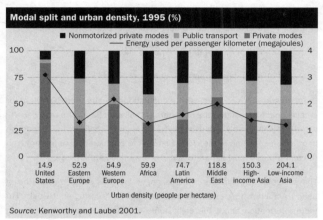

Modal split and urban density, 1995 (%)

■ Nonmotorized private modes ■ Public transport ■ Private modes
— Energy used per passenger kilometer (megajoules)

Urban density (people per hectare)

| 14.9 United States | 52.9 Eastern Europe | 54.9 Western Europe | 59.9 Africa | 74.7 Latin America | 118.8 Middle East | 150.3 High-income Asia | 204.1 Low-income Asia |

Source: Kenworthy and Laube 2001.

Improvements in air quality

Concentrations of PM10 (particulate matter 10 microns in diameter), a standard used to measure air quality, decreased significantly in all regions in 1990–2005, with the most pronounced drops in developing countries. This may be a result of multiple factors, such as policies to improve air quality standards in urban areas (through incentives to switch from diesel to compressed natural gas), fuel and vehicle quality improvements, and greater awareness of the impacts of air pollution on public health.

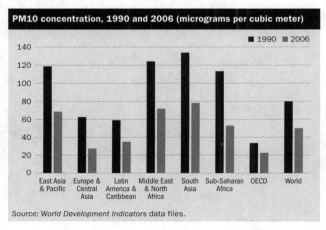

PM10 concentration, 1990 and 2006 (micrograms per cubic meter)

■ 1990 ■ 2006

East Asia & Pacific · Europe & Central Asia · Latin America & Caribbean · Middle East & North Africa · South Asia · Sub-Saharan Africa · OECD · World

Source: World Development Indicators data files.

Data notes

The data in this book are for the most recent year available; for details, see the *Glossary*. Regional aggregates include data for low- and middle-income economies only. Aggregates for regions and income groups are shown only if data are available for 66 percent of the economies in that group.

Symbols used:

0 or 0.0   indicates zero or small enough that the number rounds to zero at the displayed number of decimal places.

..   indicates that data are not available.

$ indicates current U.S. dollars.

Data are shown for economies with populations greater than 30,000 or for smaller economies if they are members of the World Bank. The word *country* (used interchangeably with *economy*) does not imply political independence or official recognition by the World Bank but refers to any economy for which the authorities report separate social or economic statistics.

The selection of indicators in these pages includes some that are being used to monitor progress toward the Millennium Development Goals. For more information about the eight goals—halving poverty and increasing well-being by 2015—please visit our Web site www.developmentgoals.org or see *World Development Indicators 2009*.

Regional tables

The country composition of regions is based on the World Bank's analytical regions and may differ from common geographic usage.

East Asia and Pacific

American Samoa, Cambodia, China, Fiji, Indonesia, Kiribati, Democratic Republic of Korea, Lao People's Democratic Republic, Malaysia, Marshall Islands, Federated States of Micronesia, Mongolia, Myanmar, Palau, Papua New Guinea, Philippines, Samoa, Solomon Islands, Thailand, Timor-Leste, Tonga, Vanuatu, Vietnam.

Europe and Central Asia

Albania, Armenia, Azerbaijan, Belarus, Bosnia and Herzegovina, Bulgaria, Croatia, Georgia, Kazakhstan, Kyrgyz Republic, Latvia, Lithuania, Former Yugoslav Republic of Macedonia, Moldova, Montenegro, Poland, Romania, Russian Federation, Serbia, Tajikistan, Turkey, Turkmenistan, Ukraine, Uzbekistan.

Latin America and the Caribbean

Argentina, Belize, Bolivia, Brazil, Chile, Colombia, Costa Rica, Cuba, Dominica, Dominican Republic, Ecuador, El Salvador, Grenada, Guatemala, Guyana, Haiti, Honduras, Jamaica, Mexico, Nicaragua, Panama, Paraguay, Peru, St. Kitts and Nevis, St. Lucia, St. Vincent and the Grenadines, Suriname, Uruguay, Bolivarian Republic of Venezuela.

Middle East and North Africa

Algeria, Djibouti, Arab Republic of Egypt, Islamic Republic of Iran, Iraq, Jordan, Lebanon, Libya, Morocco, Syrian Arab Republic, Tunisia, West Bank and Gaza, Republic of Yemen.

South Asia

Afghanistan, Bangladesh, Bhutan, India, Maldives, Nepal, Pakistan, Sri Lanka.

Sub-Saharan Africa

Angola, Benin, Botswana, Burkina Faso, Burundi, Cameroon, Cape Verde, Central African Republic, Chad, Comoros, Democratic Republic of the Congo, Republic of Congo, Côte d'Ivoire, Eritrea, Ethiopia, Gabon, The Gambia, Ghana, Guinea, Guinea-Bissau, Kenya, Lesotho, Liberia, Madagascar, Malawi, Mali, Mauritania, Mauritius, Mayotte, Mozambique, Namibia, Niger, Nigeria, Rwanda, São Tomé and Principe, Senegal, Seychelles, Sierra Leone, Somalia, South Africa, Sudan, Swaziland, Tanzania, Togo, Uganda, Zambia, Zimbabwe.

World

Population (millions) **6,610** Land area (1,000 sq. km) **129,645** GDP ($ billions) **54,583.8**

GNI per capita, *World Bank Atlas* method ($)	7,995
Urban population (% of total)	50
Urban population growth (average annual %, 1990–2007)	2.2
Population growth (average annual %, 1990–2007)	1.3

Agriculture
Agricultural land (% of land area)	38
Agricultural productivity (value added per worker, 2000 $)	939
Food production index (1999–2001 = 100)	111
Population density, rural (people/sq. km of arable land)	496

Forests and biodiversity
Forest area (% of land area)	30.4
Deforestation (average annual %, 1990–2005)	0.2
Nationally protected area (% of land area)	11.0
Animal species, total known	
Animal species, threatened	
Higher plant species, total known	
Higher plant species, threatened	
GEF benefits index for biodiversity (0–100, median is 1.5)	

Energy
GDP per unit of energy use (2005 PPP $/kg oil equivalent)	5.2
Energy use per capita (kg oil equivalent)	1,820
Energy from biomass products and waste (% of total)	9.8
Electric power consumption per capita (kWh)	2,751
Electricity generated using fossil fuel (% of total)	66.4
Electricity generated by hydropower (% of total)	15.9

Emissions and pollution
CO_2 emissions per unit of GDP (kg/2005 PPP $)	0.5
CO_2 emissions per capita (metric tons)	4.5
CO_2 emissions growth (%, 1990–2005)	29.5
Particulate matter (urban-pop.-weighted avg., µg/cu. m)	50
Transport sector fuel consumption per capita (liters)	291

Water and sanitation
Internal freshwater resources per capita (cu. m)	6,624
Freshwater withdrawal	
Total (% of internal resources)	9.0
Agriculture (% of total freshwater withdrawal)	70
Access to improved water source (% of total population)	86
Rural (% of rural population)	77
Urban (% of urban population)	96
Access to improved sanitation (% of total population)	60
Rural (% of rural population)	44
Urban (% of urban population)	78

Environment and health
Acute resp. infection prevalence (% of children under five)	
Diarrhea prevalence (% of children under five)	
Under-five mortality rate (per 1,000 live births)	68

National accounting aggregates
Gross savings (% of GNI)	22.7
Consumption of fixed capital (% of GNI)	13.7
Education expenditure (% of GNI)	4.3
Energy depletion (% of GNI)	3.0
Mineral depletion (% of GNI)	0.4
Net forest depletion (% of GNI)	0.0
CO_2 damage (% of GNI)	0.4
Particulate emission damage (% of GNI)	0.4
Adjusted net savings (% of GNI)	8.8

East Asia & Pacific

Population (millions) **1,912** Land area (1,000 sq. km) **15,871** GDP ($ billions) **4,365.5**

GNI per capita, *World Bank Atlas* method ($)	2,182
Urban population (% of total)	43
Urban population growth (average annual %, 1990–2007)	3.5
Population growth (average annual %, 1990–2007)	1.1

Agriculture

Agricultural land (% of land area)	51
Agricultural productivity (value added per worker, 2000 $)	458
Food production index (1999–2001 = 100)	120
Population density, rural (people/sq. km of arable land)	547

Forests and biodiversity

Forest area (% of land area)	28.4
Deforestation (average annual %, 1990–2005)	–0.1
Nationally protected area (% of land area)	14.0
Animal species, total known	
Animal species, threatened	
Higher plant species, total known	
Higher plant species, threatened	
GEF benefits index for biodiversity (0–100, median is 1.5)	

Energy

GDP per unit of energy use (2005 PPP $/kg oil equivalent)	3.4
Energy use per capita (kg oil equivalent)	1,258
Energy from biomass products and waste (% of total)	14.7
Electric power consumption per capita (kWh)	1,669
Electricity generated using fossil fuel (% of total)	82.0
Electricity generated by hydropower (% of total)	15.0

Emissions and pollution

CO_2 emissions per unit of GDP (kg/2005 PPP $)	0.9
CO_2 emissions per capita (metric tons)	3.6
CO_2 emissions growth (%, 1990–2005)	123.4
Particulate matter (urban-pop.-weighted avg., µg/cu. m)	69
Transport sector fuel consumption per capita (liters)	106

Water and sanitation

Internal freshwater resources per capita (cu. m)	4,948
Freshwater withdrawal	
Total (% of internal resources)	10.2
Agriculture (% of total freshwater withdrawal)	74
Access to improved water source (% of total population)	87
Rural (% of rural population)	81
Urban (% of urban population)	96
Access to improved sanitation (% of total population)	66
Rural (% of rural population)	59
Urban (% of urban population)	75

Environment and health

Acute resp. infection prevalence (% of children under five)	
Diarrhea prevalence (% of children under five)	
Under-five mortality rate (per 1,000 live births)	27

National accounting aggregates

Gross savings (% of GNI)	48.0
Consumption of fixed capital (% of GNI)	10.7
Education expenditure (% of GNI)	2.1
Energy depletion (% of GNI)	4.9
Mineral depletion (% of GNI)	1.3
Net forest depletion (% of GNI)	0.0
CO_2 damage (% of GNI)	1.3
Particulate emission damage (% of GNI)	1.3
Adjusted net savings (% of GNI)	30.6

Europe & Central Asia

Population (millions) **446** Land area (1,000 sq. km) **23,110** GDP ($ billions) **3,156.1**

GNI per capita, *World Bank Atlas* method ($)	6,052
Urban population (% of total)	64
Urban population growth (average annual %, 1990–2007)	0.2
Population growth (average annual %, 1990–2007)	0.1

Agriculture

Agricultural land (% of land area)	28
Agricultural productivity (value added per worker, 2000 $)	2,228
Food production index (1999–2001 = 100)	110
Population density, rural (people/sq. km of arable land)	129

Forests and biodiversity

Forest area (% of land area)	38.3
Deforestation (average annual %, 1990–2005)	0.0
Nationally protected area (% of land area)	6.1
Animal species, total known	
Animal species, threatened	
Higher plant species, total known	
Higher plant species, threatened	
GEF benefits index for biodiversity (0–100, median is 1.5)	

Energy

GDP per unit of energy use (2005 PPP $/kg oil equivalent)	3.5
Energy use per capita (kg oil equivalent)	2,930
Energy from biomass products and waste (% of total)	2.2
Electric power consumption per capita (kWh)	3,835
Electricity generated using fossil fuel (% of total)	67.7
Electricity generated by hydropower (% of total)	17.4

Emissions and pollution

CO_2 emissions per unit of GDP (kg/2005 PPP $)	0.7
CO_2 emissions per capita (metric tons)	7.0
CO_2 emissions growth (%, 1990–2005)	−29.3
Particulate matter (urban-pop.-weighted avg., μg/cu. m)	27
Transport sector fuel consumption per capita (liters)	255

Water and sanitation

Internal freshwater resources per capita (cu. m)	11,806
Freshwater withdrawal	
Total (% of internal resources)	7.2
Agriculture (% of total freshwater withdrawal)	60
Access to improved water source (% of total population)	95
Rural (% of rural population)	88
Urban (% of urban population)	99
Access to improved sanitation (% of total population)	89
Rural (% of rural population)	79
Urban (% of urban population)	94

Environment and health

Acute resp. infection prevalence (% of children under five)	
Diarrhea prevalence (% of children under five)	
Under-five mortality rate (per 1,000 live births)	23

National accounting aggregates

Gross savings (% of GNI)	24.0
Consumption of fixed capital (% of GNI)	12.8
Education expenditure (% of GNI)	4.0
Energy depletion (% of GNI)	9.8
Mineral depletion (% of GNI)	0.7
Net forest depletion (% of GNI)	0.0
CO_2 damage (% of GNI)	1.0
Particulate emission damage (% of GNI)	0.5
Adjusted net savings (% of GNI)	3.2

Latin America & Caribbean

Population (millions)	**561**	Land area (1,000 sq. km)	**20,156**	GDP ($ billions)	**3,615.9**

GNI per capita, *World Bank Atlas* method ($)	5,801
Urban population (% of total)	78
Urban population growth (average annual %, 1990–2007)	2.1
Population growth (average annual %, 1990–2007)	1.5

Agriculture

Agricultural land (% of land area)	36
Agricultural productivity (value added per worker, 2000 $)	3,158
Food production index (1999–2001 = 100)	117
Population density, rural (people/sq. km of arable land)	232

Forests and biodiversity

Forest area (% of land area)	45.4
Deforestation (average annual %, 1990–2005)	0.5
Nationally protected area (% of land area)	16.7
Animal species, total known	
Animal species, threatened	
Higher plant species, total known	
Higher plant species, threatened	
GEF benefits index for biodiversity (0–100, median is 1.5)	

Energy

GDP per unit of energy use (2005 PPP $/kg oil equivalent)	7.3
Energy use per capita (kg oil equivalent)	1,240
Energy from biomass products and waste (% of total)	15.9
Electric power consumption per capita (kWh)	1,808
Electricity generated using fossil fuel (% of total)	37.0
Electricity generated by hydropower (% of total)	57.3

Emissions and pollution

CO_2 emissions per unit of GDP (kg/2005 PPP $)	0.3
CO_2 emissions per capita (metric tons)	2.5
CO_2 emissions growth (%, 1990–2005)	33.4
Particulate matter (urban-pop.-weighted avg., µg/cu. m)	35
Transport sector fuel consumption per capita (liters)	295

Water and sanitation

Internal freshwater resources per capita (cu. m)	23,965
Freshwater withdrawal	
Total (% of internal resources)	2.0
Agriculture (% of total freshwater withdrawal)	71
Access to improved water source (% of total population)	91
Rural (% of rural population)	73
Urban (% of urban population)	97
Access to improved sanitation (% of total population)	78
Rural (% of rural population)	51
Urban (% of urban population)	86

Environment and health

Acute resp. infection prevalence (% of children under five)	
Diarrhea prevalence (% of children under five)	
Under-five mortality rate (per 1,000 live births)	26

National accounting aggregates

Gross savings (% of GNI)	22.9
Consumption of fixed capital (% of GNI)	12.6
Education expenditure (% of GNI)	4.5
Energy depletion (% of GNI)	5.4
Mineral depletion (% of GNI)	1.9
Net forest depletion (% of GNI)	0.0
CO_2 damage (% of GNI)	0.3
Particulate emission damage (% of GNI)	0.4
Adjusted net savings (% of GNI)	6.7

Middle East & North Africa

Population (millions) **313** Land area (1,000 sq. km) **8,644** GDP ($ billions) **850.2**

GNI per capita, *World Bank Atlas* method ($)	2,820
Urban population (% of total)	57
Urban population growth (average annual %, 1990–2007)	2.6
Population growth (average annual %, 1990–2007)	2.0

Agriculture

Agricultural land (% of land area)	22
Agricultural productivity (value added per worker, 2000 $)	2,313
Food production index (1999–2001 = 100)	116
Population density, rural (people/sq. km of arable land)	665

Forests and biodiversity

Forest area (% of land area)	2.4
Deforestation (average annual %, 1990–2005)	–0.4
Nationally protected area (% of land area)	3.6
Animal species, total known	
Animal species, threatened	
Higher plant species, total known	
Higher plant species, threatened	
GEF benefits index for biodiversity (0–100, median is 1.5)	

Energy

GDP per unit of energy use (2005 PPP $/kg oil equivalent)	5.0
Energy use per capita (kg oil equivalent)	1,254
Energy from biomass products and waste (% of total)	1.2
Electric power consumption per capita (kWh)	1,418
Electricity generated using fossil fuel (% of total)	91.1
Electricity generated by hydropower (% of total)	7.4

Emissions and pollution

CO_2 emissions per unit of GDP (kg/2005 PPP $)	0.6
CO_2 emissions per capita (metric tons)	3.7
CO_2 emissions growth (%, 1990–2005)	96.8
Particulate matter (urban-pop.-weighted avg., µg/cu. m)	72
Transport sector fuel consumption per capita (liters)	277

Water and sanitation

Internal freshwater resources per capita (cu. m)	728
Freshwater withdrawal	
Total (% of internal resources)	122.3
Agriculture (% of total freshwater withdrawal)	86
Access to improved water source (% of total population)	89
Rural (% of rural population)	81
Urban (% of urban population)	95
Access to improved sanitation (% of total population)	77
Rural (% of rural population)	62
Urban (% of urban population)	88

Environment and health

Acute resp. infection prevalence (% of children under five)	
Diarrhea prevalence (% of children under five)	
Under-five mortality rate (per 1,000 live births)	38

National accounting aggregates

Gross savings (% of GNI)	33.3
Consumption of fixed capital (% of GNI)	11.3
Education expenditure (% of GNI)	4.7
Energy depletion (% of GNI)	21.3
Mineral depletion (% of GNI)	0.4
Net forest depletion (% of GNI)	0.0
CO_2 damage (% of GNI)	1.0
Particulate emission damage (% of GNI)	0.6
Adjusted net savings (% of GNI)	3.4

South Asia

Population (millions) **1,522** Land area (1,000 sq. km) **4,781** GDP ($ billions) **1,443.5**

GNI per capita, *World Bank Atlas* method ($)	880
Urban population (% of total)	29
Urban population growth (average annual %, 1990–2007)	2.7
Population growth (average annual %, 1990–2007)	1.8

Agriculture

Agricultural land (% of land area)	55
Agricultural productivity (value added per worker, 2000 $)	417
Food production index (1999–2001 = 100)	107
Population density, rural (people/sq. km of arable land)	617

Forests and biodiversity

Forest area (% of land area)	16.8
Deforestation (average annual %, 1990–2005)	-0.1
Nationally protected area (% of land area)	5.6
Animal species, total known	
Animal species, threatened	
Higher plant species, total known	
Higher plant species, threatened	
GEF benefits index for biodiversity (0–100, median is 1.5)	

Energy

GDP per unit of energy use (2005 PPP $/kg oil equivalent)	4.8
Energy use per capita (kg oil equivalent)	468
Energy from biomass products and waste (% of total)	30.4
Electric power consumption per capita (kWh)	453
Electricity generated using fossil fuel (% of total)	78.3
Electricity generated by hydropower (% of total)	17.4

Emissions and pollution

CO_2 emissions per unit of GDP (kg/2005 PPP $)	0.5
CO_2 emissions per capita (metric tons)	1.1
CO_2 emissions growth (%, 1990–2005)	106.7
Particulate matter (urban-pop.-weighted avg., µg/cu. m)	78
Transport sector fuel consumption per capita (liters)	33

Water and sanitation

Internal freshwater resources per capita (cu. m)	1,196
Freshwater withdrawal	
Total (% of internal resources)	51.7
Agriculture (% of total freshwater withdrawal)	89
Access to improved water source (% of total population)	87
Rural (% of rural population)	84
Urban (% of urban population)	94
Access to improved sanitation (% of total population)	33
Rural (% of rural population)	23
Urban (% of urban population)	57

Environment and health

Acute resp. infection prevalence (% of children under five)	
Diarrhea prevalence (% of children under five)	
Under-five mortality rate (per 1,000 live births)	78

National accounting aggregates

Gross savings (% of GNI)	36.2
Consumption of fixed capital (% of GNI)	9.5
Education expenditure (% of GNI)	3.0
Energy depletion (% of GNI)	2.7
Mineral depletion (% of GNI)	0.6
Net forest depletion (% of GNI)	0.9
CO_2 damage (% of GNI)	1.0
Particulate emission damage (% of GNI)	0.8
Adjusted net savings (% of GNI)	23.9

Sub-Saharan Africa

Population (millions) **800** Land area (1,000 sq. km) **23,578** GDP ($ billions) **847.4**

GNI per capita, *World Bank Atlas* method ($)	951
Urban population (% of total)	36
Urban population growth (average annual %, 1990–2007)	4.0
Population growth (average annual %, 1990–2007)	2.6

Agriculture

Agricultural land (% of land area)	44
Agricultural productivity (value added per worker, 2000 $)	287
Food production index (1999–2001 = 100)	109
Population density, rural (people/sq. km of arable land)	351

Forests and biodiversity

Forest area (% of land area)	26.5
Deforestation (average annual %, 1990–2005)	0.6
Nationally protected area (% of land area)	11.3
Animal species, total known	
Animal species, threatened	
Higher plant species, total known	
Higher plant species, threatened	
GEF benefits index for biodiversity (0–100, median is 1.5)	

Energy

GDP per unit of energy use (2005 PPP $/kg oil equivalent)	3.0
Energy use per capita (kg oil equivalent)	670
Energy from biomass products and waste (% of total)	56.3
Electric power consumption per capita (kWh)	531
Electricity generated using fossil fuel (% of total)	65.6
Electricity generated by hydropower (% of total)	18.0

Emissions and pollution

CO_2 emissions per unit of GDP (kg/2005 PPP $)	0.5
CO_2 emissions per capita (metric tons)	0.8
CO_2 emissions growth (%, 1990–2005)	40.1
Particulate matter (urban-pop.-weighted avg., µg/cu. m)	53
Transport sector fuel consumption per capita (liters)	64

Water and sanitation

Internal freshwater resources per capita (cu. m)	4,824
Freshwater withdrawal	
Total (% of internal resources)	3.2
Agriculture (% of total freshwater withdrawal)	87
Access to improved water source (% of total population)	58
Rural (% of rural population)	46
Urban (% of urban population)	81
Access to improved sanitation (% of total population)	31
Rural (% of rural population)	24
Urban (% of urban population)	42

Environment and health

Acute resp. infection prevalence (% of children under five)	
Diarrhea prevalence (% of children under five)	
Under-five mortality rate (per 1,000 live births)	146

National accounting aggregates

Gross savings (% of GNI)	17.4
Consumption of fixed capital (% of GNI)	11.1
Education expenditure (% of GNI)	3.6
Energy depletion (% of GNI)	11.7
Mineral depletion (% of GNI)	1.5
Net forest depletion (% of GNI)	0.5
CO_2 damage (% of GNI)	0.7
Particulate emission damage (% of GNI)	0.4
Adjusted net savings (% of GNI)	-5.0

Income group tables

For operational and analytical purposes the World Bank's main criterion for classifying economies is gross national income (GNI) per capita. Each economy in *The Little Green Data Book* is classified as low income, middle income, or high income. Low- and middle-income economies are sometimes referred to as developing economies. The use of the term is convenient; it is not intended to imply that all economies in the group are experiencing similar development or that other economies have reached a preferred or final stage of development. Classification by income does not necessarily reflect development status.

Low-income economies are those with a GNI per capita of $935 or less in 2007.

Middle-income economies are those with a GNI per capita of more than $935 but less than $11,456. Lower-middle-income and upper-middle-income economies are separated at a GNI per capita of $3,705.

High-income economies are those with a GNI per capita of $11,456 or more.

Euro area includes the member states of the Economic and Monetary Union of the European Union that have adopted the euro as their currency: Austria, Belgium, Cyprus, Finland, France, Germany, Greece, Ireland, Italy, Luxembourg, Malta, Netherlands, Portugal, Slovenia, Slovak Republic, and Spain.

Low income

Population (millions) **1,296**   Land area (1,000 sq. km) **21,217**   GDP ($ billions) **801.4**

GNI per capita, *World Bank Atlas* method ($)	574
Urban population (% of total)	32
Urban population growth (average annual %, 1990–2007)	3.7
Population growth (average annual %, 1990–2007)	2.4

Agriculture

Agricultural land (% of land area)	39
Agricultural productivity (value added per worker, 2000 $)	330
Food production index (1999–2001 = 100)	112
Population density, rural (people/sq. km of arable land)	603

Forests and biodiversity

Forest area (% of land area)	24.7
Deforestation (average annual %, 1990–2005)	0.7
Nationally protected area (% of land area)	10.8
Animal species, total known	
Animal species, threatened	
Higher plant species, total known	
Higher plant species, threatened	
GEF benefits index for biodiversity (0–100, median is 1.5)	

Energy

GDP per unit of energy use (2005 PPP $/kg oil equivalent)	3.2
Energy use per capita (kg oil equivalent)	478
Energy from biomass products and waste (% of total)	53.8
Electric power consumption per capita (kWh)	309
Electricity generated using fossil fuel (% of total)	48.4
Electricity generated by hydropower (% of total)	38.8

Emissions and pollution

CO_2 emissions per unit of GDP (kg/2005 PPP $)	0.4
CO_2 emissions per capita (metric tons)	0.6
CO_2 emissions growth (%, 1990–2005)	39.3
Particulate matter (urban-pop.-weighted avg., µg/cu. m)	69
Transport sector fuel consumption per capita (liters)	41

Water and sanitation

Internal freshwater resources per capita (cu. m)	4,619
Freshwater withdrawal	
Total (% of internal resources)	9.4
Agriculture (% of total freshwater withdrawal)	90
Access to improved water source (% of total population)	68
Rural (% of rural population)	60
Urban (% of urban population)	84
Access to improved sanitation (% of total population)	39
Rural (% of rural population)	33
Urban (% of urban population)	54

Environment and health

Acute resp. infection prevalence (% of children under five)	
Diarrhea prevalence (% of children under five)	
Under-five mortality rate (per 1,000 live births)	126

National accounting aggregates

Gross savings (% of GNI)	25.4
Consumption of fixed capital (% of GNI)	9.3
Education expenditure (% of GNI)	2.6
Energy depletion (% of GNI)	9.8
Mineral depletion (% of GNI)	0.9
Net forest depletion (% of GNI)	0.8
CO_2 damage (% of GNI)	0.7
Particulate emission damage (% of GNI)	0.7
Adjusted net savings (% of GNI)	5.8

Middle income

Population (millions) **4,258** Land area (1,000 sq. km) **74,923** GDP ($ billions) **13,490.0**

GNI per capita, *World Bank Atlas* method ($)	2,910
Urban population (% of total)	48
Urban population growth (average annual %, 1990–2007)	2.4
Population growth (average annual %, 1990–2007)	1.2

Agriculture

Agricultural land (% of land area)	38
Agricultural productivity (value added per worker, 2000 $)	673
Food production index (1999–2001 = 100)	115
Population density, rural (people/sq. km of arable land)	473

Forests and biodiversity

Forest area (% of land area)	32.7
Deforestation (average annual %, 1990–2005)	0.2
Nationally protected area (% of land area)	10.6
Animal species, total known	
Animal species, threatened	
Higher plant species, total known	
Higher plant species, threatened	
GEF benefits index for biodiversity (0–100, median is 1.5)	

Energy

GDP per unit of energy use (2005 PPP $/kg oil equivalent)	4.2
Energy use per capita (kg oil equivalent)	1,267
Energy from biomass products and waste (% of total)	12.3
Electric power consumption per capita (kWh)	1,651
Electricity generated using fossil fuel (% of total)	72.9
Electricity generated by hydropower (% of total)	20.6

Emissions and pollution

CO_2 emissions per unit of GDP (kg/2005 PPP $)	0.7
CO_2 emissions per capita (metric tons)	3.3
CO_2 emissions growth (%, 1990–2005)	43.1
Particulate matter (urban-pop.-weighted avg., µg/cu. m)	56
Transport sector fuel consumption per capita (liters)	144

Water and sanitation

Internal freshwater resources per capita (cu. m)	6,589
Freshwater withdrawal	
Total (% of internal resources)	8.5
Agriculture (% of total freshwater withdrawal)	76
Access to improved water source (% of total population)	89
Rural (% of rural population)	83
Urban (% of urban population)	97
Access to improved sanitation (% of total population)	60
Rural (% of rural population)	45
Urban (% of urban population)	76

Environment and health

Acute resp. infection prevalence (% of children under five)	
Diarrhea prevalence (% of children under five)	
Under-five mortality rate (per 1,000 live births)	45

National accounting aggregates

Gross savings (% of GNI)	32.3
Consumption of fixed capital (% of GNI)	11.7
Education expenditure (% of GNI)	3.5
Energy depletion (% of GNI)	7.1
Mineral depletion (% of GNI)	1.2
Net forest depletion (% of GNI)	0.1
CO_2 damage (% of GNI)	0.9
Particulate emission damage (% of GNI)	0.8
Adjusted net savings (% of GNI)	14.0

Lower middle income

Population (millions) **3,435** Land area (1,000 sq. km) **34,405** GDP ($ billions) **6,896.1**

GNI per capita, *World Bank Atlas* method ($)	1,905
Urban population (% of total)	42
Urban population growth (average annual %, 1990–2007)	2.9
Population growth (average annual %, 1990–2007)	1.3

Agriculture

Agricultural land (% of land area)	47
Agricultural productivity (value added per worker, 2000 $)	532
Food production index (1999–2001 = 100)	116
Population density, rural (people/sq. km of arable land)	511

Forests and biodiversity

Forest area (% of land area)	25.0
Deforestation (average annual %, 1990–2005)	0.1
Nationally protected area (% of land area)	11.0
Animal species, total known	
Animal species, threatened	
Higher plant species, total known	
Higher plant species, threatened	
GEF benefits index for biodiversity (0–100, median is 1.5)	

Energy

GDP per unit of energy use (2005 PPP $/kg oil equivalent)	3.9
Energy use per capita (kg oil equivalent)	1,019
Energy from biomass products and waste (% of total)	15.2
Electric power consumption per capita (kWh)	1,269
Electricity generated using fossil fuel (% of total)	79.0
Electricity generated by hydropower (% of total)	16.3

Emissions and pollution

CO_2 emissions per unit of GDP (kg/2005 PPP $)	0.8
CO_2 emissions per capita (metric tons)	2.8
CO_2 emissions growth (%, 1990–2005)	93.5
Particulate matter (urban-pop.-weighted avg., µg/cu. m)	67
Transport sector fuel consumption per capita (liters)	99

Water and sanitation

Internal freshwater resources per capita (cu. m)	4,117
Freshwater withdrawal	
Total (% of internal resources)	8.7
Agriculture (% of total freshwater withdrawal)	80
Access to improved water source (% of total population)	88
Rural (% of rural population)	82
Urban (% of urban population)	96
Access to improved sanitation (% of total population)	55
Rural (% of rural population)	43
Urban (% of urban population)	71

Environment and health

Acute resp. infection prevalence (% of children under five)	
Diarrhea prevalence (% of children under five)	
Under-five mortality rate (per 1,000 live births)	50

National accounting aggregates

Gross savings (% of GNI)	41.7
Consumption of fixed capital (% of GNI)	10.7
Education expenditure (% of GNI)	2.6
Energy depletion (% of GNI)	6.6
Mineral depletion (% of GNI)	1.2
Net forest depletion (% of GNI)	0.2
CO_2 damage (% of GNI)	1.2
Particulate emission damage (% of GNI)	1.1
Adjusted net savings (% of GNI)	23.5

Upper middle income

Population (millions) **824** Land area (1,000 sq. km) **40,518** GDP ($ billions) **6,594.6**

GNI per capita, *World Bank Atlas* method ($)	7,107
Urban population (% of total)	75
Urban population growth (average annual %, 1990–2007)	1.4
Population growth (average annual %, 1990–2007)	0.9

Agriculture

Agricultural land (% of land area)	31
Agricultural productivity (value added per worker, 2000 $)	2,947
Food production index (1999–2001 = 100)	113
Population density, rural (people/sq. km of arable land)	110

Forests and biodiversity

Forest area (% of land area)	39.3
Deforestation (average annual %, 1990–2005)	0.2
Nationally protected area (% of land area)	10.3
Animal species, total known	
Animal species, threatened	
Higher plant species, total known	
Higher plant species, threatened	
GEF benefits index for biodiversity (0–100, median is 1.5)	

Energy

GDP per unit of energy use (2005 PPP $/kg oil equivalent)	4.8
Energy use per capita (kg oil equivalent)	2,300
Energy from biomass products and waste (% of total)	7.0
Electric power consumption per capita (kWh)	3,242
Electricity generated using fossil fuel (% of total)	62.8
Electricity generated by hydropower (% of total)	27.6

Emissions and pollution

CO_2 emissions per unit of GDP (kg/2005 PPP $)	0.5
CO_2 emissions per capita (metric tons)	5.5
CO_2 emissions growth (%, 1990–2005)	−8.3
Particulate matter (urban-pop.-weighted avg., µg/cu. m)	30
Transport sector fuel consumption per capita (liters)	332

Water and sanitation

Internal freshwater resources per capita (cu. m)	16,993
Freshwater withdrawal	
Total (% of internal resources)	13.8
Agriculture (% of total freshwater withdrawal)	57
Access to improved water source (% of total population)	95
Rural (% of rural population)	83
Urban (% of urban population)	98
Access to improved sanitation (% of total population)	83
Rural (% of rural population)	64
Urban (% of urban population)	89

Environment and health

Acute resp. infection prevalence (% of children under five)	
Diarrhea prevalence (% of children under five)	
Under-five mortality rate (per 1,000 live births)	24

National accounting aggregates

Gross savings (% of GNI)	23.2
Consumption of fixed capital (% of GNI)	12.8
Education expenditure (% of GNI)	4.4
Energy depletion (% of GNI)	7.6
Mineral depletion (% of GNI)	1.3
Net forest depletion (% of GNI)	0.0
CO_2 damage (% of GNI)	0.6
Particulate emission damage (% of GNI)	0.4
Adjusted net savings (% of GNI)	4.9

Low and middle income

Population (millions) **5,554** Land area (1,000 sq. km) **96,140** GDP ($ billions) **14,296.3**

GNI per capita, *World Bank Atlas* method ($)	2,366
Urban population (% of total)	44
Urban population growth (average annual %, 1990–2007)	2.6
Population growth (average annual %, 1990–2007)	1.5

Agriculture

Agricultural land (% of land area)	38
Agricultural productivity (value added per worker, 2000 $)	599
Food production index (1999–2001 = 100)	115
Population density, rural (people/sq. km of arable land)	510

Forests and biodiversity

Forest area (% of land area)	31.0
Deforestation (average annual %, 1990–2005)	0.3
Nationally protected area (% of land area)	10.7
Animal species, total known	
Animal species, threatened	
Higher plant species, total known	
Higher plant species, threatened	
GEF benefits index for biodiversity (0–100, median is 1.5)	

Energy

GDP per unit of energy use (2005 PPP $/kg oil equivalent)	4.1
Energy use per capita (kg oil equivalent)	1,108
Energy from biomass products and waste (% of total)	15.9
Electric power consumption per capita (kWh)	1,380
Electricity generated using fossil fuel (% of total)	71.5
Electricity generated by hydropower (% of total)	21.5

Emissions and pollution

CO_2 emissions per unit of GDP (kg/2005 PPP $)	0.6
CO_2 emissions per capita (metric tons)	2.7
CO_2 emissions growth (%, 1990–2005)	42.9
Particulate matter (urban-pop.-weighted avg., µg/cu. m)	58
Transport sector fuel consumption per capita (liters)	123

Water and sanitation

Internal freshwater resources per capita (cu. m)	6,128
Freshwater withdrawal	
Total (% of internal resources)	3.2
Agriculture (% of total freshwater withdrawal)	78
Access to improved water source (% of total population)	84
Rural (% of rural population)	76
Urban (% of urban population)	94
Access to improved sanitation (% of total population)	55
Rural (% of rural population)	41
Urban (% of urban population)	73

Environment and health

Acute resp. infection prevalence (% of children under five)	
Diarrhea prevalence (% of children under five)	
Under-five mortality rate (per 1,000 live births)	74

National accounting aggregates

Gross savings (% of GNI)	32.0
Consumption of fixed capital (% of GNI)	11.6
Education expenditure (% of GNI)	3.4
Energy depletion (% of GNI)	7.2
Mineral depletion (% of GNI)	1.2
Net forest depletion (% of GNI)	0.1
CO_2 damage (% of GNI)	0.9
Particulate emission damage (% of GNI)	0.8
Adjusted net savings (% of GNI)	13.6

Euro area

Population (millions) **324** Land area (1,000 sq. km) **2,513** GDP ($ billions) **12,277.6**

GNI per capita, *World Bank Atlas* method ($)	35,818
Urban population (% of total)	73
Urban population growth (average annual %, 1990–2007)	0.6
Population growth (average annual %, 1990–2007)	0.4

Agriculture
Agricultural land (% of land area)	47
Agricultural productivity (value added per worker, 2000 $)	22,860
Food production index (1999–2001 = 100)	98
Population density, rural (people/sq. km of arable land)	183

Forests and biodiversity
Forest area (% of land area)	37.2
Deforestation (average annual %, 1990–2005)	–0.8
Nationally protected area (% of land area)	10.6
Animal species, total known	
Animal species, threatened	
Higher plant species, total known	
Higher plant species, threatened	
GEF benefits index for biodiversity (0–100, median is 1.5)	

Energy
GDP per unit of energy use (2005 PPP $/kg oil equivalent)	7.7
Energy use per capita (kg oil equivalent)	3,936
Energy from biomass products and waste (% of total)	4.9
Electric power consumption per capita (kWh)	6,956
Electricity generated using fossil fuel (% of total)	50.8
Electricity generated by hydropower (% of total)	9.1

Emissions and pollution
CO_2 emissions per unit of GDP (kg/2005 PPP $)	0.3
CO_2 emissions per capita (metric tons)	8.1
CO_2 emissions growth (%, 1990–2005)	2.2
Particulate matter (urban-pop.-weighted avg., µg/cu. m)	23
Transport sector fuel consumption per capita (liters)	771

Water and sanitation
Internal freshwater resources per capita (cu. m)	2,907
Freshwater withdrawal	
Total (% of internal resources)	22.3
Agriculture (% of total freshwater withdrawal)	38
Access to improved water source (% of total population)	100
Rural (% of rural population)	100
Urban (% of urban population)	100
Access to improved sanitation (% of total population)	..
Rural (% of rural population)	..
Urban (% of urban population)	..

Environment and health
Acute resp. infection prevalence (% of children under five)	
Diarrhea prevalence (% of children under five)	
Under-five mortality rate (per 1,000 live births)	4

National accounting aggregates
Gross savings (% of GNI)	22.3
Consumption of fixed capital (% of GNI)	14.4
Education expenditure (% of GNI)	4.6
Energy depletion (% of GNI)	0.2
Mineral depletion (% of GNI)	0.0
Net forest depletion (% of GNI)	0.0
CO_2 damage (% of GNI)	0.2
Particulate emission damage (% of GNI)	0.2
Adjusted net savings (% of GNI)	11.9

High income

Population (millions) **1,056**   Land area (1,000 sq. km) **33,505**   GDP ($ billions) **40,309.7**

GNI per capita, *World Bank Atlas* method ($)	37,572
Urban population (% of total)	78
Urban population growth (average annual %, 1990–2007)	1.0
Population growth (average annual %, 1990–2007)	0.7

Agriculture

Agricultural land (% of land area)	38
Agricultural productivity (value added per worker, 2000 $)	27,680
Food production index (1999–2001 = 100)	102
Population density, rural (people/sq. km of arable land)	323

Forests and biodiversity

Forest area (% of land area)	28.8
Deforestation (average annual %, 1990–2005)	–0.1
Nationally protected area (% of land area)	11.8
Animal species, total known	
Animal species, threatened	
Higher plant species, total known	
Higher plant species, threatened	
GEF benefits index for biodiversity (0–100, median is 1.5)	

Energy

GDP per unit of energy use (2005 PPP $/kg oil equivalent)	6.3
Energy use per capita (kg oil equivalent)	5,416
Energy from biomass products and waste (% of total)	3.4
Electric power consumption per capita (kWh)	9,675
Electricity generated using fossil fuel (% of total)	62.0
Electricity generated by hydropower (% of total)	11.4

Emissions and pollution

CO_2 emissions per unit of GDP (kg/2005 PPP $)	0.4
CO_2 emissions per capita (metric tons)	12.6
CO_2 emissions growth (%, 1990–2005)	19.1
Particulate matter (urban-pop.-weighted avg., µg/cu. m)	26
Transport sector fuel consumption per capita (liters)	1,159

Water and sanitation

Internal freshwater resources per capita (cu. m)	9,313
Freshwater withdrawal	
Total (% of internal resources)	10.4
Agriculture (% of total freshwater withdrawal)	43
Access to improved water source (% of total population)	100
Rural (% of rural population)	98
Urban (% of urban population)	100
Access to improved sanitation (% of total population)	100
Rural (% of rural population)	99
Urban (% of urban population)	100

Environment and health

Acute resp. infection prevalence (% of children under five)	
Diarrhea prevalence (% of children under five)	
Under-five mortality rate (per 1,000 live births)	7

National accounting aggregates

Gross savings (% of GNI)	20.6
Consumption of fixed capital (% of GNI)	14.5
Education expenditure (% of GNI)	4.6
Energy depletion (% of GNI)	1.5
Mineral depletion (% of GNI)	0.2
Net forest depletion (% of GNI)	0.0
CO_2 damage (% of GNI)	0.3
Particulate emission damage (% of GNI)	0.3
Adjusted net savings (% of GNI)	8.5

Country tables

China

Unless otherwise noted, data for China do not include data for Hong Kong, China; Macao, China; or Taiwan, China.

Serbia and Montenegro

Montenegro declared independence from Serbia and Montenegro on June 3, 2006. Where available, data for each country are shown separately. However, some indicators for Serbia prior to 2006 include data for Montenegro. Moreover, data for most indicators from 1999 onward for Serbia exclude data for Kosovo, which in 1999 became a territory under international administration pursuant to UN Security Council Resolution 1244 (1999).

Afghanistan

| Population (millions) | .. | Land area (1,000 sq. km) | **652** | GDP ($ billions) | **8.4** |

	Country data	South Asia group	Low-income group
GNI per capita, *World Bank Atlas* method ($)	..	880	574
Urban population (% of total)	..	29	32
Urban population growth (average annual %, 1990–2007)	..	2.7	3.7
Population growth (average annual %, 1990–2007)	..	1.8	2.4
Agriculture			
Agricultural land (% of land area)	58	55	39
Agricultural productivity (value added per worker, 2000 $)	..	417	330
Food production index (1999–2001 = 100)	114	107	112
Population density, rural (people/sq. km of arable land)	..	617	603
Forests and biodiversity			
Forest area (% of land area)	1.3	16.8	24.7
Deforestation (average annual %, 1990–2005)	2.7	–0.1	0.7
Nationally protected area (% of land area)	0.3	5.6	10.8
Animal species, total known	578		
Animal species, threatened	30		
Higher plant species, total known	4,000		
Higher plant species, threatened	2		
GEF benefits index for biodiversity (0–100, median is 1.5)	3.4		
Energy			
GDP per unit of energy use (2005 PPP $/kg oil equivalent)	..	4.8	3.2
Energy use per capita (kg oil equivalent)	..	468	478
Energy from biomass products and waste (% of total)	..	30.4	53.8
Electric power consumption per capita (kWh)	..	453	309
Electricity generated using fossil fuel (% of total)	..	78.3	48.4
Electricity generated by hydropower (% of total)	..	17.4	38.8
Emissions and pollution			
CO_2 emissions per unit of GDP (kg/2005 PPP $)	0.03	0.52	0.39
CO_2 emissions per capita (metric tons)	..	1.08	0.58
CO_2 emissions growth (%, 1990–2005)	–73.5	106.7	39.3
Particulate matter (urban-pop.-weighted avg., µg/cu. m)	41	78	69
Transport sector fuel consumption per capita (liters)	..	33	41
Water and sanitation			
Internal freshwater resources per capita (cu. m)	..	1,196	4,619
Freshwater withdrawal			
Total (% of internal resources)	42.3	51.7	9.4
Agriculture (% of total freshwater withdrawal)	98	89	90
Access to improved water source (% of total population)	..	87	68
Rural (% of rural population)	..	84	60
Urban (% of urban population)	..	94	84
Access to improved sanitation (% of total population)	..	33	39
Rural (% of rural population)	..	23	33
Urban (% of urban population)	..	57	54
Environment and health			
Acute resp. infection prevalence (% of children under five)	19.0		
Diarrhea prevalence (% of children under five)	20.0		
Under-five mortality rate (per 1,000 live births)		78	126
National accounting aggregates			
Gross savings (% of GNI)	..	36.2	25.4
Consumption of fixed capital (% of GNI)	..	9.5	9.3
Education expenditure (% of GNI)	..	3.0	2.6
Energy depletion (% of GNI)	..	2.7	9.8
Mineral depletion (% of GNI)	..	0.6	0.9
Net forest depletion (% of GNI)	..	0.9	0.8
CO_2 damage (% of GNI)	..	1.0	0.7
Particulate emission damage (% of GNI)	..	0.8	0.7
Adjusted net savings (% of GNI)	..	23.9	5.8

Albania

Population (millions)	**3.2**	Land area (1,000 sq. km)	**27.4**	GDP ($ billions)	**10.8**

	Country data	Europe & Central Asia group	Lower middle-income group
GNI per capita, *World Bank Atlas* method ($)	3,300	6,052	1,905
Urban population (% of total)	46	64	42
Urban population growth (average annual %, 1990–2007)	1.2	0.2	2.9
Population growth (average annual %, 1990–2007)	–0.2	0.1	1.3
Agriculture			
Agricultural land (% of land area)	41	28	47
Agricultural productivity (value added per worker, 2000 $)	1,495	2,228	532
Food production index (1999–2001 = 100)	108	110	116
Population density, rural (people/sq. km of arable land)	301	129	511
Forests and biodiversity			
Forest area (% of land area)	29.0	38.3	25.0
Deforestation (average annual %, 1990–2005)	0.0	0.0	0.1
Nationally protected area (% of land area)	0.7	6.1	11.0
Animal species, total known	376		
Animal species, threatened	52		
Higher plant species, total known	3,031		
Higher plant species, threatened	0		
GEF benefits index for biodiversity (0–100, median is 1.5)	0.2		
Energy			
GDP per unit of energy use (2005 PPP $/kg oil equivalent)	8.9	3.5	3.9
Energy use per capita (kg oil equivalent)	715	2,930	1,019
Energy from biomass products and waste (% of total)	10.1	2.2	15.2
Electric power consumption per capita (kWh)	961	3,835	1,269
Electricity generated using fossil fuel (% of total)	1.8	67.7	79.0
Electricity generated by hydropower (% of total)	98.2	17.4	16.3
Emissions and pollution			
CO_2 emissions per unit of GDP (kg/2005 PPP $)	0.2	0.7	0.8
CO_2 emissions per capita (metric tons)	1.1	7.0	2.8
CO_2 emissions growth (%, 1990–2005)	–51.9	–29.3	93.5
Particulate matter (urban-pop.-weighted avg., µg/cu. m)	44	27	67
Transport sector fuel consumption per capita (liters)	233	255	99
Water and sanitation			
Internal freshwater resources per capita (cu. m)	8,456	11,806	4,117
Freshwater withdrawal			
Total (% of internal resources)	6.4	7.2	8.7
Agriculture (% of total freshwater withdrawal)	62	60	80
Access to improved water source (% of total population)	97	95	88
Rural (% of rural population)	97	88	82
Urban (% of urban population)	97	99	96
Access to improved sanitation (% of total population)	97	89	55
Rural (% of rural population)	97	79	43
Urban (% of urban population)	98	94	71
Environment and health			
Acute resp. infection prevalence (% of children under five)	1.0		
Diarrhea prevalence (% of children under five)	7.3		
Under-five mortality rate (per 1,000 live births)	15	23	50
National accounting aggregates			
Gross savings (% of GNI)	19.2	24.0	41.7
Consumption of fixed capital (% of GNI)	10.9	12.8	10.7
Education expenditure (% of GNI)	2.8	4.0	2.6
Energy depletion (% of GNI)	0.0	9.8	6.6
Mineral depletion (% of GNI)	0.0	0.7	1.2
Net forest depletion (% of GNI)	0.0	0.0	0.2
CO_2 damage (% of GNI)	0.2	1.0	1.2
Particulate emission damage (% of GNI)	0.2	0.5	1.1
Adjusted net savings (% of GNI)	10.7	3.2	23.5

Algeria

	Country data	Middle East & N. Africa group	Lower middle-income group
Population (millions) **34**	Land area (1,000 sq. km) **2,382**	GDP ($ billions) **135.3**	

	Country data	Middle East & N. Africa group	Lower middle-income group
GNI per capita, *World Bank Atlas* method ($)	3,620	2,820	1,905
Urban population (% of total)	65	57	42
Urban population growth (average annual %, 1990–2007)	3.0	2.6	2.9
Population growth (average annual %, 1990–2007)	1.7	2.0	1.3
Agriculture			
Agricultural land (% of land area)	17	22	47
Agricultural productivity (value added per worker, 2000 $)	2,219	2,313	532
Food production index (1999–2001 = 100)	123	116	116
Population density, rural (people/sq. km of arable land)	162	665	511
Forests and biodiversity			
Forest area (% of land area)	1.0	2.4	25.0
Deforestation (average annual %, 1990–2005)	-1.6	-0.4	0.1
Nationally protected area (% of land area)	5.0	3.6	11.0
Animal species, total known	472		
Animal species, threatened	72		
Higher plant species, total known	3,164		
Higher plant species, threatened	3		
GEF benefits index for biodiversity (0–100, median is 1.5)	2.9		
Energy			
GDP per unit of energy use (2005 PPP $/kg oil equivalent)	6.5	5.0	3.9
Energy use per capita (kg oil equivalent)	1,100	1,254	1,019
Energy from biomass products and waste (% of total)	0.2	1.2	15.2
Electric power consumption per capita (kWh)	870	1,418	1,269
Electricity generated using fossil fuel (% of total)	99.4	91.1	79.0
Electricity generated by hydropower (% of total)	0.6	7.4	16.3
Emissions and pollution			
CO_2 emissions per unit of GDP (kg/2005 PPP $)	0.6	0.6	0.8
CO_2 emissions per capita (metric tons)	4.2	3.7	2.8
CO_2 emissions growth (%, 1990–2005)	78.6	96.8	93.5
Particulate matter (urban-pop.-weighted avg., µg/cu. m)	71	72	67
Transport sector fuel consumption per capita (liters)	158	277	99
Water and sanitation			
Internal freshwater resources per capita (cu. m)	332	728	4,117
Freshwater withdrawal			
Total (% of internal resources)	54.0	122.3	8.7
Agriculture (% of total freshwater withdrawal)	65	86	80
Access to improved water source (% of total population)	85	89	88
Rural (% of rural population)	81	81	82
Urban (% of urban population)	87	95	96
Access to improved sanitation (% of total population)	94	77	55
Rural (% of rural population)	87	62	43
Urban (% of urban population)	98	88	71
Environment and health			
Acute resp. infection prevalence (% of children under five)	9.0		
Diarrhea prevalence (% of children under five)	19.8		
Under-five mortality rate (per 1,000 live births)	37	38	50
National accounting aggregates			
Gross savings (% of GNI)	57.9	33.3	41.7
Consumption of fixed capital (% of GNI)	11.6	11.3	10.7
Education expenditure (% of GNI)	4.5	4.7	2.6
Energy depletion (% of GNI)	29.7	21.3	6.6
Mineral depletion (% of GNI)	0.1	0.4	1.2
Net forest depletion (% of GNI)	0.1	0.0	0.2
CO_2 damage (% of GNI)	1.2	1.0	1.2
Particulate emission damage (% of GNI)	0.3	0.6	1.1
Adjusted net savings (% of GNI)	19.4	3.4	23.5

American Samoa

Population (thousands)	65	Land area (sq. km)	200	GDP ($ millions)	..

	Country data	East Asia & Pacific group	Upper middle-income group
GNI per capita, *World Bank Atlas* method ($)	..	2,182	7,107
Urban population (% of total)	92	43	75
Urban population growth (average annual %, 1990–2007)	..	3.5	1.4
Population growth (average annual %, 1990–2007)	..	1.1	0.9
Agriculture			
Agricultural land (% of land area)	25	51	31
Agricultural productivity (value added per worker, 2000 $)	..	458	2,947
Food production index (1999–2001 = 100)	100	120	113
Population density, rural (people/sq. km of arable land)	273	547	110
Forests and biodiversity			
Forest area (% of land area)	89.5	28.4	39.3
Deforestation (average annual %, 1990–2005)	0.0	–0.1	0.2
Nationally protected area (% of land area)	..	14.0	10.3
Animal species, total known	46		
Animal species, threatened	76		
Higher plant species, total known	471		
Higher plant species, threatened	1		
GEF benefits index for biodiversity (0–100, median is 1.5)	0.3		
Energy			
GDP per unit of energy use (2005 PPP $/kg oil equivalent)	..	3.4	4.8
Energy use per capita (kg oil equivalent)	..	1,258	2,300
Energy from biomass products and waste (% of total)	..	14.7	7.0
Electric power consumption per capita (kWh)	..	1,669	3,242
Electricity generated using fossil fuel (% of total)	..	82.0	62.8
Electricity generated by hydropower (% of total)	..	15.0	27.6
Emissions and pollution			
CO_2 emissions per unit of GDP (kg/2005 PPP $)	..	0.9	0.5
CO_2 emissions per capita (metric tons)	..	3.6	5.5
CO_2 emissions growth (%, 1990–2005)	..	123.4	–8.3
Particulate matter (urban-pop.-weighted avg., µg/cu. m)	..	69	30
Transport sector fuel consumption per capita (liters)	..	106	332
Water and sanitation			
Internal freshwater resources per capita (cu. m)	..	4,948	16,993
Freshwater withdrawal			
Total (% of internal resources)	..	10.2	13.8
Agriculture (% of total freshwater withdrawal)	..	74	57
Access to improved water source (% of total population)	..	87	95
Rural (% of rural population)	..	81	83
Urban (% of urban population)	..	96	98
Access to improved sanitation (% of total population)	..	66	83
Rural (% of rural population)	..	59	64
Urban (% of urban population)	..	75	89
Environment and health			
Acute resp. infection prevalence (% of children under five)	..		
Diarrhea prevalence (% of children under five)	..		
Under-five mortality rate (per 1,000 live births)	..	27	24
National accounting aggregates			
Gross savings (% of GNI)	..	48.0	23.2
Consumption of fixed capital (% of GNI)	..	10.7	12.8
Education expenditure (% of GNI)	..	2.1	4.4
Energy depletion (% of GNI)	..	4.9	7.6
Mineral depletion (% of GNI)	..	1.3	1.3
Net forest depletion (% of GNI)	..	0.0	0.0
CO_2 damage (% of GNI)	..	1.3	0.6
Particulate emission damage (% of GNI)	..	1.3	0.4
Adjusted net savings (% of GNI)	..	30.6	4.9

Andorra

| | Population (thousands) **82** | Land area (sq. km) | **470** | GDP ($ millions) | .. |

	Country data	High-income group
GNI per capita, *World Bank Atlas* method ($)	..	37,572
Urban population (% of total)	89	78
Urban population growth (average annual %, 1990–2007)	..	1.0
Population growth (average annual %, 1990–2007)	..	0.7
Agriculture		
Agricultural land (% of land area)	55	38
Agricultural productivity (value added per worker, 2000 $)	..	27,680
Food production index (1999–2001 = 100)	..	102
Population density, rural (people/sq. km of arable land)	754	323
Forests and biodiversity		
Forest area (% of land area)	34.0	28.8
Deforestation (average annual %, 1990–2005)	0.0	−0.1
Nationally protected area (% of land area)	7.0	11.8
Animal species, total known	..	
Animal species, threatened	9	
Higher plant species, total known	..	
Higher plant species, threatened	0	
GEF benefits index for biodiversity (0–100, median is 1.5)	0.0	
Energy		
GDP per unit of energy use (2005 PPP $/kg oil equivalent)	..	6.3
Energy use per capita (kg oil equivalent)	..	5,416
Energy from biomass products and waste (% of total)	..	3.4
Electric power consumption per capita (kWh)	..	9,675
Electricity generated using fossil fuel (% of total)	..	62.0
Electricity generated by hydropower (% of total)	..	11.4
Emissions and pollution		
CO_2 emissions per unit of GDP (kg/2005 PPP $)	..	0.4
CO_2 emissions per capita (metric tons)	..	12.6
CO_2 emissions growth (%, 1990–2005)	..	19.1
Particulate matter (urban-pop.-weighted avg., µg/cu. m)	25	26
Transport sector fuel consumption per capita (liters)	..	1,159
Water and sanitation		
Internal freshwater resources per capita (cu. m)	..	9,313
Freshwater withdrawal		
Total (% of internal resources)	..	10.4
Agriculture (% of total freshwater withdrawal)	..	43
Access to improved water source (% of total population)	100	100
Rural (% of rural population)	100	98
Urban (% of urban population)	100	100
Access to improved sanitation (% of total population)	100	100
Rural (% of rural population)	100	99
Urban (% of urban population)	100	100
Environment and health		
Acute resp. infection prevalence (% of children under five)	..	
Diarrhea prevalence (% of children under five)	..	
Under-five mortality rate (per 1,000 live births)	3	7
National accounting aggregates		
Gross savings (% of GNI)	..	20.6
Consumption of fixed capital (% of GNI)	..	14.5
Education expenditure (% of GNI)	..	4.6
Energy depletion (% of GNI)	..	1.5
Mineral depletion (% of GNI)	..	0.2
Net forest depletion (% of GNI)	..	0.0
CO_2 damage (% of GNI)	..	0.3
Particulate emission damage (% of GNI)	..	0.3
Adjusted net savings (% of GNI)	..	8.5

Angola

	Country data	Sub-Saharan Africa group	Lower middle-income group
Population (millions) **17** Land area (1,000 sq. km) **1,247** GDP ($ billions) **61.4**			

	Country data	Sub-Saharan Africa group	Lower middle-income group
GNI per capita, *World Bank Atlas* method ($)	2,540	951	1,905
Urban population (% of total)	56	36	42
Urban population growth (average annual %, 1990–2007)	5.2	4.0	2.9
Population growth (average annual %, 1990–2007)	2.8	2.6	1.3
Agriculture			
Agricultural land (% of land area)	46	44	47
Agricultural productivity (value added per worker, 2000 $)	196	287	532
Food production index (1999–2001 = 100)	148	109	116
Population density, rural (people/sq. km of arable land)	224	351	511
Forests and biodiversity			
Forest area (% of land area)	47.4	26.5	25.0
Deforestation (average annual %, 1990–2005)	0.2	0.6	0.1
Nationally protected area (% of land area)	10.1	11.3	11.0
Animal species, total known	1,226		
Animal species, threatened	63		
Higher plant species, total known	5,185		
Higher plant species, threatened	26		
GEF benefits index for biodiversity (0–100, median is 1.5)	8.3		
Energy			
GDP per unit of energy use (2005 PPP $/kg oil equivalent)	6.9	3.0	3.9
Energy use per capita (kg oil equivalent)	620	670	1,019
Energy from biomass products and waste (% of total)	63.9	56.3	15.2
Electric power consumption per capita (kWh)	153	531	1,269
Electricity generated using fossil fuel (% of total)	9.9	65.6	79.0
Electricity generated by hydropower (% of total)	90.1	18.0	16.3
Emissions and pollution			
CO_2 emissions per unit of GDP (kg/2005 PPP $)	0.1	0.5	0.8
CO_2 emissions per capita (metric tons)	0.6	0.8	2.8
CO_2 emissions growth (%, 1990–2005)	93.5	40.1	93.5
Particulate matter (urban-pop.-weighted avg., μg/cu. m)	66	53	67
Transport sector fuel consumption per capita (liters)	78	64	99
Water and sanitation			
Internal freshwater resources per capita (cu. m)	8,696	4,824	4,117
Freshwater withdrawal			
Total (% of internal resources)	0.2	3.2	8.7
Agriculture (% of total freshwater withdrawal)	60	87	80
Access to improved water source (% of total population)	51	58	88
Rural (% of rural population)	39	46	82
Urban (% of urban population)	62	81	96
Access to improved sanitation (% of total population)	50	31	55
Rural (% of rural population)	16	24	43
Urban (% of urban population)	79	42	71
Environment and health			
Acute resp. infection prevalence (% of children under five)	8.0		
Diarrhea prevalence (% of children under five)	28.4		
Under-five mortality rate (per 1,000 live births)	158	146	50
National accounting aggregates			
Gross savings (% of GNI)	31.8	17.4	41.7
Consumption of fixed capital (% of GNI)	14.3	11.1	10.7
Education expenditure (% of GNI)	2.3	3.6	2.6
Energy depletion (% of GNI)	55.6	11.7	6.6
Mineral depletion (% of GNI)	0.0	1.5	1.2
Net forest depletion (% of GNI)	0.0	0.5	0.2
CO_2 damage (% of GNI)	0.2	0.7	1.2
Particulate emission damage (% of GNI)	1.3	0.4	1.1
Adjusted net savings (% of GNI)	-37.3	-5.0	23.5

Antigua and Barbuda

Population (thousands) **85**   Land area (sq. km)   **440** GDP ($ millions)   **981**

	Country data	High-income group
GNI per capita, *World Bank Atlas* method ($)	11,650	37,572
Urban population (% of total)	31	78
Urban population growth (average annual %, 1990–2007)	1.0	1.0
Population growth (average annual %, 1990–2007)	1.9	0.7
Agriculture		
Agricultural land (% of land area)	32	38
Agricultural productivity (value added per worker, 2000 $)	2,751	27,680
Food production index (1999–2001 = 100)	108	102
Population density, rural (people/sq. km of arable land)	719	323
Forests and biodiversity		
Forest area (% of land area)	21.4	28.8
Deforestation (average annual %, 1990–2005)	0.0	–0.1
Nationally protected area (% of land area)	0.0	11.8
Animal species, total known	186	
Animal species, threatened	34	
Higher plant species, total known	1,158	
Higher plant species, threatened	4	
GEF benefits index for biodiversity (0–100, median is 1.5)	0.7	
Energy		
GDP per unit of energy use (2005 PPP $/kg oil equivalent)	..	6.3
Energy use per capita (kg oil equivalent)	..	5,416
Energy from biomass products and waste (% of total)	..	3.4
Electric power consumption per capita (kWh)	..	9,675
Electricity generated using fossil fuel (% of total)	..	62.0
Electricity generated by hydropower (% of total)	..	11.4
Emissions and pollution		
CO_2 emissions per unit of GDP (kg/2005 PPP $)	0.3	0.4
CO_2 emissions per capita (metric tons)	5.1	12.6
CO_2 emissions growth (%, 1990–2005)	40.2	19.1
Particulate matter (urban-pop.-weighted avg., µg/cu. m)	12	26
Transport sector fuel consumption per capita (liters)	..	1,159
Water and sanitation		
Internal freshwater resources per capita (cu. m)	613	9,313
Freshwater withdrawal		
Total (% of internal resources)	9.6	10.4
Agriculture (% of total freshwater withdrawal)	20	43
Access to improved water source (% of total population)	..	100
Rural (% of rural population)	..	98
Urban (% of urban population)	95	100
Access to improved sanitation (% of total population)	..	100
Rural (% of rural population)	..	99
Urban (% of urban population)	98	100
Environment and health		
Acute resp. infection prevalence (% of children under five)	..	
Diarrhea prevalence (% of children under five)	..	
Under-five mortality rate (per 1,000 live births)	11	7
National accounting aggregates		
Gross savings (% of GNI)	..	20.6
Consumption of fixed capital (% of GNI)	..	14.5
Education expenditure (% of GNI)	3.9	4.6
Energy depletion (% of GNI)	0.0	1.5
Mineral depletion (% of GNI)	0.0	0.2
Net forest depletion (% of GNI)	..	0.0
CO_2 damage (% of GNI)	0.4	0.3
Particulate emission damage (% of GNI)	..	0.3
Adjusted net savings (% of GNI)	..	8.5

Argentina

	Country data	Latin America & Caribbean group	Upper middle-income group
Population (millions) **40**	Land area (1,000 sq. km) **2,737**	GDP ($ billions) **262.5**	

	Country data	Latin America & Caribbean group	Upper middle-income group
GNI per capita, *World Bank Atlas* method ($)	6,040	5,801	7,107
Urban population (% of total)	92	78	75
Urban population growth (average annual %, 1990-2007)	1.4	2.1	1.4
Population growth (average annual %, 1990-2007)	1.1	1.5	0.9
Agriculture			
Agricultural land (% of land area)	47	36	31
Agricultural productivity (value added per worker, 2000 $)	10,762	3,158	2,947
Food production index (1999-2001 = 100)	114	117	113
Population density, rural (people/sq. km of arable land)	12	232	110
Forests and biodiversity			
Forest area (% of land area)	12.1	45.4	39.3
Deforestation (average annual %, 1990-2005)	0.4	0.5	0.2
Nationally protected area (% of land area)	6.3	16.7	10.3
Animal species, total known	1,413		
Animal species, threatened	159		
Higher plant species, total known	9,372		
Higher plant species, threatened	44		
GEF benefits index for biodiversity (0-100, median is 1.5)	17.7		
Energy			
GDP per unit of energy use (2005 PPP $/kg oil equivalent)	6.6	7.3	4.8
Energy use per capita (kg oil equivalent)	1,766	1,240	2,300
Energy from biomass products and waste (% of total)	3.7	15.9	7.0
Electric power consumption per capita (kWh)	2,620	1,808	3,242
Electricity generated using fossil fuel (% of total)	59.0	37.0	62.8
Electricity generated by hydropower (% of total)	33.0	57.3	27.6
Emissions and pollution			
CO_2 emissions per unit of GDP (kg/2005 PPP $)	0.4	0.3	0.5
CO_2 emissions per capita (metric tons)	3.9	2.5	5.5
CO_2 emissions growth (%, 1990-2005)	39.2	33.4	-8.3
Particulate matter (urban-pop.-weighted avg., µg/cu. m)	73	35	30
Transport sector fuel consumption per capita (liters)	312	295	332
Water and sanitation			
Internal freshwater resources per capita (cu. m)	6,987	23,965	16,993
Freshwater withdrawal			
Total (% of internal resources)	10.6	2.0	13.8
Agriculture (% of total freshwater withdrawal)	74	71	57
Access to improved water source (% of total population)	96	91	95
Rural (% of rural population)	80	73	83
Urban (% of urban population)	98	97	98
Access to improved sanitation (% of total population)	91	78	83
Rural (% of rural population)	83	51	64
Urban (% of urban population)	92	86	89
Environment and health			
Acute resp. infection prevalence (% of children under five)	..		
Diarrhea prevalence (% of children under five)	..		
Under-five mortality rate (per 1,000 live births)	16	26	24
National accounting aggregates			
Gross savings (% of GNI)	27.2	22.9	23.2
Consumption of fixed capital (% of GNI)	12.4	12.6	12.8
Education expenditure (% of GNI)	4.0	4.5	4.4
Energy depletion (% of GNI)	7.7	5.4	7.6
Mineral depletion (% of GNI)	0.6	1.9	1.3
Net forest depletion (% of GNI)	0.0	0.0	0.0
CO_2 damage (% of GNI)	0.5	0.3	0.6
Particulate emission damage (% of GNI)	1.6	0.4	0.4
Adjusted net savings (% of GNI)	8.3	6.7	4.9

Armenia

	Population (millions)	**3.0**	Land area (1,000 sq. km)	**28.2**	GDP ($ billions)	**9.2**

	Country data	Europe & Central Asia group	Lower middle-income group
GNI per capita, *World Bank Atlas* method ($)	2,630	6,052	1,905
Urban population (% of total)	64	64	42
Urban population growth (average annual %, 1990–2007)	-1.3	0.2	2.9
Population growth (average annual %, 1990–2007)	-1.0	0.1	1.3
Agriculture			
Agricultural land (% of land area)	49	28	47
Agricultural productivity (value added per worker, 2000 $)	4,198	2,228	532
Food production index (1999–2001 = 100)	124	110	116
Population density, rural (people/sq. km of arable land)	219	129	511
Forests and biodiversity			
Forest area (% of land area)	10.0	38.3	25.0
Deforestation (average annual %, 1990–2005)	1.3	0.0	0.1
Nationally protected area (% of land area)	8.7	6.1	11.0
Animal species, total known	380		
Animal species, threatened	36		
Higher plant species, total known	3,553		
Higher plant species, threatened	1		
GEF benefits index for biodiversity (0–100, median is 1.5)	0.2		
Energy			
GDP per unit of energy use (2005 PPP $/kg oil equivalent)	5.5	3.5	3.9
Energy use per capita (kg oil equivalent)	859	2,930	1,019
Energy from biomass products and waste (% of total)	0.0	2.2	15.2
Electric power consumption per capita (kWh)	1,612	3,835	1,269
Electricity generated using fossil fuel (% of total)	24.8	67.7	79.0
Electricity generated by hydropower (% of total)	30.7	17.4	16.3
Emissions and pollution			
CO_2 emissions per unit of GDP (kg/2005 PPP $)	0.3	0.7	0.8
CO_2 emissions per capita (metric tons)	1.4	7.0	2.8
CO_2 emissions growth (%, 1990–2005)	3.6	-29.3	93.5
Particulate matter (urban-pop.-weighted avg., µg/cu. m)	59	27	67
Transport sector fuel consumption per capita (liters)	67	255	99
Water and sanitation			
Internal freshwater resources per capita (cu. m)	3,023	11,806	4,117
Freshwater withdrawal			
Total (% of internal resources)	32.5	7.2	8.7
Agriculture (% of total freshwater withdrawal)	66	60	80
Access to improved water source (% of total population)	98	95	88
Rural (% of rural population)	96	88	82
Urban (% of urban population)	99	99	96
Access to improved sanitation (% of total population)	91	89	55
Rural (% of rural population)	81	79	43
Urban (% of urban population)	96	94	71
Environment and health			
Acute resp. infection prevalence (% of children under five)	8.0		
Diarrhea prevalence (% of children under five)	7.8		
Under-five mortality rate (per 1,000 live births)	24	23	50
National accounting aggregates			
Gross savings (% of GNI)	29.7	24.0	41.7
Consumption of fixed capital (% of GNI)	10.7	12.8	10.7
Education expenditure (% of GNI)	2.2	4.0	2.6
Energy depletion (% of GNI)	0.0	9.8	6.6
Mineral depletion (% of GNI)	1.1	0.7	1.2
Net forest depletion (% of GNI)	0.0	0.0	0.2
CO_2 damage (% of GNI)	0.4	1.0	1.2
Particulate emission damage (% of GNI)	1.6	0.5	1.1
Adjusted net savings (% of GNI)	18.1	3.2	23.5

Aruba

Population (thousands) **101** Land area (sq. km) **180** GDP ($ billions) **1.9**

	Country data	High-income group
GNI per capita, *World Bank Atlas* method ($)	..	37,572
Urban population (% of total)	47	78
Urban population growth (average annual %, 1990–2007)	..	1.0
Population growth (average annual %, 1990–2007)	..	0.7
Agriculture		
Agricultural land (% of land area)	11	38
Agricultural productivity (value added per worker, 2000 $)	..	27,680
Food production index (1999–2001 = 100)	104	102
Population density, rural (people/sq. km of arable land)	2,678	323
Forests and biodiversity		
Forest area (% of land area)	2.2	28.8
Deforestation (average annual %, 1990–2005)	..	–0.1
Nationally protected area (% of land area)	..	11.8
Animal species, total known	92	
Animal species, threatened	22	
Higher plant species, total known	460	
Higher plant species, threatened	..	
GEF benefits index for biodiversity (0–100, median is 1.5)	0.3	
Energy		
GDP per unit of energy use (2005 PPP $/kg oil equivalent)	..	6.3
Energy use per capita (kg oil equivalent)	..	5,416
Energy from biomass products and waste (% of total)	..	3.4
Electric power consumption per capita (kWh)	..	9,675
Electricity generated using fossil fuel (% of total)	..	62.0
Electricity generated by hydropower (% of total)	..	11.4
Emissions and pollution		
CO_2 emissions per unit of GDP (kg/2005 PPP $)	..	0.4
CO_2 emissions per capita (metric tons)	23.0	12.6
CO_2 emissions growth (%, 1990–2005)	25.5	19.1
Particulate matter (urban-pop.-weighted avg., µg/cu. m)	..	26
Transport sector fuel consumption per capita (liters)	..	1,159
Water and sanitation		
Internal freshwater resources per capita (cu. m)	..	9,313
Freshwater withdrawal		
Total (% of internal resources)	..	10.4
Agriculture (% of total freshwater withdrawal)	..	43
Access to improved water source (% of total population)	100	100
Rural (% of rural population)	100	98
Urban (% of urban population)	100	100
Access to improved sanitation (% of total population)	..	100
Rural (% of rural population)	..	99
Urban (% of urban population)	..	100
Environment and health		
Acute resp. infection prevalence (% of children under five)	..	
Diarrhea prevalence (% of children under five)	..	
Under-five mortality rate (per 1,000 live births)	..	7
National accounting aggregates		
Gross savings (% of GNI)	..	20.6
Consumption of fixed capital (% of GNI)	..	14.5
Education expenditure (% of GNI)	..	4.6
Energy depletion (% of GNI)	..	1.5
Mineral depletion (% of GNI)	..	0.2
Net forest depletion (% of GNI)	..	0.0
CO_2 damage (% of GNI)	..	0.3
Particulate emission damage (% of GNI)	..	0.3
Adjusted net savings (% of GNI)	..	8.5

Australia

Population (millions)	**21**	Land area (1,000 sq. km)	**7,682**	GDP ($ billions)	**821.0**

	Country data	High-income group
GNI per capita, *World Bank Atlas* method ($)	35,760	37,572
Urban population (% of total)	89	78
Urban population growth (average annual %, 1990–2007)	1.4	1.0
Population growth (average annual %, 1990–2007)	1.2	0.7
Agriculture		
Agricultural land (% of land area)	58	38
Agricultural productivity (value added per worker, 2000 $)	33,252	27,680
Food production index (1999–2001 = 100)	101	102
Population density, rural (people/sq. km of arable land)	5	323
Forests and biodiversity		
Forest area (% of land area)	21.3	28.8
Deforestation (average annual %, 1990–2005)	0.2	-0.1
Nationally protected area (% of land area)	9.6	11.8
Animal species, total known	1,227	
Animal species, threatened	733	
Higher plant species, total known	15,638	
Higher plant species, threatened	55	
GEF benefits index for biodiversity (0–100, median is 1.5)	87.7	
Energy		
GDP per unit of energy use (2005 PPP $/kg oil equivalent)	5.4	6.3
Energy use per capita (kg oil equivalent)	5,917	5,416
Energy from biomass products and waste (% of total)	4.1	3.4
Electric power consumption per capita (kWh)	11,332	9,675
Electricity generated using fossil fuel (% of total)	92.3	62.0
Electricity generated by hydropower (% of total)	6.2	11.4
Emissions and pollution		
CO_2 emissions per unit of GDP (kg/2005 PPP $)	0.6	0.4
CO_2 emissions per capita (metric tons)	18.1	12.6
CO_2 emissions growth (%, 1990–2005)	25.9	19.1
Particulate matter (urban-pop.-weighted avg., µg/cu. m)	15	26
Transport sector fuel consumption per capita (liters)	1,199	1,159
Water and sanitation		
Internal freshwater resources per capita (cu. m)	23,412	9,313
Freshwater withdrawal		
Total (% of internal resources)	4.9	10.4
Agriculture (% of total freshwater withdrawal)	75	43
Access to improved water source (% of total population)	100	100
Rural (% of rural population)	100	98
Urban (% of urban population)	100	100
Access to improved sanitation (% of total population)	100	100
Rural (% of rural population)	100	99
Urban (% of urban population)	100	100
Environment and health		
Acute resp. infection prevalence (% of children under five)	..	
Diarrhea prevalence (% of children under five)	..	
Under-five mortality rate (per 1,000 live births)	6	7
National accounting aggregates		
Gross savings (% of GNI)	22.8	20.6
Consumption of fixed capital (% of GNI)	15.3	14.5
Education expenditure (% of GNI)	4.8	4.6
Energy depletion (% of GNI)	2.9	1.5
Mineral depletion (% of GNI)	3.8	0.2
Net forest depletion (% of GNI)	0.0	0.0
CO_2 damage (% of GNI)	0.3	0.3
Particulate emission damage (% of GNI)	0.1	0.3
Adjusted net savings (% of GNI)	5.2	8.5

Austria

| Population (millions) | **8.3** | Land area (1,000 sq. km) | **82.5** | GDP ($ billions) | **373.2** |

	Country data	High-income group
GNI per capita, *World Bank Atlas* method ($)	41,960	37,572
Urban population (% of total)	67	78
Urban population growth (average annual %, 1990–2007)	0.5	1.0
Population growth (average annual %, 1990–2007)	0.4	0.7
Agriculture		
Agricultural land (% of land area)	40	38
Agricultural productivity (value added per worker, 2000 $)	22,775	27,680
Food production index (1999–2001 = 100)	99	102
Population density, rural (people/sq. km of arable land)	199	323
Forests and biodiversity		
Forest area (% of land area)	46.8	28.8
Deforestation (average annual %, 1990–2005)	–0.2	–0.1
Nationally protected area (% of land area)	28.5	11.8
Animal species, total known	513	
Animal species, threatened	66	
Higher plant species, total known	3,100	
Higher plant species, threatened	4	
GEF benefits index for biodiversity (0–100, median is 1.5)	0.3	
Energy		
GDP per unit of energy use (2005 PPP $/kg oil equivalent)	8.4	6.3
Energy use per capita (kg oil equivalent)	4,132	5,416
Energy from biomass products and waste (% of total)	13.1	3.4
Electric power consumption per capita (kWh)	8,090	9,675
Electricity generated using fossil fuel (% of total)	34.0	62.0
Electricity generated by hydropower (% of total)	57.4	11.4
Emissions and pollution		
CO_2 emissions per unit of GDP (kg/2005 PPP $)	0.3	0.4
CO_2 emissions per capita (metric tons)	8.9	12.6
CO_2 emissions growth (%, 1990–2005)	27.8	19.1
Particulate matter (urban-pop.-weighted avg., µg/cu. m)	33	26
Transport sector fuel consumption per capita (liters)	906	1,159
Water and sanitation		
Internal freshwater resources per capita (cu. m)	6,614	9,313
Freshwater withdrawal		
Total (% of internal resources)	3.8	10.4
Agriculture (% of total freshwater withdrawal)	1	43
Access to improved water source (% of total population)	100	100
Rural (% of rural population)	100	98
Urban (% of urban population)	100	100
Access to improved sanitation (% of total population)	100	100
Rural (% of rural population)	100	99
Urban (% of urban population)	100	100
Environment and health		
Acute resp. infection prevalence (% of children under five)	..	
Diarrhea prevalence (% of children under five)	..	
Under-five mortality rate (per 1,000 live births)	4	7
National accounting aggregates		
Gross savings (% of GNI)	26.2	20.6
Consumption of fixed capital (% of GNI)	15.1	14.5
Education expenditure (% of GNI)	5.3	4.6
Energy depletion (% of GNI)	0.2	1.5
Mineral depletion (% of GNI)	0.0	0.2
Net forest depletion (% of GNI)	0.0	0.0
CO_2 damage (% of GNI)	0.1	0.3
Particulate emission damage (% of GNI)	0.3	0.3
Adjusted net savings (% of GNI)	15.7	8.5

Azerbaijan

Population (millions)	8.6	Land area (1,000 sq. km)	82.7	GDP ($ billions)	31.2

	Country data	Europe & Central Asia group	Lower middle-income group
GNI per capita, *World Bank Atlas* method ($)	2,640	6,052	1,905
Urban population (% of total)	52	64	42
Urban population growth (average annual %, 1990–2007)	0.8	0.2	2.9
Population growth (average annual %, 1990–2007)	1.0	0.1	1.3
Agriculture			
Agricultural land (% of land area)	58	28	47
Agricultural productivity (value added per worker, 2000 $)	1,212	2,228	532
Food production index (1999–2001 = 100)	137	110	116
Population density, rural (people/sq. km of arable land)	221	129	511
Forests and biodiversity			
Forest area (% of land area)	11.3	38.3	25.0
Deforestation (average annual %, 1990–2005)	0.0	0.0	0.1
Nationally protected area (% of land area)	4.8	6.1	11.0
Animal species, total known	446		
Animal species, threatened	40		
Higher plant species, total known	4,300		
Higher plant species, threatened	0		
GEF benefits index for biodiversity (0–100, median is 1.5)	0.8		
Energy			
GDP per unit of energy use (2005 PPP $/kg oil equivalent)	3.6	3.5	3.9
Energy use per capita (kg oil equivalent)	1,659	2,930	1,019
Energy from biomass products and waste (% of total)	0.0	2.2	15.2
Electric power consumption per capita (kWh)	2,514	3,835	1,269
Electricity generated using fossil fuel (% of total)	89.3	67.7	79.0
Electricity generated by hydropower (% of total)	10.7	17.4	16.3
Emissions and pollution			
CO_2 emissions per unit of GDP (kg/2005 PPP $)	1.0	0.7	0.8
CO_2 emissions per capita (metric tons)	4.4	7.0	2.5
CO_2 emissions growth (%, 1990–2005)	-20.5	-29.3	93.5
Particulate matter (urban-pop.-weighted avg., µg/cu. m)	60	27	67
Transport sector fuel consumption per capita (liters)	192	255	99
Water and sanitation			
Internal freshwater resources per capita (cu. m)	948	11,806	4,117
Freshwater withdrawal			
Total (% of internal resources)	150.5	7.2	8.7
Agriculture (% of total freshwater withdrawal)	76	60	80
Access to improved water source (% of total population)	78	95	88
Rural (% of rural population)	59	88	82
Urban (% of urban population)	95	99	96
Access to improved sanitation (% of total population)	80	89	55
Rural (% of rural population)	70	79	43
Urban (% of urban population)	90	94	71
Environment and health			
Acute resp. infection prevalence (% of children under five)	3.0		
Diarrhea prevalence (% of children under five)	21.7		
Under-five mortality rate (per 1,000 live births)	39	23	50
National accounting aggregates			
Gross savings (% of GNI)	59.9	24.0	41.7
Consumption of fixed capital (% of GNI)	13.5	12.8	10.7
Education expenditure (% of GNI)	2.8	4.0	2.6
Energy depletion (% of GNI)	52.6	9.8	6.6
Mineral depletion (% of GNI)	0.0	0.7	1.2
Net forest depletion (% of GNI)	0.0	0.0	0.2
CO_2 damage (% of GNI)	2.0	1.0	1.2
Particulate emission damage (% of GNI)	1.2	0.5	1.1
Adjusted net savings (% of GNI)	-6.6	3.2	23.5

Bahamas, The

Population (thousands) **331**   Land area (1,000 sq. km)   **10**   GDP ($ billions)   **6.6**

	Country data	High-income group
GNI per capita, *World Bank Atlas* method ($)	17,160	37,572
Urban population (% of total)	84	78
Urban population growth (average annual %, 1990–2007)	1.8	1.0
Population growth (average annual %, 1990–2007)	1.5	0.7
Agriculture		
Agricultural land (% of land area)	1	38
Agricultural productivity (value added per worker, 2000 $)	28,961	27,680
Food production index (1999–2001 = 100)	105	102
Population density, rural (people/sq. km of arable land)	683	323
Forests and biodiversity		
Forest area (% of land area)	51.4	28.8
Deforestation (average annual %, 1990–2005)	0.0	−0.1
Nationally protected area (% of land area)	0.1	11.8
Animal species, total known	347	
Animal species, threatened	49	
Higher plant species, total known	1,111	
Higher plant species, threatened	5	
GEF benefits index for biodiversity (0–100, median is 1.5)	3.6	
Energy		
GDP per unit of energy use (2005 PPP $/kg oil equivalent)	..	6.3
Energy use per capita (kg oil equivalent)	..	5,416
Energy from biomass products and waste (% of total)	..	3.4
Electric power consumption per capita (kWh)	..	9,675
Electricity generated using fossil fuel (% of total)	..	62.0
Electricity generated by hydropower (% of total)	..	11.4
Emissions and pollution		
CO_2 emissions per unit of GDP (kg/2005 PPP $)	..	0.4
CO_2 emissions per capita (metric tons)	6.5	12.6
CO_2 emissions growth (%, 1990–2005)	8.1	19.1
Particulate matter (urban-pop.-weighted avg., µg/cu. m)	37	26
Transport sector fuel consumption per capita (liters)	..	1,159
Water and sanitation		
Internal freshwater resources per capita (cu. m)	60	9,313
Freshwater withdrawal		
Total (% of internal resources)	..	10.4
Agriculture (% of total freshwater withdrawal)	..	43
Access to improved water source (% of total population)	..	100
Rural (% of rural population)	..	98
Urban (% of urban population)	98	100
Access to improved sanitation (% of total population)	100	100
Rural (% of rural population)	100	99
Urban (% of urban population)	100	100
Environment and health		
Acute resp. infection prevalence (% of children under five)	..	
Diarrhea prevalence (% of children under five)	..	
Under-five mortality rate (per 1,000 live births)	13	7
National accounting aggregates		
Gross savings (% of GNI)	..	20.6
Consumption of fixed capital (% of GNI)	..	14.5
Education expenditure (% of GNI)	..	4.6
Energy depletion (% of GNI)	..	1.5
Mineral depletion (% of GNI)	..	0.2
Net forest depletion (% of GNI)	..	0.0
CO_2 damage (% of GNI)	..	0.3
Particulate emission damage (% of GNI)	..	0.3
Adjusted net savings (% of GNI)	..	8.5

Bahrain

Population (thousands) **753** Land area (sq. km) **710** GDP ($ millions) **15.8**

	Country data	High-income group
GNI per capita, *World Bank Atlas* method ($)	17,390	37,572
Urban population (% of total)	88	78
Urban population growth (average annual %, 1990–2007)	2.5	1.0
Population growth (average annual %, 1990–2007)	2.5	0.7
Agriculture		
Agricultural land (% of land area)	14	38
Agricultural productivity (value added per worker, 2000 $)	..	27,680
Food production index (1999–2001 = 100)	131	102
Population density, rural (people/sq. km of arable land)	4,204	323
Forests and biodiversity		
Forest area (% of land area)	0.7	28.8
Deforestation (average annual %, 1990–2005)	..	-0.1
Nationally protected area (% of land area)	1.1	11.8
Animal species, total known	210	
Animal species, threatened	30	
Higher plant species, total known	195	
Higher plant species, threatened	..	
GEF benefits index for biodiversity (0–100, median is 1.5)	0.0	
Energy		
GDP per unit of energy use (2005 PPP $/kg oil equivalent)	2.5	6.3
Energy use per capita (kg oil equivalent)	11,874	5,416
Energy from biomass products and waste (% of total)	0.0	3.4
Electric power consumption per capita (kWh)	12,628	9,675
Electricity generated using fossil fuel (% of total)	100.0	62.0
Electricity generated by hydropower (% of total)	0.0	11.4
Emissions and pollution		
CO_2 emissions per unit of GDP (kg/2005 PPP $)	1.0	0.4
CO_2 emissions per capita (metric tons)	27.1	12.6
CO_2 emissions growth (%, 1990–2005)	68.0	19.1
Particulate matter (urban-pop.-weighted avg., µg/cu. m)	68	26
Transport sector fuel consumption per capita (liters)	1,385	1,159
Water and sanitation		
Internal freshwater resources per capita (cu. m)	5	9,313
Freshwater withdrawal		
Total (% of internal resources)	8,935.0	10.4
Agriculture (% of total freshwater withdrawal)	45	43
Access to improved water source (% of total population)	..	100
Rural (% of rural population)	..	98
Urban (% of urban population)	100	100
Access to improved sanitation (% of total population)	..	100
Rural (% of rural population)	..	99
Urban (% of urban population)	100	100
Environment and health		
Acute resp. infection prevalence (% of children under five)	8.3	
Diarrhea prevalence (% of children under five)	8.4	
Under-five mortality rate (per 1,000 live births)	10	7
National accounting aggregates		
Gross savings (% of GNI)	..	20.6
Consumption of fixed capital (% of GNI)	..	14.5
Education expenditure (% of GNI)	..	4.6
Energy depletion (% of GNI)	..	1.5
Mineral depletion (% of GNI)	..	0.2
Net forest depletion (% of GNI)	..	0.0
CO_2 damage (% of GNI)	..	0.3
Particulate emission damage (% of GNI)	..	0.3
Adjusted net savings (% of GNI)	..	8.5

Bangladesh

| | Population (millions) | **159** | Land area (1,000 sq. km) | **130** | GDP ($ billions) | **68.4** |

	Country data	South Asia group	Low-income group
GNI per capita, *World Bank Atlas* method ($)	470	880	574
Urban population (% of total)	27	29	32
Urban population growth (average annual %, 1990–2007)	3.7	2.7	3.7
Population growth (average annual %, 1990–2007)	2.0	1.8	2.4
Agriculture			
Agricultural land (% of land area)	69	55	39
Agricultural productivity (value added per worker, 2000 $)	346	417	330
Food production index (1999–2001 = 100)	110	107	112
Population density, rural (people/sq. km of arable land)	1,432	617	603
Forests and biodiversity			
Forest area (% of land area)	6.7	16.8	24.7
Deforestation (average annual %, 1990–2005)	0.1	–0.1	0.7
Nationally protected area (% of land area)	0.7	5.6	10.8
Animal species, total known	735		
Animal species, threatened	97		
Higher plant species, total known	5,000		
Higher plant species, threatened	12		
GEF benefits index for biodiversity (0–100, median is 1.5)	1.4		
Energy			
GDP per unit of energy use (2005 PPP $/kg oil equivalent)	7.0	4.8	3.2
Energy use per capita (kg oil equivalent)	161	468	478
Energy from biomass products and waste (% of total)	33.7	30.4	53.8
Electric power consumption per capita (kWh)	146	453	309
Electricity generated using fossil fuel (% of total)	94.3	78.3	48.4
Electricity generated by hydropower (% of total)	5.7	17.4	38.8
Emissions and pollution			
CO_2 emissions per unit of GDP (kg/2005 PPP $)	0.2	0.5	0.4
CO_2 emissions per capita (metric tons)	0.3	1.1	0.6
CO_2 emissions growth (%, 1990–2005)	160.1	106.7	39.3
Particulate matter (urban-pop.-weighted avg., µg/cu. m)	135	78	69
Transport sector fuel consumption per capita (liters)	11	33	41
Water and sanitation			
Internal freshwater resources per capita (cu. m)	662	1,196	4,619
Freshwater withdrawal			
Total (% of internal resources)	75.6	51.7	9.4
Agriculture (% of total freshwater withdrawal)	96	89	90
Access to improved water source (% of total population)	80	87	68
Rural (% of rural population)	78	84	60
Urban (% of urban population)	85	94	84
Access to improved sanitation (% of total population)	36	33	39
Rural (% of rural population)	32	23	33
Urban (% of urban population)	48	57	54
Environment and health			
Acute resp. infection prevalence (% of children under five)	20.8		
Diarrhea prevalence (% of children under five)	6.1		
Under-five mortality rate (per 1,000 live births)	61	78	126
National accounting aggregates			
Gross savings (% of GNI)	32.2	36.2	25.4
Consumption of fixed capital (% of GNI)	7.7	9.5	9.3
Education expenditure (% of GNI)	1.8	3.0	2.6
Energy depletion (% of GNI)	2.9	2.7	9.8
Mineral depletion (% of GNI)	0.0	0.6	0.9
Net forest depletion (% of GNI)	0.7	0.9	0.8
CO_2 damage (% of GNI)	0.4	1.0	0.7
Particulate emission damage (% of GNI)	0.5	0.8	0.7
Adjusted net savings (% of GNI)	21.8	23.9	5.8

Barbados

Population (thousands) **294** Land area (sq. km)	**430** GDP ($ billions)	**3.0**

	Country data	High-income group
GNI per capita, *World Bank Atlas* method ($)	8,080	37,572
Urban population (% of total)	39	78
Urban population growth (average annual %, 1990–2007)	1.6	1.0
Population growth (average annual %, 1990–2007)	0.5	0.7
Agriculture		
Agricultural land (% of land area)	44	38
Agricultural productivity (value added per worker, 2000 $)	15,533	27,680
Food production index (1999–2001 = 100)	105	102
Population density, rural (people/sq. km of arable land)	1,124	323
Forests and biodiversity		
Forest area (% of land area)	4.0	28.8
Deforestation (average annual %, 1990–2005)	0.0	–0.1
Nationally protected area (% of land area)	0.0	11.8
Animal species, total known	236	
Animal species, threatened	33	
Higher plant species, total known	572	
Higher plant species, threatened	2	
GEF benefits index for biodiversity (0–100, median is 1.5)	0.4	
Energy		
GDP per unit of energy use (2005 PPP $/kg oil equivalent)	..	6.3
Energy use per capita (kg oil equivalent)	..	5,416
Energy from biomass products and waste (% of total)	..	3.4
Electric power consumption per capita (kWh)	..	9,675
Electricity generated using fossil fuel (% of total)	..	62.0
Electricity generated by hydropower (% of total)	..	11.4
Emissions and pollution		
CO_2 emissions per unit of GDP (kg/2005 PPP $)	0.3	0.4
CO_2 emissions per capita (metric tons)	4.5	12.6
CO_2 emissions growth (%, 1990–2005)	22.1	19.1
Particulate matter (urban-pop.-weighted avg., µg/cu. m)	40	26
Transport sector fuel consumption per capita (liters)	..	1,159
Water and sanitation		
Internal freshwater resources per capita (cu. m)	272	9,313
Freshwater withdrawal		
Total (% of internal resources)	112.5	10.4
Agriculture (% of total freshwater withdrawal)	22	43
Access to improved water source (% of total population)	100	100
Rural (% of rural population)	100	98
Urban (% of urban population)	100	100
Access to improved sanitation (% of total population)	99	100
Rural (% of rural population)	100	99
Urban (% of urban population)	99	100
Environment and health		
Acute resp. infection prevalence (% of children under five)	..	
Diarrhea prevalence (% of children under five)	..	
Under-five mortality rate (per 1,000 live births)	12	7
National accounting aggregates		
Gross savings (% of GNI)	..	20.6
Consumption of fixed capital (% of GNI)	..	14.5
Education expenditure (% of GNI)	..	4.6
Energy depletion (% of GNI)	..	1.5
Mineral depletion (% of GNI)	..	0.2
Net forest depletion (% of GNI)	..	0.0
CO_2 damage (% of GNI)	..	0.3
Particulate emission damage (% of GNI)	..	0.3
Adjusted net savings (% of GNI)	..	8.5

Belarus

	Country data	Europe & Central Asia group	Upper middle-income group
Population (millions) **9.7** Land area (1,000 sq. km) **207.5** GDP ($ billions) **44.8**			

	Country data	Europe & Central Asia group	Upper middle-income group
GNI per capita, *World Bank Atlas* method ($)	4,220	6,052	7,107
Urban population (% of total)	73	64	75
Urban population growth (average annual %, 1990–2007)	0.3	0.2	1.4
Population growth (average annual %, 1990–2007)	−0.3	0.1	0.9
Agriculture			
Agricultural land (% of land area)	43	28	31
Agricultural productivity (value added per worker, 2000 $)	3,445	2,228	2,947
Food production index (1999–2001 = 100)	118	110	113
Population density, rural (people/sq. km of arable land)	50	129	110
Forests and biodiversity			
Forest area (% of land area)	38.0	38.3	39.3
Deforestation (average annual %, 1990–2005)	−0.5	0.0	0.2
Nationally protected area (% of land area)	5.2	6.1	10.3
Animal species, total known	297		
Animal species, threatened	17		
Higher plant species, total known	2,100		
Higher plant species, threatened	..		
GEF benefits index for biodiversity (0–100, median is 1.5)	0.0		
Energy			
GDP per unit of energy use (2005 PPP $/kg oil equivalent)	3.2	3.5	4.8
Energy use per capita (kg oil equivalent)	2,939	2,930	2,300
Energy from biomass products and waste (% of total)	5.0	2.2	7.0
Electric power consumption per capita (kWh)	3,322	3,835	3,242
Electricity generated using fossil fuel (% of total)	99.6	67.7	62.8
Electricity generated by hydropower (% of total)	0.1	17.4	27.6
Emissions and pollution			
CO_2 emissions per unit of GDP (kg/2005 PPP $)	0.8	0.7	0.5
CO_2 emissions per capita (metric tons)	6.5	7.0	5.5
CO_2 emissions growth (%, 1990–2005)	−41.3	−29.3	−8.3
Particulate matter (urban-pop.-weighted avg., μg/cu. m)	6	27	30
Transport sector fuel consumption per capita (liters)	192	255	332
Water and sanitation			
Internal freshwater resources per capita (cu. m)	3,834	11,806	16,993
Freshwater withdrawal			
Total (% of internal resources)	7.5	7.2	13.8
Agriculture (% of total freshwater withdrawal)	30	60	57
Access to improved water source (% of total population)	100	95	95
Rural (% of rural population)	99	88	83
Urban (% of urban population)	100	99	98
Access to improved sanitation (% of total population)	93	89	83
Rural (% of rural population)	97	79	64
Urban (% of urban population)	91	94	89
Environment and health			
Acute resp. infection prevalence (% of children under five)	..		
Diarrhea prevalence (% of children under five)	..		
Under-five mortality rate (per 1,000 live births)	13	23	24
National accounting aggregates			
Gross savings (% of GNI)	26.9	24.0	23.2
Consumption of fixed capital (% of GNI)	11.8	12.8	12.8
Education expenditure (% of GNI)	4.9	4.0	4.4
Energy depletion (% of GNI)	0.1	9.8	7.6
Mineral depletion (% of GNI)	0.0	0.7	1.3
Net forest depletion (% of GNI)	0.0	0.0	0.0
CO_2 damage (% of GNI)	1.4	1.0	0.6
Particulate emission damage (% of GNI)	..	0.5	0.4
Adjusted net savings (% of GNI)	18.5	3.2	4.9

Belgium

| | Population (millions) | **11** | Land area (1,000 sq. km) | **30** | GDP ($ billions) | **452.8** |

	Country data	High-income group
GNI per capita, *World Bank Atlas* method ($)	41,110	37,572
Urban population (% of total)	97	78
Urban population growth (average annual %, 1990–2007)	0.4	1.0
Population growth (average annual %, 1990–2007)	0.4	0.7
Agriculture		
Agricultural land (% of land area)	46	38
Agricultural productivity (value added per worker, 2000 $)	39,812	27,680
Food production index (1999–2001 = 100)	97	102
Population density, rural (people/sq. km of arable land)	34	323
Forests and biodiversity		
Forest area (% of land area)	22.1	28.8
Deforestation (average annual %, 1990–2005)	0.1	-0.1
Nationally protected area (% of land area)	3.2	11.8
Animal species, total known	519	
Animal species, threatened	26	
Higher plant species, total known	1,550	
Higher plant species, threatened	1	
GEF benefits index for biodiversity (0–100, median is 1.5)	0.0	
Energy		
GDP per unit of energy use (2005 PPP $/kg oil equivalent)	5.7	6.3
Energy use per capita (kg oil equivalent)	5,782	5,416
Energy from biomass products and waste (% of total)	5.9	3.4
Electric power consumption per capita (kWh)	8,684	9,675
Electricity generated using fossil fuel (% of total)	39.9	62.0
Electricity generated by hydropower (% of total)	0.4	11.4
Emissions and pollution		
CO_2 emissions per unit of GDP (kg/2005 PPP $)	0.3	0.4
CO_2 emissions per capita (metric tons)	9.8	12.6
CO_2 emissions growth (%, 1990–2005)	3.6	19.1
Particulate matter (urban-pop.-weighted avg., µg/cu. m)	22	26
Transport sector fuel consumption per capita (liters)	894	1,159
Water and sanitation		
Internal freshwater resources per capita (cu. m)	1,129	9,313
Freshwater withdrawal		
Total (% of internal resources)	..	10.4
Agriculture (% of total freshwater withdrawal)	..	43
Access to improved water source (% of total population)	..	100
Rural (% of rural population)	..	98
Urban (% of urban population)	100	100
Access to improved sanitation (% of total population)	..	100
Rural (% of rural population)	..	99
Urban (% of urban population)	..	100
Environment and health		
Acute resp. infection prevalence (% of children under five)	..	
Diarrhea prevalence (% of children under five)	..	
Under-five mortality rate (per 1,000 live births)	5	7
National accounting aggregates		
Gross savings (% of GNI)	24.8	20.6
Consumption of fixed capital (% of GNI)	14.6	14.5
Education expenditure (% of GNI)	5.8	4.6
Energy depletion (% of GNI)	0.0	1.5
Mineral depletion (% of GNI)	0.0	0.2
Net forest depletion (% of GNI)	0.0	0.0
CO_2 damage (% of GNI)	0.2	0.3
Particulate emission damage (% of GNI)	0.2	0.3
Adjusted net savings (% of GNI)	15.7	8.5

Belize

	Country data	Latin America & Caribbean group	Upper middle-income group
Population (thousands) **304** Land area (1,000 sq. km) **23** GDP ($ billions) **1.3**			

	Country data	Latin America & Caribbean group	Upper middle-income group
GNI per capita, *World Bank Atlas* method ($)	3,760	5,801	7,107
Urban population (% of total)	51	78	75
Urban population growth (average annual %, 1990–2007)	3.2	2.1	1.4
Population growth (average annual %, 1990–2007)	2.8	1.5	0.9
Agriculture			
Agricultural land (% of land area)	7	36	31
Agricultural productivity (value added per worker, 2000 $)	6,696	3,158	2,947
Food production index (1999–2001 = 100)	116	117	113
Population density, rural (people/sq. km of arable land)	208	232	110
Forests and biodiversity			
Forest area (% of land area)	72.5	45.4	39.3
Deforestation (average annual %, 1990–2005)	0.0	0.5	0.2
Nationally protected area (% of land area)	35.8	16.7	10.3
Animal species, total known	691		
Animal species, threatened	55		
Higher plant species, total known	2,894		
Higher plant species, threatened	30		
GEF benefits index for biodiversity (0–100, median is 1.5)	1.7		
Energy			
GDP per unit of energy use (2005 PPP $/kg oil equivalent)	..	7.3	4.8
Energy use per capita (kg oil equivalent)	..	1,240	2,300
Energy from biomass products and waste (% of total)	..	15.9	7.0
Electric power consumption per capita (kWh)	..	1,808	3,242
Electricity generated using fossil fuel (% of total)	..	37.0	62.8
Electricity generated by hydropower (% of total)	..	57.3	27.6
Emissions and pollution			
CO_2 emissions per unit of GDP (kg/2005 PPP $)	0.4	0.3	0.5
CO_2 emissions per capita (metric tons)	2.8	2.5	5.5
CO_2 emissions growth (%, 1990–2005)	162.4	33.4	-8.3
Particulate matter (urban-pop.-weighted avg., μg/cu. m)	15	35	30
Transport sector fuel consumption per capita (liters)	..	295	332
Water and sanitation			
Internal freshwater resources per capita (cu. m)	52,633	23,965	16,993
Freshwater withdrawal			
Total (% of internal resources)	0.9	2.0	13.8
Agriculture (% of total freshwater withdrawal)	20	71	57
Access to improved water source (% of total population)	..	91	95
Rural (% of rural population)	..	73	83
Urban (% of urban population)	100	97	98
Access to improved sanitation (% of total population)	..	78	83
Rural (% of rural population)	..	51	64
Urban (% of urban population)	..	86	89
Environment and health			
Acute resp. infection prevalence (% of children under five)	6.7		
Diarrhea prevalence (% of children under five)	11.0		
Under-five mortality rate (per 1,000 live births)	25	26	24
National accounting aggregates			
Gross savings (% of GNI)	..	22.9	23.2
Consumption of fixed capital (% of GNI)	12.8	12.6	12.8
Education expenditure (% of GNI)	5.1	4.5	4.4
Energy depletion (% of GNI)	0.0	5.4	7.6
Mineral depletion (% of GNI)	0.0	1.9	1.3
Net forest depletion (% of GNI)	0.0	0.0	0.0
CO_2 damage (% of GNI)	0.6	0.3	0.6
Particulate emission damage (% of GNI)	0.0	0.4	0.4
Adjusted net savings (% of GNI)	..	6.7	4.9

Benin

	Country data	Sub-Saharan Africa group	Low-income group
Population (millions) **9.0** Land area (1,000 sq. km) **110.6** GDP ($ billions) **5.4**			

	Country data	Sub-Saharan Africa group	Low-income group
GNI per capita, *World Bank Atlas* method ($)	570	951	574
Urban population (% of total)	41	36	32
Urban population growth (average annual %, 1990–2007)	4.3	4.0	3.7
Population growth (average annual %, 1990–2007)	3.3	2.6	2.4
Agriculture			
Agricultural land (% of land area)	32	44	39
Agricultural productivity (value added per worker, 2000 $)	536	287	330
Food production index (1999–2001 = 100)	123	109	112
Population density, rural (people/sq. km of arable land)	185	351	603
Forests and biodiversity			
Forest area (% of land area)	21.3	26.5	24.7
Deforestation (average annual %, 1990–2005)	2.3	0.6	0.7
Nationally protected area (% of land area)	23.6	11.3	10.8
Animal species, total known	644		
Animal species, threatened	33		
Higher plant species, total known	2,500		
Higher plant species, threatened	14		
GEF benefits index for biodiversity (0–100, median is 1.5)	0.2		
Energy			
GDP per unit of energy use (2005 PPP $/kg oil equivalent)	3.8	3.0	3.2
Energy use per capita (kg oil equivalent)	321	670	478
Energy from biomass products and waste (% of total)	61.1	56.3	53.8
Electric power consumption per capita (kWh)	69	531	309
Electricity generated using fossil fuel (% of total)	100.0	65.6	48.4
Electricity generated by hydropower (% of total)	0.0	18.0	38.8
Emissions and pollution			
CO_2 emissions per unit of GDP (kg/2005 PPP $)	0.2	0.5	0.4
CO_2 emissions per capita (metric tons)	0.3	0.8	0.6
CO_2 emissions growth (%, 1990–2005)	259.0	40.1	39.3
Particulate matter (urban-pop.-weighted avg., µg/cu. m)	46	53	69
Transport sector fuel consumption per capita (liters)	79	64	41
Water and sanitation			
Internal freshwater resources per capita (cu. m)	1,141	4,824	4,619
Freshwater withdrawal			
Total (% of internal resources)	1.3	3.2	9.4
Agriculture (% of total freshwater withdrawal)	45	87	90
Access to improved water source (% of total population)	65	58	68
Rural (% of rural population)	57	46	60
Urban (% of urban population)	78	81	84
Access to improved sanitation (% of total population)	30	31	39
Rural (% of rural population)	11	24	33
Urban (% of urban population)	59	42	54
Environment and health			
Acute resp. infection prevalence (% of children under five)	12.0		
Diarrhea prevalence (% of children under five)	13.4		
Under-five mortality rate (per 1,000 live births)	123	146	126
National accounting aggregates			
Gross savings (% of GNI)	..	17.4	25.4
Consumption of fixed capital (% of GNI)	8.8	11.1	9.3
Education expenditure (% of GNI)	3.6	3.6	2.6
Energy depletion (% of GNI)	0.0	11.7	9.8
Mineral depletion (% of GNI)	0.0	1.5	0.9
Net forest depletion (% of GNI)	0.9	0.5	0.8
CO_2 damage (% of GNI)	0.3	0.7	0.7
Particulate emission damage (% of GNI)	0.4	0.4	0.7
Adjusted net savings (% of GNI)	..	-5.0	5.8

Bermuda

Population (thousands) **64** Land area (sq. km) **50** GDP ($ billions) **5.9**

	Country data	High-income group
GNI per capita, *World Bank Atlas* method ($)	..	37,572
Urban population (% of total)	100	78
Urban population growth (average annual %, 1990–2007)	0.3	1.0
Population growth (average annual %, 1990–2007)	0.3	0.7
Agriculture		
Agricultural land (% of land area)	20	38
Agricultural productivity (value added per worker, 2000 $)	..	27,680
Food production index (1999–2001 = 100)	93	102
Population density, rural (people/sq. km of arable land)	0	323
Forests and biodiversity		
Forest area (% of land area)	20.0	28.8
Deforestation (average annual %, 1990–2005)	0.0	–0.1
Nationally protected area (% of land area)	2.0	11.8
Animal species, total known	243	
Animal species, threatened	47	
Higher plant species, total known	167	
Higher plant species, threatened	4	
GEF benefits index for biodiversity (0–100, median is 1.5)	1.2	
Energy		
GDP per unit of energy use (2005 PPP $/kg oil equivalent)	..	6.3
Energy use per capita (kg oil equivalent)	..	5,416
Energy from biomass products and waste (% of total)	..	3.4
Electric power consumption per capita (kWh)	..	9,675
Electricity generated using fossil fuel (% of total)	..	62.0
Electricity generated by hydropower (% of total)	..	11.4
Emissions and pollution		
CO_2 emissions per unit of GDP (kg/2005 PPP $)	..	0.4
CO_2 emissions per capita (metric tons)	9.0	12.6
CO_2 emissions growth (%, 1990–2005)	–3.1	19.1
Particulate matter (urban-pop.-weighted avg., µg/cu. m)	..	26
Transport sector fuel consumption per capita (liters)	..	1,159
Water and sanitation		
Internal freshwater resources per capita (cu. m)	..	9,313
Freshwater withdrawal		
Total (% of internal resources)	..	10.4
Agriculture (% of total freshwater withdrawal)	..	43
Access to improved water source (% of total population)	..	100
Rural (% of rural population)	..	98
Urban (% of urban population)	..	100
Access to improved sanitation (% of total population)	..	100
Rural (% of rural population)	..	99
Urban (% of urban population)	..	100
Environment and health		
Acute resp. infection prevalence (% of children under five)	..	
Diarrhea prevalence (% of children under five)	..	
Under-five mortality rate (per 1,000 live births)	..	7
National accounting aggregates		
Gross savings (% of GNI)	..	20.6
Consumption of fixed capital (% of GNI)	..	14.5
Education expenditure (% of GNI)	..	4.6
Energy depletion (% of GNI)	..	1.5
Mineral depletion (% of GNI)	..	0.2
Net forest depletion (% of GNI)	..	0.0
CO_2 damage (% of GNI)	..	0.3
Particulate emission damage (% of GNI)	..	0.3
Adjusted net savings (% of GNI)	..	8.5

Bhutan

| Population (thousands) **657** | Land area (1,000 sq. km) | **47** | GDP ($ billions) | **1.1** |

	Country data	South Asia group	Lower middle-income group
GNI per capita, *World Bank Atlas* method ($)	1,770	880	1,905
Urban population (% of total)	33	29	42
Urban population growth (average annual %, 1990–2007)	5.2	2.7	2.9
Population growth (average annual %, 1990–2007)	1.1	1.8	1.3
Agriculture			
Agricultural land (% of land area)	13	55	47
Agricultural productivity (value added per worker, 2000 $)	138	417	532
Food production index (1999–2001 = 100)	102	107	116
Population density, rural (people/sq. km of arable land)	276	617	511
Forests and biodiversity			
Forest area (% of land area)	68.0	16.8	25.0
Deforestation (average annual %, 1990–2005)	–0.3	–0.1	0.1
Nationally protected area (% of land area)	26.4	5.6	11.0
Animal species, total known	717		
Animal species, threatened	48		
Higher plant species, total known	5,468		
Higher plant species, threatened	7		
GEF benefits index for biodiversity (0–100, median is 1.5)	1.1		
Energy			
GDP per unit of energy use (2005 PPP $/kg oil equivalent)	..	4.8	3.9
Energy use per capita (kg oil equivalent)	..	468	1,019
Energy from biomass products and waste (% of total)	..	30.4	15.2
Electric power consumption per capita (kWh)	..	453	1,269
Electricity generated using fossil fuel (% of total)	..	78.3	79.0
Electricity generated by hydropower (% of total)	..	17.4	16.3
Emissions and pollution			
CO_2 emissions per unit of GDP (kg/2005 PPP $)	0.2	0.5	0.8
CO_2 emissions per capita (metric tons)	0.6	1.1	2.8
CO_2 emissions growth (%, 1990–2005)	222.9	106.7	93.5
Particulate matter (urban-pop.-weighted avg., µg/cu. m)	26	78	67
Transport sector fuel consumption per capita (liters)	..	33	99
Water and sanitation			
Internal freshwater resources per capita (cu. m)	144,509	1,196	4,117
Freshwater withdrawal			
Total (% of internal resources)	0.4	51.7	8.7
Agriculture (% of total freshwater withdrawal)	94	89	80
Access to improved water source (% of total population)	81	87	88
Rural (% of rural population)	79	84	82
Urban (% of urban population)	98	94	96
Access to improved sanitation (% of total population)	52	33	55
Rural (% of rural population)	50	23	43
Urban (% of urban population)	71	57	71
Environment and health			
Acute resp. infection prevalence (% of children under five)	..		
Diarrhea prevalence (% of children under five)	..		
Under-five mortality rate (per 1,000 live births)	84	78	50
National accounting aggregates			
Gross savings (% of GNI)	70.0	36.2	41.7
Consumption of fixed capital (% of GNI)	9.9	9.5	10.7
Education expenditure (% of GNI)	4.2	3.0	2.6
Energy depletion (% of GNI)	0.0	2.7	6.6
Mineral depletion (% of GNI)	0.0	0.6	1.2
Net forest depletion (% of GNI)	3.8	0.9	0.2
CO_2 damage (% of GNI)	0.4	1.0	1.2
Particulate emission damage (% of GNI)	0.2	0.8	1.1
Adjusted net savings (% of GNI)	60.0	23.9	23.5

Bolivia

	Country data	Latin America & Caribbean group	Lower middle-income group
Population (millions) **9.5**	Land area (1,000 sq. km) **1,084.4**	GDP ($ billions) **13.1**	

	Country data	Latin America & Caribbean group	Lower middle-income group
GNI per capita, *World Bank Atlas* method ($)	1,260	5,801	1,905
Urban population (% of total)	65	78	42
Urban population growth (average annual %, 1990–2007)	3.0	2.1	2.9
Population growth (average annual %, 1990–2007)	2.1	1.5	1.3
Agriculture			
Agricultural land (% of land area)	35	36	47
Agricultural productivity (value added per worker, 2000 $)	783	3,158	532
Food production index (1999–2001 = 100)	116	117	116
Population density, rural (people/sq. km of arable land)	108	232	511
Forests and biodiversity			
Forest area (% of land area)	54.2	45.4	25.0
Deforestation (average annual %, 1990–2005)	0.4	0.5	0.1
Nationally protected area (% of land area)	20.2	16.7	11.0
Animal species, total known	1,775		
Animal species, threatened	90		
Higher plant species, total known	17,367		
Higher plant species, threatened	71		
GEF benefits index for biodiversity (0–100, median is 1.5)	12.5		
Energy			
GDP per unit of energy use (2005 PPP $/kg oil equivalent)	6.2	7.3	3.9
Energy use per capita (kg oil equivalent)	625	1,240	1,019
Energy from biomass products and waste (% of total)	13.8	15.9	15.2
Electric power consumption per capita (kWh)	485	1,808	1,269
Electricity generated using fossil fuel (% of total)	56.0	37.0	79.0
Electricity generated by hydropower (% of total)	40.8	57.3	16.3
Emissions and pollution			
CO_2 emissions per unit of GDP (kg/2005 PPP $)	0.3	0.3	0.8
CO_2 emissions per capita (metric tons)	1.0	2.5	2.8
CO_2 emissions growth (%, 1990–2005)	68.2	33.4	93.5
Particulate matter (urban-pop.-weighted avg., µg/cu. m)	94	35	67
Transport sector fuel consumption per capita (liters)	126	295	99
Water and sanitation			
Internal freshwater resources per capita (cu. m)	31,892	23,965	4,117
Freshwater withdrawal			
Total (% of internal resources)	0.5	2.0	8.7
Agriculture (% of total freshwater withdrawal)	81	71	80
Access to improved water source (% of total population)	86	91	88
Rural (% of rural population)	69	73	82
Urban (% of urban population)	96	97	96
Access to improved sanitation (% of total population)	43	78	55
Rural (% of rural population)	22	51	43
Urban (% of urban population)	54	86	71
Environment and health			
Acute resp. infection prevalence (% of children under five)	22.0		
Diarrhea prevalence (% of children under five)	24.8		
Under-five mortality rate (per 1,000 live births)	57	26	50
National accounting aggregates			
Gross savings (% of GNI)	30.1	22.9	41.7
Consumption of fixed capital (% of GNI)	10.1	12.6	10.7
Education expenditure (% of GNI)	6.3	4.5	2.6
Energy depletion (% of GNI)	21.6	5.4	6.6
Mineral depletion (% of GNI)	2.4	1.9	1.2
Net forest depletion (% of GNI)	0.0	0.0	0.2
CO_2 damage (% of GNI)	0.5	0.3	1.2
Particulate emission damage (% of GNI)	1.4	0.4	1.1
Adjusted net savings (% of GNI)	0.4	6.7	23.5

Bosnia and Herzegovina

Population (millions)	**3.8**	Land area (1,000 sq. km)	**51.2**	GDP ($ billions)	**15.1**

	Country data	Europe & Central Asia group	Lower middle-income group
GNI per capita, *World Bank Atlas* method ($)	3,790	6,052	1,905
Urban population (% of total)	47	64	42
Urban population growth (average annual %, 1990–2007)	0.3	0.2	2.9
Population growth (average annual %, 1990–2007)	–0.8	0.1	1.3
Agriculture			
Agricultural land (% of land area)	42	28	47
Agricultural productivity (value added per worker, 2000 $)	10,051	2,228	532
Food production index (1999–2001 = 100)	110	110	116
Population density, rural (people/sq. km of arable land)	205	129	511
Forests and biodiversity			
Forest area (% of land area)	42.7	38.3	25.0
Deforestation (average annual %, 1990–2005)	0.1	0.0	0.1
Nationally protected area (% of land area)	0.5	6.1	11.0
Animal species, total known	390		
Animal species, threatened	50		
Higher plant species, total known	..		
Higher plant species, threatened	1		
GEF benefits index for biodiversity (0–100, median is 1.5)	0.4		
Energy			
GDP per unit of energy use (2005 PPP $/kg oil equivalent)	4.6	3.5	3.9
Energy use per capita (kg oil equivalent)	1,427	2,930	1,019
Energy from biomass products and waste (% of total)	3.4	2.2	15.2
Electric power consumption per capita (kWh)	2,385	3,835	1,269
Electricity generated using fossil fuel (% of total)	56.1	67.7	79.0
Electricity generated by hydropower (% of total)	43.9	17.4	16.3
Emissions and pollution			
CO_2 emissions per unit of GDP (kg/2005 PPP $)	1.1	0.7	0.8
CO_2 emissions per capita (metric tons)	6.9	7.0	2.8
CO_2 emissions growth (%, 1990–2005)	280.2	–29.3	93.5
Particulate matter (urban-pop.-weighted avg., µg/cu. m)	19	27	67
Transport sector fuel consumption per capita (liters)	245	255	99
Water and sanitation			
Internal freshwater resources per capita (cu. m)	9,409	11,806	4,117
Freshwater withdrawal			
Total (% of internal resources)	..	7.2	8.7
Agriculture (% of total freshwater withdrawal)	..	60	80
Access to improved water source (% of total population)	99	95	88
Rural (% of rural population)	98	88	82
Urban (% of urban population)	100	99	96
Access to improved sanitation (% of total population)	95	89	55
Rural (% of rural population)	92	79	43
Urban (% of urban population)	99	94	71
Environment and health			
Acute resp. infection prevalence (% of children under five)	2.0		
Diarrhea prevalence (% of children under five)	8.9		
Under-five mortality rate (per 1,000 live births)	14	23	50
National accounting aggregates			
Gross savings (% of GNI)	8.9	24.0	41.7
Consumption of fixed capital (% of GNI)	11.1	12.8	10.7
Education expenditure (% of GNI)	..	4.0	2.6
Energy depletion (% of GNI)	0.2	9.8	6.6
Mineral depletion (% of GNI)	0.0	0.7	1.2
Net forest depletion (% of GNI)	..	0.0	0.2
CO_2 damage (% of GNI)	0.9	1.0	1.2
Particulate emission damage (% of GNI)	0.1	0.5	1.1
Adjusted net savings (% of GNI)	..	3.2	23.5

Botswana

Population (millions)	**1.9**	Land area (1,000 sq. km)	**566.7**	GDP ($ billions)	**12.3**

	Country data	Sub-Saharan Africa group	Upper middle-income group
GNI per capita, *World Bank Atlas* method ($)	6,120	951	7,107
Urban population (% of total)	59	36	75
Urban population growth (average annual %, 1990–2007)	3.9	4.0	1.4
Population growth (average annual %, 1990–2007)	1.9	2.6	0.9
Agriculture			
Agricultural land (% of land area)	46	44	31
Agricultural productivity (value added per worker, 2000 $)	367	287	2,947
Food production index (1999–2001 = 100)	107	109	113
Population density, rural (people/sq. km of arable land)	208	351	110
Forests and biodiversity			
Forest area (% of land area)	21.1	26.5	39.3
Deforestation (average annual %, 1990–2005)	0.9	0.6	0.2
Nationally protected area (% of land area)	30.8	11.3	10.3
Animal species, total known	739		
Animal species, threatened	15		
Higher plant species, total known	2,151		
Higher plant species, threatened	0		
GEF benefits index for biodiversity (0–100, median is 1.5)	1.4		
Energy			
GDP per unit of energy use (2005 PPP $/kg oil equivalent)	11.7	3.0	4.8
Energy use per capita (kg oil equivalent)	1,054	670	2,300
Energy from biomass products and waste (% of total)	23.2	56.3	7.0
Electric power consumption per capita (kWh)	1,419	531	3,242
Electricity generated using fossil fuel (% of total)	100.0	65.6	62.8
Electricity generated by hydropower (% of total)	0.0	18.0	27.6
Emissions and pollution			
CO_2 emissions per unit of GDP (kg/2005 PPP $)	0.2	0.5	0.5
CO_2 emissions per capita (metric tons)	2.5	0.8	5.5
CO_2 emissions growth (%, 1990–2005)	110.0	40.1	-8.3
Particulate matter (urban-pop.-weighted avg., µg/cu. m)	67	53	30
Transport sector fuel consumption per capita (liters)	313	64	332
Water and sanitation			
Internal freshwater resources per capita (cu. m)	1,276	4,824	16,993
Freshwater withdrawal			
Total (% of internal resources)	8.1	3.2	13.8
Agriculture (% of total freshwater withdrawal)	41	87	57
Access to improved water source (% of total population)	96	58	95
Rural (% of rural population)	90	46	83
Urban (% of urban population)	100	81	98
Access to improved sanitation (% of total population)	47	31	83
Rural (% of rural population)	30	24	64
Urban (% of urban population)	60	42	89
Environment and health			
Acute resp. infection prevalence (% of children under five)	40.0		
Diarrhea prevalence (% of children under five)	6.5		
Under-five mortality rate (per 1,000 live births)	40	146	24
National accounting aggregates			
Gross savings (% of GNI)	57.9	17.4	23.2
Consumption of fixed capital (% of GNI)	12.8	11.1	12.8
Education expenditure (% of GNI)	6.6	3.6	4.4
Energy depletion (% of GNI)	0.2	11.7	7.6
Mineral depletion (% of GNI)	8.2	1.5	1.3
Net forest depletion (% of GNI)	0.0	0.5	0.0
CO_2 damage (% of GNI)	0.3	0.7	0.6
Particulate emission damage (% of GNI)	..	0.4	0.4
Adjusted net savings (% of GNI)	42.9	-5.0	4.9

Brazil

Population (millions)	**192**	Land area (1,000 sq. km)	**8,459**	GDP ($ billions)	**1,313.4**

	Country data	Latin America & Caribbean group	Upper middle-income group
GNI per capita, *World Bank Atlas* method ($)	5,860	5,801	7,107
Urban population (% of total)	85	78	75
Urban population growth (average annual %, 1990–2007)	2.2	2.1	1.4
Population growth (average annual %, 1990–2007)	1.5	1.5	0.9
Agriculture			
Agricultural land (% of land area)	31	36	31
Agricultural productivity (value added per worker, 2000 $)	3,218	3,158	2,947
Food production index (1999–2001 = 100)	124	117	113
Population density, rural (people/sq. km of arable land)	50	232	110
Forests and biodiversity			
Forest area (% of land area)	56.5	45.4	39.3
Deforestation (average annual %, 1990–2005)	0.6	0.5	0.2
Nationally protected area (% of land area)	17.9	16.7	10.3
Animal species, total known	2,290		
Animal species, threatened	356		
Higher plant species, total known	56,215		
Higher plant species, threatened	382		
GEF benefits index for biodiversity (0–100, median is 1.5)	100.0		
Energy			
GDP per unit of energy use (2005 PPP $/kg oil equivalent)	7.3	7.3	4.8
Energy use per capita (kg oil equivalent)	1,184	1,240	2,300
Energy from biomass products and waste (% of total)	29.6	15.9	7.0
Electric power consumption per capita (kWh)	2,060	1,808	3,242
Electricity generated using fossil fuel (% of total)	9.8	37.0	62.8
Electricity generated by hydropower (% of total)	83.2	57.3	27.6
Emissions and pollution			
CO_2 emissions per unit of GDP (kg/2005 PPP $)	0.2	0.3	0.5
CO_2 emissions per capita (metric tons)	1.7	2.5	5.5
CO_2 emissions growth (%, 1990–2005)	60.6	33.4	–8.3
Particulate matter (urban-pop.-weighted avg., µg/cu. m)	23	35	30
Transport sector fuel consumption per capita (liters)	253	295	332
Water and sanitation			
Internal freshwater resources per capita (cu. m)	28,277	23,965	16,993
Freshwater withdrawal			
Total (% of internal resources)	1.1	2.0	13.8
Agriculture (% of total freshwater withdrawal)	62	71	57
Access to improved water source (% of total population)	91	91	95
Rural (% of rural population)	58	73	83
Urban (% of urban population)	97	97	98
Access to improved sanitation (% of total population)	77	78	83
Rural (% of rural population)	37	51	64
Urban (% of urban population)	84	86	89
Environment and health			
Acute resp. infection prevalence (% of children under five)	24.0		
Diarrhea prevalence (% of children under five)	13.1		
Under-five mortality rate (per 1,000 live births)	22	26	24
National accounting aggregates			
Gross savings (% of GNI)	17.0	22.9	23.2
Consumption of fixed capital (% of GNI)	12.6	12.6	12.8
Education expenditure (% of GNI)	4.4	4.5	4.4
Energy depletion (% of GNI)	2.3	5.4	7.6
Mineral depletion (% of GNI)	1.6	1.9	1.3
Net forest depletion (% of GNI)	0.0	0.0	0.0
CO_2 damage (% of GNI)	0.2	0.3	0.6
Particulate emission damage (% of GNI)	0.2	0.4	0.4
Adjusted net savings (% of GNI)	4.5	6.7	4.9

Brunei Darussalam

Population (thousands) **389** Land area (1,000 sq. km) **5** GDP ($ billions) **11.5**

	Country data	High-income group
GNI per capita, *World Bank Atlas* method ($)	26,740	37,572
Urban population (% of total)	74	78
Urban population growth (average annual %, 1990–2007)	3.2	1.0
Population growth (average annual %, 1990–2007)	2.4	0.7
Agriculture		
Agricultural land (% of land area)	5	38
Agricultural productivity (value added per worker, 2000 $)	86,426	27,680
Food production index (1999–2001 = 100)	142	102
Population density, rural (people/sq. km of arable land)	708	323
Forests and biodiversity		
Forest area (% of land area)	52.8	28.8
Deforestation (average annual %, 1990–2005)	0.8	–0.1
Nationally protected area (% of land area)	61.5	11.8
Animal species, total known	567	
Animal species, threatened	72	
Higher plant species, total known	6,000	
Higher plant species, threatened	99	
GEF benefits index for biodiversity (0–100, median is 1.5)	0.1	
Energy		
GDP per unit of energy use (2005 PPP $/kg oil equivalent)	6.5	6.3
Energy use per capita (kg oil equivalent)	7,346	5,416
Energy from biomass products and waste (% of total)	0.0	3.4
Electric power consumption per capita (kWh)	8,174	9,675
Electricity generated using fossil fuel (% of total)	100.0	62.0
Electricity generated by hydropower (% of total)	0.0	11.4
Emissions and pollution		
CO_2 emissions per unit of GDP (kg/2005 PPP $)	0.3	0.4
CO_2 emissions per capita (metric tons)	15.8	12.6
CO_2 emissions growth (%, 1990–2005)	–7.9	19.1
Particulate matter (urban-pop.-weighted avg., µg/cu. m)	54	26
Transport sector fuel consumption per capita (liters)	1,010	1,159
Water and sanitation		
Internal freshwater resources per capita (cu. m)	21,837	9,313
Freshwater withdrawal		
Total (% of internal resources)	..	10.4
Agriculture (% of total freshwater withdrawal)	..	43
Access to improved water source (% of total population)	99	100
Rural (% of rural population)	..	98
Urban (% of urban population)	..	100
Access to improved sanitation (% of total population)	..	100
Rural (% of rural population)	..	99
Urban (% of urban population)	..	100
Environment and health		
Acute resp. infection prevalence (% of children under five)	..	
Diarrhea prevalence (% of children under five)	..	
Under-five mortality rate (per 1,000 live births)	9	7
National accounting aggregates		
Gross savings (% of GNI)	..	20.6
Consumption of fixed capital (% of GNI)	..	14.5
Education expenditure (% of GNI)	..	4.6
Energy depletion (% of GNI)	..	1.5
Mineral depletion (% of GNI)	..	0.2
Net forest depletion (% of GNI)	..	0.0
CO_2 damage (% of GNI)	..	0.3
Particulate emission damage (% of GNI)	..	0.3
Adjusted net savings (% of GNI)	..	8.5

Bulgaria

| | Population (millions) | **7.7** | Land area (1,000 sq. km) | **108.6** | GDP ($ billions) | **39.5** |

	Country data	Europe & Central Asia group	Upper middle-income group
GNI per capita, *World Bank Atlas* method ($)	4,580	6,052	7,107
Urban population (% of total)	71	64	75
Urban population growth (average annual %, 1990–2007)	–0.4	0.2	1.4
Population growth (average annual %, 1990–2007)	–0.8	0.1	0.9
Agriculture			
Agricultural land (% of land area)	48	28	31
Agricultural productivity (value added per worker, 2000 $)	7,239	2,228	2,947
Food production index (1999–2001 = 100)	95	110	113
Population density, rural (people/sq. km of arable land)	73	129	110
Forests and biodiversity			
Forest area (% of land area)	33.4	38.3	39.3
Deforestation (average annual %, 1990–2005)	–0.6	0.0	0.2
Nationally protected area (% of land area)	10.1	6.1	10.3
Animal species, total known	485		
Animal species, threatened	45		
Higher plant species, total known	3,572		
Higher plant species, threatened	0		
GEF benefits index for biodiversity (0–100, median is 1.5)	0.8		
Energy			
GDP per unit of energy use (2005 PPP $/kg oil equivalent)	3.7	3.5	4.8
Energy use per capita (kg oil equivalent)	2,688	2,930	2,300
Energy from biomass products and waste (% of total)	3.9	2.2	7.0
Electric power consumption per capita (kWh)	4,311	3,835	3,242
Electricity generated using fossil fuel (% of total)	47.8	67.7	62.8
Electricity generated by hydropower (% of total)	9.3	17.4	27.6
Emissions and pollution			
CO_2 emissions per unit of GDP (kg/2005 PPP $)	0.6	0.7	0.5
CO_2 emissions per capita (metric tons)	5.7	7.0	5.5
CO_2 emissions growth (%, 1990–2005)	–41.0	–29.3	–8.3
Particulate matter (urban-pop.-weighted avg., μg/cu. m)	57	27	30
Transport sector fuel consumption per capita (liters)	313	255	332
Water and sanitation			
Internal freshwater resources per capita (cu. m)	2,742	11,806	16,993
Freshwater withdrawal			
Total (% of internal resources)	50.0	7.2	13.8
Agriculture (% of total freshwater withdrawal)	19	60	57
Access to improved water source (% of total population)	99	95	95
Rural (% of rural population)	97	88	83
Urban (% of urban population)	100	99	98
Access to improved sanitation (% of total population)	99	89	83
Rural (% of rural population)	96	79	64
Urban (% of urban population)	100	94	89
Environment and health			
Acute resp. infection prevalence (% of children under five)	..		
Diarrhea prevalence (% of children under five)	..		
Under-five mortality rate (per 1,000 live births)	12	23	24
National accounting aggregates			
Gross savings (% of GNI)	17.8	24.0	23.2
Consumption of fixed capital (% of GNI)	11.9	12.8	12.8
Education expenditure (% of GNI)	4.1	4.0	4.4
Energy depletion (% of GNI)	0.6	9.8	7.6
Mineral depletion (% of GNI)	1.1	0.7	1.3
Net forest depletion (% of GNI)	0.0	0.0	0.0
CO_2 damage (% of GNI)	1.0	1.0	0.6
Particulate emission damage (% of GNI)	1.5	0.5	0.4
Adjusted net savings (% of GNI)	5.7	3.2	4.9

Burkina Faso

Population (millions)	**15**	Land area (1,000 sq. km)	**274**	GDP ($ billions)	**6.8**

	Country data	Sub-Saharan Africa group	Low-income group
GNI per capita, *World Bank Atlas* method ($)	430	951	574
Urban population (% of total)	19	36	32
Urban population growth (average annual %, 1990–2007)	4.9	4.0	3.7
Population growth (average annual %, 1990–2007)	3.0	2.6	2.4
Agriculture			
Agricultural land (% of land area)	40	44	39
Agricultural productivity (value added per worker, 2000 $)	179	287	330
Food production index (1999–2001 = 100)	109	109	112
Population density, rural (people/sq. km of arable land)	235	351	603
Forests and biodiversity			
Forest area (% of land area)	24.8	26.5	24.7
Deforestation (average annual %, 1990–2005)	0.3	0.6	0.7
Nationally protected area (% of land area)	14.0	11.3	10.8
Animal species, total known	581		
Animal species, threatened	14		
Higher plant species, total known	1,100		
Higher plant species, threatened	2		
GEF benefits index for biodiversity (0–100, median is 1.5)	0.3		
Energy			
GDP per unit of energy use (2005 PPP $/kg oil equivalent)	..	3.0	3.2
Energy use per capita (kg oil equivalent)	..	670	478
Energy from biomass products and waste (% of total)	..	56.3	53.8
Electric power consumption per capita (kWh)	..	531	309
Electricity generated using fossil fuel (% of total)	..	65.6	48.4
Electricity generated by hydropower (% of total)	..	18.0	38.8
Emissions and pollution			
CO_2 emissions per unit of GDP (kg/2005 PPP $)	0.05	0.49	0.39
CO_2 emissions per capita (metric tons)	0.05	0.85	0.58
CO_2 emissions growth (%, 1990–2005)	33.6	40.1	39.3
Particulate matter (urban-pop.-weighted avg., µg/cu. m)	84	53	69
Transport sector fuel consumption per capita (liters)	..	64	41
Water and sanitation			
Internal freshwater resources per capita (cu. m)	846	4,824	4,619
Freshwater withdrawal			
Total (% of internal resources)	6.4	3.2	9.4
Agriculture (% of total freshwater withdrawal)	86	87	90
Access to improved water source (% of total population)	72	58	68
Rural (% of rural population)	66	46	60
Urban (% of urban population)	97	81	84
Access to improved sanitation (% of total population)	13	31	39
Rural (% of rural population)	6	24	33
Urban (% of urban population)	41	42	54
Environment and health			
Acute resp. infection prevalence (% of children under five)	9.0		
Diarrhea prevalence (% of children under five)	20.0		
Under-five mortality rate (per 1,000 live births)	191	146	126
National accounting aggregates			
Gross savings (% of GNI)	..	17.4	25.4
Consumption of fixed capital (% of GNI)	8.4	11.1	9.3
Education expenditure (% of GNI)	4.3	3.6	2.6
Energy depletion (% of GNI)	0.0	11.7	9.8
Mineral depletion (% of GNI)	0.0	1.5	0.9
Net forest depletion (% of GNI)	1.1	0.5	0.8
CO_2 damage (% of GNI)	0.1	0.7	0.7
Particulate emission damage (% of GNI)	1.3	0.4	0.7
Adjusted net savings (% of GNI)	..	–5.0	5.8

Burundi

	Country data	Sub-Saharan Africa group	Low-income group
Population (millions)	**8.5**		
Land area (1,000 sq. km)	**25.7**		
GDP ($ millions)	**974**		

	Country data	Sub-Saharan Africa group	Low-income group
GNI per capita, *World Bank Atlas* method ($)	110	951	574
Urban population (% of total)	10	36	32
Urban population growth (average annual %, 1990–2007)	5.1	4.0	3.7
Population growth (average annual %, 1990–2007)	2.4	2.6	2.4
Agriculture			
Agricultural land (% of land area)	91	44	39
Agricultural productivity (value added per worker, 2000 $)	64	287	330
Food production index (1999–2001 = 100)	104	109	112
Population density, rural (people/sq. km of arable land)	732	351	603
Forests and biodiversity			
Forest area (% of land area)	5.9	26.5	24.7
Deforestation (average annual %, 1990–2005)	4.2	0.6	0.7
Nationally protected area (% of land area)	6.0	11.3	10.8
Animal species, total known	713		
Animal species, threatened	46		
Higher plant species, total known	2,500		
Higher plant species, threatened	2		
GEF benefits index for biodiversity (0–100, median is 1.5)	0.3		
Energy			
GDP per unit of energy use (2005 PPP $/kg oil equivalent)	..	3.0	3.2
Energy use per capita (kg oil equivalent)	..	670	478
Energy from biomass products and waste (% of total)	..	56.3	53.8
Electric power consumption per capita (kWh)	..	531	309
Electricity generated using fossil fuel (% of total)	..	65.6	48.4
Electricity generated by hydropower (% of total)	..	18.0	38.8
Emissions and pollution			
CO_2 emissions per unit of GDP (kg/2005 PPP $)	0.09	0.49	0.39
CO_2 emissions per capita (metric tons)	0.03	0.85	0.58
CO_2 emissions growth (%, 1990–2005)	15.1	40.1	39.3
Particulate matter (urban-pop.-weighted avg., μg/cu. m)	29	53	69
Transport sector fuel consumption per capita (liters)	..	64	41
Water and sanitation			
Internal freshwater resources per capita (cu. m)	1,184	4,824	4,619
Freshwater withdrawal			
Total (% of internal resources)	2.9	3.2	9.4
Agriculture (% of total freshwater withdrawal)	77	87	90
Access to improved water source (% of total population)	71	58	68
Rural (% of rural population)	70	46	60
Urban (% of urban population)	84	81	84
Access to improved sanitation (% of total population)	41	31	39
Rural (% of rural population)	41	24	33
Urban (% of urban population)	44	42	54
Environment and health			
Acute resp. infection prevalence (% of children under five)	13.0		
Diarrhea prevalence (% of children under five)	..		
Under-five mortality rate (per 1,000 live births)	180	146	126
National accounting aggregates			
Gross savings (% of GNI)	..	17.4	25.4
Consumption of fixed capital (% of GNI)	6.6	11.1	9.3
Education expenditure (% of GNI)	5.1	3.6	2.6
Energy depletion (% of GNI)	0.0	11.7	9.8
Mineral depletion (% of GNI)	0.8	1.5	0.9
Net forest depletion (% of GNI)	11.5	0.5	0.8
CO_2 damage (% of GNI)	0.2	0.7	0.7
Particulate emission damage (% of GNI)	0.1	0.4	0.7
Adjusted net savings (% of GNI)	..	−5.0	5.8

Cambodia

	Population (millions)	**14**	Land area (1,000 sq. km)	**177**	GDP ($ billions)	**8.3**

	Country data	East Asia & Pacific group	Low-income group
GNI per capita, *World Bank Atlas* method ($)	550	2,182	574
Urban population (% of total)	21	43	32
Urban population growth (average annual %, 1990–2007)	5.3	3.5	3.7
Population growth (average annual %, 1990–2007)	2.3	1.1	2.4
Agriculture			
Agricultural land (% of land area)	30	51	39
Agricultural productivity (value added per worker, 2000 $)	337	458	330
Food production index (1999–2001 = 100)	110	120	112
Population density, rural (people/sq. km of arable land)	303	547	603
Forests and biodiversity			
Forest area (% of land area)	59.2	28.4	24.7
Deforestation (average annual %, 1990–2005)	1.4	-0.1	0.7
Nationally protected area (% of land area)	23.5	14.0	10.8
Animal species, total known	648		
Animal species, threatened	162		
Higher plant species, total known	..		
Higher plant species, threatened	31		
GEF benefits index for biodiversity (0–100, median is 1.5)	3.5		
Energy			
GDP per unit of energy use (2005 PPP $/kg oil equivalent)	4.5	3.4	3.2
Energy use per capita (kg oil equivalent)	351	1,258	478
Energy from biomass products and waste (% of total)	71.3	14.7	53.8
Electric power consumption per capita (kWh)	88	1,669	309
Electricity generated using fossil fuel (% of total)	95.7	82.0	48.4
Electricity generated by hydropower (% of total)	4.1	15.0	38.8
Emissions and pollution			
CO_2 emissions per unit of GDP (kg/2005 PPP $)	0.03	0.92	0.39
CO_2 emissions per capita (metric tons)	0.04	3.59	0.58
CO_2 emissions growth (%, 1990–2005)	19.5	123.4	39.3
Particulate matter (urban-pop.-weighted avg., µg/cu. m)	46	69	69
Transport sector fuel consumption per capita (liters)	31	106	41
Water and sanitation			
Internal freshwater resources per capita (cu. m)	8,346	4,948	4,619
Freshwater withdrawal			
Total (% of internal resources)	3.4	10.2	9.4
Agriculture (% of total freshwater withdrawal)	98	74	90
Access to improved water source (% of total population)	65	87	68
Rural (% of rural population)	61	81	60
Urban (% of urban population)	80	96	84
Access to improved sanitation (% of total population)	28	66	39
Rural (% of rural population)	19	59	33
Urban (% of urban population)	62	75	54
Environment and health			
Acute resp. infection prevalence (% of children under five)	20.0		
Diarrhea prevalence (% of children under five)	18.9		
Under-five mortality rate (per 1,000 live births)	91	27	126
National accounting aggregates			
Gross savings (% of GNI)	15.9	48.0	25.4
Consumption of fixed capital (% of GNI)	9.1	10.7	9.3
Education expenditure (% of GNI)	1.7	2.1	2.6
Energy depletion (% of GNI)	0.0	4.9	9.8
Mineral depletion (% of GNI)	0.0	1.3	0.9
Net forest depletion (% of GNI)	0.2	0.0	0.8
CO_2 damage (% of GNI)	0.1	1.3	0.7
Particulate emission damage (% of GNI)	0.3	1.3	0.7
Adjusted net savings (% of GNI)	7.9	30.6	5.8

Cameroon

	Population (millions)	**19**	Land area (1,000 sq. km)	**465**	GDP ($ billions)	**20.7**

	Country data	Sub-Saharan Africa group	Lower middle-income group
GNI per capita, *World Bank Atlas* method ($)	1,050	951	1,905
Urban population (% of total)	56	36	42
Urban population growth (average annual %, 1990–2007)	4.3	4.0	2.9
Population growth (average annual %, 1990–2007)	2.4	2.6	1.3
Agriculture			
Agricultural land (% of land area)	20	44	47
Agricultural productivity (value added per worker, 2000 $)	666	287	532
Food production index (1999–2001 = 100)	108	109	116
Population density, rural (people/sq. km of arable land)	136	351	511
Forests and biodiversity			
Forest area (% of land area)	45.6	26.5	25.0
Deforestation (average annual %, 1990–2005)	1.0	0.6	0.1
Nationally protected area (% of land area)	8.6	11.3	11.0
Animal species, total known	1,258		
Animal species, threatened	159		
Higher plant species, total known	8,260		
Higher plant species, threatened	355		
GEF benefits index for biodiversity (0–100, median is 1.5)	12.5		
Energy			
GDP per unit of energy use (2005 PPP $/kg oil equivalent)	5.1	3.0	3.9
Energy use per capita (kg oil equivalent)	390	670	1,019
Energy from biomass products and waste (% of total)	79.2	56.3	15.2
Electric power consumption per capita (kWh)	186	531	1,269
Electricity generated using fossil fuel (% of total)	5.9	65.6	79.0
Electricity generated by hydropower (% of total)	94.1	18.0	16.3
Emissions and pollution			
CO_2 emissions per unit of GDP (kg/2005 PPP $)	0.1	0.5	0.8
CO_2 emissions per capita (metric tons)	0.2	0.8	2.8
CO_2 emissions growth (%, 1990–2005)	131.5	40.1	93.5
Particulate matter (urban-pop.-weighted avg., µg/cu. m)	62	53	67
Transport sector fuel consumption per capita (liters)	44	64	99
Water and sanitation			
Internal freshwater resources per capita (cu. m)	14,731	4,824	4,117
Freshwater withdrawal			
Total (% of internal resources)	0.4	3.2	8.7
Agriculture (% of total freshwater withdrawal)	74	87	80
Access to improved water source (% of total population)	70	58	88
Rural (% of rural population)	47	46	82
Urban (% of urban population)	88	81	96
Access to improved sanitation (% of total population)	51	31	55
Rural (% of rural population)	42	24	43
Urban (% of urban population)	58	42	71
Environment and health			
Acute resp. infection prevalence (% of children under five)	11.0		
Diarrhea prevalence (% of children under five)	18.9		
Under-five mortality rate (per 1,000 live births)	148	146	50
National accounting aggregates			
Gross savings (% of GNI)	19.7	17.4	41.7
Consumption of fixed capital (% of GNI)	9.7	11.1	10.7
Education expenditure (% of GNI)	2.6	3.6	2.6
Energy depletion (% of GNI)	6.4	11.7	6.6
Mineral depletion (% of GNI)	0.1	1.5	1.2
Net forest depletion (% of GNI)	0.0	0.5	0.2
CO_2 damage (% of GNI)	0.2	0.7	1.2
Particulate emission damage (% of GNI)	0.8	0.4	1.1
Adjusted net savings (% of GNI)	5.3	–5.0	23.5

Canada

Population (millions) **33** Land area (1,000 sq. km) **9,094** GDP ($ billions) **1,329.9**

	Country data	High-income group
GNI per capita, *World Bank Atlas* method ($)	39,650	37,572
Urban population (% of total)	80	78
Urban population growth (average annual %, 1990–2007)	1.3	1.0
Population growth (average annual %, 1990–2007)	1.0	0.7
Agriculture		
Agricultural land (% of land area)	7	38
Agricultural productivity (value added per worker, 2000 $)	47,181	27,680
Food production index (1999–2001 = 100)	..	102
Population density, rural (people/sq. km of arable land)	14	323
Forests and biodiversity		
Forest area (% of land area)	34.1	28.8
Deforestation (average annual %, 1990–2005)	0.0	−0.1
Nationally protected area (% of land area)	5.2	11.8
Animal species, total known	683	
Animal species, threatened	70	
Higher plant species, total known	3,270	
Higher plant species, threatened	2	
GEF benefits index for biodiversity (0–100, median is 1.5)	21.5	
Energy		
GDP per unit of energy use (2005 PPP $/kg oil equivalent)	4.3	6.3
Energy use per capita (kg oil equivalent)	8,262	5,416
Energy from biomass products and waste (% of total)	4.7	3.4
Electric power consumption per capita (kWh)	16,753	9,675
Electricity generated using fossil fuel (% of total)	24.1	62.0
Electricity generated by hydropower (% of total)	58.0	11.4
Emissions and pollution		
CO_2 emissions per unit of GDP (kg/2005 PPP $)	0.5	0.4
CO_2 emissions per capita (metric tons)	16.6	12.6
CO_2 emissions growth (%, 1990–2005)	25.4	19.1
Particulate matter (urban-pop.-weighted avg., µg/cu. m)	17	26
Transport sector fuel consumption per capita (liters)	1,536	1,159
Water and sanitation		
Internal freshwater resources per capita (cu. m)	86,426	9,313
Freshwater withdrawal		
Total (% of internal resources)	1.6	10.4
Agriculture (% of total freshwater withdrawal)	12	43
Access to improved water source (% of total population)	100	100
Rural (% of rural population)	99	98
Urban (% of urban population)	100	100
Access to improved sanitation (% of total population)	100	100
Rural (% of rural population)	99	99
Urban (% of urban population)	100	100
Environment and health		
Acute resp. infection prevalence (% of children under five)	..	
Diarrhea prevalence (% of children under five)	..	
Under-five mortality rate (per 1,000 live births)	6	7
National accounting aggregates		
Gross savings (% of GNI)	23.0	20.6
Consumption of fixed capital (% of GNI)	14.9	14.5
Education expenditure (% of GNI)	4.8	4.6
Energy depletion (% of GNI)	4.1	1.5
Mineral depletion (% of GNI)	0.9	0.2
Net forest depletion (% of GNI)	0.0	0.0
CO_2 damage (% of GNI)	0.4	0.3
Particulate emission damage (% of GNI)	0.1	0.3
Adjusted net savings (% of GNI)	7.4	8.5

Cape Verde

Population (thousands) **530**	Land area (1,000 sq. km)	**4**	GDP ($ billions) **1.4**

	Country data	Sub-Saharan Africa group	Lower middle-income group
GNI per capita, *World Bank Atlas* method ($)	2,430	951	1,905
Urban population (% of total)	59	36	42
Urban population growth (average annual %, 1990–2007)	4.1	4.0	2.9
Population growth (average annual %, 1990–2007)	2.4	2.6	1.3
Agriculture			
Agricultural land (% of land area)	18	44	47
Agricultural productivity (value added per worker, 2000 $)	1,510	287	532
Food production index (1999–2001 = 100)	95	109	116
Population density, rural (people/sq. km of arable land)	469	351	511
Forests and biodiversity			
Forest area (% of land area)	20.7	26.5	25.0
Deforestation (average annual %, 1990–2005)	-2.5	0.6	0.1
Nationally protected area (% of land area)	..	11.3	11.0
Animal species, total known	186		
Animal species, threatened	26		
Higher plant species, total known	774		
Higher plant species, threatened	2		
GEF benefits index for biodiversity (0–100, median is 1.5)	2.4		
Energy			
GDP per unit of energy use (2005 PPP $/kg oil equivalent)	..	3.0	3.9
Energy use per capita (kg oil equivalent)	..	670	1,019
Energy from biomass products and waste (% of total)	..	56.3	15.2
Electric power consumption per capita (kWh)	..	531	1,269
Electricity generated using fossil fuel (% of total)	..	65.6	79.0
Electricity generated by hydropower (% of total)	..	18.0	16.3
Emissions and pollution			
CO_2 emissions per unit of GDP (kg/2005 PPP $)	0.2	0.5	0.8
CO_2 emissions per capita (metric tons)	0.6	0.8	2.8
CO_2 emissions growth (%, 1990–2005)	225.0	40.1	93.5
Particulate matter (urban-pop.-weighted avg., μg/cu. m)	..	53	67
Transport sector fuel consumption per capita (liters)	..	64	99
Water and sanitation			
Internal freshwater resources per capita (cu. m)	566	4,824	4,117
Freshwater withdrawal			
Total (% of internal resources)	..	3.2	8.7
Agriculture (% of total freshwater withdrawal)	..	87	80
Access to improved water source (% of total population)	..	58	88
Rural (% of rural population)	..	46	82
Urban (% of urban population)	..	81	96
Access to improved sanitation (% of total population)	..	31	55
Rural (% of rural population)	..	24	43
Urban (% of urban population)	..	42	71
Environment and health			
Acute resp. infection prevalence (% of children under five)	..		
Diarrhea prevalence (% of children under five)	..		
Under-five mortality rate (per 1,000 live births)	32	146	50
National accounting aggregates			
Gross savings (% of GNI)	24.0	17.4	41.7
Consumption of fixed capital (% of GNI)	11.3	11.1	10.7
Education expenditure (% of GNI)	5.0	3.6	2.6
Energy depletion (% of GNI)	0.0	11.7	6.6
Mineral depletion (% of GNI)	0.0	1.5	1.2
Net forest depletion (% of GNI)	0.0	0.5	0.2
CO_2 damage (% of GNI)	0.2	0.7	1.2
Particulate emission damage (% of GNI)	..	0.4	1.1
Adjusted net savings (% of GNI)	17.6	-5.0	23.5

Cayman Islands

| Population (thousands) **54** | Land area (sq. km) | **260** GDP ($ millions) | .. |

	Country data	High-income group
GNI per capita, *World Bank Atlas* method ($)	..	37,572
Urban population (% of total)	100	78
Urban population growth (average annual %, 1990–2007)	4.2	1.0
Population growth (average annual %, 1990–2007)	4.2	0.7
Agriculture		
Agricultural land (% of land area)	12	38
Agricultural productivity (value added per worker, 2000 $)	..	27,680
Food production index (1999–2001 = 100)	100	102
Population density, rural (people/sq. km of arable land)	0	323
Forests and biodiversity		
Forest area (% of land area)	47.7	28.8
Deforestation (average annual %, 1990–2005)	0.0	–0.1
Nationally protected area (% of land area)	1.5	11.8
Animal species, total known	221	
Animal species, threatened	31	
Higher plant species, total known	539	
Higher plant species, threatened	2	
GEF benefits index for biodiversity (0–100, median is 1.5)	0.6	
Energy		
GDP per unit of energy use (2005 PPP $/kg oil equivalent)	..	6.3
Energy use per capita (kg oil equivalent)	..	5,416
Energy from biomass products and waste (% of total)	..	3.4
Electric power consumption per capita (kWh)	..	9,675
Electricity generated using fossil fuel (% of total)	..	62.0
Electricity generated by hydropower (% of total)	..	11.4
Emissions and pollution		
CO_2 emissions per unit of GDP (kg/2005 PPP $)	..	0.4
CO_2 emissions per capita (metric tons)	7.1	12.6
CO_2 emissions growth (%, 1990–2005)	26.5	19.1
Particulate matter (urban-pop.-weighted avg., µg/cu. m)	24	26
Transport sector fuel consumption per capita (liters)	..	1,159
Water and sanitation		
Internal freshwater resources per capita (cu. m)	..	9,313
Freshwater withdrawal		
Total (% of internal resources)	..	10.4
Agriculture (% of total freshwater withdrawal)	..	43
Access to improved water source (% of total population)	..	100
Rural (% of rural population)	..	98
Urban (% of urban population)	..	100
Access to improved sanitation (% of total population)	..	100
Rural (% of rural population)	..	99
Urban (% of urban population)	..	100
Environment and health		
Acute resp. infection prevalence (% of children under five)	..	
Diarrhea prevalence (% of children under five)	..	
Under-five mortality rate (per 1,000 live births)	..	7
National accounting aggregates		
Gross savings (% of GNI)	..	20.6
Consumption of fixed capital (% of GNI)	..	14.5
Education expenditure (% of GNI)	..	4.6
Energy depletion (% of GNI)	..	1.5
Mineral depletion (% of GNI)	..	0.2
Net forest depletion (% of GNI)	..	0.0
CO_2 damage (% of GNI)	..	0.3
Particulate emission damage (% of GNI)	..	0.3
Adjusted net savings (% of GNI)	..	8.5

Central African Republic

| | Population (millions) | **4.3** | Land area (1,000 sq. km) | **623.0** | GDP ($ billions) | **1.7** |

	Country data	Sub-Saharan Africa group	Low-income group
GNI per capita, *World Bank Atlas* method ($)	370	951	574
Urban population (% of total)	38	36	32
Urban population growth (average annual %, 1990–2007)	2.4	4.0	3.7
Population growth (average annual %, 1990–2007)	2.2	2.6	2.4
Agriculture			
Agricultural land (% of land area)	8	44	39
Agricultural productivity (value added per worker, 2000 $)	384	287	330
Food production index (1999–2001 = 100)	111	109	112
Population density, rural (people/sq. km of arable land)	134	351	603
Forests and biodiversity			
Forest area (% of land area)	36.5	26.5	24.7
Deforestation (average annual %, 1990–2005)	0.1	0.6	0.7
Nationally protected area (% of land area)	15.2	11.3	10.8
Animal species, total known	850		
Animal species, threatened	13		
Higher plant species, total known	3,602		
Higher plant species, threatened	15		
GEF benefits index for biodiversity (0–100, median is 1.5)	1.5		
Energy			
GDP per unit of energy use (2005 PPP $/kg oil equivalent)	..	3.0	3.2
Energy use per capita (kg oil equivalent)	..	670	478
Energy from biomass products and waste (% of total)	..	56.3	53.8
Electric power consumption per capita (kWh)	..	531	309
Electricity generated using fossil fuel (% of total)	..	65.6	48.4
Electricity generated by hydropower (% of total)	..	18.0	38.8
Emissions and pollution			
CO_2 emissions per unit of GDP (kg/2005 PPP $)	0.09	0.49	0.39
CO_2 emissions per capita (metric tons)	0.06	0.85	0.58
CO_2 emissions growth (%, 1990–2005)	27.8	40.1	39.3
Particulate matter (urban-pop.-weighted avg., µg/cu. m)	44	53	69
Transport sector fuel consumption per capita (liters)	..	64	41
Water and sanitation			
Internal freshwater resources per capita (cu. m)	32,463	4,824	4,619
Freshwater withdrawal			
Total (% of internal resources)	0.0	3.2	9.4
Agriculture (% of total freshwater withdrawal)	4	87	90
Access to improved water source (% of total population)	66	58	68
Rural (% of rural population)	51	46	60
Urban (% of urban population)	90	81	84
Access to improved sanitation (% of total population)	31	31	39
Rural (% of rural population)	25	24	33
Urban (% of urban population)	40	42	54
Environment and health			
Acute resp. infection prevalence (% of children under five)	10.0		
Diarrhea prevalence (% of children under five)	26.5		
Under-five mortality rate (per 1,000 live births)	172	146	126
National accounting aggregates			
Gross savings (% of GNI)	4.5	17.4	25.4
Consumption of fixed capital (% of GNI)	8.2	11.1	9.3
Education expenditure (% of GNI)	1.3	3.6	2.6
Energy depletion (% of GNI)	0.0	11.7	9.8
Mineral depletion (% of GNI)	0.0	1.5	0.9
Net forest depletion (% of GNI)	0.0	0.5	0.8
CO_2 damage (% of GNI)	0.1	0.7	0.7
Particulate emission damage (% of GNI)	0.4	0.4	0.7
Adjusted net savings (% of GNI)	-2.9	-5.0	5.8

Chad

	Country data	Sub-Saharan Africa group	Low-income group
Population (millions) **11** Land area (1,000 sq. km) **1,259** GDP ($ billions) **7.1**			

	Country data	Sub-Saharan Africa group	Low-income group
GNI per capita, *World Bank Atlas* method ($)	540	951	574
Urban population (% of total)	26	36	32
Urban population growth (average annual %, 1990–2007)	4.7	4.0	3.7
Population growth (average annual %, 1990–2007)	3.3	2.6	2.4
Agriculture			
Agricultural land (% of land area)	39	44	39
Agricultural productivity (value added per worker, 2000 $)	225	287	330
Food production index (1999–2001 = 100)	109	109	112
Population density, rural (people/sq. km of arable land)	180	351	603
Forests and biodiversity			
Forest area (% of land area)	9.5	26.5	24.7
Deforestation (average annual %, 1990–2005)	0.6	0.6	0.7
Nationally protected area (% of land area)	9.1	11.3	10.8
Animal species, total known	635		
Animal species, threatened	21		
Higher plant species, total known	1,600		
Higher plant species, threatened	2		
GEF benefits index for biodiversity (0–100, median is 1.5)	2.2		
Energy			
GDP per unit of energy use (2005 PPP $/kg oil equivalent)	..	3.0	3.2
Energy use per capita (kg oil equivalent)	..	670	478
Energy from biomass products and waste (% of total)	..	56.3	53.8
Electric power consumption per capita (kWh)	..	531	309
Electricity generated using fossil fuel (% of total)	..	65.6	48.4
Electricity generated by hydropower (% of total)	..	18.0	38.8
Emissions and pollution			
CO_2 emissions per unit of GDP (kg/2005 PPP $)	0.01	0.49	0.39
CO_2 emissions per capita (metric tons)	0.01	0.85	0.58
CO_2 emissions growth (%, 1990–2005)	-2.6	40.1	39.3
Particulate matter (urban-pop.-weighted avg., μg/cu. m)	109	53	69
Transport sector fuel consumption per capita (liters)	..	64	41
Water and sanitation			
Internal freshwater resources per capita (cu. m)	1,394	4,824	4,619
Freshwater withdrawal			
Total (% of internal resources)	1.5	3.2	9.4
Agriculture (% of total freshwater withdrawal)	83	87	90
Access to improved water source (% of total population)	48	58	68
Rural (% of rural population)	40	46	60
Urban (% of urban population)	71	81	84
Access to improved sanitation (% of total population)	9	31	39
Rural (% of rural population)	4	24	33
Urban (% of urban population)	23	42	54
Environment and health			
Acute resp. infection prevalence (% of children under five)	9.2		
Diarrhea prevalence (% of children under five)	31.2		
Under-five mortality rate (per 1,000 live births)	209	146	126
National accounting aggregates			
Gross savings (% of GNI)	26.9	17.4	25.4
Consumption of fixed capital (% of GNI)	10.2	11.1	9.3
Education expenditure (% of GNI)	1.2	3.6	2.6
Energy depletion (% of GNI)	40.7	11.7	9.8
Mineral depletion (% of GNI)	0.0	1.5	0.9
Net forest depletion (% of GNI)	0.0	0.5	0.8
CO_2 damage (% of GNI)	0.0	0.7	0.7
Particulate emission damage (% of GNI)	1.1	0.4	0.7
Adjusted net savings (% of GNI)	-24.0	-5.0	5.8

Channel Islands

Population (thousands) **149** Land area (sq. km) **190** GDP ($ billions) **11.5**

	Country data	High-income group
GNI per capita, *World Bank Atlas* method ($)	68,640	37,572
Urban population (% of total)	31	78
Urban population growth (average annual %, 1990–2007)	0.2	1.0
Population growth (average annual %, 1990–2007)	0.3	0.7
Agriculture		
Agricultural land (% of land area)	40	38
Agricultural productivity (value added per worker, 2000 $)	..	27,680
Food production index (1999–2001 = 100)	..	102
Population density, rural (people/sq. km of arable land)	2,710	323
Forests and biodiversity		
Forest area (% of land area)	4.2	28.8
Deforestation (average annual %, 1990–2005)	0.0	–0.1
Nationally protected area (% of land area)	..	11.8
Animal species, total known	..	
Animal species, threatened	..	
Higher plant species, total known	..	
Higher plant species, threatened	..	
GEF benefits index for biodiversity (0–100, median is 1.5)	0.0	
Energy		
GDP per unit of energy use (2005 PPP $/kg oil equivalent)	..	6.3
Energy use per capita (kg oil equivalent)	..	5,416
Energy from biomass products and waste (% of total)	..	3.4
Electric power consumption per capita (kWh)	..	9,675
Electricity generated using fossil fuel (% of total)	..	62.0
Electricity generated by hydropower (% of total)	..	11.4
Emissions and pollution		
CO_2 emissions per unit of GDP (kg/2005 PPP $)	..	0.4
CO_2 emissions per capita (metric tons)	..	12.6
CO_2 emissions growth (%, 1990–2005)	..	19.1
Particulate matter (urban-pop.-weighted avg., µg/cu. m)	..	26
Transport sector fuel consumption per capita (liters)	..	1,159
Water and sanitation		
Internal freshwater resources per capita (cu. m)	..	9,313
Freshwater withdrawal		
Total (% of internal resources)	..	10.4
Agriculture (% of total freshwater withdrawal)	..	43
Access to improved water source (% of total population)	..	100
Rural (% of rural population)	..	98
Urban (% of urban population)	..	100
Access to improved sanitation (% of total population)	..	100
Rural (% of rural population)	..	99
Urban (% of urban population)	..	100
Environment and health		
Acute resp. infection prevalence (% of children under five)	..	
Diarrhea prevalence (% of children under five)	..	
Under-five mortality rate (per 1,000 live births)	..	7
National accounting aggregates		
Gross savings (% of GNI)	..	20.6
Consumption of fixed capital (% of GNI)	..	14.5
Education expenditure (% of GNI)	..	4.6
Energy depletion (% of GNI)	..	1.5
Mineral depletion (% of GNI)	..	0.2
Net forest depletion (% of GNI)	..	0.0
CO_2 damage (% of GNI)	..	0.3
Particulate emission damage (% of GNI)	..	0.3
Adjusted net savings (% of GNI)	..	8.5

Chile

	Country data	Latin America & Caribbean group	Upper middle-income group
Population (millions) 17 **Land area (1,000 sq. km)** 749 **GDP ($ billions)** 163.9			

	Country data	Latin America & Caribbean group	Upper middle-income group
GNI per capita, *World Bank Atlas* method ($)	8,190	5,801	7,107
Urban population (% of total)	88	78	75
Urban population growth (average annual %, 1990–2007)	1.7	2.1	1.4
Population growth (average annual %, 1990–2007)	1.4	1.5	0.9
Agriculture			
Agricultural land (% of land area)	20	36	31
Agricultural productivity (value added per worker, 2000 $)	5,720	3,158	2,947
Food production index (1999–2001 = 100)	120	117	113
Population density, rural (people/sq. km of arable land)	104	232	110
Forests and biodiversity			
Forest area (% of land area)	21.5	45.4	39.3
Deforestation (average annual %, 1990–2005)	-0.4	0.5	0.2
Nationally protected area (% of land area)	3.7	16.7	10.3
Animal species, total known	604		
Animal species, threatened	101		
Higher plant species, total known	5,284		
Higher plant species, threatened	40		
GEF benefits index for biodiversity (0–100, median is 1.5)	15.3		
Energy			
GDP per unit of energy use (2005 PPP $/kg oil equivalent)	7.0	7.3	4.8
Energy use per capita (kg oil equivalent)	1,812	1,240	2,300
Energy from biomass products and waste (% of total)	15.9	15.9	7.0
Electric power consumption per capita (kWh)	3,207	1,808	3,242
Electricity generated using fossil fuel (% of total)	38.5	37.0	62.8
Electricity generated by hydropower (% of total)	59.5	57.3	27.6
Emissions and pollution			
CO_2 emissions per unit of GDP (kg/2005 PPP $)	0.3	0.3	0.5
CO_2 emissions per capita (metric tons)	4.1	2.5	5.5
CO_2 emissions growth (%, 1990–2005)	87.1	33.4	-8.3
Particulate matter (urban-pop.-weighted avg., µg/cu. m)	48	35	30
Transport sector fuel consumption per capita (liters)	381	295	332
Water and sanitation			
Internal freshwater resources per capita (cu. m)	53,270	23,965	16,993
Freshwater withdrawal			
Total (% of internal resources)	1.4	2.0	13.8
Agriculture (% of total freshwater withdrawal)	64	71	57
Access to improved water source (% of total population)	95	91	95
Rural (% of rural population)	72	73	83
Urban (% of urban population)	98	97	98
Access to improved sanitation (% of total population)	94	78	83
Rural (% of rural population)	74	51	64
Urban (% of urban population)	97	86	89
Environment and health			
Acute resp. infection prevalence (% of children under five)	..		
Diarrhea prevalence (% of children under five)	..		
Under-five mortality rate (per 1,000 live births)	9	26	24
National accounting aggregates			
Gross savings (% of GNI)	28.7	22.9	23.2
Consumption of fixed capital (% of GNI)	14.3	12.6	12.8
Education expenditure (% of GNI)	3.4	4.5	4.4
Energy depletion (% of GNI)	0.2	5.4	7.6
Mineral depletion (% of GNI)	16.7	1.9	1.3
Net forest depletion (% of GNI)	0.0	0.0	0.0
CO_2 damage (% of GNI)	0.4	0.3	0.6
Particulate emission damage (% of GNI)	0.6	0.4	0.4
Adjusted net savings (% of GNI)	-0.1	6.7	4.9

China

Population (millions) **1,318** Land area (1,000 sq. km) **9,327** GDP ($ billions) **3,205.5**

	Country data	East Asia & Pacific group	Lower middle-income group
GNI per capita, *World Bank Atlas* method ($)	2,370	2,182	1,905
Urban population (% of total)	42	43	42
Urban population growth (average annual %, 1990–2007)	3.4	3.5	2.9
Population growth (average annual %, 1990–2007)	0.9	1.1	1.3
Agriculture			
Agricultural land (% of land area)	60	51	47
Agricultural productivity (value added per worker, 2000 $)	430	458	532
Food production index (1999–2001 = 100)	121	120	116
Population density, rural (people/sq. km of arable land)	542	547	511
Forests and biodiversity			
Forest area (% of land area)	21.2	28.4	25.0
Deforestation (average annual %, 1990–2005)	-1.5	-0.1	0.1
Nationally protected area (% of land area)	15.4	14.0	11.0
Animal species, total known	1,801		
Animal species, threatened	370		
Higher plant species, total known	32,200		
Higher plant species, threatened	446		
GEF benefits index for biodiversity (0–100, median is 1.5)	66.6		
Energy			
GDP per unit of energy use (2005 PPP $/kg oil equivalent)	3.2	3.4	3.9
Energy use per capita (kg oil equivalent)	1,433	1,258	1,019
Energy from biomass products and waste (% of total)	12.0	14.7	15.2
Electric power consumption per capita (kWh)	2,041	1,669	1,269
Electricity generated using fossil fuel (% of total)	82.6	82.0	79.0
Electricity generated by hydropower (% of total)	15.2	15.0	16.3
Emissions and pollution			
CO_2 emissions per unit of GDP (kg/2005 PPP $)	1.0	0.9	0.8
CO_2 emissions per capita (metric tons)	4.3	3.6	2.8
CO_2 emissions growth (%, 1990–2005)	131.2	123.4	93.5
Particulate matter (urban-pop.-weighted avg., µg/cu. m)	73	69	67
Transport sector fuel consumption per capita (liters)	93	106	99
Water and sanitation			
Internal freshwater resources per capita (cu. m)	2,133	4,948	4,117
Freshwater withdrawal			
Total (% of internal resources)	22.4	10.2	8.7
Agriculture (% of total freshwater withdrawal)	68	74	80
Access to improved water source (% of total population)	88	87	88
Rural (% of rural population)	81	81	82
Urban (% of urban population)	98	96	96
Access to improved sanitation (% of total population)	65	66	55
Rural (% of rural population)	59	59	43
Urban (% of urban population)	74	75	71
Environment and health			
Acute resp. infection prevalence (% of children under five)	..		
Diarrhea prevalence (% of children under five)	..		
Under-five mortality rate (per 1,000 live births)	22	27	50
National accounting aggregates			
Gross savings (% of GNI)	54.4	48.0	41.7
Consumption of fixed capital (% of GNI)	10.7	10.7	10.7
Education expenditure (% of GNI)	1.8	2.1	2.6
Energy depletion (% of GNI)	4.5	4.9	6.6
Mineral depletion (% of GNI)	1.3	1.3	1.2
Net forest depletion (% of GNI)	0.0	0.0	0.2
CO_2 damage (% of GNI)	1.4	1.3	1.2
Particulate emission damage (% of GNI)	1.6	1.3	1.1
Adjusted net savings (% of GNI)	36.8	30.6	23.5

Colombia

	Country data	Latin America & Caribbean group	Lower middle-income group
Population (millions) **44** Land area (1,000 sq. km) **1,110** GDP ($ billions) **207.8**			

	Country data	Latin America & Caribbean group	Lower middle-income group
GNI per capita, *World Bank Atlas* method ($)	4,100	5,801	1,905
Urban population (% of total)	74	78	42
Urban population growth (average annual %, 1990–2007)	2.2	2.1	2.9
Population growth (average annual %, 1990–2007)	1.7	1.5	1.3
Agriculture			
Agricultural land (% of land area)	38	36	47
Agricultural productivity (value added per worker, 2000 $)	2,821	3,158	532
Food production index (1999–2001 = 100)	115	117	116
Population density, rural (people/sq. km of arable land)	565	232	511
Forests and biodiversity			
Forest area (% of land area)	54.7	45.4	25.0
Deforestation (average annual %, 1990–2005)	0.1	0.5	0.1
Nationally protected area (% of land area)	25.5	16.7	11.0
Animal species, total known	2,288		
Animal species, threatened	429		
Higher plant species, total known	51,220		
Higher plant species, threatened	223		
GEF benefits index for biodiversity (0–100, median is 1.5)	51.5		
Energy			
GDP per unit of energy use (2005 PPP $/kg oil equivalent)	11.0	7.3	3.9
Energy use per capita (kg oil equivalent)	695	1,240	1,019
Energy from biomass products and waste (% of total)	14.9	15.9	15.2
Electric power consumption per capita (kWh)	968	1,808	1,269
Electricity generated using fossil fuel (% of total)	20.1	37.0	79.0
Electricity generated by hydropower (% of total)	78.7	57.3	16.3
Emissions and pollution			
CO_2 emissions per unit of GDP (kg/2005 PPP $)	0.2	0.3	0.8
CO_2 emissions per capita (metric tons)	1.4	2.5	2.8
CO_2 emissions growth (%, 1990–2005)	2.1	33.4	93.5
Particulate matter (urban-pop.-weighted avg., μg/cu. m)	22	35	67
Transport sector fuel consumption per capita (liters)	173	295	99
Water and sanitation			
Internal freshwater resources per capita (cu. m)	48,014	23,965	4,117
Freshwater withdrawal			
Total (% of internal resources)	0.5	2.0	8.7
Agriculture (% of total freshwater withdrawal)	46	71	80
Access to improved water source (% of total population)	93	91	88
Rural (% of rural population)	77	73	82
Urban (% of urban population)	99	97	96
Access to improved sanitation (% of total population)	78	78	55
Rural (% of rural population)	58	51	43
Urban (% of urban population)	85	86	71
Environment and health			
Acute resp. infection prevalence (% of children under five)	9.6		
Diarrhea prevalence (% of children under five)	13.9		
Under-five mortality rate (per 1,000 live births)	20	26	50
National accounting aggregates			
Gross savings (% of GNI)	19.6	22.9	41.7
Consumption of fixed capital (% of GNI)	12.1	12.6	10.7
Education expenditure (% of GNI)	4.8	4.5	2.6
Energy depletion (% of GNI)	6.6	5.4	6.6
Mineral depletion (% of GNI)	1.7	1.9	1.2
Net forest depletion (% of GNI)	0.0	0.0	0.2
CO_2 damage (% of GNI)	0.3	0.3	1.2
Particulate emission damage (% of GNI)	0.1	0.4	1.1
Adjusted net savings (% of GNI)	3.6	6.7	23.5

Comoros

Population (thousands) **628**   Land area (1,000 sq. km)   **2**   GDP ($ millions)   **449**

	Country data	Sub-Saharan Africa group	Low-income group
GNI per capita, *World Bank Atlas* method ($)	680	951	574
Urban population (% of total)	28	36	32
Urban population growth (average annual %, 1990–2007)	2.2	4.0	3.7
Population growth (average annual %, 1990–2007)	2.2	2.6	2.4
Agriculture			
Agricultural land (% of land area)	80	44	39
Agricultural productivity (value added per worker, 2000 $)	436	287	330
Food production index (1999–2001 = 100)	104	109	112
Population density, rural (people/sq. km of arable land)	541	351	603
Forests and biodiversity			
Forest area (% of land area)	3.0	26.5	24.7
Deforestation (average annual %, 1990–2005)	5.7	0.6	0.7
Nationally protected area (% of land area)	..	11.3	10.8
Animal species, total known	153		
Animal species, threatened	84		
Higher plant species, total known	721		
Higher plant species, threatened	5		
GEF benefits index for biodiversity (0–100, median is 1.5)	2.3		
Energy			
GDP per unit of energy use (2005 PPP $/kg oil equivalent)	..	3.0	3.2
Energy use per capita (kg oil equivalent)	..	670	478
Energy from biomass products and waste (% of total)	..	56.3	53.8
Electric power consumption per capita (kWh)	..	531	309
Electricity generated using fossil fuel (% of total)	..	65.6	48.4
Electricity generated by hydropower (% of total)	..	18.0	38.8
Emissions and pollution			
CO_2 emissions per unit of GDP (kg/2005 PPP $)	0.1	0.5	0.4
CO_2 emissions per capita (metric tons)	0.1	0.8	0.6
CO_2 emissions growth (%, 1990–2005)	33.3	40.1	39.3
Particulate matter (urban-pop.-weighted avg., µg/cu. m)	33	53	69
Transport sector fuel consumption per capita (liters)	..	64	41
Water and sanitation			
Internal freshwater resources per capita (cu. m)	1,910	4,824	4,619
Freshwater withdrawal			
Total (% of internal resources)	0.8	3.2	9.4
Agriculture (% of total freshwater withdrawal)	47	87	90
Access to improved water source (% of total population)	85	58	68
Rural (% of rural population)	81	46	60
Urban (% of urban population)	91	81	84
Access to improved sanitation (% of total population)	35	31	39
Rural (% of rural population)	26	24	33
Urban (% of urban population)	49	42	54
Environment and health			
Acute resp. infection prevalence (% of children under five)	10.0		
Diarrhea prevalence (% of children under five)	18.3		
Under-five mortality rate (per 1,000 live births)	66	146	126
National accounting aggregates			
Gross savings (% of GNI)	7.9	17.4	25.4
Consumption of fixed capital (% of GNI)	9.0	11.1	9.3
Education expenditure (% of GNI)	4.2	3.6	2.6
Energy depletion (% of GNI)	0.0	11.7	9.8
Mineral depletion (% of GNI)	0.0	1.5	0.9
Net forest depletion (% of GNI)	0.1	0.5	0.8
CO_2 damage (% of GNI)	0.1	0.7	0.7
Particulate emission damage (% of GNI)	0.0	0.4	0.7
Adjusted net savings (% of GNI)	2.8	−5.0	5.8

Congo, Dem. Rep.

Population (millions)	**62** Land area (1,000 sq. km)	**2,267** GDP ($ billions)	**9.0**

	Country data	Sub-Saharan Africa group	Low-income group
GNI per capita, *World Bank Atlas* method ($)	140	951	574
Urban population (% of total)	33	36	32
Urban population growth (average annual %, 1990–2007)	4.0	4.0	3.7
Population growth (average annual %, 1990–2007)	2.9	2.6	2.4
Agriculture			
Agricultural land (% of land area)	10	44	39
Agricultural productivity (value added per worker, 2000 $)	149	287	330
Food production index (1999–2001 = 100)	97	109	112
Population density, rural (people/sq. km of arable land)	595	351	603
Forests and biodiversity			
Forest area (% of land area)	58.9	26.5	24.7
Deforestation (average annual %, 1990–2005)	0.3	0.6	0.7
Nationally protected area (% of land area)	8.6	11.3	10.8
Animal species, total known	1,578		
Animal species, threatened	125		
Higher plant species, total known	11,007		
Higher plant species, threatened	65		
GEF benefits index for biodiversity (0–100, median is 1.5)	19.9		
Energy			
GDP per unit of energy use (2005 PPP $/kg oil equivalent)	0.9	3.0	3.2
Energy use per capita (kg oil equivalent)	289	670	478
Energy from biomass products and waste (% of total)	92.4	56.3	53.8
Electric power consumption per capita (kWh)	96	531	309
Electricity generated using fossil fuel (% of total)	0.3	65.6	48.4
Electricity generated by hydropower (% of total)	99.7	18.0	38.8
Emissions and pollution			
CO_2 emissions per unit of GDP (kg/2005 PPP $)	0.1	0.5	0.4
CO_2 emissions per capita (metric tons)	0.04	0.85	0.58
CO_2 emissions growth (%, 1990–2005)	-46.0	40.1	39.3
Particulate matter (urban-pop.-weighted avg., μg/cu. m)	47	53	69
Transport sector fuel consumption per capita (liters)	3	64	41
Water and sanitation			
Internal freshwater resources per capita (cu. m)	14,423	4,824	4,619
Freshwater withdrawal			
Total (% of internal resources)	0.0	3.2	9.4
Agriculture (% of total freshwater withdrawal)	31	87	90
Access to improved water source (% of total population)	46	58	68
Rural (% of rural population)	29	46	60
Urban (% of urban population)	82	81	84
Access to improved sanitation (% of total population)	31	31	39
Rural (% of rural population)	25	24	33
Urban (% of urban population)	42	42	54
Environment and health			
Acute resp. infection prevalence (% of children under five)	11.0		
Diarrhea prevalence (% of children under five)	22.7		
Under-five mortality rate (per 1,000 live births)	161	146	126
National accounting aggregates			
Gross savings (% of GNI)	12.1	17.4	25.4
Consumption of fixed capital (% of GNI)	7.0	11.1	9.3
Education expenditure (% of GNI)	0.9	3.6	2.6
Energy depletion (% of GNI)	3.1	11.7	9.8
Mineral depletion (% of GNI)	2.9	1.5	0.9
Net forest depletion (% of GNI)	0.0	0.5	0.8
CO_2 damage (% of GNI)	0.2	0.7	0.7
Particulate emission damage (% of GNI)	0.6	0.4	0.7
Adjusted net savings (% of GNI)	-0.8	-5.0	5.8

Congo, Rep.

Population (millions)	**3.8**	Land area (1,000 sq. km)	**341.5**	GDP ($ billions)	**7.6**

	Country data	Sub-Saharan Africa group	Lower middle-income group
GNI per capita, *World Bank Atlas* method ($)	1,540	951	1,905
Urban population (% of total)	61	36	42
Urban population growth (average annual %, 1990–2007)	3.3	4.0	2.9
Population growth (average annual %, 1990–2007)	2.6	2.6	1.3
Agriculture			
Agricultural land (% of land area)	31	44	47
Agricultural productivity (value added per worker, 2000 $)	..	287	532
Food production index (1999–2001 = 100)	110	109	116
Population density, rural (people/sq. km of arable land)	290	351	511
Forests and biodiversity			
Forest area (% of land area)	65.8	26.5	25.0
Deforestation (average annual %, 1990–2005)	0.1	0.6	0.1
Nationally protected area (% of land area)	14.3	11.3	11.0
Animal species, total known	763		
Animal species, threatened	35		
Higher plant species, total known	6,000		
Higher plant species, threatened	35		
GEF benefits index for biodiversity (0–100, median is 1.5)	3.6		
Energy			
GDP per unit of energy use (2005 PPP $/kg oil equivalent)	10.5	3.0	3.9
Energy use per capita (kg oil equivalent)	327	670	1,019
Energy from biomass products and waste (% of total)	57.6	56.3	15.2
Electric power consumption per capita (kWh)	155	531	1,269
Electricity generated using fossil fuel (% of total)	17.9	65.6	79.0
Electricity generated by hydropower (% of total)	82.1	18.0	16.3
Emissions and pollution			
CO_2 emissions per unit of GDP (kg/2005 PPP $)	0.2	0.5	0.8
CO_2 emissions per capita (metric tons)	0.6	0.8	2.8
CO_2 emissions growth (%, 1990–2005)	70.6	40.1	93.5
Particulate matter (urban-pop.-weighted avg., µg/cu. m)	64	53	67
Transport sector fuel consumption per capita (liters)	81	64	99
Water and sanitation			
Internal freshwater resources per capita (cu. m)	58,937	4,824	4,117
Freshwater withdrawal			
Total (% of internal resources)	0.0	3.2	8.7
Agriculture (% of total freshwater withdrawal)	9	87	80
Access to improved water source (% of total population)	71	58	88
Rural (% of rural population)	35	46	82
Urban (% of urban population)	95	81	96
Access to improved sanitation (% of total population)	20	31	55
Rural (% of rural population)	21	24	43
Urban (% of urban population)	19	42	71
Environment and health			
Acute resp. infection prevalence (% of children under five)	..		
Diarrhea prevalence (% of children under five)	..		
Under-five mortality rate (per 1,000 live births)	125	146	50
National accounting aggregates			
Gross savings (% of GNI)	45.4	17.4	41.7
Consumption of fixed capital (% of GNI)	13.4	11.1	10.7
Education expenditure (% of GNI)	2.3	3.6	2.6
Energy depletion (% of GNI)	56.5	11.7	6.6
Mineral depletion (% of GNI)	0.0	1.5	1.2
Net forest depletion (% of GNI)	0.0	0.5	0.2
CO_2 damage (% of GNI)	0.4	0.7	1.2
Particulate emission damage (% of GNI)	0.7	0.4	1.1
Adjusted net savings (% of GNI)	-23.4	-5.0	23.5

Costa Rica

Population (millions)	**4.5**	Land area (1,000 sq. km)	**51.1**	GDP ($ billions)	**26.3**

	Country data	Latin America & Caribbean group	Upper middle-income group
GNI per capita, *World Bank Atlas* method ($)	5,520	5,801	7,107
Urban population (% of total)	63	78	75
Urban population growth (average annual %, 1990–2007)	3.4	2.1	1.4
Population growth (average annual %, 1990–2007)	2.2	1.5	0.9
Agriculture			
Agricultural land (% of land area)	57	36	31
Agricultural productivity (value added per worker, 2000 $)	4,643	3,158	2,947
Food production index (1999–2001 = 100)	110	117	113
Population density, rural (people/sq. km of arable land)	737	232	110
Forests and biodiversity			
Forest area (% of land area)	46.8	45.4	39.3
Deforestation (average annual %, 1990–2005)	0.5	0.5	0.2
Nationally protected area (% of land area)	21.8	16.7	10.3
Animal species, total known	1,070		
Animal species, threatened	139		
Higher plant species, total known	12,119		
Higher plant species, threatened	111		
GEF benefits index for biodiversity (0–100, median is 1.5)	9.7		
Energy			
GDP per unit of energy use (2005 PPP $/kg oil equivalent)	9.3	7.3	4.8
Energy use per capita (kg oil equivalent)	1,040	1,240	2,300
Energy from biomass products and waste (% of total)	15.5	15.9	7.0
Electric power consumption per capita (kWh)	1,801	1,808	3,242
Electricity generated using fossil fuel (% of total)	6.1	37.0	62.8
Electricity generated by hydropower (% of total)	75.9	57.3	27.6
Emissions and pollution			
CO_2 emissions per unit of GDP (kg/2005 PPP $)	0.2	0.3	0.5
CO_2 emissions per capita (metric tons)	1.7	2.5	5.5
CO_2 emissions growth (%, 1990–2005)	150.4	33.4	-8.3
Particulate matter (urban-pop.-weighted avg., µg/cu. m)	36	35	30
Transport sector fuel consumption per capita (liters)	339	295	332
Water and sanitation			
Internal freshwater resources per capita (cu. m)	25,189	23,965	16,993
Freshwater withdrawal			
Total (% of internal resources)	2.4	2.0	13.8
Agriculture (% of total freshwater withdrawal)	53	71	57
Access to improved water source (% of total population)	98	91	95
Rural (% of rural population)	96	73	83
Urban (% of urban population)	99	97	98
Access to improved sanitation (% of total population)	96	78	83
Rural (% of rural population)	95	51	64
Urban (% of urban population)	96	86	89
Environment and health			
Acute resp. infection prevalence (% of children under five)	..		
Diarrhea prevalence (% of children under five)	..		
Under-five mortality rate (per 1,000 live births)	11	26	24
National accounting aggregates			
Gross savings (% of GNI)	19.2	22.9	23.2
Consumption of fixed capital (% of GNI)	12.4	12.6	12.8
Education expenditure (% of GNI)	4.1	4.5	4.4
Energy depletion (% of GNI)	0.0	5.4	7.6
Mineral depletion (% of GNI)	0.0	1.9	1.3
Net forest depletion (% of GNI)	0.1	0.0	0.0
CO_2 damage (% of GNI)	0.2	0.3	0.6
Particulate emission damage (% of GNI)	0.3	0.4	0.4
Adjusted net savings (% of GNI)	10.2	6.7	4.9

Côte d'Ivoire

Population (millions)	**19**	Land area (1,000 sq. km)	**318**	GDP ($ billions)	**19.8**

	Country data	Sub-Saharan Africa group	Low-income group
GNI per capita, *World Bank Atlas* method ($)	920	951	574
Urban population (% of total)	48	36	32
Urban population growth (average annual %, 1990–2007)	3.5	4.0	3.7
Population growth (average annual %, 1990–2007)	2.4	2.6	2.4
Agriculture			
Agricultural land (% of land area)	64	44	39
Agricultural productivity (value added per worker, 2000 $)	817	287	330
Food production index (1999–2001 = 100)	102	109	112
Population density, rural (people/sq. km of arable land)	282	351	603
Forests and biodiversity			
Forest area (% of land area)	32.7	26.5	24.7
Deforestation (average annual %, 1990–2005)	−0.1	0.6	0.7
Nationally protected area (% of land area)	12.2	11.3	10.8
Animal species, total known	931		
Animal species, threatened	75		
Higher plant species, total known	3,660		
Higher plant species, threatened	105		
GEF benefits index for biodiversity (0–100, median is 1.5)	3.4		
Energy			
GDP per unit of energy use (2005 PPP $/kg oil equivalent)	4.1	3.0	3.2
Energy use per capita (kg oil equivalent)	385	670	478
Energy from biomass products and waste (% of total)	63.8	56.3	53.8
Electric power consumption per capita (kWh)	182	531	309
Electricity generated using fossil fuel (% of total)	72.7	65.6	48.4
Electricity generated by hydropower (% of total)	27.3	18.0	38.8
Emissions and pollution			
CO_2 emissions per unit of GDP (kg/2005 PPP $)	0.3	0.5	0.4
CO_2 emissions per capita (metric tons)	0.5	0.8	0.6
CO_2 emissions growth (%, 1990–2005)	61.5	40.1	39.3
Particulate matter (urban-pop.-weighted avg., μg/cu. m)	36	53	69
Transport sector fuel consumption per capita (liters)	27	64	41
Water and sanitation			
Internal freshwater resources per capita (cu. m)	3,988	4,824	4,619
Freshwater withdrawal			
Total (% of internal resources)	1.2	3.2	9.4
Agriculture (% of total freshwater withdrawal)	65	87	90
Access to improved water source (% of total population)	81	58	68
Rural (% of rural population)	66	46	60
Urban (% of urban population)	98	81	84
Access to improved sanitation (% of total population)	24	31	39
Rural (% of rural population)	12	24	33
Urban (% of urban population)	38	42	54
Environment and health			
Acute resp. infection prevalence (% of children under five)	4.0		
Diarrhea prevalence (% of children under five)	20.1		
Under-five mortality rate (per 1,000 live births)	127	146	126
National accounting aggregates			
Gross savings (% of GNI)	9.6	17.4	25.4
Consumption of fixed capital (% of GNI)	10.0	11.1	9.3
Education expenditure (% of GNI)	4.7	3.6	2.6
Energy depletion (% of GNI)	7.0	11.7	9.8
Mineral depletion (% of GNI)	0.0	1.5	0.9
Net forest depletion (% of GNI)	0.0	0.5	0.8
CO_2 damage (% of GNI)	0.2	0.7	0.7
Particulate emission damage (% of GNI)	0.3	0.4	0.7
Adjusted net savings (% of GNI)	−3.2	−5.0	5.8

Croatia

	Country data	Europe & Central Asia group	Upper middle-income group
Population (millions) **4.4**	Land area (1,000 sq. km) **55.9**	GDP ($ billions)	**51.3**

	Country data	Europe & Central Asia group	Upper middle-income group
GNI per capita, *World Bank Atlas* method ($)	10,460	6,052	7,107
Urban population (% of total)	57	64	75
Urban population growth (average annual %, 1990–2007)	-0.1	0.2	1.4
Population growth (average annual %, 1990–2007)	-0.4	0.1	0.9
Agriculture			
Agricultural land (% of land area)	48	28	31
Agricultural productivity (value added per worker, 2000 $)	10,916	2,228	2,947
Food production index (1999–2001 = 100)	97	110	113
Population density, rural (people/sq. km of arable land)	174	129	110
Forests and biodiversity			
Forest area (% of land area)	38.2	38.3	39.3
Deforestation (average annual %, 1990–2005)	-0.1	0.0	0.2
Nationally protected area (% of land area)	5.6	6.1	10.3
Animal species, total known	461		
Animal species, threatened	83		
Higher plant species, total known	4,288		
Higher plant species, threatened	1		
GEF benefits index for biodiversity (0–100, median is 1.5)	0.6		
Energy			
GDP per unit of energy use (2005 PPP $/kg oil equivalent)	6.9	3.5	4.8
Energy use per capita (kg oil equivalent)	2,017	2,930	2,300
Energy from biomass products and waste (% of total)	4.1	2.2	7.0
Electric power consumption per capita (kWh)	3,636	3,835	3,242
Electricity generated using fossil fuel (% of total)	51.0	67.7	62.8
Electricity generated by hydropower (% of total)	48.8	17.4	27.6
Emissions and pollution			
CO_2 emissions per unit of GDP (kg/2005 PPP $)	0.4	0.7	0.5
CO_2 emissions per capita (metric tons)	5.2	7.0	5.5
CO_2 emissions growth (%, 1990–2005)	-7.0	-29.3	-8.3
Particulate matter (urban-pop.-weighted avg., μg/cu. m)	30	27	30
Transport sector fuel consumption per capita (liters)	479	255	332
Water and sanitation			
Internal freshwater resources per capita (cu. m)	8,499	11,806	16,993
Freshwater withdrawal			
Total (% of internal resources)	..	7.2	13.8
Agriculture (% of total freshwater withdrawal)	..	60	57
Access to improved water source (% of total population)	99	95	95
Rural (% of rural population)	98	88	83
Urban (% of urban population)	100	99	98
Access to improved sanitation (% of total population)	99	89	83
Rural (% of rural population)	98	79	64
Urban (% of urban population)	99	94	89
Environment and health			
Acute resp. infection prevalence (% of children under five)	..		
Diarrhea prevalence (% of children under five)	11.3		
Under-five mortality rate (per 1,000 live births)	6	23	24
National accounting aggregates			
Gross savings (% of GNI)	24.6	24.0	23.2
Consumption of fixed capital (% of GNI)	13.4	12.8	12.8
Education expenditure (% of GNI)	4.3	4.0	4.4
Energy depletion (% of GNI)	0.7	9.8	7.6
Mineral depletion (% of GNI)	0.0	0.7	1.3
Net forest depletion (% of GNI)	0.2	0.0	0.0
CO_2 damage (% of GNI)	0.4	1.0	0.6
Particulate emission damage (% of GNI)	0.5	0.5	0.4
Adjusted net savings (% of GNI)	13.8	3.2	4.9

Cuba

	Population (millions)	**11**	Land area (1,000 sq. km)	**110**	GDP ($ billions)	..

	Country data	Latin America & Caribbean group	Upper middle-income group
GNI per capita, *World Bank Atlas* method ($)	..	5,801	7,107
Urban population (% of total)	76	78	75
Urban population growth (average annual %, 1990–2007)	0.5	2.1	1.4
Population growth (average annual %, 1990–2007)	0.4	1.5	0.9
Agriculture			
Agricultural land (% of land area)	60	36	31
Agricultural productivity (value added per worker, 2000 $)	..	3,158	2,947
Food production index (1999–2001 = 100)	102	117	113
Population density, rural (people/sq. km of arable land)	75	232	110
Forests and biodiversity			
Forest area (% of land area)	24.7	45.4	39.3
Deforestation (average annual %, 1990–2005)	-1.9	0.5	0.2
Nationally protected area (% of land area)	1.4	16.7	10.3
Animal species, total known	423		
Animal species, threatened	131		
Higher plant species, total known	6,522		
Higher plant species, threatened	163		
GEF benefits index for biodiversity (0–100, median is 1.5)	12.5		
Energy			
GDP per unit of energy use (2005 PPP $/kg oil equivalent)	..	7.3	4.8
Energy use per capita (kg oil equivalent)	944	1,240	2,300
Energy from biomass products and waste (% of total)	11.9	15.9	7.0
Electric power consumption per capita (kWh)	1,231	1,808	3,242
Electricity generated using fossil fuel (% of total)	96.7	37.0	62.8
Electricity generated by hydropower (% of total)	0.6	57.3	27.6
Emissions and pollution			
CO_2 emissions per unit of GDP (kg/2005 PPP $)	..	0.3	0.5
CO_2 emissions per capita (metric tons)	2.2	2.5	5.5
CO_2 emissions growth (%, 1990–2005)	-24.1	33.4	-8.3
Particulate matter (urban-pop.-weighted avg., µg/cu. m)	17	35	30
Transport sector fuel consumption per capita (liters)	70	295	332
Water and sanitation			
Internal freshwater resources per capita (cu. m)	3,386	23,965	16,993
Freshwater withdrawal			
Total (% of internal resources)	21.5	2.0	13.8
Agriculture (% of total freshwater withdrawal)	69	71	57
Access to improved water source (% of total population)	91	91	95
Rural (% of rural population)	78	73	83
Urban (% of urban population)	95	97	98
Access to improved sanitation (% of total population)	98	78	83
Rural (% of rural population)	95	51	64
Urban (% of urban population)	99	86	89
Environment and health			
Acute resp. infection prevalence (% of children under five)	..		
Diarrhea prevalence (% of children under five)	..		
Under-five mortality rate (per 1,000 live births)	7	26	24
National accounting aggregates			
Gross savings (% of GNI)	..	22.9	23.2
Consumption of fixed capital (% of GNI)	..	12.6	12.8
Education expenditure (% of GNI)	8.2	4.5	4.4
Energy depletion (% of GNI)	..	5.4	7.6
Mineral depletion (% of GNI)	..	1.9	1.3
Net forest depletion (% of GNI)	..	0.0	0.0
CO_2 damage (% of GNI)	..	0.3	0.6
Particulate emission damage (% of GNI)	0.1	0.4	0.4
Adjusted net savings (% of GNI)	..	6.7	4.9

Cyprus

Population (thousands) **855**   Land area (1,000 sq. km)   **9**   GDP ($ billions)   **21.3**

	Country data	High-income group
GNI per capita, *World Bank Atlas* method ($)	24,940	37,572
Urban population (% of total)	70	78
Urban population growth (average annual %, 1990–2007)	1.6	1.0
Population growth (average annual %, 1990–2007)	1.3	0.7
Agriculture		
Agricultural land (% of land area)	18	38
Agricultural productivity (value added per worker, 2000 $)	..	27,680
Food production index (1999–2001 = 100)	101	102
Population density, rural (people/sq. km of arable land)	214	323
Forests and biodiversity		
Forest area (% of land area)	18.9	28.8
Deforestation (average annual %, 1990–2005)	–0.5	–0.1
Nationally protected area (% of land area)	9.7	11.8
Animal species, total known	370	
Animal species, threatened	26	
Higher plant species, total known	1,682	
Higher plant species, threatened	7	
GEF benefits index for biodiversity (0–100, median is 1.5)	0.5	
Energy		
GDP per unit of energy use (2005 PPP $/kg oil equivalent)	7.4	6.3
Energy use per capita (kg oil equivalent)	3,094	5,416
Energy from biomass products and waste (% of total)	0.5	3.4
Electric power consumption per capita (kWh)	5,239	9,675
Electricity generated using fossil fuel (% of total)	100.0	62.0
Electricity generated by hydropower (% of total)	0.0	11.4
Emissions and pollution		
CO_2 emissions per unit of GDP (kg/2005 PPP $)	0.4	0.4
CO_2 emissions per capita (metric tons)	8.4	12.6
CO_2 emissions growth (%, 1990–2005)	51.0	19.1
Particulate matter (urban-pop.-weighted avg., μg/cu. m)	44	26
Transport sector fuel consumption per capita (liters)	831	1,159
Water and sanitation		
Internal freshwater resources per capita (cu. m)	913	9,313
Freshwater withdrawal		
Total (% of internal resources)	31.6	10.4
Agriculture (% of total freshwater withdrawal)	71	43
Access to improved water source (% of total population)	100	100
Rural (% of rural population)	100	98
Urban (% of urban population)	100	100
Access to improved sanitation (% of total population)	100	100
Rural (% of rural population)	100	99
Urban (% of urban population)	100	100
Environment and health		
Acute resp. infection prevalence (% of children under five)	..	
Diarrhea prevalence (% of children under five)	..	
Under-five mortality rate (per 1,000 live births)	5	7
National accounting aggregates		
Gross savings (% of GNI)	..	20.6
Consumption of fixed capital (% of GNI)	14.5	14.5
Education expenditure (% of GNI)	5.7	4.6
Energy depletion (% of GNI)	0.0	1.5
Mineral depletion (% of GNI)	0.0	0.2
Net forest depletion (% of GNI)	0.0	0.0
CO_2 damage (% of GNI)	0.3	0.3
Particulate emission damage (% of GNI)	0.7	0.3
Adjusted net savings (% of GNI)	..	8.5

Czech Republic

| | Population (millions) | **10** | Land area (1,000 sq. km) | **77** | GDP ($ billions) | **175.0** |

	Country data	High-income group
GNI per capita, *World Bank Atlas* method ($)	14,580	37,572
Urban population (% of total)	74	78
Urban population growth (average annual %, 1990–2007)	–0.2	1.0
Population growth (average annual %, 1990–2007)	0.0	0.7
Agriculture		
Agricultural land (% of land area)	55	38
Agricultural productivity (value added per worker, 2000 $)	6,241	27,680
Food production index (1999–2001 = 100)	95	102
Population density, rural (people/sq. km of arable land)	89	323
Forests and biodiversity		
Forest area (% of land area)	34.3	28.8
Deforestation (average annual %, 1990–2005)	0.0	–0.1
Nationally protected area (% of land area)	16.1	11.8
Animal species, total known	474	
Animal species, threatened	31	
Higher plant species, total known	1,900	
Higher plant species, threatened	4	
GEF benefits index for biodiversity (0–100, median is 1.5)	0.1	
Energy		
GDP per unit of energy use (2005 PPP $/kg oil equivalent)	4.8	6.3
Energy use per capita (kg oil equivalent)	4,485	5,416
Energy from biomass products and waste (% of total)	4.0	3.4
Electric power consumption per capita (kWh)	6,509	9,675
Electricity generated using fossil fuel (% of total)	64.6	62.0
Electricity generated by hydropower (% of total)	3.0	11.4
Emissions and pollution		
CO_2 emissions per unit of GDP (kg/2005 PPP $)	0.6	0.4
CO_2 emissions per capita (metric tons)	11.7	12.6
CO_2 emissions growth (%, 1990–2005)	–26.0	19.1
Particulate matter (urban-pop.-weighted avg., μg/cu. m)	21	26
Transport sector fuel consumption per capita (liters)	629	1,159
Water and sanitation		
Internal freshwater resources per capita (cu. m)	1,272	9,313
Freshwater withdrawal		
Total (% of internal resources)	19.6	10.4
Agriculture (% of total freshwater withdrawal)	2	43
Access to improved water source (% of total population)	100	100
Rural (% of rural population)	100	98
Urban (% of urban population)	100	100
Access to improved sanitation (% of total population)	99	100
Rural (% of rural population)	98	99
Urban (% of urban population)	100	100
Environment and health		
Acute resp. infection prevalence (% of children under five)	..	
Diarrhea prevalence (% of children under five)	..	
Under-five mortality rate (per 1,000 live births)	4	7
National accounting aggregates		
Gross savings (% of GNI)	27.0	20.6
Consumption of fixed capital (% of GNI)	14.4	14.5
Education expenditure (% of GNI)	4.0	4.6
Energy depletion (% of GNI)	0.4	1.5
Mineral depletion (% of GNI)	0.0	0.2
Net forest depletion (% of GNI)	0.1	0.0
CO_2 damage (% of GNI)	0.6	0.3
Particulate emission damage (% of GNI)	0.1	0.3
Adjusted net savings (% of GNI)	15.4	8.5

Denmark

| Population (millions) | **5.5** | Land area (1,000 sq. km) | **42.4** | GDP ($ billions) | **311.6** |

	Country data	High-income group
GNI per capita, *World Bank Atlas* method ($)	55,440	37,572
Urban population (% of total)	86	78
Urban population growth (average annual %, 1990–2007)	0.5	1.0
Population growth (average annual %, 1990–2007)	0.4	0.7
Agriculture		
Agricultural land (% of land area)	61	38
Agricultural productivity (value added per worker, 2000 $)	40,052	27,680
Food production index (1999–2001 = 100)	103	102
Population density, rural (people/sq. km of arable land)	34	323
Forests and biodiversity		
Forest area (% of land area)	11.8	28.8
Deforestation (average annual %, 1990–2005)	–0.8	–0.1
Nationally protected area (% of land area)	5.8	11.8
Animal species, total known	508	
Animal species, threatened	28	
Higher plant species, total known	1,450	
Higher plant species, threatened	3	
GEF benefits index for biodiversity (0–100, median is 1.5)	0.2	
Energy		
GDP per unit of energy use (2005 PPP $/kg oil equivalent)	8.9	6.3
Energy use per capita (kg oil equivalent)	3,850	5,416
Energy from biomass products and waste (% of total)	12.9	3.4
Electric power consumption per capita (kWh)	6,864	9,675
Electricity generated using fossil fuel (% of total)	78.0	62.0
Electricity generated by hydropower (% of total)	0.1	11.4
Emissions and pollution		
CO_2 emissions per unit of GDP (kg/2005 PPP $)	0.3	0.4
CO_2 emissions per capita (metric tons)	8.5	12.6
CO_2 emissions growth (%, 1990–2005)	–7.4	19.1
Particulate matter (urban-pop.-weighted avg., µg/cu. m)	19	26
Transport sector fuel consumption per capita (liters)	910	1,159
Water and sanitation		
Internal freshwater resources per capita (cu. m)	1,099	9,313
Freshwater withdrawal		
Total (% of internal resources)	21.2	10.4
Agriculture (% of total freshwater withdrawal)	43	43
Access to improved water source (% of total population)	100	100
Rural (% of rural population)	100	98
Urban (% of urban population)	100	100
Access to improved sanitation (% of total population)	100	100
Rural (% of rural population)	100	99
Urban (% of urban population)	100	100
Environment and health		
Acute resp. infection prevalence (% of children under five)	..	
Diarrhea prevalence (% of children under five)	..	
Under-five mortality rate (per 1,000 live births)	4	7
National accounting aggregates		
Gross savings (% of GNI)	24.0	20.6
Consumption of fixed capital (% of GNI)	14.9	14.5
Education expenditure (% of GNI)	7.8	4.6
Energy depletion (% of GNI)	2.3	1.5
Mineral depletion (% of GNI)	0.0	0.2
Net forest depletion (% of GNI)	0.0	0.0
CO_2 damage (% of GNI)	0.1	0.3
Particulate emission damage (% of GNI)	0.1	0.3
Adjusted net savings (% of GNI)	14.4	8.5

Djibouti

Population (thousands) **833** Land area (1,000 sq. km) **23** GDP ($ millions) **830**

	Country data	Middle East & N. Africa group	Lower middle-income group
GNI per capita, *World Bank Atlas* method ($)	1,090	2,820	1,905
Urban population (% of total)	87	57	42
Urban population growth (average annual %, 1990–2007)	3.1	2.6	2.9
Population growth (average annual %, 1990–2007)	2.3	2.0	1.3
Agriculture			
Agricultural land (% of land area)	73	22	47
Agricultural productivity (value added per worker, 2000 $)	65	2,313	532
Food production index (1999–2001 = 100)	131	116	116
Population density, rural (people/sq. km of arable land)	11,178	665	511
Forests and biodiversity			
Forest area (% of land area)	0.2	2.4	25.0
Deforestation (average annual %, 1990–2005)	0.0	-0.4	0.1
Nationally protected area (% of land area)	..	3.6	11.0
Animal species, total known	418		
Animal species, threatened	79		
Higher plant species, total known	826		
Higher plant species, threatened	2		
GEF benefits index for biodiversity (0–100, median is 1.5)	0.5		
Energy			
GDP per unit of energy use (2005 PPP $/kg oil equivalent)	..	5.0	3.9
Energy use per capita (kg oil equivalent)	..	1,254	1,019
Energy from biomass products and waste (% of total)	..	1.2	15.2
Electric power consumption per capita (kWh)	..	1,418	1,269
Electricity generated using fossil fuel (% of total)	..	91.1	79.0
Electricity generated by hydropower (% of total)	..	7.4	16.3
Emissions and pollution			
CO_2 emissions per unit of GDP (kg/2005 PPP $)	0.3	0.6	0.8
CO_2 emissions per capita (metric tons)	0.5	3.7	2.8
CO_2 emissions growth (%, 1990–2005)	6.2	96.8	93.5
Particulate matter (urban-pop.-weighted avg., μg/cu. m)	45	72	67
Transport sector fuel consumption per capita (liters)	..	277	99
Water and sanitation			
Internal freshwater resources per capita (cu. m)	360	728	4,117
Freshwater withdrawal			
Total (% of internal resources)	6.3	122.3	8.7
Agriculture (% of total freshwater withdrawal)	16	86	80
Access to improved water source (% of total population)	92	89	88
Rural (% of rural population)	54	81	82
Urban (% of urban population)	98	95	96
Access to improved sanitation (% of total population)	67	77	55
Rural (% of rural population)	11	62	43
Urban (% of urban population)	76	88	71
Environment and health			
Acute resp. infection prevalence (% of children under five)	..		
Diarrhea prevalence (% of children under five)	..		
Under-five mortality rate (per 1,000 live births)	127	38	50
National accounting aggregates			
Gross savings (% of GNI)	..	33.3	41.7
Consumption of fixed capital (% of GNI)	8.6	11.3	10.7
Education expenditure (% of GNI)	..	4.7	2.6
Energy depletion (% of GNI)	0.0	21.3	6.6
Mineral depletion (% of GNI)	0.0	0.4	1.2
Net forest depletion (% of GNI)	0.0	0.0	0.2
CO_2 damage (% of GNI)	0.3	1.0	1.2
Particulate emission damage (% of GNI)	..	0.6	1.1
Adjusted net savings (% of GNI)	..	3.4	23.5

Dominica

| | Population (thousands) | **73** | Land area (sq. km) | **750** | GDP ($ millions) | **314** |

	Country data	Latin America & Caribbean group	Upper middle-income group
GNI per capita, *World Bank Atlas* method ($)	4,030	5,801	7,107
Urban population (% of total)	74	78	75
Urban population growth (average annual %, 1990–2007)	0.5	2.1	1.4
Population growth (average annual %, 1990–2007)	0.0	1.5	0.9
Agriculture			
Agricultural land (% of land area)	31	36	31
Agricultural productivity (value added per worker, 2000 $)	4,817	3,158	2,947
Food production index (1999–2001 = 100)	99	117	113
Population density, rural (people/sq. km of arable land)	390	232	110
Forests and biodiversity			
Forest area (% of land area)	61.3	45.4	39.3
Deforestation (average annual %, 1990–2005)	0.6	0.5	0.2
Nationally protected area (% of land area)	26.5	16.7	10.3
Animal species, total known	180		
Animal species, threatened	37		
Higher plant species, total known	1,228		
Higher plant species, threatened	11		
GEF benefits index for biodiversity (0–100, median is 1.5)	0.9		
Energy			
GDP per unit of energy use (2005 PPP $/kg oil equivalent)	..	7.3	4.8
Energy use per capita (kg oil equivalent)	..	1,240	2,300
Energy from biomass products and waste (% of total)	..	15.9	7.0
Electric power consumption per capita (kWh)	..	1,808	3,242
Electricity generated using fossil fuel (% of total)	..	37.0	62.8
Electricity generated by hydropower (% of total)	..	57.3	27.6
Emissions and pollution			
CO_2 emissions per unit of GDP (kg/2005 PPP $)	0.2	0.3	0.5
CO_2 emissions per capita (metric tons)	1.6	2.5	5.5
CO_2 emissions growth (%, 1990–2005)	93.8	33.4	-8.3
Particulate matter (urban-pop.-weighted avg., µg/cu. m)	26	35	30
Transport sector fuel consumption per capita (liters)	..	295	332
Water and sanitation			
Internal freshwater resources per capita (cu. m)	..	23,965	16,993
Freshwater withdrawal			
Total (% of internal resources)	..	2.0	13.8
Agriculture (% of total freshwater withdrawal)	..	71	57
Access to improved water source (% of total population)	..	91	95
Rural (% of rural population)	..	73	83
Urban (% of urban population)	100	97	98
Access to improved sanitation (% of total population)	..	78	83
Rural (% of rural population)	..	51	64
Urban (% of urban population)	..	86	89
Environment and health			
Acute resp. infection prevalence (% of children under five)	..		
Diarrhea prevalence (% of children under five)	..		
Under-five mortality rate (per 1,000 live births)	11	26	24
National accounting aggregates			
Gross savings (% of GNI)	..	22.9	23.2
Consumption of fixed capital (% of GNI)	..	12.6	12.8
Education expenditure (% of GNI)	..	4.5	4.4
Energy depletion (% of GNI)	..	5.4	7.6
Mineral depletion (% of GNI)	..	1.9	1.3
Net forest depletion (% of GNI)	..	0.0	0.0
CO_2 damage (% of GNI)	..	0.3	0.6
Particulate emission damage (% of GNI)	..	0.4	0.4
Adjusted net savings (% of GNI)	..	6.7	4.9

Dominican Republic

	Population (millions)	**9.7**	Land area (1,000 sq. km)	**48.4**	GDP ($ billions)	**36.7**

	Country data	Latin America & Caribbean group	Lower middle-income group
GNI per capita, *World Bank Atlas* method ($)	3,560	5,801	1,905
Urban population (% of total)	68	78	42
Urban population growth (average annual %, 1990–2007)	2.9	2.1	2.9
Population growth (average annual %, 1990–2007)	1.7	1.5	1.3
Agriculture			
Agricultural land (% of land area)	71	36	47
Agricultural productivity (value added per worker, 2000 $)	4,943	3,158	532
Food production index (1999–2001 = 100)	108	117	116
Population density, rural (people/sq. km of arable land)	383	232	511
Forests and biodiversity			
Forest area (% of land area)	28.4	45.4	25.0
Deforestation (average annual %, 1990–2005)	0.0	0.5	0.1
Nationally protected area (% of land area)	24.4	16.7	11.0
Animal species, total known	260		
Animal species, threatened	94		
Higher plant species, total known	5,657		
Higher plant species, threatened	30		
GEF benefits index for biodiversity (0–100, median is 1.5)	6.0		
Energy			
GDP per unit of energy use (2005 PPP $/kg oil equivalent)	7.2	7.3	3.9
Energy use per capita (kg oil equivalent)	816	1,240	1,019
Energy from biomass products and waste (% of total)	18.0	15.9	15.2
Electric power consumption per capita (kWh)	1,309	1,808	1,269
Electricity generated using fossil fuel (% of total)	89.8	37.0	79.0
Electricity generated by hydropower (% of total)	10.0	57.3	16.3
Emissions and pollution			
CO_2 emissions per unit of GDP (kg/2005 PPP $)	0.4	0.3	0.8
CO_2 emissions per capita (metric tons)	2.0	2.5	2.8
CO_2 emissions growth (%, 1990–2005)	96.3	33.4	93.5
Particulate matter (urban-pop.-weighted avg., μg/cu. m)	20	35	67
Transport sector fuel consumption per capita (liters)	182	295	99
Water and sanitation			
Internal freshwater resources per capita (cu. m)	2,159	23,965	4,117
Freshwater withdrawal			
Total (% of internal resources)	16.1	2.0	8.7
Agriculture (% of total freshwater withdrawal)	66	71	80
Access to improved water source (% of total population)	95	91	88
Rural (% of rural population)	91	73	82
Urban (% of urban population)	97	97	96
Access to improved sanitation (% of total population)	79	78	55
Rural (% of rural population)	74	51	43
Urban (% of urban population)	81	86	71
Environment and health			
Acute resp. infection prevalence (% of children under five)	20.0		
Diarrhea prevalence (% of children under five)	20.1		
Under-five mortality rate (per 1,000 live births)	38	26	50
National accounting aggregates			
Gross savings (% of GNI)	21.0	22.9	41.7
Consumption of fixed capital (% of GNI)	12.0	12.6	10.7
Education expenditure (% of GNI)	3.5	4.5	2.6
Energy depletion (% of GNI)	0.0	5.4	6.6
Mineral depletion (% of GNI)	3.5	1.9	1.2
Net forest depletion (% of GNI)	0.0	0.0	0.2
CO_2 damage (% of GNI)	0.6	0.3	1.2
Particulate emission damage (% of GNI)	0.1	0.4	1.1
Adjusted net savings (% of GNI)	8.4	6.7	23.5

Ecuador

	Country data	Latin America & Caribbean group	Lower middle-income group
Population (millions) **13** Land area (1,000 sq. km) **277** GDP ($ billions) **44.5**			

	Country data	Latin America & Caribbean group	Lower middle-income group
GNI per capita, *World Bank Atlas* method ($)	3,110	5,801	1,905
Urban population (% of total)	65	78	42
Urban population growth (average annual %, 1990–2007)	2.5	2.1	2.9
Population growth (average annual %, 1990–2007)	1.5	1.5	1.3
Agriculture			
Agricultural land (% of land area)	27	36	47
Agricultural productivity (value added per worker, 2000 $)	1,778	3,158	532
Food production index (1999–2001 = 100)	114	117	116
Population density, rural (people/sq. km of arable land)	353	232	511
Forests and biodiversity			
Forest area (% of land area)	39.2	45.4	25.0
Deforestation (average annual %, 1990–2005)	1.6	0.5	0.1
Nationally protected area (% of land area)	22.6	16.7	11.0
Animal species, total known	1,856		
Animal species, threatened	369		
Higher plant species, total known	19,362		
Higher plant species, threatened	1,839		
GEF benefits index for biodiversity (0–100, median is 1.5)	29.3		
Energy			
GDP per unit of energy use (2005 PPP $/kg oil equivalent)	8.1	7.3	3.9
Energy use per capita (kg oil equivalent)	851	1,240	1,019
Energy from biomass products and waste (% of total)	5.2	15.9	15.2
Electric power consumption per capita (kWh)	759	1,808	1,269
Electricity generated using fossil fuel (% of total)	53.7	37.0	79.0
Electricity generated by hydropower (% of total)	46.3	57.3	16.3
Emissions and pollution			
CO_2 emissions per unit of GDP (kg/2005 PPP $)	0.3	0.3	0.8
CO_2 emissions per capita (metric tons)	2.2	2.5	2.8
CO_2 emissions growth (%, 1990–2005)	76.8	33.4	93.5
Particulate matter (urban-pop.-weighted avg., µg/cu. m)	25	35	67
Transport sector fuel consumption per capita (liters)	328	295	99
Water and sanitation			
Internal freshwater resources per capita (cu. m)	32,385	23,965	4,117
Freshwater withdrawal			
Total (% of internal resources)	3.9	2.0	8.7
Agriculture (% of total freshwater withdrawal)	82	71	80
Access to improved water source (% of total population)	95	91	88
Rural (% of rural population)	91	73	82
Urban (% of urban population)	98	97	96
Access to improved sanitation (% of total population)	84	78	55
Rural (% of rural population)	72	51	43
Urban (% of urban population)	91	86	71
Environment and health			
Acute resp. infection prevalence (% of children under five)	57.2		
Diarrhea prevalence (% of children under five)	19.9		
Under-five mortality rate (per 1,000 live births)	22	26	50
National accounting aggregates			
Gross savings (% of GNI)	26.9	22.9	41.7
Consumption of fixed capital (% of GNI)	11.7	12.6	10.7
Education expenditure (% of GNI)	1.4	4.5	2.6
Energy depletion (% of GNI)	18.4	5.4	6.6
Mineral depletion (% of GNI)	0.5	1.9	1.2
Net forest depletion (% of GNI)	0.0	0.0	0.2
CO_2 damage (% of GNI)	0.5	0.3	1.2
Particulate emission damage (% of GNI)	0.1	0.4	1.1
Adjusted net savings (% of GNI)	-2.9	6.7	23.5

Egypt, Arab Rep.

Population (millions)	**75**	Land area (1,000 sq. km)	**995**	GDP ($ billions)	**130.5**

	Country data	Middle East & N. Africa group	Lower middle-income group
GNI per capita, *World Bank Atlas* method ($)	1,580	2,820	1,905
Urban population (% of total)	43	57	42
Urban population growth (average annual %, 1990–2007)	1.7	2.6	2.9
Population growth (average annual %, 1990–2007)	1.8	2.0	1.3
Agriculture			
Agricultural land (% of land area)	4	22	47
Agricultural productivity (value added per worker, 2000 $)	2,128	2,313	532
Food production index (1999–2001 = 100)	116	116	116
Population density, rural (people/sq. km of arable land)	1,394	665	511
Forests and biodiversity			
Forest area (% of land area)	0.1	2.4	25.0
Deforestation (average annual %, 1990–2005)	-2.8	-0.4	0.1
Nationally protected area (% of land area)	5.3	3.6	11.0
Animal species, total known	599		
Animal species, threatened	108		
Higher plant species, total known	2,076		
Higher plant species, threatened	2		
GEF benefits index for biodiversity (0–100, median is 1.5)	2.9		
Energy			
GDP per unit of energy use (2005 PPP $/kg oil equivalent)	5.7	5.0	3.9
Energy use per capita (kg oil equivalent)	843	1,254	1,019
Energy from biomass products and waste (% of total)	2.3	1.2	15.2
Electric power consumption per capita (kWh)	1,382	1,418	1,269
Electricity generated using fossil fuel (% of total)	88.3	91.1	79.0
Electricity generated by hydropower (% of total)	11.2	7.4	16.3
Emissions and pollution			
CO_2 emissions per unit of GDP (kg/2005 PPP $)	0.5	0.6	0.8
CO_2 emissions per capita (metric tons)	2.4	3.7	2.8
CO_2 emissions growth (%, 1990–2005)	130.0	96.8	93.5
Particulate matter (urban-pop.-weighted avg., μg/cu. m)	119	72	67
Transport sector fuel consumption per capita (liters)	146	277	99
Water and sanitation			
Internal freshwater resources per capita (cu. m)	24	728	4,117
Freshwater withdrawal			
Total (% of internal resources)	3,794.4	122.3	8.7
Agriculture (% of total freshwater withdrawal)	86	86	80
Access to improved water source (% of total population)	98	89	88
Rural (% of rural population)	98	81	82
Urban (% of urban population)	99	95	96
Access to improved sanitation (% of total population)	66	77	55
Rural (% of rural population)	52	62	43
Urban (% of urban population)	85	88	71
Environment and health			
Acute resp. infection prevalence (% of children under five)	9.0		
Diarrhea prevalence (% of children under five)	18.4		
Under-five mortality rate (per 1,000 live births)	36	38	50
National accounting aggregates			
Gross savings (% of GNI)	22.4	33.3	41.7
Consumption of fixed capital (% of GNI)	10.2	11.3	10.7
Education expenditure (% of GNI)	4.4	4.7	2.6
Energy depletion (% of GNI)	13.4	21.3	6.6
Mineral depletion (% of GNI)	0.1	0.4	1.2
Net forest depletion (% of GNI)	0.2	0.0	0.2
CO_2 damage (% of GNI)	1.0	1.0	1.2
Particulate emission damage (% of GNI)	1.0	0.6	1.1
Adjusted net savings (% of GNI)	0.9	3.4	23.5

El Salvador

Population (millions)	**6.9**	Land area (1,000 sq. km)	**20.7**	GDP ($ billions)	**20.4**

	Country data	Latin America & Caribbean group	Lower middle-income group
GNI per capita, *World Bank Atlas* method ($)	2,850	5,801	1,905
Urban population (% of total)	60	78	42
Urban population growth (average annual %, 1990–2007)	2.9	2.1	2.9
Population growth (average annual %, 1990–2007)	1.7	1.5	1.3
Agriculture			
Agricultural land (% of land area)	82	36	47
Agricultural productivity (value added per worker, 2000 $)	1,700	3,158	532
Food production index (1999–2001 = 100)	105	117	116
Population density, rural (people/sq. km of arable land)	406	232	511
Forests and biodiversity			
Forest area (% of land area)	14.4	45.4	25.0
Deforestation (average annual %, 1990–2005)	1.5	0.5	0.1
Nationally protected area (% of land area)	1.0	16.7	11.0
Animal species, total known	571		
Animal species, threatened	38		
Higher plant species, total known	2,911		
Higher plant species, threatened	26		
GEF benefits index for biodiversity (0–100, median is 1.5)	0.9		
Energy			
GDP per unit of energy use (2005 PPP $/kg oil equivalent)	7.6	7.3	3.9
Energy use per capita (kg oil equivalent)	697	1,240	1,019
Energy from biomass products and waste (% of total)	31.6	15.9	15.2
Electric power consumption per capita (kWh)	721	1,808	1,269
Electricity generated using fossil fuel (% of total)	44.2	37.0	79.0
Electricity generated by hydropower (% of total)	35.1	57.3	16.3
Emissions and pollution			
CO_2 emissions per unit of GDP (kg/2005 PPP $)	0.2	0.3	0.8
CO_2 emissions per capita (metric tons)	1.0	2.5	2.8
CO_2 emissions growth (%, 1990–2005)	144.5	33.4	93.5
Particulate matter (urban-pop.-weighted avg., µg/cu. m)	33	35	67
Transport sector fuel consumption per capita (liters)	153	295	99
Water and sanitation			
Internal freshwater resources per capita (cu. m)	2,590	23,965	4,117
Freshwater withdrawal			
Total (% of internal resources)	7.2	2.0	8.7
Agriculture (% of total freshwater withdrawal)	59	71	80
Access to improved water source (% of total population)	84	91	88
Rural (% of rural population)	68	73	82
Urban (% of urban population)	94	97	96
Access to improved sanitation (% of total population)	86	78	55
Rural (% of rural population)	80	51	43
Urban (% of urban population)	90	86	71
Environment and health			
Acute resp. infection prevalence (% of children under five)	42.0		
Diarrhea prevalence (% of children under five)	19.8		
Under-five mortality rate (per 1,000 live births)	24	26	50
National accounting aggregates			
Gross savings (% of GNI)	12.5	22.9	41.7
Consumption of fixed capital (% of GNI)	11.3	12.6	10.7
Education expenditure (% of GNI)	2.8	4.5	2.6
Energy depletion (% of GNI)	0.0	5.4	6.6
Mineral depletion (% of GNI)	0.0	1.9	1.2
Net forest depletion (% of GNI)	0.5	0.0	0.2
CO_2 damage (% of GNI)	0.3	0.3	1.2
Particulate emission damage (% of GNI)	0.2	0.4	1.1
Adjusted net savings (% of GNI)	3.0	6.7	23.5

Equatorial Guinea

Population (thousands) **508** Land area (1,000 sq. km) **28** GDP ($ billions) **9.9**

	Country data	High-income group
GNI per capita, *World Bank Atlas* method ($)	12,860	37,572
Urban population (% of total)	39	78
Urban population growth (average annual %, 1990–2007)	3.1	1.0
Population growth (average annual %, 1990–2007)	2.4	0.7
Agriculture		
Agricultural land (% of land area)	12	38
Agricultural productivity (value added per worker, 2000 $)	1,198	27,680
Food production index (1999–2001 = 100)	95	102
Population density, rural (people/sq. km of arable land)	228	323
Forests and biodiversity		
Forest area (% of land area)	58.2	28.8
Deforestation (average annual %, 1990–2005)	0.9	–0.1
Nationally protected area (% of land area)	16.2	11.8
Animal species, total known	571	
Animal species, threatened	44	
Higher plant species, total known	3,250	
Higher plant species, threatened	63	
GEF benefits index for biodiversity (0–100, median is 1.5)	1.5	
Energy		
GDP per unit of energy use (2005 PPP $/kg oil equivalent)	..	6.3
Energy use per capita (kg oil equivalent)	..	5,416
Energy from biomass products and waste (% of total)	..	3.4
Electric power consumption per capita (kWh)	..	9,675
Electricity generated using fossil fuel (% of total)	..	62.0
Electricity generated by hydropower (% of total)	..	11.4
Emissions and pollution		
CO_2 emissions per unit of GDP (kg/2005 PPP $)	0.3	0.4
CO_2 emissions per capita (metric tons)	9.0	12.6
CO_2 emissions growth (%, 1990–2005)	3,596.9	19.1
Particulate matter (urban-pop.-weighted avg., µg/cu. m)	8	26
Transport sector fuel consumption per capita (liters)	..	1,159
Water and sanitation		
Internal freshwater resources per capita (cu. m)	51,227	9,313
Freshwater withdrawal		
Total (% of internal resources)	0.4	10.4
Agriculture (% of total freshwater withdrawal)	1	43
Access to improved water source (% of total population)	43	100
Rural (% of rural population)	42	98
Urban (% of urban population)	45	100
Access to improved sanitation (% of total population)	51	100
Rural (% of rural population)	46	99
Urban (% of urban population)	60	100
Environment and health		
Acute resp. infection prevalence (% of children under five)	..	
Diarrhea prevalence (% of children under five)	..	
Under-five mortality rate (per 1,000 live births)	206	7
National accounting aggregates		
Gross savings (% of GNI)	73.0	20.6
Consumption of fixed capital (% of GNI)	19.8	14.5
Education expenditure (% of GNI)	1.1	4.6
Energy depletion (% of GNI)	93.1	1.5
Mineral depletion (% of GNI)	0.0	0.2
Net forest depletion (% of GNI)	0.0	0.0
CO_2 damage (% of GNI)	0.6	0.3
Particulate emission damage (% of GNI)	..	0.3
Adjusted net savings (% of GNI)	–39.3	8.5

Eritrea

| | Population (millions) | **4.8** | Land area (1,000 sq. km) | **101.0** | GDP ($ billions) | **1.4** |

	Country data	Sub-Saharan Africa group	Low-income group
GNI per capita, *World Bank Atlas* method ($)	270	951	574
Urban population (% of total)	20	36	32
Urban population growth (average annual %, 1990–2007)	4.0	4.0	3.7
Population growth (average annual %, 1990–2007)	2.5	2.6	2.4
Agriculture			
Agricultural land (% of land area)	75	44	39
Agricultural productivity (value added per worker, 2000 $)	94	287	330
Food production index (1999–2001 = 100)	100	109	112
Population density, rural (people/sq. km of arable land)	573	351	603
Forests and biodiversity			
Forest area (% of land area)	15.4	26.5	24.7
Deforestation (average annual %, 1990–2005)	0.3	0.6	0.7
Nationally protected area (% of land area)	5.0	11.3	10.8
Animal species, total known	607		
Animal species, threatened	88		
Higher plant species, total known	..		
Higher plant species, threatened	3		
GEF benefits index for biodiversity (0–100, median is 1.5)	0.8		
Energy			
GDP per unit of energy use (2005 PPP $/kg oil equivalent)	4.0	3.0	3.2
Energy use per capita (kg oil equivalent)	150	670	478
Energy from biomass products and waste (% of total)	73.0	56.3	53.8
Electric power consumption per capita (kWh)	49	531	309
Electricity generated using fossil fuel (% of total)	99.3	65.6	48.4
Electricity generated by hydropower (% of total)	0.0	18.0	38.8
Emissions and pollution			
CO_2 emissions per unit of GDP (kg/2005 PPP $)	0.3	0.5	0.4
CO_2 emissions per capita (metric tons)	0.2	0.8	0.6
CO_2 emissions growth (%, 1990–2005)	..	40.1	39.3
Particulate matter (urban-pop.-weighted avg., µg/cu. m)	56	53	69
Transport sector fuel consumption per capita (liters)	11	64	41
Water and sanitation			
Internal freshwater resources per capita (cu. m)	578	4,824	4,619
Freshwater withdrawal			
Total (% of internal resources)	20.8	3.2	9.4
Agriculture (% of total freshwater withdrawal)	95	87	90
Access to improved water source (% of total population)	60	58	68
Rural (% of rural population)	57	46	60
Urban (% of urban population)	74	81	84
Access to improved sanitation (% of total population)	5	31	39
Rural (% of rural population)	3	24	33
Urban (% of urban population)	14	42	54
Environment and health			
Acute resp. infection prevalence (% of children under five)	19.0		
Diarrhea prevalence (% of children under five)	23.6		
Under-five mortality rate (per 1,000 live births)	70	146	126
National accounting aggregates			
Gross savings (% of GNI)	..	17.4	25.4
Consumption of fixed capital (% of GNI)	7.8	11.1	9.3
Education expenditure (% of GNI)	1.9	3.6	2.6
Energy depletion (% of GNI)	0.0	11.7	9.8
Mineral depletion (% of GNI)	0.0	1.5	0.9
Net forest depletion (% of GNI)	0.9	0.5	0.8
CO_2 damage (% of GNI)	0.4	0.7	0.7
Particulate emission damage (% of GNI)	0.4	0.4	0.7
Adjusted net savings (% of GNI)	..	-5.0	5.8

Estonia

| Population (millions) | **1.3** | Land area (1,000 sq. km) | **42.4** | GDP ($ billions) | **20.9** |

	Country data	High-income group
GNI per capita, *World Bank Atlas* method ($)	12,830	37,572
Urban population (% of total)	69	78
Urban population growth (average annual %, 1990–2007)	–1.1	1.0
Population growth (average annual %, 1990–2007)	–0.9	0.7
Agriculture		
Agricultural land (% of land area)	20	38
Agricultural productivity (value added per worker, 2000 $)	3,021	27,680
Food production index (1999–2001 = 100)	104	102
Population density, rural (people/sq. km of arable land)	70	323
Forests and biodiversity		
Forest area (% of land area)	53.9	28.8
Deforestation (average annual %, 1990–2005)	–0.4	–0.1
Nationally protected area (% of land area)	47.1	11.8
Animal species, total known	334	
Animal species, threatened	12	
Higher plant species, total known	1,630	
Higher plant species, threatened	0	
GEF benefits index for biodiversity (0–100, median is 1.5)	0.1	
Energy		
GDP per unit of energy use (2005 PPP $/kg oil equivalent)	5.0	6.3
Energy use per capita (kg oil equivalent)	3,638	5,416
Energy from biomass products and waste (% of total)	10.7	3.4
Electric power consumption per capita (kWh)	5,883	9,675
Electricity generated using fossil fuel (% of total)	98.5	62.0
Electricity generated by hydropower (% of total)	0.1	11.4
Emissions and pollution		
CO_2 emissions per unit of GDP (kg/2005 PPP $)	0.8	0.4
CO_2 emissions per capita (metric tons)	13.5	12.6
CO_2 emissions growth (%, 1990–2005)	–35.7	19.1
Particulate matter (urban-pop.-weighted avg., µg/cu. m)	13	26
Transport sector fuel consumption per capita (liters)	644	1,159
Water and sanitation		
Internal freshwater resources per capita (cu. m)	9,475	9,313
Freshwater withdrawal		
Total (% of internal resources)	1.2	10.4
Agriculture (% of total freshwater withdrawal)	5	43
Access to improved water source (% of total population)	100	100
Rural (% of rural population)	99	98
Urban (% of urban population)	100	100
Access to improved sanitation (% of total population)	95	100
Rural (% of rural population)	94	99
Urban (% of urban population)	96	100
Environment and health		
Acute resp. infection prevalence (% of children under five)	..	
Diarrhea prevalence (% of children under five)	..	
Under-five mortality rate (per 1,000 live births)	6	7
National accounting aggregates		
Gross savings (% of GNI)	21.9	20.6
Consumption of fixed capital (% of GNI)	14.5	14.5
Education expenditure (% of GNI)	4.6	4.6
Energy depletion (% of GNI)	23.0	1.5
Mineral depletion (% of GNI)	0.0	0.2
Net forest depletion (% of GNI)	0.1	0.0
CO_2 damage (% of GNI)	0.9	0.3
Particulate emission damage (% of GNI)	0.0	0.3
Adjusted net savings (% of GNI)	–11.9	8.5

Ethiopia

| | Population (millions) | 79 | Land area (1,000 sq. km) | **1,000** | GDP ($ billions) | **19.4** |

	Country data	Sub-Saharan Africa group	Low-income group
GNI per capita, *World Bank Atlas* method ($)	220	951	574
Urban population (% of total)	17	36	32
Urban population growth (average annual %, 1990–2007)	4.6	4.0	3.7
Population growth (average annual %, 1990–2007)	2.9	2.6	2.4
Agriculture			
Agricultural land (% of land area)	34	44	39
Agricultural productivity (value added per worker, 2000 $)	177	287	330
Food production index (1999–2001 = 100)	113	109	112
Population density, rural (people/sq. km of arable land)	481	351	603
Forests and biodiversity			
Forest area (% of land area)	13.0	26.5	24.7
Deforestation (average annual %, 1990–2005)	1.0	0.6	0.7
Nationally protected area (% of land area)	18.6	11.3	10.8
Animal species, total known	1,127		
Animal species, threatened	79		
Higher plant species, total known	6,603		
Higher plant species, threatened	22		
GEF benefits index for biodiversity (0–100, median is 1.5)	8.4		
Energy			
GDP per unit of energy use (2005 PPP $/kg oil equivalent)	2.3	3.0	3.2
Energy use per capita (kg oil equivalent)	289	670	478
Energy from biomass products and waste (% of total)	90.0	56.3	53.8
Electric power consumption per capita (kWh)	38	531	309
Electricity generated using fossil fuel (% of total)	0.3	65.6	48.4
Electricity generated by hydropower (% of total)	99.7	18.0	38.8
Emissions and pollution			
CO_2 emissions per unit of GDP (kg/2005 PPP $)	0.2	0.5	0.4
CO_2 emissions per capita (metric tons)	0.1	0.8	0.6
CO_2 emissions growth (%, 1990–2005)	165.9	40.1	39.3
Particulate matter (urban-pop.-weighted avg., µg/cu. m)	68	53	69
Transport sector fuel consumption per capita (liters)	15	64	41
Water and sanitation			
Internal freshwater resources per capita (cu. m)	1,543	4,824	4,619
Freshwater withdrawal			
Total (% of internal resources)	4.6	3.2	9.4
Agriculture (% of total freshwater withdrawal)	94	87	90
Access to improved water source (% of total population)	42	58	68
Rural (% of rural population)	31	46	60
Urban (% of urban population)	96	81	84
Access to improved sanitation (% of total population)	11	31	39
Rural (% of rural population)	8	24	33
Urban (% of urban population)	27	42	54
Environment and health			
Acute resp. infection prevalence (% of children under five)	12.6		
Diarrhea prevalence (% of children under five)	23.6		
Under-five mortality rate (per 1,000 live births)	119	146	126
National accounting aggregates			
Gross savings (% of GNI)	20.9	17.4	25.4
Consumption of fixed capital (% of GNI)	7.5	11.1	9.3
Education expenditure (% of GNI)	3.7	3.6	2.6
Energy depletion (% of GNI)	0.0	11.7	9.8
Mineral depletion (% of GNI)	0.4	1.5	0.9
Net forest depletion (% of GNI)	5.4	0.5	0.8
CO_2 damage (% of GNI)	0.4	0.7	0.7
Particulate emission damage (% of GNI)	0.3	0.4	0.7
Adjusted net savings (% of GNI)	10.6	-5.0	5.8

Faeroe Islands

Population (thousands) **48** Land area (1,000 sq. km) **1.4** GDP ($ billions) ..

	Country data	High-income group
GNI per capita, *World Bank Atlas* method ($)	..	37,572
Urban population (% of total)	41	78
Urban population growth (average annual %, 1990–2007)	1.8	1.0
Population growth (average annual %, 1990–2007)	0.1	0.7
Agriculture		
Agricultural land (% of land area)	2	38
Agricultural productivity (value added per worker, 2000 $)	..	27,680
Food production index (1999–2001 = 100)	100	102
Population density, rural (people/sq. km of arable land)	968	323
Forests and biodiversity		
Forest area (% of land area)	0.1	28.8
Deforestation (average annual %, 1990–2005)	..	–0.1
Nationally protected area (% of land area)	..	11.8
Animal species, total known	268	
Animal species, threatened	..	
Higher plant species, total known	236	
Higher plant species, threatened	..	
GEF benefits index for biodiversity (0–100, median is 1.5)	0.3	
Energy		
GDP per unit of energy use (2005 PPP $/kg oil equivalent)	..	6.3
Energy use per capita (kg oil equivalent)	..	5,416
Energy from biomass products and waste (% of total)	..	3.4
Electric power consumption per capita (kWh)	..	9,675
Electricity generated using fossil fuel (% of total)	..	62.0
Electricity generated by hydropower (% of total)	..	11.4
Emissions and pollution		
CO_2 emissions per unit of GDP (kg/2005 PPP $)	..	0.4
CO_2 emissions per capita (metric tons)	13.6	12.6
CO_2 emissions growth (%, 1990–2005)	6.5	19.1
Particulate matter (urban-pop.-weighted avg., µg/cu. m)	14	26
Transport sector fuel consumption per capita (liters)	..	1,159
Water and sanitation		
Internal freshwater resources per capita (cu. m)	..	9,313
Freshwater withdrawal		
Total (% of internal resources)	..	10.4
Agriculture (% of total freshwater withdrawal)	..	43
Access to improved water source (% of total population)	..	100
Rural (% of rural population)	..	98
Urban (% of urban population)	..	100
Access to improved sanitation (% of total population)	..	100
Rural (% of rural population)	..	99
Urban (% of urban population)	..	100
Environment and health		
Acute resp. infection prevalence (% of children under five)	..	
Diarrhea prevalence (% of children under five)	..	
Under-five mortality rate (per 1,000 live births)	..	7
National accounting aggregates		
Gross savings (% of GNI)	..	20.6
Consumption of fixed capital (% of GNI)	..	14.5
Education expenditure (% of GNI)	..	4.6
Energy depletion (% of GNI)	..	1.5
Mineral depletion (% of GNI)	..	0.2
Net forest depletion (% of GNI)	..	0.0
CO_2 damage (% of GNI)	..	0.3
Particulate emission damage (% of GNI)	..	0.3
Adjusted net savings (% of GNI)	..	8.5

Fiji

| | Population (thousands) **834** | Land area (1,000 sq. km) | **18** | GDP ($ billions) | **3.4** |

	Country data	East Asia & Pacific group	Upper middle-income group
GNI per capita, *World Bank Atlas* method ($)	3,750	2,182	7,107
Urban population (% of total)	52	43	75
Urban population growth (average annual %, 1990–2007)	2.1	3.5	1.4
Population growth (average annual %, 1990–2007)	0.8	1.1	0.9
Agriculture			
Agricultural land (% of land area)	25	51	31
Agricultural productivity (value added per worker, 2000 $)	1,867	458	2,947
Food production index (1999–2001 = 100)	96	120	113
Population density, rural (people/sq. km of arable land)	203	547	110
Forests and biodiversity			
Forest area (% of land area)	54.7	28.4	39.3
Deforestation (average annual %, 1990–2005)	-0.1	-0.1	0.2
Nationally protected area (% of land area)	0.8	14.0	10.3
Animal species, total known	127		
Animal species, threatened	124		
Higher plant species, total known	1,518		
Higher plant species, threatened	66		
GEF benefits index for biodiversity (0–100, median is 1.5)	3.9		
Energy			
GDP per unit of energy use (2005 PPP $/kg oil equivalent)	..	3.4	4.8
Energy use per capita (kg oil equivalent)	..	1,258	2,300
Energy from biomass products and waste (% of total)	..	14.7	7.0
Electric power consumption per capita (kWh)	..	1,669	3,242
Electricity generated using fossil fuel (% of total)	..	82.0	62.8
Electricity generated by hydropower (% of total)	..	15.0	27.6
Emissions and pollution			
CO_2 emissions per unit of GDP (kg/2005 PPP $)	0.5	0.9	0.5
CO_2 emissions per capita (metric tons)	2.0	3.6	5.5
CO_2 emissions growth (%, 1990–2005)	101.8	123.4	-8.3
Particulate matter (urban-pop.-weighted avg., µg/cu. m)	22	69	30
Transport sector fuel consumption per capita (liters)	..	106	332
Water and sanitation			
Internal freshwater resources per capita (cu. m)	34,221	4,948	16,993
Freshwater withdrawal			
Total (% of internal resources)	0.2	10.2	13.8
Agriculture (% of total freshwater withdrawal)	71	74	57
Access to improved water source (% of total population)	47	87	95
Rural (% of rural population)	51	81	83
Urban (% of urban population)	43	96	98
Access to improved sanitation (% of total population)	71	66	83
Rural (% of rural population)	55	59	64
Urban (% of urban population)	87	75	89
Environment and health			
Acute resp. infection prevalence (% of children under five)	..		
Diarrhea prevalence (% of children under five)	..		
Under-five mortality rate (per 1,000 live births)	18	27	24
National accounting aggregates			
Gross savings (% of GNI)	..	48.0	23.2
Consumption of fixed capital (% of GNI)	11.7	10.7	12.8
Education expenditure (% of GNI)	6.0	2.1	4.4
Energy depletion (% of GNI)	0.0	4.9	7.6
Mineral depletion (% of GNI)	0.9	1.3	1.3
Net forest depletion (% of GNI)	0.0	0.0	0.0
CO_2 damage (% of GNI)	0.2	1.3	0.6
Particulate emission damage (% of GNI)	0.1	1.3	0.4
Adjusted net savings (% of GNI)	..	30.6	4.9

Finland

| Population (millions) | **5.3** | Land area (1,000 sq. km) | **304.6** | GDP ($ billions) | **244.7** |

	Country data	High-income group
GNI per capita, *World Bank Atlas* method ($)	44,300	37,572
Urban population (% of total)	63	78
Urban population growth (average annual %, 1990–2007)	0.5	1.0
Population growth (average annual %, 1990–2007)	0.3	0.7
Agriculture		
Agricultural land (% of land area)	7	38
Agricultural productivity (value added per worker, 2000 $)	33,738	27,680
Food production index (1999–2001 = 100)	109	102
Population density, rural (people/sq. km of arable land)	88	323
Forests and biodiversity		
Forest area (% of land area)	73.9	28.8
Deforestation (average annual %, 1990–2005)	-0.1	-0.1
Nationally protected area (% of land area)	9.7	11.8
Animal species, total known	501	
Animal species, threatened	20	
Higher plant species, total known	1,102	
Higher plant species, threatened	1	
GEF benefits index for biodiversity (0–100, median is 1.5)	0.2	
Energy		
GDP per unit of energy use (2005 PPP $/kg oil equivalent)	4.5	6.3
Energy use per capita (kg oil equivalent)	7,108	5,416
Energy from biomass products and waste (% of total)	20.4	3.4
Electric power consumption per capita (kWh)	17,177	9,675
Electricity generated using fossil fuel (% of total)	36.2	62.0
Electricity generated by hydropower (% of total)	14.0	11.4
Emissions and pollution		
CO_2 emissions per unit of GDP (kg/2005 PPP $)	0.3	0.4
CO_2 emissions per capita (metric tons)	10.1	12.6
CO_2 emissions growth (%, 1990–2005)	5.1	19.1
Particulate matter (urban-pop.-weighted avg., µg/cu. m)	18	26
Transport sector fuel consumption per capita (liters)	915	1,159
Water and sanitation		
Internal freshwater resources per capita (cu. m)	20,232	9,313
Freshwater withdrawal		
Total (% of internal resources)	2.3	10.4
Agriculture (% of total freshwater withdrawal)	3	43
Access to improved water source (% of total population)	100	100
Rural (% of rural population)	100	98
Urban (% of urban population)	100	100
Access to improved sanitation (% of total population)	100	100
Rural (% of rural population)	100	99
Urban (% of urban population)	100	100
Environment and health		
Acute resp. infection prevalence (% of children under five)	..	
Diarrhea prevalence (% of children under five)	..	
Under-five mortality rate (per 1,000 live births)	4	7
National accounting aggregates		
Gross savings (% of GNI)	26.5	20.6
Consumption of fixed capital (% of GNI)	14.8	14.5
Education expenditure (% of GNI)	5.9	4.6
Energy depletion (% of GNI)	0.0	1.5
Mineral depletion (% of GNI)	0.1	0.2
Net forest depletion (% of GNI)	0.0	0.0
CO_2 damage (% of GNI)	0.2	0.3
Particulate emission damage (% of GNI)	0.1	0.3
Adjusted net savings (% of GNI)	17.1	8.5

France

| Population (millions) | **62** | Land area (1,000 sq. km) | **550** | GDP ($ billions) | **2,589.8** |

	Country data	High-income group
GNI per capita, *World Bank Atlas* method ($)	38,810	37,572
Urban population (% of total)	77	78
Urban population growth (average annual %, 1990–2007)	0.7	1.0
Population growth (average annual %, 1990–2007)	0.5	0.7
Agriculture		
Agricultural land (% of land area)	54	38
Agricultural productivity (value added per worker, 2000 $)	47,153	27,680
Food production index (1999–2001 = 100)	98	102
Population density, rural (people/sq. km of arable land)	77	323
Forests and biodiversity		
Forest area (% of land area)	28.3	28.8
Deforestation (average annual %, 1990–2005)	-0.5	-0.1
Nationally protected area (% of land area)	10.1	11.8
Animal species, total known	665	
Animal species, threatened	127	
Higher plant species, total known	4,630	
Higher plant species, threatened	8	
GEF benefits index for biodiversity (0–100, median is 1.5)	5.3	
Energy		
GDP per unit of energy use (2005 PPP $/kg oil equivalent)	7.0	6.3
Energy use per capita (kg oil equivalent)	4,444	5,416
Energy from biomass products and waste (% of total)	4.4	3.4
Electric power consumption per capita (kWh)	7,813	9,675
Electricity generated using fossil fuel (% of total)	9.7	62.0
Electricity generated by hydropower (% of total)	9.8	11.4
Emissions and pollution		
CO_2 emissions per unit of GDP (kg/2005 PPP $)	0.2	0.4
CO_2 emissions per capita (metric tons)	6.2	12.6
CO_2 emissions growth (%, 1990–2005)	4.0	19.1
Particulate matter (urban-pop.-weighted avg., µg/cu. m)	13	26
Transport sector fuel consumption per capita (liters)	781	1,159
Water and sanitation		
Internal freshwater resources per capita (cu. m)	2,893	9,313
Freshwater withdrawal		
Total (% of internal resources)	22.4	10.4
Agriculture (% of total freshwater withdrawal)	10	43
Access to improved water source (% of total population)	100	100
Rural (% of rural population)	100	98
Urban (% of urban population)	100	100
Access to improved sanitation (% of total population)	..	100
Rural (% of rural population)	..	99
Urban (% of urban population)	..	100
Environment and health		
Acute resp. infection prevalence (% of children under five)	..	
Diarrhea prevalence (% of children under five)	..	
Under-five mortality rate (per 1,000 live births)	4	7
National accounting aggregates		
Gross savings (% of GNI)	19.2	20.6
Consumption of fixed capital (% of GNI)	13.3	14.5
Education expenditure (% of GNI)	5.1	4.6
Energy depletion (% of GNI)	0.0	1.5
Mineral depletion (% of GNI)	0.0	0.2
Net forest depletion (% of GNI)	0.0	0.0
CO_2 damage (% of GNI)	0.1	0.3
Particulate emission damage (% of GNI)	0.0	0.3
Adjusted net savings (% of GNI)	10.9	8.5

French Polynesia

Population (thousands) **263**	Land area (1,000 sq. km)	**4**	GDP ($ billions)	**3.4**

	Country data	High-income group
GNI per capita, *World Bank Atlas* method ($)	16,070	37,572
Urban population (% of total)	52	78
Urban population growth (average annual %, 1990–2007)	1.3	1.0
Population growth (average annual %, 1990–2007)	1.7	0.7
Agriculture		
Agricultural land (% of land area)	12	38
Agricultural productivity (value added per worker, 2000 $)	..	27,680
Food production index (1999–2001 = 100)	109	102
Population density, rural (people/sq. km of arable land)	4,116	323
Forests and biodiversity		
Forest area (% of land area)	28.7	28.8
Deforestation (average annual %, 1990–2005)	0.0	–0.1
Nationally protected area (% of land area)	0.2	11.8
Animal species, total known	137	
Animal species, threatened	102	
Higher plant species, total known	959	
Higher plant species, threatened	47	
GEF benefits index for biodiversity (0–100, median is 1.5)	4.6	
Energy		
GDP per unit of energy use (2005 PPP $/kg oil equivalent)	..	6.3
Energy use per capita (kg oil equivalent)	..	5,416
Energy from biomass products and waste (% of total)	..	3.4
Electric power consumption per capita (kWh)	..	9,675
Electricity generated using fossil fuel (% of total)	..	62.0
Electricity generated by hydropower (% of total)	..	11.4
Emissions and pollution		
CO_2 emissions per unit of GDP (kg/2005 PPP $)	..	0.4
CO_2 emissions per capita (metric tons)	2.7	12.6
CO_2 emissions growth (%, 1990–2005)	12.0	19.1
Particulate matter (urban-pop.-weighted avg., µg/cu. m)	..	26
Transport sector fuel consumption per capita (liters)	..	1,159
Water and sanitation		
Internal freshwater resources per capita (cu. m)	38,078	9,313
Freshwater withdrawal		
Total (% of internal resources)	..	10.4
Agriculture (% of total freshwater withdrawal)	..	43
Access to improved water source (% of total population)	100	100
Rural (% of rural population)	100	98
Urban (% of urban population)	100	100
Access to improved sanitation (% of total population)	98	100
Rural (% of rural population)	97	99
Urban (% of urban population)	99	100
Environment and health		
Acute resp. infection prevalence (% of children under five)	..	
Diarrhea prevalence (% of children under five)	..	
Under-five mortality rate (per 1,000 live births)	..	7
National accounting aggregates		
Gross savings (% of GNI)	..	20.6
Consumption of fixed capital (% of GNI)	..	14.5
Education expenditure (% of GNI)	..	4.6
Energy depletion (% of GNI)	..	1.5
Mineral depletion (% of GNI)	..	0.2
Net forest depletion (% of GNI)	..	0.0
CO_2 damage (% of GNI)	..	0.3
Particulate emission damage (% of GNI)	..	0.3
Adjusted net savings (% of GNI)	..	8.5

Gabon

| Population (millions) | **1.3** | Land area (1,000 sq. km) | **257.7** | GDP ($ billions) | **11.6** |

	Country data	Sub-Saharan Africa group	Upper middle-income group
GNI per capita, *World Bank Atlas* method ($)	7,020	951	7,107
Urban population (% of total)	85	36	75
Urban population growth (average annual %, 1990–2007)	3.4	4.0	1.4
Population growth (average annual %, 1990–2007)	2.2	2.6	0.9
Agriculture			
Agricultural land (% of land area)	20	44	31
Agricultural productivity (value added per worker, 2000 $)	1,663	287	2,947
Food production index (1999–2001 = 100)	102	109	113
Population density, rural (people/sq. km of arable land)	65	351	110
Forests and biodiversity			
Forest area (% of land area)	84.5	26.5	39.3
Deforestation (average annual %, 1990–2005)	0.0	0.6	0.2
Nationally protected area (% of land area)	13.5	11.3	10.3
Animal species, total known	798		
Animal species, threatened	45		
Higher plant species, total known	6,651		
Higher plant species, threatened	108		
GEF benefits index for biodiversity (0–100, median is 1.5)	3.0		
Energy			
GDP per unit of energy use (2005 PPP $/kg oil equivalent)	9.9	3.0	4.8
Energy use per capita (kg oil equivalent)	1,391	670	2,300
Energy from biomass products and waste (% of total)	56.3	56.3	7.0
Electric power consumption per capita (kWh)	1,083	531	3,242
Electricity generated using fossil fuel (% of total)	44.8	65.6	62.8
Electricity generated by hydropower (% of total)	54.8	18.0	27.6
Emissions and pollution			
CO_2 emissions per unit of GDP (kg/2005 PPP $)	0.08	0.49	0.52
CO_2 emissions per capita (metric tons)	1.2	0.8	5.5
CO_2 emissions growth (%, 1990–2005)	–74.9	40.1	–8.3
Particulate matter (urban-pop.-weighted avg., µg/cu. m)	8	53	30
Transport sector fuel consumption per capita (liters)	123	64	332
Water and sanitation			
Internal freshwater resources per capita (cu. m)	123,291	4,824	16,993
Freshwater withdrawal			
Total (% of internal resources)	0.1	3.2	13.8
Agriculture (% of total freshwater withdrawal)	42	87	57
Access to improved water source (% of total population)	87	58	95
Rural (% of rural population)	47	46	83
Urban (% of urban population)	95	81	98
Access to improved sanitation (% of total population)	36	31	83
Rural (% of rural population)	30	24	64
Urban (% of urban population)	37	42	89
Environment and health			
Acute resp. infection prevalence (% of children under five)	13.0		
Diarrhea prevalence (% of children under five)	15.7		
Under-five mortality rate (per 1,000 live births)	91	146	24
National accounting aggregates			
Gross savings (% of GNI)	46.3	17.4	23.2
Consumption of fixed capital (% of GNI)	14.2	11.1	12.8
Education expenditure (% of GNI)	3.1	3.6	4.4
Energy depletion (% of GNI)	33.3	11.7	7.6
Mineral depletion (% of GNI)	0.0	1.5	1.3
Net forest depletion (% of GNI)	0.0	0.5	0.0
CO_2 damage (% of GNI)	0.1	0.7	0.6
Particulate emission damage (% of GNI)	..	0.4	0.4
Adjusted net savings (% of GNI)	1.7	–5.0	4.9

Gambia, The

| Population (millions) | 1.7 | Land area (1,000 sq. km) | 10.0 | GDP ($ millions) | 644 |

	Country data	Sub-Saharan Africa group	Low-income group
GNI per capita, *World Bank Atlas* method ($)	320	951	574
Urban population (% of total)	56	36	32
Urban population growth (average annual %, 1990–2007)	5.6	4.0	3.7
Population growth (average annual %, 1990–2007)	3.4	2.6	2.4
Agriculture			
Agricultural land (% of land area)	81	44	39
Agricultural productivity (value added per worker, 2000 $)	244	287	330
Food production index (1999–2001 = 100)	104	109	112
Population density, rural (people/sq. km of arable land)	213	351	603
Forests and biodiversity			
Forest area (% of land area)	47.1	26.5	24.7
Deforestation (average annual %, 1990–2005)	-0.4	0.6	0.7
Nationally protected area (% of land area)	..	11.3	10.8
Animal species, total known	668		
Animal species, threatened	32		
Higher plant species, total known	974		
Higher plant species, threatened	4		
GEF benefits index for biodiversity (0–100, median is 1.5)	0.1		
Energy			
GDP per unit of energy use (2005 PPP $/kg oil equivalent)	..	3.0	3.2
Energy use per capita (kg oil equivalent)	..	670	478
Energy from biomass products and waste (% of total)	..	56.3	53.8
Electric power consumption per capita (kWh)	..	531	309
Electricity generated using fossil fuel (% of total)	..	65.6	48.4
Electricity generated by hydropower (% of total)	..	18.0	38.8
Emissions and pollution			
CO_2 emissions per unit of GDP (kg/2005 PPP $)	0.2	0.5	0.4
CO_2 emissions per capita (metric tons)	0.2	0.8	0.6
CO_2 emissions growth (%, 1990–2005)	50.0	40.1	39.3
Particulate matter (urban-pop.-weighted avg., µg/cu. m)	86	53	69
Transport sector fuel consumption per capita (liters)	..	64	41
Water and sanitation			
Internal freshwater resources per capita (cu. m)	1,758	4,824	4,619
Freshwater withdrawal			
Total (% of internal resources)	1.0	3.2	9.4
Agriculture (% of total freshwater withdrawal)	65	87	90
Access to improved water source (% of total population)	86	58	68
Rural (% of rural population)	81	46	60
Urban (% of urban population)	91	81	84
Access to improved sanitation (% of total population)	52	31	39
Rural (% of rural population)	55	24	33
Urban (% of urban population)	50	42	54
Environment and health			
Acute resp. infection prevalence (% of children under five)	8.0		
Diarrhea prevalence (% of children under five)	21.5		
Under-five mortality rate (per 1,000 live births)	109	146	126
National accounting aggregates			
Gross savings (% of GNI)	12.6	17.4	25.4
Consumption of fixed capital (% of GNI)	8.7	11.1	9.3
Education expenditure (% of GNI)	2.0	3.6	2.6
Energy depletion (% of GNI)	0.0	11.7	9.8
Mineral depletion (% of GNI)	0.0	1.5	0.9
Net forest depletion (% of GNI)	0.6	0.5	0.8
CO_2 damage (% of GNI)	0.4	0.7	0.7
Particulate emission damage (% of GNI)	0.7	0.4	0.7
Adjusted net savings (% of GNI)	4.2	-5.0	5.8

Georgia

Population (millions)	**4.4**	Land area (1,000 sq. km)	**69.5**	GDP ($ billions)	**10.2**

	Country data	Europe & Central Asia group	Lower middle-income group
GNI per capita, *World Bank Atlas* method ($)	2,120	6,052	1,905
Urban population (% of total)	53	64	42
Urban population growth (average annual %, 1990–2007)	–1.5	0.2	2.9
Population growth (average annual %, 1990–2007)	–1.3	0.1	1.3
Agriculture			
Agricultural land (% of land area)	43	28	47
Agricultural productivity (value added per worker, 2000 $)	1,937	2,228	532
Food production index (1999–2001 = 100)	103	110	116
Population density, rural (people/sq. km of arable land)	265	129	511
Forests and biodiversity			
Forest area (% of land area)	39.7	38.3	25.0
Deforestation (average annual %, 1990–2005)	0.0	0.0	0.1
Nationally protected area (% of land area)	3.9	6.1	11.0
Animal species, total known	366		
Animal species, threatened	49		
Higher plant species, total known	4,350		
Higher plant species, threatened	0		
GEF benefits index for biodiversity (0–100, median is 1.5)	0.6		
Energy			
GDP per unit of energy use (2005 PPP $/kg oil equivalent)	5.2	3.5	3.9
Energy use per capita (kg oil equivalent)	754	2,930	1,019
Energy from biomass products and waste (% of total)	19.3	2.2	15.2
Electric power consumption per capita (kWh)	1,549	3,835	1,269
Electricity generated using fossil fuel (% of total)	27.1	67.7	79.0
Electricity generated by hydropower (% of total)	72.9	17.4	16.3
Emissions and pollution			
CO_2 emissions per unit of GDP (kg/2005 PPP $)	0.3	0.7	0.8
CO_2 emissions per capita (metric tons)	1.1	7.0	2.8
CO_2 emissions growth (%, 1990–2005)	–72.4	–29.3	93.5
Particulate matter (urban-pop.-weighted avg., µg/cu. m)	47	27	67
Transport sector fuel consumption per capita (liters)	131	255	99
Water and sanitation			
Internal freshwater resources per capita (cu. m)	13,216	11,806	4,117
Freshwater withdrawal			
Total (% of internal resources)	2.8	7.2	8.7
Agriculture (% of total freshwater withdrawal)	65	60	80
Access to improved water source (% of total population)	99	95	88
Rural (% of rural population)	97	88	82
Urban (% of urban population)	100	99	96
Access to improved sanitation (% of total population)	93	89	55
Rural (% of rural population)	92	79	43
Urban (% of urban population)	94	94	71
Environment and health			
Acute resp. infection prevalence (% of children under five)	4.0		
Diarrhea prevalence (% of children under five)	6.0		
Under-five mortality rate (per 1,000 live births)	30	23	50
National accounting aggregates			
Gross savings (% of GNI)	17.0	24.0	41.7
Consumption of fixed capital (% of GNI)	10.4	12.8	10.7
Education expenditure (% of GNI)	2.8	4.0	2.6
Energy depletion (% of GNI)	0.0	9.8	6.6
Mineral depletion (% of GNI)	0.0	0.7	1.2
Net forest depletion (% of GNI)	0.0	0.0	0.2
CO_2 damage (% of GNI)	0.4	1.0	1.2
Particulate emission damage (% of GNI)	1.3	0.5	1.1
Adjusted net savings (% of GNI)	7.7	3.2	23.5

Germany

| | Population (millions) | **82** | Land area (1,000 sq. km) | **349** | GDP ($ billions) | **3,317.4** |

	Country data	High-income group
GNI per capita, *World Bank Atlas* method ($)	38,990	37,572
Urban population (% of total)	74	78
Urban population growth (average annual %, 1990–2007)	0.2	1.0
Population growth (average annual %, 1990–2007)	0.2	0.7

Agriculture
Agricultural land (% of land area)	49	38
Agricultural productivity (value added per worker, 2000 $)	26,418	27,680
Food production index (1999–2001 = 100)	99	102
Population density, rural (people/sq. km of arable land)	184	323

Forests and biodiversity
Forest area (% of land area)	31.8	28.8
Deforestation (average annual %, 1990–2005)	-0.2	-0.1
Nationally protected area (% of land area)	21.7	11.8
Animal species, total known	613	
Animal species, threatened	62	
Higher plant species, total known	2,682	
Higher plant species, threatened	12	
GEF benefits index for biodiversity (0–100, median is 1.5)	0.6	

Energy
GDP per unit of energy use (2005 PPP $/kg oil equivalent)	7.6	6.3
Energy use per capita (kg oil equivalent)	4,231	5,416
Energy from biomass products and waste (% of total)	4.6	3.4
Electric power consumption per capita (kWh)	7,174	9,675
Electricity generated using fossil fuel (% of total)	61.6	62.0
Electricity generated by hydropower (% of total)	3.2	11.4

Emissions and pollution
CO_2 emissions per unit of GDP (kg/2005 PPP $)	0.3	0.4
CO_2 emissions per capita (metric tons)	9.5	12.6
CO_2 emissions growth (%, 1990–2005)	-20.0	19.1
Particulate matter (urban-pop.-weighted avg., µg/cu. m)	19	26
Transport sector fuel consumption per capita (liters)	686	1,159

Water and sanitation
Internal freshwater resources per capita (cu. m)	1,301	9,313
Freshwater withdrawal		
Total (% of internal resources)	44.0	10.4
Agriculture (% of total freshwater withdrawal)	20	43
Access to improved water source (% of total population)	100	100
Rural (% of rural population)	100	98
Urban (% of urban population)	100	100
Access to improved sanitation (% of total population)	100	100
Rural (% of rural population)	100	99
Urban (% of urban population)	100	100

Environment and health
Acute resp. infection prevalence (% of children under five)	..	
Diarrhea prevalence (% of children under five)	..	
Under-five mortality rate (per 1,000 live births)	4	7

National accounting aggregates
Gross savings (% of GNI)	24.9	20.6
Consumption of fixed capital (% of GNI)	14.6	14.5
Education expenditure (% of GNI)	4.4	4.6
Energy depletion (% of GNI)	0.2	1.5
Mineral depletion (% of GNI)	0.0	0.2
Net forest depletion (% of GNI)	0.0	0.0
CO_2 damage (% of GNI)	0.2	0.3
Particulate emission damage (% of GNI)	0.1	0.3
Adjusted net savings (% of GNI)	14.3	8.5

Ghana

| Population (millions) | **23** | Land area (1,000 sq. km) | **228** | GDP ($ billions) | **15.1** |

	Country data	Sub-Saharan Africa group	Low-income group
GNI per capita, *World Bank Atlas* method ($)	590	951	574
Urban population (% of total)	49	36	32
Urban population growth (average annual %, 1990–2007)	4.2	4.0	3.7
Population growth (average annual %, 1990–2007)	2.4	2.6	2.4
Agriculture			
Agricultural land (% of land area)	65	44	39
Agricultural productivity (value added per worker, 2000 $)	332	287	330
Food production index (1999–2001 = 100)	117	109	112
Population density, rural (people/sq. km of arable land)	281	351	603
Forests and biodiversity			
Forest area (% of land area)	24.2	26.5	24.7
Deforestation (average annual %, 1990–2005)	2.0	0.6	0.7
Nationally protected area (% of land area)	15.9	11.3	10.8
Animal species, total known	978		
Animal species, threatened	57		
Higher plant species, total known	3,725		
Higher plant species, threatened	117		
GEF benefits index for biodiversity (0–100, median is 1.5)	1.9		
Energy			
GDP per unit of energy use (2005 PPP $/kg oil equivalent)	2.9	3.0	3.2
Energy use per capita (kg oil equivalent)	413	670	478
Energy from biomass products and waste (% of total)	63.3	56.3	53.8
Electric power consumption per capita (kWh)	304	531	309
Electricity generated using fossil fuel (% of total)	33.3	65.6	48.4
Electricity generated by hydropower (% of total)	66.7	18.0	38.8
Emissions and pollution			
CO_2 emissions per unit of GDP (kg/2005 PPP $)	0.3	0.5	0.4
CO_2 emissions per capita (metric tons)	0.3	0.8	0.6
CO_2 emissions growth (%, 1990–2005)	94.3	40.1	39.3
Particulate matter (urban-pop.-weighted avg., µg/cu. m)	34	53	69
Transport sector fuel consumption per capita (liters)	58	64	41
Water and sanitation			
Internal freshwater resources per capita (cu. m)	1,291	4,824	4,619
Freshwater withdrawal			
Total (% of internal resources)	3.2	3.2	9.4
Agriculture (% of total freshwater withdrawal)	66	87	90
Access to improved water source (% of total population)	80	58	68
Rural (% of rural population)	71	46	60
Urban (% of urban population)	90	81	84
Access to improved sanitation (% of total population)	10	31	39
Rural (% of rural population)	6	24	33
Urban (% of urban population)	15	42	54
Environment and health			
Acute resp. infection prevalence (% of children under five)	10.0		
Diarrhea prevalence (% of children under five)	17.9		
Under-five mortality rate (per 1,000 live births)	115	146	126
National accounting aggregates			
Gross savings (% of GNI)	23.2	17.4	25.4
Consumption of fixed capital (% of GNI)	8.9	11.1	9.3
Education expenditure (% of GNI)	4.7	3.6	2.6
Energy depletion (% of GNI)	0.0	11.7	9.8
Mineral depletion (% of GNI)	4.5	1.5	0.9
Net forest depletion (% of GNI)	2.3	0.5	0.8
CO_2 damage (% of GNI)	0.4	0.7	0.7
Particulate emission damage (% of GNI)	0.1	0.4	0.7
Adjusted net savings (% of GNI)	11.5	–5.0	5.8

Greece

| Population (millions) | **11** | Land area (1,000 sq. km) | **129** | GDP ($ billions) | **313.4** |

	Country data	High-income group
GNI per capita, *World Bank Atlas* method ($)	25,740	37,572
Urban population (% of total)	61	78
Urban population growth (average annual %, 1990–2007)	0.8	1.0
Population growth (average annual %, 1990–2007)	0.6	0.7
Agriculture		
Agricultural land (% of land area)	65	38
Agricultural productivity (value added per worker, 2000 $)	9,105	27,680
Food production index (1999–2001 = 100)	96	102
Population density, rural (people/sq. km of arable land)	167	323
Forests and biodiversity		
Forest area (% of land area)	29.1	28.8
Deforestation (average annual %, 1990–2005)	-0.9	-0.1
Nationally protected area (% of land area)	3.1	11.8
Animal species, total known	530	
Animal species, threatened	107	
Higher plant species, total known	4,992	
Higher plant species, threatened	11	
GEF benefits index for biodiversity (0–100, median is 1.5)	2.8	
Energy		
GDP per unit of energy use (2005 PPP $/kg oil equivalent)	9.3	6.3
Energy use per capita (kg oil equivalent)	2,792	5,416
Energy from biomass products and waste (% of total)	3.3	3.4
Electric power consumption per capita (kWh)	5,372	9,675
Electricity generated using fossil fuel (% of total)	87.2	62.0
Electricity generated by hydropower (% of total)	9.7	11.4
Emissions and pollution		
CO_2 emissions per unit of GDP (kg/2005 PPP $)	0.3	0.4
CO_2 emissions per capita (metric tons)	8.6	12.6
CO_2 emissions growth (%, 1990–2005)	32.0	19.1
Particulate matter (urban-pop.-weighted avg., µg/cu. m)	36	26
Transport sector fuel consumption per capita (liters)	684	1,159
Water and sanitation		
Internal freshwater resources per capita (cu. m)	5,182	9,313
Freshwater withdrawal		
Total (% of internal resources)	13.4	10.4
Agriculture (% of total freshwater withdrawal)	80	43
Access to improved water source (% of total population)	100	100
Rural (% of rural population)	99	98
Urban (% of urban population)	100	100
Access to improved sanitation (% of total population)	98	100
Rural (% of rural population)	97	99
Urban (% of urban population)	99	100
Environment and health		
Acute resp. infection prevalence (% of children under five)	..	
Diarrhea prevalence (% of children under five)	..	
Under-five mortality rate (per 1,000 live births)	4	7
National accounting aggregates		
Gross savings (% of GNI)	9.5	20.6
Consumption of fixed capital (% of GNI)	14.6	14.5
Education expenditure (% of GNI)	2.8	4.6
Energy depletion (% of GNI)	0.2	1.5
Mineral depletion (% of GNI)	0.2	0.2
Net forest depletion (% of GNI)	0.0	0.0
CO_2 damage (% of GNI)	0.3	0.3
Particulate emission damage (% of GNI)	0.7	0.3
Adjusted net savings (% of GNI)	-3.7	8.5

Greenland

Population (thousands) **57** Land area (1,000 sq. km) **410** GDP ($ billions) ..

	Country data	High-income group
GNI per capita, *World Bank Atlas* method ($)	..	37,572
Urban population (% of total)	83	78
Urban population growth (average annual %, 1990–2007)	0.4	1.0
Population growth (average annual %, 1990–2007)	0.1	0.7
Agriculture		
Agricultural land (% of land area)	1	38
Agricultural productivity (value added per worker, 2000 $)	..	27,680
Food production index (1999–2001 = 100)	100	102
Population density, rural (people/sq. km of arable land)	..	323
Forests and biodiversity		
Forest area (% of land area)	0.0	28.8
Deforestation (average annual %, 1990–2005)	..	-0.1
Nationally protected area (% of land area)	0.0	11.8
Animal species, total known	166	
Animal species, threatened	12	
Higher plant species, total known	529	
Higher plant species, threatened	1	
GEF benefits index for biodiversity (0–100, median is 1.5)	1.1	
Energy		
GDP per unit of energy use (2005 PPP $/kg oil equivalent)	..	6.3
Energy use per capita (kg oil equivalent)	..	5,416
Energy from biomass products and waste (% of total)	..	3.4
Electric power consumption per capita (kWh)	..	9,675
Electricity generated using fossil fuel (% of total)	..	62.0
Electricity generated by hydropower (% of total)	..	11.4
Emissions and pollution		
CO_2 emissions per unit of GDP (kg/2005 PPP $)	..	0.4
CO_2 emissions per capita (metric tons)	9.8	12.6
CO_2 emissions growth (%, 1990–2005)	0.7	19.1
Particulate matter (urban-pop.-weighted avg., µg/cu. m)	..	26
Transport sector fuel consumption per capita (liters)	..	1,159
Water and sanitation		
Internal freshwater resources per capita (cu. m)	10,624,264	9,313
Freshwater withdrawal		
Total (% of internal resources)	..	10.4
Agriculture (% of total freshwater withdrawal)	..	43
Access to improved water source (% of total population)	..	100
Rural (% of rural population)	..	98
Urban (% of urban population)	..	100
Access to improved sanitation (% of total population)	..	100
Rural (% of rural population)	..	99
Urban (% of urban population)	..	100
Environment and health		
Acute resp. infection prevalence (% of children under five)	..	
Diarrhea prevalence (% of children under five)	..	
Under-five mortality rate (per 1,000 live births)	..	7
National accounting aggregates		
Gross savings (% of GNI)	..	20.6
Consumption of fixed capital (% of GNI)	..	14.5
Education expenditure (% of GNI)	..	4.6
Energy depletion (% of GNI)	..	1.5
Mineral depletion (% of GNI)	..	0.2
Net forest depletion (% of GNI)	..	0.0
CO_2 damage (% of GNI)	..	0.3
Particulate emission damage (% of GNI)	..	0.3
Adjusted net savings (% of GNI)	..	8.5

Grenada

	Country data	Latin America & Caribbean group	Upper middle-income group
Population (thousands) **106**	Land area (sq. km) **340**	GDP ($ millions) **605**	

	Country data	Latin America & Caribbean group	Upper middle-income group
GNI per capita, *World Bank Atlas* method ($)	3,920	5,801	7,107
Urban population (% of total)	31	78	75
Urban population growth (average annual %, 1990–2007)	0.3	2.1	1.4
Population growth (average annual %, 1990–2007)	0.6	1.5	0.9
Agriculture			
Agricultural land (% of land area)	38	36	31
Agricultural productivity (value added per worker, 2000 $)	1,522	3,158	2,947
Food production index (1999–2001 = 100)	103	117	113
Population density, rural (people/sq. km of arable land)	3,652	232	110
Forests and biodiversity			
Forest area (% of land area)	12.1	45.4	39.3
Deforestation (average annual %, 1990–2005)	0.0	0.5	0.2
Nationally protected area (% of land area)	1.8	16.7	10.3
Animal species, total known	181		
Animal species, threatened	34		
Higher plant species, total known	1,068		
Higher plant species, threatened	3		
GEF benefits index for biodiversity (0–100, median is 1.5)	0.6		
Energy			
GDP per unit of energy use (2005 PPP $/kg oil equivalent)	..	7.3	4.8
Energy use per capita (kg oil equivalent)	..	1,240	2,300
Energy from biomass products and waste (% of total)	..	15.9	7.0
Electric power consumption per capita (kWh)	..	1,808	3,242
Electricity generated using fossil fuel (% of total)	..	37.0	62.8
Electricity generated by hydropower (% of total)	..	57.3	27.6
Emissions and pollution			
CO_2 emissions per unit of GDP (kg/2005 PPP $)	0.3	0.3	0.5
CO_2 emissions per capita (metric tons)	2.2	2.5	5.5
CO_2 emissions growth (%, 1990–2005)	93.9	33.4	-8.3
Particulate matter (urban-pop.-weighted avg., µg/cu. m)	20	35	30
Transport sector fuel consumption per capita (liters)	..	295	332
Water and sanitation			
Internal freshwater resources per capita (cu. m)	..	23,965	16,993
Freshwater withdrawal			
Total (% of internal resources)	..	2.0	13.8
Agriculture (% of total freshwater withdrawal)	..	71	57
Access to improved water source (% of total population)	..	91	95
Rural (% of rural population)	..	73	83
Urban (% of urban population)	97	97	98
Access to improved sanitation (% of total population)	97	78	83
Rural (% of rural population)	97	51	64
Urban (% of urban population)	96	86	89
Environment and health			
Acute resp. infection prevalence (% of children under five)	..		
Diarrhea prevalence (% of children under five)	..		
Under-five mortality rate (per 1,000 live births)	19	26	24
National accounting aggregates			
Gross savings (% of GNI)	..	22.9	23.2
Consumption of fixed capital (% of GNI)	16.0	12.6	12.8
Education expenditure (% of GNI)	5.1	4.5	4.4
Energy depletion (% of GNI)	0.0	5.4	7.6
Mineral depletion (% of GNI)	0.0	1.9	1.3
Net forest depletion (% of GNI)	0.0	0.0	0.0
CO_2 damage (% of GNI)	0.4	0.3	0.6
Particulate emission damage (% of GNI)	..	0.4	0.4
Adjusted net savings (% of GNI)	..	6.7	4.9

Guam

Population (thousands) **173** Land area (sq. km) **540** GDP ($ millions) ..

	Country data	High-income group
GNI per capita, *World Bank Atlas* method ($)	..	37,572
Urban population (% of total)	93	78
Urban population growth (average annual %, 1990–2007)	1.7	1.0
Population growth (average annual %, 1990–2007)	1.5	0.7

Agriculture
Agricultural land (% of land area)	37	38
Agricultural productivity (value added per worker, 2000 $)	..	27,680
Food production index (1999–2001 = 100)	107	102
Population density, rural (people/sq. km of arable land)	582	323

Forests and biodiversity
Forest area (% of land area)	48.0	28.8
Deforestation (average annual %, 1990–2005)	0.0	–0.1
Nationally protected area (% of land area)	2.2	11.8
Animal species, total known	71	
Animal species, threatened	31	
Higher plant species, total known	330	
Higher plant species, threatened	4	
GEF benefits index for biodiversity (0–100, median is 1.5)	0.2	

Energy
GDP per unit of energy use (2005 PPP $/kg oil equivalent)	..	6.3
Energy use per capita (kg oil equivalent)	..	5,416
Energy from biomass products and waste (% of total)	..	3.4
Electric power consumption per capita (kWh)	..	9,675
Electricity generated using fossil fuel (% of total)	..	62.0
Electricity generated by hydropower (% of total)	..	11.4

Emissions and pollution
CO_2 emissions per unit of GDP (kg/2005 PPP $)	..	0.4
CO_2 emissions per capita (metric tons)	..	12.6
CO_2 emissions growth (%, 1990–2005)	..	19.1
Particulate matter (urban-pop.-weighted avg., µg/cu. m)	..	26
Transport sector fuel consumption per capita (liters)	..	1,159

Water and sanitation
Internal freshwater resources per capita (cu. m)	..	9,313
Freshwater withdrawal		
Total (% of internal resources)	..	10.4
Agriculture (% of total freshwater withdrawal)	..	43
Access to improved water source (% of total population)	100	100
Rural (% of rural population)	100	98
Urban (% of urban population)	100	100
Access to improved sanitation (% of total population)	99	100
Rural (% of rural population)	98	99
Urban (% of urban population)	99	100

Environment and health
Acute resp. infection prevalence (% of children under five)	..	
Diarrhea prevalence (% of children under five)	..	
Under-five mortality rate (per 1,000 live births)	..	7

National accounting aggregates
Gross savings (% of GNI)	..	20.6
Consumption of fixed capital (% of GNI)	..	14.5
Education expenditure (% of GNI)	..	4.6
Energy depletion (% of GNI)	..	1.5
Mineral depletion (% of GNI)	..	0.2
Net forest depletion (% of GNI)	..	0.0
CO_2 damage (% of GNI)	..	0.3
Particulate emission damage (% of GNI)	..	0.3
Adjusted net savings (% of GNI)	..	8.5

Guatemala

| | Population (millions) | **13** | Land area (1,000 sq. km) | **108** | GDP ($ billions) | **33.9** |

	Country data	Latin America & Caribbean group	Lower middle-income group
GNI per capita, *World Bank Atlas* method ($)	2,450	5,801	1,905
Urban population (% of total)	48	78	42
Urban population growth (average annual %, 1990–2007)	3.3	2.1	2.9
Population growth (average annual %, 1990–2007)	2.4	1.5	1.3
Agriculture			
Agricultural land (% of land area)	43	36	47
Agricultural productivity (value added per worker, 2000 $)	2,652	3,158	532
Food production index (1999–2001 = 100)	108	117	116
Population density, rural (people/sq. km of arable land)	466	232	511
Forests and biodiversity			
Forest area (% of land area)	36.3	45.4	25.0
Deforestation (average annual %, 1990–2005)	1.2	0.5	0.1
Nationally protected area (% of land area)	32.6	16.7	11.0
Animal species, total known	877		
Animal species, threatened	145		
Higher plant species, total known	8,681		
Higher plant species, threatened	83		
GEF benefits index for biodiversity (0–100, median is 1.5)	8.0		
Energy			
GDP per unit of energy use (2005 PPP $/kg oil equivalent)	6.6	7.3	3.9
Energy use per capita (kg oil equivalent)	628	1,240	1,019
Energy from biomass products and waste (% of total)	51.5	15.9	15.2
Electric power consumption per capita (kWh)	529	1,808	1,269
Electricity generated using fossil fuel (% of total)	39.0	37.0	79.0
Electricity generated by hydropower (% of total)	48.3	57.3	16.3
Emissions and pollution			
CO_2 emissions per unit of GDP (kg/2005 PPP $)	0.2	0.3	0.8
CO_2 emissions per capita (metric tons)	0.9	2.5	2.8
CO_2 emissions growth (%, 1990–2005)	125.0	33.4	93.5
Particulate matter (urban-pop.-weighted avg., µg/cu. m)	62	35	67
Transport sector fuel consumption per capita (liters)	142	295	99
Water and sanitation			
Internal freshwater resources per capita (cu. m)	8,181	23,965	4,117
Freshwater withdrawal			
Total (% of internal resources)	1.8	2.0	8.7
Agriculture (% of total freshwater withdrawal)	80	71	80
Access to improved water source (% of total population)	96	91	88
Rural (% of rural population)	94	73	82
Urban (% of urban population)	99	97	96
Access to improved sanitation (% of total population)	84	78	55
Rural (% of rural population)	79	51	43
Urban (% of urban population)	90	86	71
Environment and health			
Acute resp. infection prevalence (% of children under five)	18.0		
Diarrhea prevalence (% of children under five)	13.3		
Under-five mortality rate (per 1,000 live births)	39	26	50
National accounting aggregates			
Gross savings (% of GNI)	16.8	22.9	41.7
Consumption of fixed capital (% of GNI)	10.9	12.6	10.7
Education expenditure (% of GNI)	2.8	4.5	2.6
Energy depletion (% of GNI)	0.6	5.4	6.6
Mineral depletion (% of GNI)	0.0	1.9	1.2
Net forest depletion (% of GNI)	0.8	0.0	0.2
CO_2 damage (% of GNI)	0.3	0.3	1.2
Particulate emission damage (% of GNI)	0.5	0.4	1.1
Adjusted net savings (% of GNI)	6.5	6.7	23.5

Guinea

	Country data	Sub-Saharan Africa group	Low-income group
Population (millions) **9.4** Land area (1,000 sq. km) **245.7** GDP ($ billions) **4.6**			
GNI per capita, *World Bank Atlas* method ($)	400	951	574
Urban population (% of total)	34	36	32
Urban population growth (average annual %, 1990–2007)	3.7	4.0	3.7
Population growth (average annual %, 1990–2007)	2.6	2.6	2.4
Agriculture			
Agricultural land (% of land area)	51	44	39
Agricultural productivity (value added per worker, 2000 $)	193	287	330
Food production index (1999–2001 = 100)	115	109	112
Population density, rural (people/sq. km of arable land)	503	351	603
Forests and biodiversity			
Forest area (% of land area)	27.4	26.5	24.7
Deforestation (average annual %, 1990–2005)	0.6	0.6	0.7
Nationally protected area (% of land area)	6.1	11.3	10.8
Animal species, total known	855		
Animal species, threatened	64		
Higher plant species, total known	3,000		
Higher plant species, threatened	22		
GEF benefits index for biodiversity (0–100, median is 1.5)	2.3		
Energy			
GDP per unit of energy use (2005 PPP $/kg oil equivalent)	..	3.0	3.2
Energy use per capita (kg oil equivalent)	..	670	478
Energy from biomass products and waste (% of total)	..	56.3	53.8
Electric power consumption per capita (kWh)	..	531	309
Electricity generated using fossil fuel (% of total)	..	65.6	48.4
Electricity generated by hydropower (% of total)	..	18.0	38.8
Emissions and pollution			
CO_2 emissions per unit of GDP (kg/2005 PPP $)	0.1	0.5	0.4
CO_2 emissions per capita (metric tons)	0.2	0.8	0.6
CO_2 emissions growth (%, 1990–2005)	34.1	40.1	39.3
Particulate matter (urban-pop.-weighted avg., μg/cu. m)	70	53	69
Transport sector fuel consumption per capita (liters)	..	64	41
Water and sanitation			
Internal freshwater resources per capita (cu. m)	24,093	4,824	4,619
Freshwater withdrawal			
Total (% of internal resources)	0.7	3.2	9.4
Agriculture (% of total freshwater withdrawal)	90	87	90
Access to improved water source (% of total population)	70	58	68
Rural (% of rural population)	59	46	60
Urban (% of urban population)	91	81	84
Access to improved sanitation (% of total population)	19	31	39
Rural (% of rural population)	12	24	33
Urban (% of urban population)	33	42	54
Environment and health			
Acute resp. infection prevalence (% of children under five)	15.0		
Diarrhea prevalence (% of children under five)	21.2		
Under-five mortality rate (per 1,000 live births)	150	146	126
National accounting aggregates			
Gross savings (% of GNI)	8.8	17.4	25.4
Consumption of fixed capital (% of GNI)	8.6	11.1	9.3
Education expenditure (% of GNI)	2.0	3.6	2.6
Energy depletion (% of GNI)	0.0	11.7	9.8
Mineral depletion (% of GNI)	4.9	1.5	0.9
Net forest depletion (% of GNI)	1.7	0.5	0.8
CO_2 damage (% of GNI)	0.2	0.7	0.7
Particulate emission damage (% of GNI)	0.3	0.4	0.7
Adjusted net savings (% of GNI)	-4.9	-5.0	5.8

Guinea-Bissau

| Population (millions) | **1.7** | Land area (1,000 sq. km) | **28.1** | GDP ($ millions) | **357** |

	Country data	Sub-Saharan Africa group	Low-income group
GNI per capita, *World Bank Atlas* method ($)	200	951	574
Urban population (% of total)	30	36	32
Urban population growth (average annual %, 1990–2007)	3.3	4.0	3.7
Population growth (average annual %, 1990–2007)	3.0	2.6	2.4
Agriculture			
Agricultural land (% of land area)	58	44	39
Agricultural productivity (value added per worker, 2000 $)	246	287	330
Food production index (1999–2001 = 100)	110	109	112
Population density, rural (people/sq. km of arable land)	375	351	603
Forests and biodiversity			
Forest area (% of land area)	73.7	26.5	24.7
Deforestation (average annual %, 1990–2005)	0.4	0.6	0.7
Nationally protected area (% of land area)	10.2	11.3	10.8
Animal species, total known	560		
Animal species, threatened	33		
Higher plant species, total known	1,000		
Higher plant species, threatened	4		
GEF benefits index for biodiversity (0–100, median is 1.5)	0.6		
Energy			
GDP per unit of energy use (2005 PPP $/kg oil equivalent)	..	3.0	3.2
Energy use per capita (kg oil equivalent)	..	670	478
Energy from biomass products and waste (% of total)	..	56.3	53.8
Electric power consumption per capita (kWh)	..	531	309
Electricity generated using fossil fuel (% of total)	..	65.6	48.4
Electricity generated by hydropower (% of total)	..	18.0	38.8
Emissions and pollution			
CO_2 emissions per unit of GDP (kg/2005 PPP $)	0.4	0.5	0.4
CO_2 emissions per capita (metric tons)	0.2	0.8	0.6
CO_2 emissions growth (%, 1990–2005)	29.8	40.1	39.3
Particulate matter (urban-pop.-weighted avg., µg/cu. m)	72	53	69
Transport sector fuel consumption per capita (liters)	..	64	41
Water and sanitation			
Internal freshwater resources per capita (cu. m)	9,441	4,824	4,619
Freshwater withdrawal			
Total (% of internal resources)	1.1	3.2	9.4
Agriculture (% of total freshwater withdrawal)	82	87	90
Access to improved water source (% of total population)	57	58	68
Rural (% of rural population)	47	46	60
Urban (% of urban population)	82	81	84
Access to improved sanitation (% of total population)	33	31	39
Rural (% of rural population)	26	24	33
Urban (% of urban population)	48	42	54
Environment and health			
Acute resp. infection prevalence (% of children under five)	10.0		
Diarrhea prevalence (% of children under five)	31.5		
Under-five mortality rate (per 1,000 live births)	198	146	126
National accounting aggregates			
Gross savings (% of GNI)	24.0	17.4	25.4
Consumption of fixed capital (% of GNI)	7.5	11.1	9.3
Education expenditure (% of GNI)	2.3	3.6	2.6
Energy depletion (% of GNI)	0.0	11.7	9.8
Mineral depletion (% of GNI)	0.0	1.5	0.9
Net forest depletion (% of GNI)	0.0	0.5	0.8
CO_2 damage (% of GNI)	0.6	0.7	0.7
Particulate emission damage (% of GNI)	0.9	0.4	0.7
Adjusted net savings (% of GNI)	17.3	-5.0	5.8

Guyana

Population (thousands) **739**	Land area (1,000 sq. km)	**197**	GDP ($ billions)	**1.1**

	Country data	Latin America & Caribbean group	Lower middle-income group
GNI per capita, *World Bank Atlas* method ($)	1,250	5,801	1,905
Urban population (% of total)	28	78	42
Urban population growth (average annual %, 1990–2007)	-0.2	2.1	2.9
Population growth (average annual %, 1990–2007)	0.1	1.5	1.3
Agriculture			
Agricultural land (% of land area)	9	36	47
Agricultural productivity (value added per worker, 2000 $)	3,383	3,158	532
Food production index (1999–2001 = 100)	106	117	116
Population density, rural (people/sq. km of arable land)	111	232	511
Forests and biodiversity			
Forest area (% of land area)	76.7	45.4	25.0
Deforestation (average annual %, 1990–2005)	0.0	0.5	0.1
Nationally protected area (% of land area)	2.5	16.7	11.0
Animal species, total known	1,023		
Animal species, threatened	46		
Higher plant species, total known	6,409		
Higher plant species, threatened	22		
GEF benefits index for biodiversity (0–100, median is 1.5)	3.0		
Energy			
GDP per unit of energy use (2005 PPP $/kg oil equivalent)	..	7.3	3.9
Energy use per capita (kg oil equivalent)	..	1,240	1,019
Energy from biomass products and waste (% of total)	..	15.9	15.2
Electric power consumption per capita (kWh)	..	1,808	1,269
Electricity generated using fossil fuel (% of total)	..	37.0	79.0
Electricity generated by hydropower (% of total)	..	57.3	16.3
Emissions and pollution			
CO_2 emissions per unit of GDP (kg/2005 PPP $)	0.8	0.3	0.8
CO_2 emissions per capita (metric tons)	2.0	2.5	2.8
CO_2 emissions growth (%, 1990–2005)	31.7	33.4	93.5
Particulate matter (urban-pop.-weighted avg., µg/cu. m)	30	35	67
Transport sector fuel consumption per capita (liters)	..	295	99
Water and sanitation			
Internal freshwater resources per capita (cu. m)	326,316	23,965	4,117
Freshwater withdrawal			
Total (% of internal resources)	0.7	2.0	8.7
Agriculture (% of total freshwater withdrawal)	98	71	80
Access to improved water source (% of total population)	93	91	88
Rural (% of rural population)	91	73	82
Urban (% of urban population)	98	97	96
Access to improved sanitation (% of total population)	81	78	55
Rural (% of rural population)	80	51	43
Urban (% of urban population)	85	86	71
Environment and health			
Acute resp. infection prevalence (% of children under five)	5.0		
Diarrhea prevalence (% of children under five)	..		
Under-five mortality rate (per 1,000 live births)	60	26	50
National accounting aggregates			
Gross savings (% of GNI)	..	22.9	41.7
Consumption of fixed capital (% of GNI)	10.8	12.6	10.7
Education expenditure (% of GNI)	7.8	4.5	2.6
Energy depletion (% of GNI)	0.0	5.4	6.6
Mineral depletion (% of GNI)	17.1	1.9	1.2
Net forest depletion (% of GNI)	0.0	0.0	0.2
CO_2 damage (% of GNI)	1.1	0.3	1.2
Particulate emission damage (% of GNI)	0.3	0.4	1.1
Adjusted net savings (% of GNI)	..	6.7	23.5

Haiti

	Country data	Latin America & Caribbean group	Low-income group
Population (millions)	9.6	Land area (1,000 sq. km)	27.6	GDP ($ billions)	6.7

	Country data	Latin America & Caribbean group	Low-income group
GNI per capita, *World Bank Atlas* method ($)	520	5,801	574
Urban population (% of total)	45	78	32
Urban population growth (average annual %, 1990–2007)	4.5	2.1	3.7
Population growth (average annual %, 1990–2007)	1.8	1.5	2.4
Agriculture			
Agricultural land (% of land area)	58	36	39
Agricultural productivity (value added per worker, 2000 $)	..	3,158	330
Food production index (1999–2001 = 100)	101	117	112
Population density, rural (people/sq. km of arable land)	683	232	603
Forests and biodiversity			
Forest area (% of land area)	3.8	45.4	24.7
Deforestation (average annual %, 1990–2005)	0.7	0.5	0.7
Nationally protected area (% of land area)	0.3	16.7	10.8
Animal species, total known	312		
Animal species, threatened	101		
Higher plant species, total known	5,242		
Higher plant species, threatened	29		
GEF benefits index for biodiversity (0–100, median is 1.5)	5.2		
Energy			
GDP per unit of energy use (2005 PPP $/kg oil equivalent)	4.0	7.3	3.2
Energy use per capita (kg oil equivalent)	272	1,240	478
Energy from biomass products and waste (% of total)	75.8	15.9	53.8
Electric power consumption per capita (kWh)	37	1,808	309
Electricity generated using fossil fuel (% of total)	52.5	37.0	48.4
Electricity generated by hydropower (% of total)	47.5	57.3	38.8
Emissions and pollution			
CO_2 emissions per unit of GDP (kg/2005 PPP $)	0.2	0.3	0.4
CO_2 emissions per capita (metric tons)	0.2	2.5	0.6
CO_2 emissions growth (%, 1990–2005)	77.9	33.4	39.3
Particulate matter (urban-pop.-weighted avg., µg/cu. m)	37	35	69
Transport sector fuel consumption per capita (liters)	34	295	41
Water and sanitation			
Internal freshwater resources per capita (cu. m)	1,354	23,965	4,619
Freshwater withdrawal			
Total (% of internal resources)	7.6	2.0	9.4
Agriculture (% of total freshwater withdrawal)	94	71	90
Access to improved water source (% of total population)	58	91	68
Rural (% of rural population)	51	73	60
Urban (% of urban population)	70	97	84
Access to improved sanitation (% of total population)	19	78	39
Rural (% of rural population)	12	51	33
Urban (% of urban population)	29	86	54
Environment and health			
Acute resp. infection prevalence (% of children under five)	39.0		
Diarrhea prevalence (% of children under five)	25.7		
Under-five mortality rate (per 1,000 live births)	76	26	126
National accounting aggregates			
Gross savings (% of GNI)	..	22.9	25.4
Consumption of fixed capital (% of GNI)	9.8	12.6	9.3
Education expenditure (% of GNI)	1.5	4.5	2.6
Energy depletion (% of GNI)	0.0	5.4	9.8
Mineral depletion (% of GNI)	0.0	1.9	0.9
Net forest depletion (% of GNI)	0.6	0.0	0.8
CO_2 damage (% of GNI)	0.2	0.3	0.7
Particulate emission damage (% of GNI)	0.4	0.4	0.7
Adjusted net savings (% of GNI)	..	6.7	5.8

Honduras

	Country data	Latin America & Caribbean group	Lower middle-income group
Population (millions) **7.1** Land area (1,000 sq. km) **111.9** GDP ($ billions) **12.2**			

	Country data	Latin America & Caribbean group	Lower middle-income group
GNI per capita, *World Bank Atlas* method ($)	1,590	5,801	1,905
Urban population (% of total)	47	78	42
Urban population growth (average annual %, 1990–2007)	3.2	2.1	2.9
Population growth (average annual %, 1990–2007)	2.2	1.5	1.3
Agriculture			
Agricultural land (% of land area)	26	36	47
Agricultural productivity (value added per worker, 2000 $)	1,489	3,158	532
Food production index (1999–2001 = 100)	165	117	116
Population density, rural (people/sq. km of arable land)	342	232	511
Forests and biodiversity			
Forest area (% of land area)	41.5	45.4	25.0
Deforestation (average annual %, 1990–2005)	3.0	0.5	0.1
Nationally protected area (% of land area)	19.6	16.7	11.0
Animal species, total known	900		
Animal species, threatened	120		
Higher plant species, total known	5,680		
Higher plant species, threatened	110		
GEF benefits index for biodiversity (0–100, median is 1.5)	7.2		
Energy			
GDP per unit of energy use (2005 PPP $/kg oil equivalent)	5.5	7.3	3.9
Energy use per capita (kg oil equivalent)	621	1,240	1,019
Energy from biomass products and waste (% of total)	41.5	15.9	15.2
Electric power consumption per capita (kWh)	642	1,808	1,269
Electricity generated using fossil fuel (% of total)	56.1	37.0	79.0
Electricity generated by hydropower (% of total)	43.2	57.3	16.3
Emissions and pollution			
CO_2 emissions per unit of GDP (kg/2005 PPP $)	0.3	0.3	0.8
CO_2 emissions per capita (metric tons)	1.1	2.5	2.8
CO_2 emissions growth (%, 1990–2005)	186.8	33.4	93.5
Particulate matter (urban-pop.-weighted avg., µg/cu. m)	43	35	67
Transport sector fuel consumption per capita (liters)	121	295	99
Water and sanitation			
Internal freshwater resources per capita (cu. m)	13,504	23,965	4,117
Freshwater withdrawal			
Total (% of internal resources)	0.9	2.0	8.7
Agriculture (% of total freshwater withdrawal)	80	71	80
Access to improved water source (% of total population)	84	91	88
Rural (% of rural population)	74	73	82
Urban (% of urban population)	95	97	96
Access to improved sanitation (% of total population)	66	78	55
Rural (% of rural population)	55	51	43
Urban (% of urban population)	78	86	71
Environment and health			
Acute resp. infection prevalence (% of children under five)	..		
Diarrhea prevalence (% of children under five)	19.3		
Under-five mortality rate (per 1,000 live births)	24	26	50
National accounting aggregates			
Gross savings (% of GNI)	23.8	22.9	41.7
Consumption of fixed capital (% of GNI)	10.8	12.6	10.7
Education expenditure (% of GNI)	3.5	4.5	2.6
Energy depletion (% of GNI)	0.0	5.4	6.6
Mineral depletion (% of GNI)	2.0	1.9	1.2
Net forest depletion (% of GNI)	0.0	0.0	0.2
CO_2 damage (% of GNI)	0.5	0.3	1.2
Particulate emission damage (% of GNI)	0.4	0.4	1.1
Adjusted net savings (% of GNI)	13.6	6.7	23.5

Hong Kong, China

| Population (millions) | **6.9** | Land area (1,000 sq. km) | **1.0** | GDP ($ billions) | **207.2** |

	Country data	High-income group
GNI per capita, *World Bank Atlas* method ($)	31,560	37,572
Urban population (% of total)	100	78
Urban population growth (average annual %, 1990–2007)	1.2	1.0
Population growth (average annual %, 1990–2007)	1.1	0.7
Agriculture		
Agricultural land (% of land area)	..	38
Agricultural productivity (value added per worker, 2000 $)	..	27,680
Food production index (1999–2001 = 100)	..	102
Population density, rural (people/sq. km of arable land)	..	323
Forests and biodiversity		
Forest area (% of land area)	..	28.8
Deforestation (average annual %, 1990–2005)	..	-0.1
Nationally protected area (% of land area)	..	11.8
Animal species, total known	363	
Animal species, threatened	42	
Higher plant species, total known	..	
Higher plant species, threatened	6	
GEF benefits index for biodiversity (0–100, median is 1.5)	..	
Energy		
GDP per unit of energy use (2005 PPP $/kg oil equivalent)	14.3	6.3
Energy use per capita (kg oil equivalent)	2,653	5,416
Energy from biomass products and waste (% of total)	0.3	3.4
Electric power consumption per capita (kWh)	5,883	9,675
Electricity generated using fossil fuel (% of total)	100.0	62.0
Electricity generated by hydropower (% of total)	0.0	11.4
Emissions and pollution		
CO_2 emissions per unit of GDP (kg/2005 PPP $)	0.2	0.4
CO_2 emissions per capita (metric tons)	5.7	12.6
CO_2 emissions growth (%, 1990–2005)	47.3	19.1
Particulate matter (urban-pop.-weighted avg., µg/cu. m)	..	26
Transport sector fuel consumption per capita (liters)	240	1,159
Water and sanitation		
Internal freshwater resources per capita (cu. m)	..	9,313
Freshwater withdrawal		
Total (% of internal resources)	..	10.4
Agriculture (% of total freshwater withdrawal)	..	43
Access to improved water source (% of total population)	..	100
Rural (% of rural population)	..	98
Urban (% of urban population)	..	100
Access to improved sanitation (% of total population)	..	100
Rural (% of rural population)	..	99
Urban (% of urban population)	..	100
Environment and health		
Acute resp. infection prevalence (% of children under five)	..	
Diarrhea prevalence (% of children under five)	..	
Under-five mortality rate (per 1,000 live births)	..	7
National accounting aggregates		
Gross savings (% of GNI)	33.8	20.6
Consumption of fixed capital (% of GNI)	13.8	14.5
Education expenditure (% of GNI)	3.0	4.6
Energy depletion (% of GNI)	0.0	1.5
Mineral depletion (% of GNI)	0.0	0.2
Net forest depletion (% of GNI)	0.0	0.0
CO_2 damage (% of GNI)	0.2	0.3
Particulate emission damage (% of GNI)	..	0.3
Adjusted net savings (% of GNI)	22.9	8.5

Hungary

| Population (millions) | **10** | Land area (1,000 sq. km) | **90** | GDP ($ billions) | **138.4** |

	Country data	High-income group
GNI per capita, *World Bank Atlas* method ($)	11,680	37,572
Urban population (% of total)	67	78
Urban population growth (average annual %, 1990–2007)	–0.1	1.0
Population growth (average annual %, 1990–2007)	–0.2	0.7
Agriculture		
Agricultural land (% of land area)	65	38
Agricultural productivity (value added per worker, 2000 $)	8,102	27,680
Food production index (1999–2001 = 100)	111	102
Population density, rural (people/sq. km of arable land)	74	323
Forests and biodiversity		
Forest area (% of land area)	22.1	28.8
Deforestation (average annual %, 1990–2005)	–0.6	–0.1
Nationally protected area (% of land area)	5.8	11.8
Animal species, total known	455	
Animal species, threatened	47	
Higher plant species, total known	2,214	
Higher plant species, threatened	1	
GEF benefits index for biodiversity (0–100, median is 1.5)	0.2	
Energy		
GDP per unit of energy use (2005 PPP $/kg oil equivalent)	6.4	6.3
Energy use per capita (kg oil equivalent)	2,740	5,416
Energy from biomass products and waste (% of total)	4.3	3.4
Electric power consumption per capita (kWh)	3,882	9,675
Electricity generated using fossil fuel (% of total)	57.9	62.0
Electricity generated by hydropower (% of total)	0.5	11.4
Emissions and pollution		
CO_2 emissions per unit of GDP (kg/2005 PPP $)	0.3	0.4
CO_2 emissions per capita (metric tons)	5.6	12.6
CO_2 emissions growth (%, 1990–2005)	–6.2	19.1
Particulate matter (urban-pop.-weighted avg., µg/cu. m)	19	26
Transport sector fuel consumption per capita (liters)	484	1,159
Water and sanitation		
Internal freshwater resources per capita (cu. m)	597	9,313
Freshwater withdrawal		
Total (% of internal resources)	127.3	10.4
Agriculture (% of total freshwater withdrawal)	32	43
Access to improved water source (% of total population)	100	100
Rural (% of rural population)	100	98
Urban (% of urban population)	100	100
Access to improved sanitation (% of total population)	100	100
Rural (% of rural population)	100	99
Urban (% of urban population)	100	100
Environment and health		
Acute resp. infection prevalence (% of children under five)	..	
Diarrhea prevalence (% of children under five)	..	
Under-five mortality rate (per 1,000 live births)	7	7
National accounting aggregates		
Gross savings (% of GNI)	17.7	20.6
Consumption of fixed capital (% of GNI)	14.2	14.5
Education expenditure (% of GNI)	5.4	4.6
Energy depletion (% of GNI)	0.6	1.5
Mineral depletion (% of GNI)	0.0	0.2
Net forest depletion (% of GNI)	0.0	0.0
CO_2 damage (% of GNI)	0.4	0.3
Particulate emission damage (% of GNI)	0.1	0.3
Adjusted net savings (% of GNI)	7.9	8.5

Iceland

| | Population (thousands) **311** | Land area (1,000 sq. km) | **100** | GDP ($ billions) | **20.0** |

	Country data	High-income group
GNI per capita, *World Bank Atlas* method ($)	57,750	37,572
Urban population (% of total)	92	78
Urban population growth (average annual %, 1990–2007)	1.3	1.0
Population growth (average annual %, 1990–2007)	1.2	0.7
Agriculture		
Agricultural land (% of land area)	23	38
Agricultural productivity (value added per worker, 2000 $)	53,483	27,680
Food production index (1999–2001 = 100)	105	102
Population density, rural (people/sq. km of arable land)	331	323
Forests and biodiversity		
Forest area (% of land area)	0.5	28.8
Deforestation (average annual %, 1990–2005)	-4.1	-0.1
Nationally protected area (% of land area)	3.9	11.8
Animal species, total known	338	
Animal species, threatened	17	
Higher plant species, total known	377	
Higher plant species, threatened	0	
GEF benefits index for biodiversity (0–100, median is 1.5)	0.7	
Energy		
GDP per unit of energy use (2005 PPP $/kg oil equivalent)	2.5	6.3
Energy use per capita (kg oil equivalent)	14,237	5,416
Energy from biomass products and waste (% of total)	0.0	3.4
Electric power consumption per capita (kWh)	31,328	9,675
Electricity generated using fossil fuel (% of total)	0.0	62.0
Electricity generated by hydropower (% of total)	73.4	11.4
Emissions and pollution		
CO_2 emissions per unit of GDP (kg/2005 PPP $)	0.2	0.4
CO_2 emissions per capita (metric tons)	7.4	12.6
CO_2 emissions growth (%, 1990–2005)	8.2	19.1
Particulate matter (urban-pop.-weighted avg., µg/cu. m)	18	26
Transport sector fuel consumption per capita (liters)	1,069	1,159
Water and sanitation		
Internal freshwater resources per capita (cu. m)	546,629	9,313
Freshwater withdrawal		
Total (% of internal resources)	0.1	10.4
Agriculture (% of total freshwater withdrawal)	0	43
Access to improved water source (% of total population)	100	100
Rural (% of rural population)	100	98
Urban (% of urban population)	100	100
Access to improved sanitation (% of total population)	100	100
Rural (% of rural population)	100	99
Urban (% of urban population)	100	100
Environment and health		
Acute resp. infection prevalence (% of children under five)	..	
Diarrhea prevalence (% of children under five)	..	
Under-five mortality rate (per 1,000 live births)	3	7
National accounting aggregates		
Gross savings (% of GNI)	12.7	20.6
Consumption of fixed capital (% of GNI)	16.1	14.5
Education expenditure (% of GNI)	7.2	4.6
Energy depletion (% of GNI)	0.0	1.5
Mineral depletion (% of GNI)	0.0	0.2
Net forest depletion (% of GNI)	0.0	0.0
CO_2 damage (% of GNI)	0.1	0.3
Particulate emission damage (% of GNI)	0.1	0.3
Adjusted net savings (% of GNI)	3.6	8.5

India

| Population (millions) **1,125** | Land area (1,000 sq. km) | **2,973** | GDP ($ billions) **1,176.9** |

	Country data	South Asia group	Lower middle-income group
GNI per capita, *World Bank Atlas* method ($)	950	880	1,905
Urban population (% of total)	29	29	42
Urban population growth (average annual %, 1990–2007)	2.5	2.7	2.9
Population growth (average annual %, 1990–2007)	1.7	1.8	1.3
Agriculture			
Agricultural land (% of land area)	61	55	47
Agricultural productivity (value added per worker, 2000 $)	402	417	532
Food production index (1999–2001 = 100)	106	107	116
Population density, rural (people/sq. km of arable land)	489	617	511
Forests and biodiversity			
Forest area (% of land area)	22.8	16.8	25.0
Deforestation (average annual %, 1990–2005)	-0.4	-0.1	0.1
Nationally protected area (% of land area)	5.1	5.6	11.0
Animal species, total known	1,602		
Animal species, threatened	413		
Higher plant species, total known	18,664		
Higher plant species, threatened	246		
GEF benefits index for biodiversity (0–100, median is 1.5)	39.9		
Energy			
GDP per unit of energy use (2005 PPP $/kg oil equivalent)	4.7	4.8	3.9
Energy use per capita (kg oil equivalent)	510	468	1,019
Energy from biomass products and waste (% of total)	28.3	30.4	15.2
Electric power consumption per capita (kWh)	503	453	1,269
Electricity generated using fossil fuel (% of total)	80.9	78.3	79.0
Electricity generated by hydropower (% of total)	15.3	17.4	16.3
Emissions and pollution			
CO_2 emissions per unit of GDP (kg/2005 PPP $)	0.6	0.5	0.8
CO_2 emissions per capita (metric tons)	1.3	1.1	2.8
CO_2 emissions growth (%, 1990–2005)	106.3	106.7	93.5
Particulate matter (urban-pop.-weighted avg., µg/cu. m)	65	78	67
Transport sector fuel consumption per capita (liters)	33	33	99
Water and sanitation			
Internal freshwater resources per capita (cu. m)	1,121	1,196	4,117
Freshwater withdrawal			
Total (% of internal resources)	51.2	51.7	8.7
Agriculture (% of total freshwater withdrawal)	86	89	80
Access to improved water source (% of total population)	89	87	88
Rural (% of rural population)	86	84	82
Urban (% of urban population)	96	94	96
Access to improved sanitation (% of total population)	28	33	55
Rural (% of rural population)	18	23	43
Urban (% of urban population)	52	57	71
Environment and health			
Acute resp. infection prevalence (% of children under five)	19.0		
Diarrhea prevalence (% of children under five)	19.2		
Under-five mortality rate (per 1,000 live births)	72	78	50
National accounting aggregates			
Gross savings (% of GNI)	38.8	36.2	41.7
Consumption of fixed capital (% of GNI)	9.6	9.5	10.7
Education expenditure (% of GNI)	3.2	3.0	2.6
Energy depletion (% of GNI)	2.7	2.7	6.6
Mineral depletion (% of GNI)	0.7	0.6	1.2
Net forest depletion (% of GNI)	0.9	0.9	0.2
CO_2 damage (% of GNI)	1.1	1.0	1.2
Particulate emission damage (% of GNI)	0.7	0.8	1.1
Adjusted net savings (% of GNI)	26.4	23.9	23.5

Indonesia

| | Population (millions) | 226 | Land area (1,000 sq. km) | **1,812** | GDP ($ billions) | **432.8** |

	Country data	East Asia & Pacific group	Lower middle-income group
GNI per capita, *World Bank Atlas* method ($)	1,650	2,182	1,905
Urban population (% of total)	50	43	42
Urban population growth (average annual %, 1990–2007)	4.3	3.5	2.9
Population growth (average annual %, 1990–2007)	1.4	1.1	1.3
Agriculture			
Agricultural land (% of land area)	26	51	47
Agricultural productivity (value added per worker, 2000 $)	596	458	532
Food production index (1999–2001 = 100)	123	120	116
Population density, rural (people/sq. km of arable land)	498	547	511
Forests and biodiversity			
Forest area (% of land area)	48.8	28.4	25.0
Deforestation (average annual %, 1990–2005)	1.8	–0.1	0.1
Nationally protected area (% of land area)	11.2	14.0	11.0
Animal species, total known	2,271		
Animal species, threatened	701		
Higher plant species, total known	29,375		
Higher plant species, threatened	386		
GEF benefits index for biodiversity (0–100, median is 1.5)	81.0		
Energy			
GDP per unit of energy use (2005 PPP $/kg oil equivalent)	4.2	3.4	3.9
Energy use per capita (kg oil equivalent)	803	1,258	1,019
Energy from biomass products and waste (% of total)	29.2	14.7	15.2
Electric power consumption per capita (kWh)	530	1,669	1,269
Electricity generated using fossil fuel (% of total)	87.8	82.0	79.0
Electricity generated by hydropower (% of total)	7.2	15.0	16.3
Emissions and pollution			
CO_2 emissions per unit of GDP (kg/2005 PPP $)	0.6	0.9	0.8
CO_2 emissions per capita (metric tons)	1.9	3.6	2.8
CO_2 emissions growth (%, 1990–2005)	181.0	123.4	93.5
Particulate matter (urban-pop.-weighted avg., µg/cu. m)	83	69	67
Transport sector fuel consumption per capita (liters)	118	106	99
Water and sanitation			
Internal freshwater resources per capita (cu. m)	12,578	4,948	4,117
Freshwater withdrawal			
Total (% of internal resources)	2.9	10.2	8.7
Agriculture (% of total freshwater withdrawal)	91	74	80
Access to improved water source (% of total population)	80	87	88
Rural (% of rural population)	71	81	82
Urban (% of urban population)	89	96	96
Access to improved sanitation (% of total population)	52	66	55
Rural (% of rural population)	37	59	43
Urban (% of urban population)	67	75	71
Environment and health			
Acute resp. infection prevalence (% of children under five)	8.0		
Diarrhea prevalence (% of children under five)	10.4		
Under-five mortality rate (per 1,000 live births)	31	27	50
National accounting aggregates			
Gross savings (% of GNI)	27.2	48.0	41.7
Consumption of fixed capital (% of GNI)	10.8	10.7	10.7
Education expenditure (% of GNI)	1.1	2.1	2.6
Energy depletion (% of GNI)	6.9	4.9	6.6
Mineral depletion (% of GNI)	2.0	1.3	1.2
Net forest depletion (% of GNI)	0.0	0.0	0.2
CO_2 damage (% of GNI)	0.8	1.3	1.2
Particulate emission damage (% of GNI)	1.1	1.3	1.1
Adjusted net savings (% of GNI)	6.7	30.6	23.5

Iran, Islamic Rep.

Population (millions)	**71**	Land area (1,000 sq. km)	**1,629** GDP ($ billions) **286.1**

	Country data	Middle East & N. Africa group	Lower middle- income group
GNI per capita, *World Bank Atlas* method ($)	3,540	2,820	1,905
Urban population (% of total)	68	57	42
Urban population growth (average annual %, 1990–2007)	2.7	2.6	2.9
Population growth (average annual %, 1990–2007)	1.6	2.0	1.3
Agriculture			
Agricultural land (% of land area)	29	22	47
Agricultural productivity (value added per worker, 2000 $)	2,687	2,313	532
Food production index (1999–2001 = 100)	115	116	116
Population density, rural (people/sq. km of arable land)	138	665	511
Forests and biodiversity			
Forest area (% of land area)	6.8	2.4	25.0
Deforestation (average annual %, 1990–2005)	0.0	-0.4	0.1
Nationally protected area (% of land area)	6.4	3.6	11.0
Animal species, total known	656		
Animal species, threatened	89		
Higher plant species, total known	8,000		
Higher plant species, threatened	1		
GEF benefits index for biodiversity (0–100, median is 1.5)	7.3		
Energy			
GDP per unit of energy use (2005 PPP $/kg oil equivalent)	4.0	5.0	3.9
Energy use per capita (kg oil equivalent)	2,438	1,254	1,019
Energy from biomass products and waste (% of total)	0.5	1.2	15.2
Electric power consumption per capita (kWh)	2,290	1,418	1,269
Electricity generated using fossil fuel (% of total)	90.9	91.1	79.0
Electricity generated by hydropower (% of total)	9.1	7.4	16.3
Emissions and pollution			
CO_2 emissions per unit of GDP (kg/2005 PPP $)	0.7	0.6	0.8
CO_2 emissions per capita (metric tons)	6.5	3.7	2.8
CO_2 emissions growth (%, 1990–2005)	106.9	96.8	93.5
Particulate matter (urban-pop.-weighted avg., μg/cu. m)	51	72	67
Transport sector fuel consumption per capita (liters)	569	277	99
Water and sanitation			
Internal freshwater resources per capita (cu. m)	1,809	728	4,117
Freshwater withdrawal			
Total (% of internal resources)	72.6	122.3	8.7
Agriculture (% of total freshwater withdrawal)	92	86	80
Access to improved water source (% of total population)	..	89	88
Rural (% of rural population)	..	81	82
Urban (% of urban population)	99	95	96
Access to improved sanitation (% of total population)	..	77	55
Rural (% of rural population)	..	62	43
Urban (% of urban population)	..	88	71
Environment and health			
Acute resp. infection prevalence (% of children under five)	24.0		
Diarrhea prevalence (% of children under five)	11.3		
Under-five mortality rate (per 1,000 live births)	33	38	50
National accounting aggregates			
Gross savings (% of GNI)	43.4	33.3	41.7
Consumption of fixed capital (% of GNI)	11.6	11.3	10.7
Education expenditure (% of GNI)	4.9	4.7	2.6
Energy depletion (% of GNI)	26.8	21.3	6.6
Mineral depletion (% of GNI)	0.6	0.4	1.2
Net forest depletion (% of GNI)	0.0	0.0	0.2
CO_2 damage (% of GNI)	1.3	1.0	1.2
Particulate emission damage (% of GNI)	0.7	0.6	1.1
Adjusted net savings (% of GNI)	7.3	3.4	23.5

Iraq

Population (millions)	..	Land area (1,000 sq. km)	**437**	GDP ($ billions)	**12.6**

	Country data	Middle East & N. Africa group	Lower middle-income group
GNI per capita, *World Bank Atlas* method ($)	..	2,820	1,905
Urban population (% of total)	..	57	42
Urban population growth (average annual %, 1990–2007)	..	2.6	2.9
Population growth (average annual %, 1990–2007)	..	2.0	1.3
Agriculture			
Agricultural land (% of land area)	23	22	47
Agricultural productivity (value added per worker, 2000 $)	1,756	2,313	532
Food production index (1999–2001 = 100)	123	116	116
Population density, rural (people/sq. km of arable land)	..	665	511
Forests and biodiversity			
Forest area (% of land area)	1.9	2.4	25.0
Deforestation (average annual %, 1990–2005)	-0.1	-0.4	0.1
Nationally protected area (% of land area)	..	3.6	11.0
Animal species, total known	498		
Animal species, threatened	55		
Higher plant species, total known	..		
Higher plant species, threatened	0		
GEF benefits index for biodiversity (0–100, median is 1.5)	1.6		
Energy			
GDP per unit of energy use (2005 PPP $/kg oil equivalent)	..	5.0	3.9
Energy use per capita (kg oil equivalent)	..	1,254	1,019
Energy from biomass products and waste (% of total)	0.1	1.2	15.2
Electric power consumption per capita (kWh)	1,091	1,418	1,269
Electricity generated using fossil fuel (% of total)	98.5	91.1	79.0
Electricity generated by hydropower (% of total)	1.5	7.4	16.3
Emissions and pollution			
CO_2 emissions per unit of GDP (kg/2005 PPP $)	..	0.6	0.8
CO_2 emissions per capita (metric tons)	3.0	3.7	2.8
CO_2 emissions growth (%, 1990–2005)	74.2	96.8	93.5
Particulate matter (urban-pop.-weighted avg., μg/cu. m)	115	72	67
Transport sector fuel consumption per capita (liters)	405	277	99
Water and sanitation			
Internal freshwater resources per capita (cu. m)	..	728	4,117
Freshwater withdrawal			
Total (% of internal resources)	187.5	122.3	8.7
Agriculture (% of total freshwater withdrawal)	..	86	80
Access to improved water source (% of total population)	..	89	88
Rural (% of rural population)	..	81	82
Urban (% of urban population)	..	95	96
Access to improved sanitation (% of total population)	..	77	55
Rural (% of rural population)	..	62	43
Urban (% of urban population)	..	88	71
Environment and health			
Acute resp. infection prevalence (% of children under five)	7.0		
Diarrhea prevalence (% of children under five)	..		
Under-five mortality rate (per 1,000 live births)	..	38	50
National accounting aggregates			
Gross savings (% of GNI)	..	33.3	41.7
Consumption of fixed capital (% of GNI)	..	11.3	10.7
Education expenditure (% of GNI)	..	4.7	2.6
Energy depletion (% of GNI)	..	21.3	6.6
Mineral depletion (% of GNI)	..	0.4	1.2
Net forest depletion (% of GNI)	..	0.0	0.2
CO_2 damage (% of GNI)	..	1.0	1.2
Particulate emission damage (% of GNI)	..	0.6	1.1
Adjusted net savings (% of GNI)	..	3.4	23.5

Ireland

Population (millions)	**4.4**	Land area (1,000 sq. km)	**68.9**	GDP ($ billions)	**259.0**

	Country data	High-income group
GNI per capita, *World Bank Atlas* method ($)	47,610	37,572
Urban population (% of total)	61	78
Urban population growth (average annual %, 1990–2007)	1.7	1.0
Population growth (average annual %, 1990–2007)	1.3	0.7
Agriculture		
Agricultural land (% of land area)	61	38
Agricultural productivity (value added per worker, 2000 $)	14,641	27,680
Food production index (1999–2001 = 100)	98	102
Population density, rural (people/sq. km of arable land)	135	323
Forests and biodiversity		
Forest area (% of land area)	9.7	28.8
Deforestation (average annual %, 1990–2005)	-2.8	-0.1
Nationally protected area (% of land area)	1.1	11.8
Animal species, total known	471	
Animal species, threatened	25	
Higher plant species, total known	950	
Higher plant species, threatened	1	
GEF benefits index for biodiversity (0–100, median is 1.5)	0.6	
Energy		
GDP per unit of energy use (2005 PPP $/kg oil equivalent)	10.9	6.3
Energy use per capita (kg oil equivalent)	3,628	5,416
Energy from biomass products and waste (% of total)	1.4	3.4
Electric power consumption per capita (kWh)	6,488	9,675
Electricity generated using fossil fuel (% of total)	83.3	62.0
Electricity generated by hydropower (% of total)	2.6	11.4
Emissions and pollution		
CO_2 emissions per unit of GDP (kg/2005 PPP $)	0.3	0.4
CO_2 emissions per capita (metric tons)	10.2	12.6
CO_2 emissions growth (%, 1990–2005)	38.3	19.1
Particulate matter (urban-pop.-weighted avg., µg/cu. m)	16	26
Transport sector fuel consumption per capita (liters)	1,194	1,159
Water and sanitation		
Internal freshwater resources per capita (cu. m)	11,223	9,313
Freshwater withdrawal		
Total (% of internal resources)	2.3	10.4
Agriculture (% of total freshwater withdrawal)	0	43
Access to improved water source (% of total population)	..	100
Rural (% of rural population)	..	98
Urban (% of urban population)	100	100
Access to improved sanitation (% of total population)	..	100
Rural (% of rural population)	..	99
Urban (% of urban population)	..	100
Environment and health		
Acute resp. infection prevalence (% of children under five)	..	
Diarrhea prevalence (% of children under five)	..	
Under-five mortality rate (per 1,000 live births)	4	7
National accounting aggregates		
Gross savings (% of GNI)	25.6	20.6
Consumption of fixed capital (% of GNI)	18.1	14.5
Education expenditure (% of GNI)	5.1	4.6
Energy depletion (% of GNI)	0.0	1.5
Mineral depletion (% of GNI)	0.2	0.2
Net forest depletion (% of GNI)	0.0	0.0
CO_2 damage (% of GNI)	0.2	0.3
Particulate emission damage (% of GNI)	0.0	0.3
Adjusted net savings (% of GNI)	12.3	8.5

Isle of Man

| Population (thousands) | **77** | Land area (sq. km) | **570** | GDP ($ billions) | **3.4** |

	Country data	High-income group
GNI per capita, *World Bank Atlas* method ($)	45,810	37,572
Urban population (% of total)	51	78
Urban population growth (average annual %, 1990–2007)	0.9	1.0
Population growth (average annual %, 1990–2007)	1.0	0.7
Agriculture		
Agricultural land (% of land area)	46	38
Agricultural productivity (value added per worker, 2000 $)	..	27,680
Food production index (1999–2001 = 100)	..	102
Population density, rural (people/sq. km of arable land)	495	323
Forests and biodiversity		
Forest area (% of land area)	6.1	28.8
Deforestation (average annual %, 1990–2005)	0.0	-0.1
Nationally protected area (% of land area)	..	11.8
Animal species, total known	..	
Animal species, threatened	3	
Higher plant species, total known	..	
Higher plant species, threatened	0	
GEF benefits index for biodiversity (0–100, median is 1.5)	0.0	
Energy		
GDP per unit of energy use (2005 PPP $/kg oil equivalent)	..	6.3
Energy use per capita (kg oil equivalent)	..	5,416
Energy from biomass products and waste (% of total)	..	3.4
Electric power consumption per capita (kWh)	..	9,675
Electricity generated using fossil fuel (% of total)	..	62.0
Electricity generated by hydropower (% of total)	..	11.4
Emissions and pollution		
CO_2 emissions per unit of GDP (kg/2005 PPP $)	..	0.4
CO_2 emissions per capita (metric tons)	..	12.6
CO_2 emissions growth (%, 1990–2005)	..	19.1
Particulate matter (urban-pop.-weighted avg., µg/cu. m)	..	26
Transport sector fuel consumption per capita (liters)	..	1,159
Water and sanitation		
Internal freshwater resources per capita (cu. m)	..	9,313
Freshwater withdrawal		
Total (% of internal resources)	..	10.4
Agriculture (% of total freshwater withdrawal)	..	43
Access to improved water source (% of total population)	..	100
Rural (% of rural population)	..	98
Urban (% of urban population)	..	100
Access to improved sanitation (% of total population)	..	100
Rural (% of rural population)	..	99
Urban (% of urban population)	..	100
Environment and health		
Acute resp. infection prevalence (% of children under five)	..	
Diarrhea prevalence (% of children under five)	..	
Under-five mortality rate (per 1,000 live births)	..	7
National accounting aggregates		
Gross savings (% of GNI)	..	20.6
Consumption of fixed capital (% of GNI)	..	14.5
Education expenditure (% of GNI)	..	4.6
Energy depletion (% of GNI)	..	1.5
Mineral depletion (% of GNI)	..	0.2
Net forest depletion (% of GNI)	..	0.0
CO_2 damage (% of GNI)	..	0.3
Particulate emission damage (% of GNI)	..	0.3
Adjusted net savings (% of GNI)	..	8.5

Israel

Population (millions)	**7.2**	Land area (1,000 sq. km)	**21.6**	GDP ($ billions)	**164.0**

	Country data	High-income group
GNI per capita, *World Bank Atlas* method ($)	22,170	37,572
Urban population (% of total)	92	78
Urban population growth (average annual %, 1990–2007)	2.6	1.0
Population growth (average annual %, 1990–2007)	2.5	0.7
Agriculture		
Agricultural land (% of land area)	24	38
Agricultural productivity (value added per worker, 2000 $)	..	27,680
Food production index (1999–2001 = 100)	118	102
Population density, rural (people/sq. km of arable land)	184	323
Forests and biodiversity		
Forest area (% of land area)	7.9	28.8
Deforestation (average annual %, 1990–2005)	-0.7	-0.1
Nationally protected area (% of land area)	15.6	11.8
Animal species, total known	649	
Animal species, threatened	127	
Higher plant species, total known	2,317	
Higher plant species, threatened	0	
GEF benefits index for biodiversity (0–100, median is 1.5)	0.8	
Energy		
GDP per unit of energy use (2005 PPP $/kg oil equivalent)	7.9	6.3
Energy use per capita (kg oil equivalent)	3,017	5,416
Energy from biomass products and waste (% of total)	0.0	3.4
Electric power consumption per capita (kWh)	6,889	9,675
Electricity generated using fossil fuel (% of total)	99.9	62.0
Electricity generated by hydropower (% of total)	0.1	11.4
Emissions and pollution		
CO_2 emissions per unit of GDP (kg/2005 PPP $)	0.4	0.4
CO_2 emissions per capita (metric tons)	9.2	12.6
CO_2 emissions growth (%, 1990–2005)	92.0	19.1
Particulate matter (urban-pop.-weighted avg., µg/cu. m)	31	26
Transport sector fuel consumption per capita (liters)	543	1,159
Water and sanitation		
Internal freshwater resources per capita (cu. m)	104	9,313
Freshwater withdrawal		
Total (% of internal resources)	260.5	10.4
Agriculture (% of total freshwater withdrawal)	58	43
Access to improved water source (% of total population)	100	100
Rural (% of rural population)	100	98
Urban (% of urban population)	100	100
Access to improved sanitation (% of total population)	..	100
Rural (% of rural population)	..	99
Urban (% of urban population)	100	100
Environment and health		
Acute resp. infection prevalence (% of children under five)	..	
Diarrhea prevalence (% of children under five)	..	
Under-five mortality rate (per 1,000 live births)	5	7
National accounting aggregates		
Gross savings (% of GNI)	..	20.6
Consumption of fixed capital (% of GNI)	13.9	14.5
Education expenditure (% of GNI)	6.0	4.6
Energy depletion (% of GNI)	0.2	1.5
Mineral depletion (% of GNI)	0.0	0.2
Net forest depletion (% of GNI)	0.0	0.0
CO_2 damage (% of GNI)	0.4	0.3
Particulate emission damage (% of GNI)	0.4	0.3
Adjusted net savings (% of GNI)	..	8.5

Italy

	Country data	High-income group
Population (millions) **59**	Land area (1,000 sq. km) **294**	GDP ($ billions) **2,101.6**

	Country data	High-income group
GNI per capita, *World Bank Atlas* method ($)	33,490	37,572
Urban population (% of total)	68	78
Urban population growth (average annual %, 1990–2007)	0.4	1.0
Population growth (average annual %, 1990–2007)	0.3	0.7

Agriculture
Agricultural land (% of land area)	50	38
Agricultural productivity (value added per worker, 2000 $)	25,416	27,680
Food production index (1999–2001 = 100)	98	102
Population density, rural (people/sq. km of arable land)	245	323

Forests and biodiversity
Forest area (% of land area)	33.9	28.8
Deforestation (average annual %, 1990–2005)	-1.2	-0.1
Nationally protected area (% of land area)	6.6	11.8
Animal species, total known	610	
Animal species, threatened	119	
Higher plant species, total known	5,599	
Higher plant species, threatened	19	
GEF benefits index for biodiversity (0–100, median is 1.5)	3.8	

Energy
GDP per unit of energy use (2005 PPP $/kg oil equivalent)	9.1	6.3
Energy use per capita (kg oil equivalent)	3,125	5,416
Energy from biomass products and waste (% of total)	2.6	3.4
Electric power consumption per capita (kWh)	5,755	9,675
Electricity generated using fossil fuel (% of total)	82.7	62.0
Electricity generated by hydropower (% of total)	12.0	11.4

Emissions and pollution
CO_2 emissions per unit of GDP (kg/2005 PPP $)	0.3	0.4
CO_2 emissions per capita (metric tons)	7.7	12.6
CO_2 emissions growth (%, 1990–2005)	14.2	19.1
Particulate matter (urban-pop.-weighted avg., µg/cu. m)	27	26
Transport sector fuel consumption per capita (liters)	732	1,159

Water and sanitation
Internal freshwater resources per capita (cu. m)	3,074	9,313
Freshwater withdrawal		
Total (% of internal resources)	24.3	10.4
Agriculture (% of total freshwater withdrawal)	45	43
Access to improved water source (% of total population)	..	100
Rural (% of rural population)	..	98
Urban (% of urban population)	100	100
Access to improved sanitation (% of total population)	..	100
Rural (% of rural population)	..	99
Urban (% of urban population)	..	100

Environment and health
Acute resp. infection prevalence (% of children under five)	..	
Diarrhea prevalence (% of children under five)	..	
Under-five mortality rate (per 1,000 live births)	4	7

National accounting aggregates
Gross savings (% of GNI)	19.8	20.6
Consumption of fixed capital (% of GNI)	14.6	14.5
Education expenditure (% of GNI)	4.2	4.6
Energy depletion (% of GNI)	0.2	1.5
Mineral depletion (% of GNI)	0.0	0.2
Net forest depletion (% of GNI)	0.0	0.0
CO_2 damage (% of GNI)	0.2	0.3
Particulate emission damage (% of GNI)	0.2	0.3
Adjusted net savings (% of GNI)	8.9	8.5

Jamaica

	Population (millions)	**2.7**	Land area (1,000 sq. km)	**10.8**	GDP ($ billions)	**11.4**

	Country data	Latin America & Caribbean group	Upper middle-income group
GNI per capita, *World Bank Atlas* method ($)	3,330	5,801	7,107
Urban population (% of total)	53	78	75
Urban population growth (average annual %, 1990–2007)	1.1	2.1	1.4
Population growth (average annual %, 1990–2007)	0.7	1.5	0.9
Agriculture			
Agricultural land (% of land area)	47	36	31
Agricultural productivity (value added per worker, 2000 $)	1,759	3,158	2,947
Food production index (1999–2001 = 100)	99	117	113
Population density, rural (people/sq. km of arable land)	720	232	110
Forests and biodiversity			
Forest area (% of land area)	31.3	45.4	39.3
Deforestation (average annual %, 1990–2005)	0.1	0.5	0.2
Nationally protected area (% of land area)	15.0	16.7	10.3
Animal species, total known	333		
Animal species, threatened	71		
Higher plant species, total known	3,308		
Higher plant species, threatened	209		
GEF benefits index for biodiversity (0–100, median is 1.5)	4.4		
Energy			
GDP per unit of energy use (2005 PPP $/kg oil equivalent)	3.6	7.3	4.8
Energy use per capita (kg oil equivalent)	1,724	1,240	2,300
Energy from biomass products and waste (% of total)	10.5	15.9	7.0
Electric power consumption per capita (kWh)	2,453	1,808	3,242
Electricity generated using fossil fuel (% of total)	96.4	37.0	62.8
Electricity generated by hydropower (% of total)	2.2	57.3	27.6
Emissions and pollution			
CO_2 emissions per unit of GDP (kg/2005 PPP $)	0.6	0.3	0.5
CO_2 emissions per capita (metric tons)	3.8	2.5	5.5
CO_2 emissions growth (%, 1990–2005)	27.6	33.4	-8.3
Particulate matter (urban-pop.-weighted avg., µg/cu. m)	43	35	30
Transport sector fuel consumption per capita (liters)	392	295	332
Water and sanitation			
Internal freshwater resources per capita (cu. m)	3,514	23,965	16,993
Freshwater withdrawal			
Total (% of internal resources)	4.4	2.0	13.8
Agriculture (% of total freshwater withdrawal)	49	71	57
Access to improved water source (% of total population)	93	91	95
Rural (% of rural population)	88	73	83
Urban (% of urban population)	97	97	98
Access to improved sanitation (% of total population)	83	78	83
Rural (% of rural population)	84	51	64
Urban (% of urban population)	82	86	89
Environment and health			
Acute resp. infection prevalence (% of children under five)	3.0		
Diarrhea prevalence (% of children under five)	..		
Under-five mortality rate (per 1,000 live births)	31	26	24
National accounting aggregates			
Gross savings (% of GNI)	..	22.9	23.2
Consumption of fixed capital (% of GNI)	13.2	12.6	12.8
Education expenditure (% of GNI)	5.4	4.5	4.4
Energy depletion (% of GNI)	0.0	5.4	7.6
Mineral depletion (% of GNI)	1.9	1.9	1.3
Net forest depletion (% of GNI)	0.0	0.0	0.0
CO_2 damage (% of GNI)	0.7	0.3	0.6
Particulate emission damage (% of GNI)	0.3	0.4	0.4
Adjusted net savings (% of GNI)	..	6.7	4.9

Japan

	Population (millions)	128	Land area (1,000 sq. km)	365	GDP ($ billions)	**4,384.3**

	Country data	High-income group
GNI per capita, *World Bank Atlas* method ($)	37,790	37,572
Urban population (% of total)	66	78
Urban population growth (average annual %, 1990–2007)	0.5	1.0
Population growth (average annual %, 1990–2007)	0.2	0.7
Agriculture		
Agricultural land (% of land area)	13	38
Agricultural productivity (value added per worker, 2000 $)	37,842	27,680
Food production index (1999–2001 = 100)	97	102
Population density, rural (people/sq. km of arable land)	996	323
Forests and biodiversity		
Forest area (% of land area)	68.2	28.8
Deforestation (average annual %, 1990–2005)	0.0	-0.1
Nationally protected area (% of land area)	9.5	11.8
Animal species, total known	763	
Animal species, threatened	297	
Higher plant species, total known	5,565	
Higher plant species, threatened	12	
GEF benefits index for biodiversity (0–100, median is 1.5)	36.0	
Energy		
GDP per unit of energy use (2005 PPP $/kg oil equivalent)	7.5	6.3
Energy use per capita (kg oil equivalent)	4,129	5,416
Energy from biomass products and waste (% of total)	1.3	3.4
Electric power consumption per capita (kWh)	8,220	9,675
Electricity generated using fossil fuel (% of total)	59.2	62.0
Electricity generated by hydropower (% of total)	7.9	11.4
Emissions and pollution		
CO_2 emissions per unit of GDP (kg/2005 PPP $)	0.3	0.4
CO_2 emissions per capita (metric tons)	9.6	12.6
CO_2 emissions growth (%, 1990–2005)	13.8	19.1
Particulate matter (urban-pop.-weighted avg., µg/cu. m)	30	26
Transport sector fuel consumption per capita (liters)	658	1,159
Water and sanitation		
Internal freshwater resources per capita (cu. m)	3,365	9,313
Freshwater withdrawal		
Total (% of internal resources)	20.6	10.4
Agriculture (% of total freshwater withdrawal)	62	43
Access to improved water source (% of total population)	100	100
Rural (% of rural population)	100	98
Urban (% of urban population)	100	100
Access to improved sanitation (% of total population)	100	100
Rural (% of rural population)	100	99
Urban (% of urban population)	100	100
Environment and health		
Acute resp. infection prevalence (% of children under five)	..	
Diarrhea prevalence (% of children under five)	..	
Under-five mortality rate (per 1,000 live births)	4	7
National accounting aggregates		
Gross savings (% of GNI)	31.0	20.6
Consumption of fixed capital (% of GNI)	14.0	14.5
Education expenditure (% of GNI)	3.2	4.6
Energy depletion (% of GNI)	0.0	1.5
Mineral depletion (% of GNI)	0.0	0.2
Net forest depletion (% of GNI)	0.0	0.0
CO_2 damage (% of GNI)	0.2	0.3
Particulate emission damage (% of GNI)	0.5	0.3
Adjusted net savings (% of GNI)	19.5	8.5

Jordan

	Country data	Middle East & N. Africa group	Lower middle-income group
Population (millions) **5.7** Land area (1,000 sq. km) **88.2** GDP ($ billions) **15.8**			

	Country data	Middle East & N. Africa group	Lower middle-income group
GNI per capita, *World Bank Atlas* method ($)	2,840	2,820	1,905
Urban population (% of total)	78	57	42
Urban population growth (average annual %, 1990–2007)	4.0	2.6	2.9
Population growth (average annual %, 1990–2007)	3.5	2.0	1.3
Agriculture			
Agricultural land (% of land area)	11	22	47
Agricultural productivity (value added per worker, 2000 $)	1,392	2,313	532
Food production index (1999–2001 = 100)	115	116	116
Population density, rural (people/sq. km of arable land)	638	665	511
Forests and biodiversity			
Forest area (% of land area)	0.9	2.4	25.0
Deforestation (average annual %, 1990–2005)	0.0	-0.4	0.1
Nationally protected area (% of land area)	10.6	3.6	11.0
Animal species, total known	490		
Animal species, threatened	89		
Higher plant species, total known	2,100		
Higher plant species, threatened	0		
GEF benefits index for biodiversity (0–100, median is 1.5)	0.4		
Energy			
GDP per unit of energy use (2005 PPP $/kg oil equivalent)	3.5	5.0	3.9
Energy use per capita (kg oil equivalent)	1,294	1,254	1,019
Energy from biomass products and waste (% of total)	0.0	1.2	15.2
Electric power consumption per capita (kWh)	1,904	1,418	1,269
Electricity generated using fossil fuel (% of total)	99.5	91.1	79.0
Electricity generated by hydropower (% of total)	0.4	7.4	16.3
Emissions and pollution			
CO_2 emissions per unit of GDP (kg/2005 PPP $)	0.9	0.6	0.8
CO_2 emissions per capita (metric tons)	3.8	3.7	2.8
CO_2 emissions growth (%, 1990–2005)	101.4	96.8	93.5
Particulate matter (urban-pop.-weighted avg., µg/cu. m)	45	72	67
Transport sector fuel consumption per capita (liters)	323	277	99
Water and sanitation			
Internal freshwater resources per capita (cu. m)	119	728	4,117
Freshwater withdrawal			
Total (% of internal resources)	138.0	122.3	8.7
Agriculture (% of total freshwater withdrawal)	65	86	80
Access to improved water source (% of total population)	98	89	88
Rural (% of rural population)	91	81	82
Urban (% of urban population)	99	95	96
Access to improved sanitation (% of total population)	85	77	55
Rural (% of rural population)	71	62	43
Urban (% of urban population)	88	88	71
Environment and health			
Acute resp. infection prevalence (% of children under five)	6.0		
Diarrhea prevalence (% of children under five)	18.0		
Under-five mortality rate (per 1,000 live births)	24	38	50
National accounting aggregates			
Gross savings (% of GNI)	8.2	33.3	41.7
Consumption of fixed capital (% of GNI)	10.4	11.3	10.7
Education expenditure (% of GNI)	5.6	4.7	2.6
Energy depletion (% of GNI)	0.3	21.3	6.6
Mineral depletion (% of GNI)	0.5	0.4	1.2
Net forest depletion (% of GNI)	0.0	0.0	0.2
CO_2 damage (% of GNI)	0.9	1.0	1.2
Particulate emission damage (% of GNI)	0.6	0.6	1.1
Adjusted net savings (% of GNI)	1.1	3.4	23.5

Kazakhstan

| Population (millions) | **15** | Land area (1,000 sq. km) | **2,700** | GDP ($ billions) | **104.9** |

	Country data	Europe & Central Asia group	Upper middle-income group
GNI per capita, *World Bank Atlas* method ($)	5,020	6,052	7,107
Urban population (% of total)	58	64	75
Urban population growth (average annual %, 1990–2007)	–0.2	0.2	1.4
Population growth (average annual %, 1990–2007)	–0.3	0.1	0.9
Agriculture			
Agricultural land (% of land area)	77	28	31
Agricultural productivity (value added per worker, 2000 $)	1,652	2,228	2,947
Food production index (1999–2001 = 100)	116	110	113
Population density, rural (people/sq. km of arable land)	29	129	110
Forests and biodiversity			
Forest area (% of land area)	1.2	38.3	39.3
Deforestation (average annual %, 1990–2005)	0.2	0.0	0.2
Nationally protected area (% of land area)	2.9	6.1	10.3
Animal species, total known	642		
Animal species, threatened	57		
Higher plant species, total known	6,000		
Higher plant species, threatened	16		
GEF benefits index for biodiversity (0–100, median is 1.5)	5.1		
Energy			
GDP per unit of energy use (2005 PPP $/kg oil equivalent)	2.4	3.5	4.8
Energy use per capita (kg oil equivalent)	4,012	2,930	2,300
Energy from biomass products and waste (% of total)	0.1	2.2	7.0
Electric power consumption per capita (kWh)	4,293	3,835	3,242
Electricity generated using fossil fuel (% of total)	89.2	67.7	62.8
Electricity generated by hydropower (% of total)	10.8	17.4	27.6
Emissions and pollution			
CO_2 emissions per unit of GDP (kg/2005 PPP $)	1.4	0.7	0.5
CO_2 emissions per capita (metric tons)	11.9	7.0	5.5
CO_2 emissions growth (%, 1990–2005)	–37.2	–29.3	–8.3
Particulate matter (urban-pop.-weighted avg., µg/cu. m)	19	27	30
Transport sector fuel consumption per capita (liters)	252	255	332
Water and sanitation			
Internal freshwater resources per capita (cu. m)	4,871	11,806	16,993
Freshwater withdrawal			
Total (% of internal resources)	46.4	7.2	13.8
Agriculture (% of total freshwater withdrawal)	82	60	57
Access to improved water source (% of total population)	96	95	95
Rural (% of rural population)	91	88	83
Urban (% of urban population)	99	99	98
Access to improved sanitation (% of total population)	97	89	83
Rural (% of rural population)	98	79	64
Urban (% of urban population)	97	94	89
Environment and health			
Acute resp. infection prevalence (% of children under five)	3.0		
Diarrhea prevalence (% of children under five)	13.4		
Under-five mortality rate (per 1,000 live births)	32	23	24
National accounting aggregates			
Gross savings (% of GNI)	32.5	24.0	23.2
Consumption of fixed capital (% of GNI)	13.8	12.8	12.8
Education expenditure (% of GNI)	4.4	4.0	4.4
Energy depletion (% of GNI)	28.3	9.8	7.6
Mineral depletion (% of GNI)	2.4	0.7	1.3
Net forest depletion (% of GNI)	0.0	0.0	0.0
CO_2 damage (% of GNI)	2.0	1.0	0.6
Particulate emission damage (% of GNI)	0.3	0.5	0.4
Adjusted net savings (% of GNI)	–9.9	3.2	4.9

Population (millions)	**38**	Land area (1,000 sq. km)	**569**	GDP ($ billions)	**24.2**

	Country data	Sub-Saharan Africa group	Low-income group
GNI per capita, *World Bank Atlas* method ($)	640	951	574
Urban population (% of total)	21	36	32
Urban population growth (average annual %, 1990–2007)	3.7	4.0	3.7
Population growth (average annual %, 1990–2007)	2.8	2.6	2.4

Agriculture
Agricultural land (% of land area)	47	44	39
Agricultural productivity (value added per worker, 2000 $)	344	287	330
Food production index (1999–2001 = 100)	106	109	112
Population density, rural (people/sq. km of arable land)	536	351	603

Forests and biodiversity
Forest area (% of land area)	6.2	26.5	24.7
Deforestation (average annual %, 1990–2005)	0.3	0.6	0.7
Nationally protected area (% of land area)	12.1	11.3	10.8
Animal species, total known	1,510		
Animal species, threatened	208		
Higher plant species, total known	6,506		
Higher plant species, threatened	103		
GEF benefits index for biodiversity (0–100, median is 1.5)	8.8		

Energy
GDP per unit of energy use (2005 PPP $/kg oil equivalent)	2.8	3.0	3.2
Energy use per capita (kg oil equivalent)	491	670	478
Energy from biomass products and waste (% of total)	73.6	56.3	53.8
Electric power consumption per capita (kWh)	145	531	309
Electricity generated using fossil fuel (% of total)	30.5	65.6	48.4
Electricity generated by hydropower (% of total)	50.6	18.0	38.8

Emissions and pollution
CO_2 emissions per unit of GDP (kg/2005 PPP $)	0.2	0.5	0.4
CO_2 emissions per capita (metric tons)	0.3	0.8	0.6
CO_2 emissions growth (%, 1990–2005)	90.5	40.1	39.3
Particulate matter (urban-pop.-weighted avg., µg/cu. m)	36	53	69
Transport sector fuel consumption per capita (liters)	34	64	41

Water and sanitation
Internal freshwater resources per capita (cu. m)	552	4,824	4,619
Freshwater withdrawal			
Total (% of internal resources)	13.2	3.2	9.4
Agriculture (% of total freshwater withdrawal)	79	87	90
Access to improved water source (% of total population)	57	58	68
Rural (% of rural population)	49	46	60
Urban (% of urban population)	85	81	84
Access to improved sanitation (% of total population)	42	31	39
Rural (% of rural population)	48	24	33
Urban (% of urban population)	19	42	54

Environment and health
Acute resp. infection prevalence (% of children under five)	18.0		
Diarrhea prevalence (% of children under five)	17.1		
Under-five mortality rate (per 1,000 live births)	121	146	126

National accounting aggregates
Gross savings (% of GNI)	17.1	17.4	25.4
Consumption of fixed capital (% of GNI)	8.8	11.1	9.3
Education expenditure (% of GNI)	6.6	3.6	2.6
Energy depletion (% of GNI)	0.0	11.7	9.8
Mineral depletion (% of GNI)	0.1	1.5	0.9
Net forest depletion (% of GNI)	1.2	0.5	0.8
CO_2 damage (% of GNI)	0.3	0.7	0.7
Particulate emission damage (% of GNI)	0.1	0.4	0.7
Adjusted net savings (% of GNI)	13.1	-5.0	5.8

Kiribati

Population (thousands)	95	Land area (sq. km)	810	GDP ($ millions)	78

	Country data	East Asia & Pacific group	Lower middle-income group
GNI per capita, *World Bank Atlas* method ($)	1,120	2,182	1,905
Urban population (% of total)	44	43	42
Urban population growth (average annual %, 1990–2007)	3.0	3.5	2.9
Population growth (average annual %, 1990–2007)	1.6	1.1	1.3
Agriculture			
Agricultural land (% of land area)	46	51	47
Agricultural productivity (value added per worker, 2000 $)	8	458	532
Food production index (1999–2001 = 100)	..	120	116
Population density, rural (people/sq. km of arable land)	2,594	547	511
Forests and biodiversity			
Forest area (% of land area)	2.7	28.4	25.0
Deforestation (average annual %, 1990–2005)	0.0	-0.1	0.1
Nationally protected area (% of land area)	..	14.0	11.0
Animal species, total known	51		
Animal species, threatened	87		
Higher plant species, total known	60		
Higher plant species, threatened	..		
GEF benefits index for biodiversity (0–100, median is 1.5)	1.1		
Energy			
GDP per unit of energy use (2005 PPP $/kg oil equivalent)	..	3.4	3.9
Energy use per capita (kg oil equivalent)	..	1,258	1,019
Energy from biomass products and waste (% of total)	..	14.7	15.2
Electric power consumption per capita (kWh)	..	1,669	1,269
Electricity generated using fossil fuel (% of total)	..	82.0	79.0
Electricity generated by hydropower (% of total)	..	15.0	16.3
Emissions and pollution			
CO_2 emissions per unit of GDP (kg/2005 PPP $)	0.2	0.9	0.8
CO_2 emissions per capita (metric tons)	0.3	3.6	2.8
CO_2 emissions growth (%, 1990–2005)	16.7	123.4	93.5
Particulate matter (urban-pop.-weighted avg., µg/cu. m)	..	69	67
Transport sector fuel consumption per capita (liters)	..	106	99
Water and sanitation			
Internal freshwater resources per capita (cu. m)	..	4,948	4,117
Freshwater withdrawal			
Total (% of internal resources)	..	10.2	8.7
Agriculture (% of total freshwater withdrawal)	..	74	80
Access to improved water source (% of total population)	65	87	88
Rural (% of rural population)	53	81	82
Urban (% of urban population)	77	96	96
Access to improved sanitation (% of total population)	33	66	55
Rural (% of rural population)	20	59	43
Urban (% of urban population)	46	75	71
Environment and health			
Acute resp. infection prevalence (% of children under five)	..		
Diarrhea prevalence (% of children under five)	..		
Under-five mortality rate (per 1,000 live births)	63	27	50
National accounting aggregates			
Gross savings (% of GNI)	..	48.0	41.7
Consumption of fixed capital (% of GNI)	5.8	10.7	10.7
Education expenditure (% of GNI)	..	2.1	2.6
Energy depletion (% of GNI)	0.0	4.9	6.6
Mineral depletion (% of GNI)	0.0	1.3	1.2
Net forest depletion (% of GNI)	..	0.0	0.2
CO_2 damage (% of GNI)	0.2	1.3	1.2
Particulate emission damage (% of GNI)	..	1.3	1.1
Adjusted net savings (% of GNI)	..	30.6	23.5

Korea, Dem. Rep.

| Population (millions) | **24** | Land area (1,000 sq. km) | **120** | GDP ($ billions) | .. |

	Country data	East Asia & Pacific group	Low-income group
GNI per capita, *World Bank Atlas* method ($)	..	2,182	574
Urban population (% of total)	62	43	32
Urban population growth (average annual %, 1990–2007)	1.4	3.5	3.7
Population growth (average annual %, 1990–2007)	1.0	1.1	2.4
Agriculture			
Agricultural land (% of land area)	25	51	39
Agricultural productivity (value added per worker, 2000 $)	..	458	330
Food production index (1999–2001 = 100)	113	120	112
Population density, rural (people/sq. km of arable land)	324	547	603
Forests and biodiversity			
Forest area (% of land area)	51.4	28.4	24.7
Deforestation (average annual %, 1990–2005)	1.9	-0.1	0.7
Nationally protected area (% of land area)	2.6	14.0	10.8
Animal species, total known	474		
Animal species, threatened	40		
Higher plant species, total known	2,898		
Higher plant species, threatened	3		
GEF benefits index for biodiversity (0–100, median is 1.5)	0.7		
Energy			
GDP per unit of energy use (2005 PPP $/kg oil equivalent)	..	3.4	3.2
Energy use per capita (kg oil equivalent)	913	1,258	478
Energy from biomass products and waste (% of total)	4.8	14.7	53.8
Electric power consumption per capita (kWh)	797	1,669	309
Electricity generated using fossil fuel (% of total)	43.8	82.0	48.4
Electricity generated by hydropower (% of total)	56.2	15.0	38.8
Emissions and pollution			
CO_2 emissions per unit of GDP (kg/2005 PPP $)	..	0.9	0.4
CO_2 emissions per capita (metric tons)	3.5	3.6	0.6
CO_2 emissions growth (%, 1990–2005)	-66.2	123.4	39.3
Particulate matter (urban-pop.-weighted avg., µg/cu. m)	68	69	69
Transport sector fuel consumption per capita (liters)	16	106	41
Water and sanitation			
Internal freshwater resources per capita (cu. m)	2,817	4,948	4,619
Freshwater withdrawal			
Total (% of internal resources)	13.5	10.2	9.4
Agriculture (% of total freshwater withdrawal)	55	74	90
Access to improved water source (% of total population)	100	87	68
Rural (% of rural population)	100	81	60
Urban (% of urban population)	100	96	84
Access to improved sanitation (% of total population)	..	66	39
Rural (% of rural population)	..	59	33
Urban (% of urban population)	..	75	54
Environment and health			
Acute resp. infection prevalence (% of children under five)	12.0		
Diarrhea prevalence (% of children under five)	..		
Under-five mortality rate (per 1,000 live births)	55	27	126
National accounting aggregates			
Gross savings (% of GNI)	..	48.0	25.4
Consumption of fixed capital (% of GNI)	..	10.7	9.3
Education expenditure (% of GNI)	..	2.1	2.6
Energy depletion (% of GNI)	..	4.9	9.8
Mineral depletion (% of GNI)	..	1.3	0.9
Net forest depletion (% of GNI)	..	0.0	0.8
CO_2 damage (% of GNI)	..	1.3	0.7
Particulate emission damage (% of GNI)	..	1.3	0.7
Adjusted net savings (% of GNI)	..	30.6	5.8

Korea, Rep.

| Population (millions) | **48** | Land area (1,000 sq. km) | **99** | GDP ($ billions) | **969.8** |

	Country data	High-income group
GNI per capita, *World Bank Atlas* method ($)	19,730	37,572
Urban population (% of total)	81	78
Urban population growth (average annual %, 1990–2007)	1.3	1.0
Population growth (average annual %, 1990–2007)	0.7	0.7
Agriculture		
Agricultural land (% of land area)	19	38
Agricultural productivity (value added per worker, 2000 $)	12,275	27,680
Food production index (1999–2001 = 100)	98	102
Population density, rural (people/sq. km of arable land)	569	323
Forests and biodiversity		
Forest area (% of land area)	63.5	28.8
Deforestation (average annual %, 1990–2005)	0.1	–0.1
Nationally protected area (% of land area)	3.5	11.8
Animal species, total known	512	
Animal species, threatened	58	
Higher plant species, total known	2,898	
Higher plant species, threatened	0	
GEF benefits index for biodiversity (0–100, median is 1.5)	1.7	
Energy		
GDP per unit of energy use (2005 PPP $/kg oil equivalent)	5.0	6.3
Energy use per capita (kg oil equivalent)	4,483	5,416
Energy from biomass products and waste (% of total)	1.1	3.4
Electric power consumption per capita (kWh)	8,063	9,675
Electricity generated using fossil fuel (% of total)	61.7	62.0
Electricity generated by hydropower (% of total)	0.9	11.4
Emissions and pollution		
CO_2 emissions per unit of GDP (kg/2005 PPP $)	0.4	0.4
CO_2 emissions per capita (metric tons)	9.4	12.6
CO_2 emissions growth (%, 1990–2005)	87.2	19.1
Particulate matter (urban-pop.-weighted avg., µg/cu. m)	35	26
Transport sector fuel consumption per capita (liters)	534	1,159
Water and sanitation		
Internal freshwater resources per capita (cu. m)	1,338	9,313
Freshwater withdrawal		
Total (% of internal resources)	28.7	10.4
Agriculture (% of total freshwater withdrawal)	48	43
Access to improved water source (% of total population)	..	100
Rural (% of rural population)	..	98
Urban (% of urban population)	97	100
Access to improved sanitation (% of total population)	..	100
Rural (% of rural population)	..	99
Urban (% of urban population)	..	100
Environment and health		
Acute resp. infection prevalence (% of children under five)	..	
Diarrhea prevalence (% of children under five)	..	
Under-five mortality rate (per 1,000 live births)	5	7
National accounting aggregates		
Gross savings (% of GNI)	29.9	20.6
Consumption of fixed capital (% of GNI)	13.7	14.5
Education expenditure (% of GNI)	3.9	4.6
Energy depletion (% of GNI)	0.0	1.5
Mineral depletion (% of GNI)	0.0	0.2
Net forest depletion (% of GNI)	0.0	0.0
CO_2 damage (% of GNI)	0.4	0.3
Particulate emission damage (% of GNI)	0.6	0.3
Adjusted net savings (% of GNI)	19.1	8.5

Kuwait

| Population (millions) | **2.7** | Land area (1,000 sq. km) | **17.8** | GDP ($ billions) | **112.1** |

	Country data	High-income group
GNI per capita, *World Bank Atlas* method ($)	38,420	37,572
Urban population (% of total)	98	78
Urban population growth (average annual %, 1990–2007)	1.3	1.0
Population growth (average annual %, 1990–2007)	1.3	0.7
Agriculture		
Agricultural land (% of land area)	9	38
Agricultural productivity (value added per worker, 2000 $)	13,521	27,680
Food production index (1999–2001 = 100)	117	102
Population density, rural (people/sq. km of arable land)	287	323
Forests and biodiversity		
Forest area (% of land area)	0.3	28.8
Deforestation (average annual %, 1990–2005)	-4.7	-0.1
Nationally protected area (% of land area)	0.0	11.8
Animal species, total known	381	
Animal species, threatened	39	
Higher plant species, total known	234	
Higher plant species, threatened	..	
GEF benefits index for biodiversity (0–100, median is 1.5)	0.1	
Energy		
GDP per unit of energy use (2005 PPP $/kg oil equivalent)	4.6	6.3
Energy use per capita (kg oil equivalent)	9,729	5,416
Energy from biomass products and waste (% of total)	0.0	3.4
Electric power consumption per capita (kWh)	16,311	9,675
Electricity generated using fossil fuel (% of total)	100.0	62.0
Electricity generated by hydropower (% of total)	0.0	11.4
Emissions and pollution		
CO_2 emissions per unit of GDP (kg/2005 PPP $)	0.8	0.4
CO_2 emissions per capita (metric tons)	36.9	12.6
CO_2 emissions growth (%, 1990–2005)	115.6	19.1
Particulate matter (urban-pop.-weighted avg., µg/cu. m)	97	26
Transport sector fuel consumption per capita (liters)	1,358	1,159
Water and sanitation		
Internal freshwater resources per capita (cu. m)	..	9,313
Freshwater withdrawal		
Total (% of internal resources)	..	10.4
Agriculture (% of total freshwater withdrawal)	54	43
Access to improved water source (% of total population)	..	100
Rural (% of rural population)	..	98
Urban (% of urban population)	..	100
Access to improved sanitation (% of total population)	..	100
Rural (% of rural population)	..	99
Urban (% of urban population)	..	100
Environment and health		
Acute resp. infection prevalence (% of children under five)	9.9	
Diarrhea prevalence (% of children under five)	10.2	
Under-five mortality rate (per 1,000 live births)	11	7
National accounting aggregates		
Gross savings (% of GNI)	..	20.6
Consumption of fixed capital (% of GNI)	13.3	14.5
Education expenditure (% of GNI)	3.0	4.6
Energy depletion (% of GNI)	32.5	1.5
Mineral depletion (% of GNI)	0.0	0.2
Net forest depletion (% of GNI)	0.0	0.0
CO_2 damage (% of GNI)	0.5	0.3
Particulate emission damage (% of GNI)	1.4	0.3
Adjusted net savings (% of GNI)	..	8.5

Kyrgyz Republic

Population (millions)	**5.2**	Land area (1,000 sq. km)	**191.8**	GDP ($ billions)	**3.7**

	Country data	Europe & Central Asia group	Low-income group
GNI per capita, *World Bank Atlas* method ($)	610	6,052	574
Urban population (% of total)	36	64	32
Urban population growth (average annual %, 1990–2007)	0.7	0.2	3.7
Population growth (average annual %, 1990–2007)	1.0	0.1	2.4
Agriculture			
Agricultural land (% of land area)	56	28	39
Agricultural productivity (value added per worker, 2000 $)	966	2,228	330
Food production index (1999–2001 = 100)	101	110	112
Population density, rural (people/sq. km of arable land)	257	129	603
Forests and biodiversity			
Forest area (% of land area)	4.5	38.3	24.7
Deforestation (average annual %, 1990–2005)	-0.3	0.0	0.7
Nationally protected area (% of land area)	3.2	6.1	10.8
Animal species, total known	265		
Animal species, threatened	26		
Higher plant species, total known	4,500		
Higher plant species, threatened	14		
GEF benefits index for biodiversity (0–100, median is 1.5)	1.1		
Energy			
GDP per unit of energy use (2005 PPP $/kg oil equivalent)	3.3	3.5	3.2
Energy use per capita (kg oil equivalent)	542	2,930	478
Energy from biomass products and waste (% of total)	0.1	2.2	53.8
Electric power consumption per capita (kWh)	2,015	3,835	309
Electricity generated using fossil fuel (% of total)	12.8	67.7	48.4
Electricity generated by hydropower (% of total)	87.2	17.4	38.8
Emissions and pollution			
CO_2 emissions per unit of GDP (kg/2005 PPP $)	0.6	0.7	0.4
CO_2 emissions per capita (metric tons)	1.1	7.0	0.6
CO_2 emissions growth (%, 1990–2005)	-55.9	-29.3	39.3
Particulate matter (urban-pop.-weighted avg., µg/cu. m)	22	27	69
Transport sector fuel consumption per capita (liters)	52	255	41
Water and sanitation			
Internal freshwater resources per capita (cu. m)	8,873	11,806	4,619
Freshwater withdrawal			
Total (% of internal resources)	21.7	7.2	9.4
Agriculture (% of total freshwater withdrawal)	94	60	90
Access to improved water source (% of total population)	89	95	68
Rural (% of rural population)	83	88	60
Urban (% of urban population)	99	99	84
Access to improved sanitation (% of total population)	93	89	39
Rural (% of rural population)	93	79	33
Urban (% of urban population)	94	94	54
Environment and health			
Acute resp. infection prevalence (% of children under five)	4.0		
Diarrhea prevalence (% of children under five)	17.6		
Under-five mortality rate (per 1,000 live births)	38	23	126
National accounting aggregates			
Gross savings (% of GNI)	6.7	24.0	25.4
Consumption of fixed capital (% of GNI)	9.1	12.8	9.3
Education expenditure (% of GNI)	5.2	4.0	2.6
Energy depletion (% of GNI)	0.1	9.8	9.8
Mineral depletion (% of GNI)	0.0	0.7	0.9
Net forest depletion (% of GNI)	0.0	0.0	0.8
CO_2 damage (% of GNI)	1.2	1.0	0.7
Particulate emission damage (% of GNI)	0.2	0.5	0.7
Adjusted net savings (% of GNI)	1.2	3.2	5.8

Lao PDR

Population (millions)	**5.9**	Land area (1,000 sq. km)	**230.8**	GDP ($ billions)	**4.1**

	Country data	East Asia & Pacific group	Low-income group
GNI per capita, *World Bank Atlas* method ($)	630	2,182	574
Urban population (% of total)	30	43	32
Urban population growth (average annual %, 1990–2007)	6.0	3.5	3.7
Population growth (average annual %, 1990–2007)	2.1	1.1	2.4
Agriculture			
Agricultural land (% of land area)	8	51	39
Agricultural productivity (value added per worker, 2000 $)	457	458	330
Food production index (1999–2001 = 100)	115	120	112
Population density, rural (people/sq. km of arable land)	411	547	603
Forests and biodiversity			
Forest area (% of land area)	69.9	28.4	24.7
Deforestation (average annual %, 1990–2005)	0.5	-0.1	0.7
Nationally protected area (% of land area)	16.3	14.0	10.8
Animal species, total known	919		
Animal species, threatened	94		
Higher plant species, total known	8,286		
Higher plant species, threatened	21		
GEF benefits index for biodiversity (0–100, median is 1.5)	5.0		
Energy			
GDP per unit of energy use (2005 PPP $/kg oil equivalent)	..	3.4	3.2
Energy use per capita (kg oil equivalent)	..	1,258	478
Energy from biomass products and waste (% of total)	..	14.7	53.8
Electric power consumption per capita (kWh)	..	1,669	309
Electricity generated using fossil fuel (% of total)	..	82.0	48.4
Electricity generated by hydropower (% of total)	..	15.0	38.8
Emissions and pollution			
CO_2 emissions per unit of GDP (kg/2005 PPP $)	0.1	0.9	0.4
CO_2 emissions per capita (metric tons)	0.3	3.6	0.6
CO_2 emissions growth (%, 1990–2005)	520.6	123.4	39.3
Particulate matter (urban-pop.-weighted avg., µg/cu. m)	49	69	69
Transport sector fuel consumption per capita (liters)	..	106	41
Water and sanitation			
Internal freshwater resources per capita (cu. m)	32,495	4,948	4,619
Freshwater withdrawal			
Total (% of internal resources)	1.6	10.2	9.4
Agriculture (% of total freshwater withdrawal)	90	74	90
Access to improved water source (% of total population)	60	87	68
Rural (% of rural population)	53	81	60
Urban (% of urban population)	86	96	84
Access to improved sanitation (% of total population)	48	66	39
Rural (% of rural population)	38	59	33
Urban (% of urban population)	87	75	54
Environment and health			
Acute resp. infection prevalence (% of children under five)	1.0		
Diarrhea prevalence (% of children under five)	6.2		
Under-five mortality rate (per 1,000 live births)	70	27	126
National accounting aggregates			
Gross savings (% of GNI)	23.5	48.0	25.4
Consumption of fixed capital (% of GNI)	9.3	10.7	9.3
Education expenditure (% of GNI)	1.3	2.1	2.6
Energy depletion (% of GNI)	0.0	4.9	9.8
Mineral depletion (% of GNI)	0.0	1.3	0.9
Net forest depletion (% of GNI)	0.0	0.0	0.8
CO_2 damage (% of GNI)	0.3	1.3	0.7
Particulate emission damage (% of GNI)	1.2	1.3	0.7
Adjusted net savings (% of GNI)	14.0	30.6	5.8

Latvia

| Population (millions) | 2.3 | Land area (1,000 sq. km) | 62.3 | GDP ($ billions) | 27.2 |

	Country data	Europe & Central Asia group	Upper middle-income group
GNI per capita, *World Bank Atlas* method ($)	9,920	6,052	7,107
Urban population (% of total)	68	64	75
Urban population growth (average annual %, 1990–2007)	–1.0	0.2	1.4
Population growth (average annual %, 1990–2007)	–0.9	0.1	0.9
Agriculture			
Agricultural land (% of land area)	28	28	31
Agricultural productivity (value added per worker, 2000 $)	2,974	2,228	2,947
Food production index (1999–2001 = 100)	119	110	113
Population density, rural (people/sq. km of arable land)	67	129	110
Forests and biodiversity			
Forest area (% of land area)	47.2	38.3	39.3
Deforestation (average annual %, 1990–2005)	–0.4	0.0	0.2
Nationally protected area (% of land area)	16.7	6.1	10.3
Animal species, total known	393		
Animal species, threatened	21		
Higher plant species, total known	1,153		
Higher plant species, threatened	0		
GEF benefits index for biodiversity (0–100, median is 1.5)	0.0		
Energy			
GDP per unit of energy use (2005 PPP $/kg oil equivalent)	7.3	3.5	4.8
Energy use per capita (kg oil equivalent)	2,017	2,930	2,300
Energy from biomass products and waste (% of total)	25.9	2.2	7.0
Electric power consumption per capita (kWh)	2,876	3,835	3,242
Electricity generated using fossil fuel (% of total)	43.0	67.7	62.8
Electricity generated by hydropower (% of total)	55.2	17.4	27.6
Emissions and pollution			
CO_2 emissions per unit of GDP (kg/2005 PPP $)	0.2	0.7	0.5
CO_2 emissions per capita (metric tons)	2.8	5.5	5.5
CO_2 emissions growth (%, 1990–2005)	–55.6	–29.3	–8.3
Particulate matter (urban-pop.-weighted avg., µg/cu. m)	16	27	30
Transport sector fuel consumption per capita (liters)	533	255	332
Water and sanitation			
Internal freshwater resources per capita (cu. m)	7,355	11,806	16,993
Freshwater withdrawal			
Total (% of internal resources)	1.8	7.2	13.8
Agriculture (% of total freshwater withdrawal)	13	60	57
Access to improved water source (% of total population)	99	95	95
Rural (% of rural population)	96	88	83
Urban (% of urban population)	100	99	98
Access to improved sanitation (% of total population)	78	89	83
Rural (% of rural population)	71	79	64
Urban (% of urban population)	82	94	89
Environment and health			
Acute resp. infection prevalence (% of children under five)	..		
Diarrhea prevalence (% of children under five)	..		
Under-five mortality rate (per 1,000 live births)	9	23	24
National accounting aggregates			
Gross savings (% of GNI)	15.4	24.0	23.2
Consumption of fixed capital (% of GNI)	13.9	12.8	12.8
Education expenditure (% of GNI)	5.6	4.0	4.4
Energy depletion (% of GNI)	0.0	9.8	7.6
Mineral depletion (% of GNI)	0.0	0.7	1.3
Net forest depletion (% of GNI)	0.6	0.0	0.0
CO_2 damage (% of GNI)	0.3	1.0	0.6
Particulate emission damage (% of GNI)	0.0	0.5	0.4
Adjusted net savings (% of GNI)	6.2	3.2	4.9

Lebanon

| Population (millions) | **4.1** | Land area (1,000 sq. km) | **10.2** | GDP ($ billions) | **24.4** |

	Country data	Middle East & N. Africa group	Upper middle-income group
GNI per capita, *World Bank Atlas* method ($)	5,800	2,820	7,107
Urban population (% of total)	87	57	75
Urban population growth (average annual %, 1990–2007)	2.1	2.6	1.4
Population growth (average annual %, 1990–2007)	1.9	2.0	0.9
Agriculture			
Agricultural land (% of land area)	38	22	31
Agricultural productivity (value added per worker, 2000 $)	32,025	2,313	2,947
Food production index (1999–2001 = 100)	105	116	113
Population density, rural (people/sq. km of arable land)	289	665	110
Forests and biodiversity			
Forest area (% of land area)	13.3	2.4	39.3
Deforestation (average annual %, 1990–2005)	-0.8	-0.4	0.2
Nationally protected area (% of land area)	0.4	3.6	10.3
Animal species, total known	447		
Animal species, threatened	40		
Higher plant species, total known	3,000		
Higher plant species, threatened	0		
GEF benefits index for biodiversity (0–100, median is 1.5)	0.2		
Energy			
GDP per unit of energy use (2005 PPP $/kg oil equivalent)	8.1	5.0	4.8
Energy use per capita (kg oil equivalent)	1,173	1,254	2,300
Energy from biomass products and waste (% of total)	2.7	1.2	7.0
Electric power consumption per capita (kWh)	2,141	1,418	3,242
Electricity generated using fossil fuel (% of total)	92.5	91.1	62.8
Electricity generated by hydropower (% of total)	7.5	7.4	27.6
Emissions and pollution			
CO_2 emissions per unit of GDP (kg/2005 PPP $)	0.4	0.6	0.5
CO_2 emissions per capita (metric tons)	4.2	3.7	5.5
CO_2 emissions growth (%, 1990–2005)	85.7	96.8	-8.3
Particulate matter (urban-pop.-weighted avg., μg/cu. m)	36	72	30
Transport sector fuel consumption per capita (liters)	359	277	332
Water and sanitation			
Internal freshwater resources per capita (cu. m)	1,172	728	16,993
Freshwater withdrawal			
Total (% of internal resources)	27.3	122.3	13.8
Agriculture (% of total freshwater withdrawal)	60	86	57
Access to improved water source (% of total population)	100	89	95
Rural (% of rural population)	100	81	83
Urban (% of urban population)	100	95	98
Access to improved sanitation (% of total population)	..	77	83
Rural (% of rural population)	..	62	64
Urban (% of urban population)	100	88	89
Environment and health			
Acute resp. infection prevalence (% of children under five)	4.0		
Diarrhea prevalence (% of children under five)	19.3		
Under-five mortality rate (per 1,000 live births)	29	38	24
National accounting aggregates			
Gross savings (% of GNI)	0.4	33.3	23.2
Consumption of fixed capital (% of GNI)	12.1	11.3	12.8
Education expenditure (% of GNI)	2.5	4.7	4.4
Energy depletion (% of GNI)	0.0	21.3	7.6
Mineral depletion (% of GNI)	0.0	0.4	1.3
Net forest depletion (% of GNI)	0.0	0.0	0.0
CO_2 damage (% of GNI)	0.5	1.0	0.6
Particulate emission damage (% of GNI)	0.8	0.6	0.4
Adjusted net savings (% of GNI)	-10.6	3.4	4.9

Lesotho

| | Population (millions) | **2.0** | Land area (1,000 sq. km) | **30.4** | GDP ($ billions) | **1.6** |

	Country data	Sub-Saharan Africa group	Lower middle-income group
GNI per capita, *World Bank Atlas* method ($)	1,030	951	1,905
Urban population (% of total)	25	36	42
Urban population growth (average annual %, 1990–2007)	4.7	4.0	2.9
Population growth (average annual %, 1990–2007)	1.3	2.6	1.3
Agriculture			
Agricultural land (% of land area)	77	44	47
Agricultural productivity (value added per worker, 2000 $)	427	287	532
Food production index (1999–2001 = 100)	106	109	116
Population density, rural (people/sq. km of arable land)	460	351	511
Forests and biodiversity			
Forest area (% of land area)	0.3	26.5	25.0
Deforestation (average annual %, 1990–2005)	-3.2	0.6	0.1
Nationally protected area (% of land area)	0.2	11.3	11.0
Animal species, total known	370		
Animal species, threatened	10		
Higher plant species, total known	1,591		
Higher plant species, threatened	1		
GEF benefits index for biodiversity (0–100, median is 1.5)	0.3		
Energy			
GDP per unit of energy use (2005 PPP $/kg oil equivalent)	..	3.0	3.9
Energy use per capita (kg oil equivalent)	..	670	1,019
Energy from biomass products and waste (% of total)	..	56.3	15.2
Electric power consumption per capita (kWh)	..	531	1,269
Electricity generated using fossil fuel (% of total)	..	65.6	79.0
Electricity generated by hydropower (% of total)	..	18.0	16.3
Emissions and pollution			
CO_2 emissions per unit of GDP (kg/2005 PPP $)	..	0.5	0.8
CO_2 emissions per capita (metric tons)	..	0.8	2.8
CO_2 emissions growth (%, 1990–2005)	..	40.1	93.5
Particulate matter (urban-pop.-weighted avg., µg/cu. m)	41	53	67
Transport sector fuel consumption per capita (liters)	..	64	99
Water and sanitation			
Internal freshwater resources per capita (cu. m)	2,607	4,824	4,117
Freshwater withdrawal			
Total (% of internal resources)	1.0	3.2	8.7
Agriculture (% of total freshwater withdrawal)	20	87	80
Access to improved water source (% of total population)	78	58	88
Rural (% of rural population)	74	46	82
Urban (% of urban population)	93	81	96
Access to improved sanitation (% of total population)	36	31	55
Rural (% of rural population)	34	24	43
Urban (% of urban population)	43	42	71
Environment and health			
Acute resp. infection prevalence (% of children under five)	18.7		
Diarrhea prevalence (% of children under five)	..		
Under-five mortality rate (per 1,000 live births)	84	146	50
National accounting aggregates			
Gross savings (% of GNI)	32.7	17.4	41.7
Consumption of fixed capital (% of GNI)	7.3	11.1	10.7
Education expenditure (% of GNI)	10.0	3.6	2.6
Energy depletion (% of GNI)	0.0	11.7	6.6
Mineral depletion (% of GNI)	0.0	1.5	1.2
Net forest depletion (% of GNI)	1.3	0.5	0.2
CO_2 damage (% of GNI)	..	0.7	1.2
Particulate emission damage (% of GNI)	0.2	0.4	1.1
Adjusted net savings (% of GNI)	..	-5.0	23.5

Liberia

	Country data	Sub-Saharan Africa group	Low-income group
Population (millions) **3.7** Land area (1,000 sq. km) **96.3** GDP ($ millions) **735**			

	Country data	Sub-Saharan Africa group	Low-income group
GNI per capita, *World Bank Atlas* method ($)	140	951	574
Urban population (% of total)	59	36	32
Urban population growth (average annual %, 1990–2007)	4.9	4.0	3.7
Population growth (average annual %, 1990–2007)	3.3	2.6	2.4
Agriculture			
Agricultural land (% of land area)	27	44	39
Agricultural productivity (value added per worker, 2000 $)	..	287	330
Food production index (1999–2001 = 100)	98	109	112
Population density, rural (people/sq. km of arable land)	378	351	603
Forests and biodiversity			
Forest area (% of land area)	32.7	26.5	24.7
Deforestation (average annual %, 1990–2005)	1.7	0.6	0.7
Nationally protected area (% of land area)	15.8	11.3	10.8
Animal species, total known	759		
Animal species, threatened	65		
Higher plant species, total known	2,200		
Higher plant species, threatened	46		
GEF benefits index for biodiversity (0–100, median is 1.5)	2.6		
Energy			
GDP per unit of energy use (2005 PPP $/kg oil equivalent)	..	3.0	3.2
Energy use per capita (kg oil equivalent)	..	670	478
Energy from biomass products and waste (% of total)	..	56.3	53.8
Electric power consumption per capita (kWh)	..	531	309
Electricity generated using fossil fuel (% of total)	..	65.6	48.4
Electricity generated by hydropower (% of total)	..	18.0	38.8
Emissions and pollution			
CO_2 emissions per unit of GDP (kg/2005 PPP $)	0.4	0.5	0.4
CO_2 emissions per capita (metric tons)	0.1	0.8	0.6
CO_2 emissions growth (%, 1990–2005)	1.6	40.1	39.3
Particulate matter (urban-pop.-weighted avg., µg/cu. m)	40	53	69
Transport sector fuel consumption per capita (liters)	..	64	41
Water and sanitation			
Internal freshwater resources per capita (cu. m)	53,852	4,824	4,619
Freshwater withdrawal			
Total (% of internal resources)	0.1	3.2	9.4
Agriculture (% of total freshwater withdrawal)	55	87	90
Access to improved water source (% of total population)	64	58	68
Rural (% of rural population)	52	46	60
Urban (% of urban population)	72	81	84
Access to improved sanitation (% of total population)	32	31	39
Rural (% of rural population)	7	24	33
Urban (% of urban population)	49	42	54
Environment and health			
Acute resp. infection prevalence (% of children under five)	39.0		
Diarrhea prevalence (% of children under five)	..		
Under-five mortality rate (per 1,000 live births)	133	146	126
National accounting aggregates			
Gross savings (% of GNI)	-19.3	17.4	25.4
Consumption of fixed capital (% of GNI)	9.4	11.1	9.3
Education expenditure (% of GNI)	..	3.6	2.6
Energy depletion (% of GNI)	0.0	11.7	9.8
Mineral depletion (% of GNI)	0.0	1.5	0.9
Net forest depletion (% of GNI)	6.6	0.5	0.8
CO_2 damage (% of GNI)	0.6	0.7	0.7
Particulate emission damage (% of GNI)	0.4	0.4	0.7
Adjusted net savings (% of GNI)	..	-5.0	5.8

Libya

| Population (millions) | **6.2** | Land area (1,000 sq. km) | **1,759.5** | GDP ($ billions) | **58.3** |

	Country data	Middle East & N. Africa group	Upper middle-income group
GNI per capita, *World Bank Atlas* method ($)	9,010	2,820	7,107
Urban population (% of total)	77	57	75
Urban population growth (average annual %, 1990–2007)	2.2	2.6	1.4
Population growth (average annual %, 1990–2007)	2.0	2.0	0.9
Agriculture			
Agricultural land (% of land area)	9	22	31
Agricultural productivity (value added per worker, 2000 $)	..	2,313	2,947
Food production index (1999–2001 = 100)	100	116	113
Population density, rural (people/sq. km of arable land)	78	665	110
Forests and biodiversity			
Forest area (% of land area)	0.1	2.4	39.3
Deforestation (average annual %, 1990–2005)	0.0	-0.4	0.2
Nationally protected area (% of land area)	0.1	3.6	10.3
Animal species, total known	413		
Animal species, threatened	35		
Higher plant species, total known	1,825		
Higher plant species, threatened	1		
GEF benefits index for biodiversity (0–100, median is 1.5)	1.6		
Energy			
GDP per unit of energy use (2005 PPP $/kg oil equivalent)	4.4	5.0	4.8
Energy use per capita (kg oil equivalent)	2,943	1,254	2,300
Energy from biomass products and waste (% of total)	0.9	1.2	7.0
Electric power consumption per capita (kWh)	3,688	1,418	3,242
Electricity generated using fossil fuel (% of total)	100.0	91.1	62.8
Electricity generated by hydropower (% of total)	0.0	7.4	27.6
Emissions and pollution			
CO_2 emissions per unit of GDP (kg/2005 PPP $)	0.8	0.6	0.5
CO_2 emissions per capita (metric tons)	9.5	3.7	5.5
CO_2 emissions growth (%, 1990–2005)	48.5	96.8	-8.3
Particulate matter (urban-pop.-weighted avg., µg/cu. m)	88	72	30
Transport sector fuel consumption per capita (liters)	591	277	332
Water and sanitation			
Internal freshwater resources per capita (cu. m)	97	728	16,993
Freshwater withdrawal			
Total (% of internal resources)	721.0	122.3	13.8
Agriculture (% of total freshwater withdrawal)	83	86	57
Access to improved water source (% of total population)	..	89	95
Rural (% of rural population)	..	81	83
Urban (% of urban population)	..	95	98
Access to improved sanitation (% of total population)	97	77	83
Rural (% of rural population)	96	62	64
Urban (% of urban population)	97	88	89
Environment and health			
Acute resp. infection prevalence (% of children under five)	4.3		
Diarrhea prevalence (% of children under five)	16.9		
Under-five mortality rate (per 1,000 live births)	18	38	24
National accounting aggregates			
Gross savings (% of GNI)	..	33.3	23.2
Consumption of fixed capital (% of GNI)	12.4	11.3	12.8
Education expenditure (% of GNI)	..	4.7	4.4
Energy depletion (% of GNI)	45.1	21.3	7.6
Mineral depletion (% of GNI)	0.0	0.4	1.3
Net forest depletion (% of GNI)	0.0	0.0	0.0
CO_2 damage (% of GNI)	0.9	1.0	0.6
Particulate emission damage (% of GNI)	..	0.6	0.4
Adjusted net savings (% of GNI)	..	3.4	4.9

Liechtenstein

Population (thousands) **35**	Land area (sq. km) **160**	GDP ($ millions) ..

	Country data	High-income group
GNI per capita, *World Bank Atlas* method ($)	..	37,572
Urban population (% of total)	14	78
Urban population growth (average annual %, 1990–2007)	..	1.0
Population growth (average annual %, 1990–2007)	..	0.7
Agriculture		
Agricultural land (% of land area)	44	38
Agricultural productivity (value added per worker, 2000 $)	..	27,680
Food production index (1999–2001 = 100)	100	102
Population density, rural (people/sq. km of arable land)	743	323
Forests and biodiversity		
Forest area (% of land area)	43.1	28.8
Deforestation (average annual %, 1990–2005)	-1.0	-0.1
Nationally protected area (% of land area)	40.0	11.8
Animal species, total known	297	
Animal species, threatened	4	
Higher plant species, total known	1,410	
Higher plant species, threatened	0	
GEF benefits index for biodiversity (0–100, median is 1.5)	0.0	
Energy		
GDP per unit of energy use (2005 PPP $/kg oil equivalent)	..	6.3
Energy use per capita (kg oil equivalent)	..	5,416
Energy from biomass products and waste (% of total)	..	3.4
Electric power consumption per capita (kWh)	..	9,675
Electricity generated using fossil fuel (% of total)	..	62.0
Electricity generated by hydropower (% of total)	..	11.4
Emissions and pollution		
CO_2 emissions per unit of GDP (kg/2005 PPP $)	..	0.4
CO_2 emissions per capita (metric tons)	..	12.6
CO_2 emissions growth (%, 1990–2005)	..	19.1
Particulate matter (urban-pop.-weighted avg., µg/cu. m)	32	26
Transport sector fuel consumption per capita (liters)	..	1,159
Water and sanitation		
Internal freshwater resources per capita (cu. m)	..	9,313
Freshwater withdrawal		
Total (% of internal resources)	..	10.4
Agriculture (% of total freshwater withdrawal)	..	43
Access to improved water source (% of total population)	..	100
Rural (% of rural population)	..	98
Urban (% of urban population)	..	100
Access to improved sanitation (% of total population)	..	100
Rural (% of rural population)	..	99
Urban (% of urban population)	..	100
Environment and health		
Acute resp. infection prevalence (% of children under five)	..	
Diarrhea prevalence (% of children under five)	..	
Under-five mortality rate (per 1,000 live births)	3	7
National accounting aggregates		
Gross savings (% of GNI)	..	20.6
Consumption of fixed capital (% of GNI)	..	14.5
Education expenditure (% of GNI)	..	4.6
Energy depletion (% of GNI)	..	1.5
Mineral depletion (% of GNI)	..	0.2
Net forest depletion (% of GNI)	..	0.0
CO_2 damage (% of GNI)	..	0.3
Particulate emission damage (% of GNI)	..	0.3
Adjusted net savings (% of GNI)	..	8.5

Lithuania

Population (millions)	3.4	Land area (1,000 sq. km)	62.7	GDP ($ billions)	38.3

	Country data	Europe & Central Asia group	Upper middle-income group
GNI per capita, *World Bank Atlas* method ($)	9,770	6,052	7,107
Urban population (% of total)	67	64	75
Urban population growth (average annual %, 1990–2007)	-0.6	0.2	1.4
Population growth (average annual %, 1990–2007)	-0.5	0.1	0.9
Agriculture			
Agricultural land (% of land area)	45	28	31
Agricultural productivity (value added per worker, 2000 $)	5,020	2,228	2,947
Food production index (1999–2001 = 100)	96	110	113
Population density, rural (people/sq. km of arable land)	60	129	110
Forests and biodiversity			
Forest area (% of land area)	33.5	38.3	39.3
Deforestation (average annual %, 1990–2005)	-0.5	0.0	0.2
Nationally protected area (% of land area)	5.7	6.1	10.3
Animal species, total known	298		
Animal species, threatened	19		
Higher plant species, total known	1,796		
Higher plant species, threatened	..		
GEF benefits index for biodiversity (0–100, median is 1.5)	0.0		
Energy			
GDP per unit of energy use (2005 PPP $/kg oil equivalent)	6.1	3.5	4.8
Energy use per capita (kg oil equivalent)	2,517	2,930	2,300
Energy from biomass products and waste (% of total)	8.8	2.2	7.0
Electric power consumption per capita (kWh)	3,233	3,835	3,242
Electricity generated using fossil fuel (% of total)	22.1	67.7	62.8
Electricity generated by hydropower (% of total)	3.3	17.4	27.6
Emissions and pollution			
CO_2 emissions per unit of GDP (kg/2005 PPP $)	0.3	0.7	0.5
CO_2 emissions per capita (metric tons)	4.1	7.0	5.5
CO_2 emissions growth (%, 1990–2005)	-42.8	-29.3	-8.3
Particulate matter (urban-pop.-weighted avg., μg/cu. m)	19	27	30
Transport sector fuel consumption per capita (liters)	403	255	332
Water and sanitation			
Internal freshwater resources per capita (cu. m)	4,610	11,806	16,993
Freshwater withdrawal			
Total (% of internal resources)	1.7	7.2	13.8
Agriculture (% of total freshwater withdrawal)	7	60	57
Access to improved water source (% of total population)	..	95	95
Rural (% of rural population)	..	88	83
Urban (% of urban population)	..	99	98
Access to improved sanitation (% of total population)	..	89	83
Rural (% of rural population)	..	79	64
Urban (% of urban population)	..	94	89
Environment and health			
Acute resp. infection prevalence (% of children under five)	..		
Diarrhea prevalence (% of children under five)	..		
Under-five mortality rate (per 1,000 live births)	8	23	24
National accounting aggregates			
Gross savings (% of GNI)	17.0	24.0	23.2
Consumption of fixed capital (% of GNI)	13.5	12.8	12.8
Education expenditure (% of GNI)	4.8	4.0	4.4
Energy depletion (% of GNI)	0.1	9.8	7.6
Mineral depletion (% of GNI)	0.0	0.7	1.3
Net forest depletion (% of GNI)	0.1	0.0	0.0
CO_2 damage (% of GNI)	0.3	1.0	0.6
Particulate emission damage (% of GNI)	0.2	0.5	0.4
Adjusted net savings (% of GNI)	7.6	3.2	4.9

Luxembourg

	Population (thousands) **480**	Land area (1,000 sq. km)	**2.6**	GDP ($ billions)	**49.5**

	Country data	High-income group
GNI per capita, *World Bank Atlas* method ($)	72,430	37,572
Urban population (% of total)	83	78
Urban population growth (average annual %, 1990–2007)	1.5	1.0
Population growth (average annual %, 1990–2007)	1.3	0.7
Agriculture		
Agricultural land (% of land area)	50	38
Agricultural productivity (value added per worker, 2000 $)	30,035	27,680
Food production index (1999–2001 = 100)	98	102
Population density, rural (people/sq. km of arable land)	131	323
Forests and biodiversity		
Forest area (% of land area)	33.5	28.8
Deforestation (average annual %, 1990–2005)	–0.1	–0.1
Nationally protected area (% of land area)	16.6	11.8
Animal species, total known	350	
Animal species, threatened	5	
Higher plant species, total known	1,246	
Higher plant species, threatened	0	
GEF benefits index for biodiversity (0–100, median is 1.5)	0.0	
Energy		
GDP per unit of energy use (2005 PPP $/kg oil equivalent)	7.1	6.3
Energy use per capita (kg oil equivalent)	9,972	5,416
Energy from biomass products and waste (% of total)	1.3	3.4
Electric power consumption per capita (kWh)	16,414	9,675
Electricity generated using fossil fuel (% of total)	92.1	62.0
Electricity generated by hydropower (% of total)	3.1	11.4
Emissions and pollution		
CO_2 emissions per unit of GDP (kg/2005 PPP $)	0.4	0.4
CO_2 emissions per capita (metric tons)	24.8	12.6
CO_2 emissions growth (%, 1990–2005)	14.3	19.1
Particulate matter (urban-pop.-weighted avg., µg/cu. m)	15	26
Transport sector fuel consumption per capita (liters)	5,382	1,159
Water and sanitation		
Internal freshwater resources per capita (cu. m)	2,083	9,313
Freshwater withdrawal		
Total (% of internal resources)	..	10.4
Agriculture (% of total freshwater withdrawal)	..	43
Access to improved water source (% of total population)	100	100
Rural (% of rural population)	100	98
Urban (% of urban population)	100	100
Access to improved sanitation (% of total population)	100	100
Rural (% of rural population)	100	99
Urban (% of urban population)	100	100
Environment and health		
Acute resp. infection prevalence (% of children under five)	..	
Diarrhea prevalence (% of children under five)	..	
Under-five mortality rate (per 1,000 live births)	3	7
National accounting aggregates		
Gross savings (% of GNI)	..	20.6
Consumption of fixed capital (% of GNI)	..	14.5
Education expenditure (% of GNI)	3.7	4.6
Energy depletion (% of GNI)	..	1.5
Mineral depletion (% of GNI)	..	0.2
Net forest depletion (% of GNI)	..	0.0
CO_2 damage (% of GNI)	..	0.3
Particulate emission damage (% of GNI)	..	0.3
Adjusted net savings (% of GNI)	..	8.5

Macao, China

| | Population (thousands) **480** Land area (sq. km) | **28** | GDP ($ billions) | **14.2** |

	Country data	High-income group
GNI per capita, *World Bank Atlas* method ($)	14,020	37,572
Urban population (% of total)	100	78
Urban population growth (average annual %, 1990–2007)	1.5	1.0
Population growth (average annual %, 1990–2007)	1.5	0.7
Agriculture		
Agricultural land (% of land area)	..	38
Agricultural productivity (value added per worker, 2000 $)	..	27,680
Food production index (1999–2001 = 100)	..	102
Population density, rural (people/sq. km of arable land)	..	323
Forests and biodiversity		
Forest area (% of land area)	..	28.8
Deforestation (average annual %, 1990–2005)	..	–0.1
Nationally protected area (% of land area)	..	11.8
Animal species, total known	60	
Animal species, threatened	10	
Higher plant species, total known	..	
Higher plant species, threatened	..	
GEF benefits index for biodiversity (0–100, median is 1.5)	..	
Energy		
GDP per unit of energy use (2005 PPP $/kg oil equivalent)	..	6.3
Energy use per capita (kg oil equivalent)	..	5,416
Energy from biomass products and waste (% of total)	..	3.4
Electric power consumption per capita (kWh)	..	9,675
Electricity generated using fossil fuel (% of total)	..	62.0
Electricity generated by hydropower (% of total)	..	11.4
Emissions and pollution		
CO_2 emissions per unit of GDP (kg/2005 PPP $)	0.1	0.4
CO_2 emissions per capita (metric tons)	4.7	12.6
CO_2 emissions growth (%, 1990–2005)	117.9	19.1
Particulate matter (urban-pop.-weighted avg., µg/cu. m)	48	26
Transport sector fuel consumption per capita (liters)	..	1,159
Water and sanitation		
Internal freshwater resources per capita (cu. m)	..	9,313
Freshwater withdrawal		
Total (% of internal resources)	..	10.4
Agriculture (% of total freshwater withdrawal)	..	43
Access to improved water source (% of total population)	..	100
Rural (% of rural population)	..	98
Urban (% of urban population)	..	100
Access to improved sanitation (% of total population)	..	100
Rural (% of rural population)	..	99
Urban (% of urban population)	..	100
Environment and health		
Acute resp. infection prevalence (% of children under five)	..	
Diarrhea prevalence (% of children under five)	..	
Under-five mortality rate (per 1,000 live births)	..	7
National accounting aggregates		
Gross savings (% of GNI)	..	20.6
Consumption of fixed capital (% of GNI)	..	14.5
Education expenditure (% of GNI)	..	4.6
Energy depletion (% of GNI)	..	1.5
Mineral depletion (% of GNI)	..	0.2
Net forest depletion (% of GNI)	..	0.0
CO_2 damage (% of GNI)	..	0.3
Particulate emission damage (% of GNI)	..	0.3
Adjusted net savings (% of GNI)	..	8.5

Macedonia, FYR

Population (millions)	**2.0**	Land area (1,000 sq. km)	**25.4**	GDP ($ billions)	**7.7**

	Country data	Europe & Central Asia group	Lower middle-income group
GNI per capita, *World Bank Atlas* method ($)	3,470	6,052	1,905
Urban population (% of total)	66	64	42
Urban population growth (average annual %, 1990–2007)	1.2	0.2	2.9
Population growth (average annual %, 1990–2007)	0.4	0.1	1.3
Agriculture			
Agricultural land (% of land area)	49	28	47
Agricultural productivity (value added per worker, 2000 $)	3,739	2,228	532
Food production index (1999–2001 = 100)	103	110	116
Population density, rural (people/sq. km of arable land)	124	129	511
Forests and biodiversity			
Forest area (% of land area)	35.6	38.3	25.0
Deforestation (average annual %, 1990–2005)	0.0	0.0	0.1
Nationally protected area (% of land area)	7.1	6.1	11.0
Animal species, total known	380		
Animal species, threatened	36		
Higher plant species, total known	3,500		
Higher plant species, threatened	0		
GEF benefits index for biodiversity (0–100, median is 1.5)	0.2		
Energy			
GDP per unit of energy use (2005 PPP $/kg oil equivalent)	5.9	3.5	3.9
Energy use per capita (kg oil equivalent)	1,355	2,930	1,019
Energy from biomass products and waste (% of total)	6.0	2.2	15.2
Electric power consumption per capita (kWh)	3,495	3,835	1,269
Electricity generated using fossil fuel (% of total)	76.4	67.7	79.0
Electricity generated by hydropower (% of total)	23.6	17.4	16.3
Emissions and pollution			
CO_2 emissions per unit of GDP (kg/2005 PPP $)	0.7	0.7	0.8
CO_2 emissions per capita (metric tons)	5.1	7.0	2.8
CO_2 emissions growth (%, 1990–2005)	-34.0	-29.3	93.5
Particulate matter (urban-pop.-weighted avg., μg/cu. m)	21	27	67
Transport sector fuel consumption per capita (liters)	171	255	99
Water and sanitation			
Internal freshwater resources per capita (cu. m)	2,651	11,806	4,117
Freshwater withdrawal			
Total (% of internal resources)	..	7.2	8.7
Agriculture (% of total freshwater withdrawal)	..	60	80
Access to improved water source (% of total population)	100	95	88
Rural (% of rural population)	99	88	82
Urban (% of urban population)	100	99	96
Access to improved sanitation (% of total population)	89	89	55
Rural (% of rural population)	81	79	43
Urban (% of urban population)	92	94	71
Environment and health			
Acute resp. infection prevalence (% of children under five)	..		
Diarrhea prevalence (% of children under five)	..		
Under-five mortality rate (per 1,000 live births)	17	23	50
National accounting aggregates			
Gross savings (% of GNI)	21.1	24.0	41.7
Consumption of fixed capital (% of GNI)	11.4	12.8	10.7
Education expenditure (% of GNI)	4.9	4.0	2.6
Energy depletion (% of GNI)	0.0	9.8	6.6
Mineral depletion (% of GNI)	0.0	0.7	1.2
Net forest depletion (% of GNI)	0.2	0.0	0.2
CO_2 damage (% of GNI)	1.2	1.0	1.2
Particulate emission damage (% of GNI)	0.1	0.5	1.1
Adjusted net savings (% of GNI)	13.1	3.2	23.5

Madagascar

Population (millions)	**20**	Land area (1,000 sq. km)	**582**	GDP ($ billions)	**7.4**

	Country data	Sub-Saharan Africa group	Low-income group
GNI per capita, *World Bank Atlas* method ($)	320	951	574
Urban population (% of total)	29	36	32
Urban population growth (average annual %, 1990–2007)	4.1	4.0	3.7
Population growth (average annual %, 1990–2007)	2.9	2.6	2.4
Agriculture			
Agricultural land (% of land area)	70	44	39
Agricultural productivity (value added per worker, 2000 $)	175	287	330
Food production index (1999–2001 = 100)	107	109	112
Population density, rural (people/sq. km of arable land)	452	351	603
Forests and biodiversity			
Forest area (% of land area)	22.1	26.5	24.7
Deforestation (average annual %, 1990–2005)	0.4	0.6	0.7
Nationally protected area (% of land area)	2.6	11.3	10.8
Animal species, total known	427		
Animal species, threatened	355		
Higher plant species, total known	9,505		
Higher plant species, threatened	281		
GEF benefits index for biodiversity (0–100, median is 1.5)	29.2		
Energy			
GDP per unit of energy use (2005 PPP $/kg oil equivalent)	..	3.0	3.2
Energy use per capita (kg oil equivalent)	..	670	478
Energy from biomass products and waste (% of total)	..	56.3	53.8
Electric power consumption per capita (kWh)	..	531	309
Electricity generated using fossil fuel (% of total)	..	65.6	48.4
Electricity generated by hydropower (% of total)	..	18.0	38.8
Emissions and pollution			
CO_2 emissions per unit of GDP (kg/2005 PPP $)	0.2	0.5	0.4
CO_2 emissions per capita (metric tons)	0.2	0.8	0.6
CO_2 emissions growth (%, 1990–2005)	198.8	40.1	39.3
Particulate matter (urban-pop.-weighted avg., µg/cu. m)	34	53	69
Transport sector fuel consumption per capita (liters)	..	64	41
Water and sanitation			
Internal freshwater resources per capita (cu. m)	17,133	4,824	4,619
Freshwater withdrawal			
Total (% of internal resources)	4.4	3.2	9.4
Agriculture (% of total freshwater withdrawal)	96	87	90
Access to improved water source (% of total population)	47	58	68
Rural (% of rural population)	36	46	60
Urban (% of urban population)	76	81	84
Access to improved sanitation (% of total population)	12	31	39
Rural (% of rural population)	10	24	33
Urban (% of urban population)	18	42	54
Environment and health			
Acute resp. infection prevalence (% of children under five)	9.0		
Diarrhea prevalence (% of children under five)	12.8		
Under-five mortality rate (per 1,000 live births)	112	146	126
National accounting aggregates			
Gross savings (% of GNI)	13.4	17.4	25.4
Consumption of fixed capital (% of GNI)	8.2	11.1	9.3
Education expenditure (% of GNI)	3.1	3.6	2.6
Energy depletion (% of GNI)	0.0	11.7	9.8
Mineral depletion (% of GNI)	0.0	1.5	0.9
Net forest depletion (% of GNI)	0.2	0.5	0.8
CO_2 damage (% of GNI)	0.3	0.7	0.7
Particulate emission damage (% of GNI)	0.2	0.4	0.7
Adjusted net savings (% of GNI)	7.7	–5.0	5.8

Malawi

| | Population (millions) | **14** | Land area (1,000 sq. km) | **94** | GDP ($ billions) | **3.6** |

	Country data	Sub-Saharan Africa group	Low-income group
GNI per capita, *World Bank Atlas* method ($)	250	951	574
Urban population (% of total)	18	36	32
Urban population growth (average annual %, 1990–2007)	5.0	4.0	3.7
Population growth (average annual %, 1990–2007)	2.3	2.6	2.4
Agriculture			
Agricultural land (% of land area)	49	44	39
Agricultural productivity (value added per worker, 2000 $)	109	287	330
Food production index (1999–2001 = 100)	100	109	112
Population density, rural (people/sq. km of arable land)	421	351	603
Forests and biodiversity			
Forest area (% of land area)	36.2	26.5	24.7
Deforestation (average annual %, 1990–2005)	0.9	0.6	0.7
Nationally protected area (% of land area)	19.5	11.3	10.8
Animal species, total known	865		
Animal species, threatened	140		
Higher plant species, total known	3,765		
Higher plant species, threatened	14		
GEF benefits index for biodiversity (0–100, median is 1.5)	3.5		
Energy			
GDP per unit of energy use (2005 PPP $/kg oil equivalent)	..	3.0	3.2
Energy use per capita (kg oil equivalent)	..	670	478
Energy from biomass products and waste (% of total)	..	56.3	53.8
Electric power consumption per capita (kWh)	..	531	309
Electricity generated using fossil fuel (% of total)	..	65.6	48.4
Electricity generated by hydropower (% of total)	..	18.0	38.8
Emissions and pollution			
CO_2 emissions per unit of GDP (kg/2005 PPP $)	0.1	0.5	0.4
CO_2 emissions per capita (metric tons)	0.08	0.85	0.58
CO_2 emissions growth (%, 1990–2005)	65.2	40.1	39.3
Particulate matter (urban-pop.-weighted avg., µg/cu. m)	33	53	69
Transport sector fuel consumption per capita (liters)	..	64	41
Water and sanitation			
Internal freshwater resources per capita (cu. m)	1,159	4,824	4,619
Freshwater withdrawal			
Total (% of internal resources)	6.3	3.2	9.4
Agriculture (% of total freshwater withdrawal)	80	87	90
Access to improved water source (% of total population)	76	58	68
Rural (% of rural population)	72	46	60
Urban (% of urban population)	96	81	84
Access to improved sanitation (% of total population)	60	31	39
Rural (% of rural population)	62	24	33
Urban (% of urban population)	51	42	54
Environment and health			
Acute resp. infection prevalence (% of children under five)	27.0		
Diarrhea prevalence (% of children under five)	17.6		
Under-five mortality rate (per 1,000 live births)	111	146	126
National accounting aggregates			
Gross savings (% of GNI)	9.6	17.4	25.4
Consumption of fixed capital (% of GNI)	7.6	11.1	9.3
Education expenditure (% of GNI)	3.5	3.6	2.6
Energy depletion (% of GNI)	0.0	11.7	9.8
Mineral depletion (% of GNI)	0.0	1.5	0.9
Net forest depletion (% of GNI)	0.8	0.5	0.8
CO_2 damage (% of GNI)	0.3	0.7	0.7
Particulate emission damage (% of GNI)	0.2	0.4	0.7
Adjusted net savings (% of GNI)	4.3	–5.0	5.8

Malaysia

| | Population (millions) | **27** | Land area (1,000 sq. km) | **329** | GDP ($ billions) | **186.7** |

	Country data	East Asia & Pacific group	Upper middle-income group
GNI per capita, *World Bank Atlas* method ($)	6,420	2,182	7,107
Urban population (% of total)	69	43	75
Urban population growth (average annual %, 1990–2007)	4.2	3.5	1.4
Population growth (average annual %, 1990–2007)	2.3	1.1	0.9
Agriculture			
Agricultural land (% of land area)	24	51	31
Agricultural productivity (value added per worker, 2000 $)	551	458	2,947
Food production index (1999–2001 = 100)	126	120	113
Population density, rural (people/sq. km of arable land)	462	547	110
Forests and biodiversity			
Forest area (% of land area)	63.6	28.4	39.3
Deforestation (average annual %, 1990–2005)	0.5	–0.1	0.2
Nationally protected area (% of land area)	18.2	14.0	10.3
Animal species, total known	1,083		
Animal species, threatened	455		
Higher plant species, total known	15,500		
Higher plant species, threatened	686		
GEF benefits index for biodiversity (0–100, median is 1.5)	13.9		
Energy			
GDP per unit of energy use (2005 PPP $/kg oil equivalent)	4.7	3.4	4.8
Energy use per capita (kg oil equivalent)	2,617	1,258	2,300
Energy from biomass products and waste (% of total)	4.1	14.7	7.0
Electric power consumption per capita (kWh)	3,388	1,669	3,242
Electricity generated using fossil fuel (% of total)	92.3	82.0	62.8
Electricity generated by hydropower (% of total)	7.7	15.0	27.6
Emissions and pollution			
CO_2 emissions per unit of GDP (kg/2005 PPP $)	0.8	0.9	0.5
CO_2 emissions per capita (metric tons)	9.3	3.6	5.5
CO_2 emissions growth (%, 1990–2005)	333.9	123.4	–8.3
Particulate matter (urban-pop.-weighted avg., µg/cu. m)	23	69	30
Transport sector fuel consumption per capita (liters)	567	106	332
Water and sanitation			
Internal freshwater resources per capita (cu. m)	21,846	4,948	16,993
Freshwater withdrawal			
Total (% of internal resources)	1.6	10.2	13.8
Agriculture (% of total freshwater withdrawal)	62	74	57
Access to improved water source (% of total population)	99	87	95
Rural (% of rural population)	96	81	83
Urban (% of urban population)	100	96	98
Access to improved sanitation (% of total population)	94	66	83
Rural (% of rural population)	93	59	64
Urban (% of urban population)	95	75	89
Environment and health			
Acute resp. infection prevalence (% of children under five)	..		
Diarrhea prevalence (% of children under five)	..		
Under-five mortality rate (per 1,000 live births)	11	27	24
National accounting aggregates			
Gross savings (% of GNI)	38.4	48.0	23.2
Consumption of fixed capital (% of GNI)	12.5	10.7	12.8
Education expenditure (% of GNI)	5.5	2.1	4.4
Energy depletion (% of GNI)	10.3	4.9	7.6
Mineral depletion (% of GNI)	0.1	1.3	1.3
Net forest depletion (% of GNI)	0.0	0.0	0.0
CO_2 damage (% of GNI)	0.8	1.3	0.6
Particulate emission damage (% of GNI)	0.1	1.3	0.4
Adjusted net savings (% of GNI)	20.2	30.6	4.9

Maldives

| Population (thousands) **305** | Land area (sq. km) | **300** | GDP ($ billions) | **1.1** |

	Country data	South Asia group	Lower middle-income group
GNI per capita, *World Bank Atlas* method ($)	3,190	880	1,905
Urban population (% of total)	37	29	42
Urban population growth (average annual %, 1990–2007)	4.1	2.7	2.9
Population growth (average annual %, 1990–2007)	2.0	1.8	1.3
Agriculture			
Agricultural land (% of land area)	47	55	47
Agricultural productivity (value added per worker, 2000 $)	..	417	532
Food production index (1999–2001 = 100)	92	107	116
Population density, rural (people/sq. km of arable land)	4,880	617	511
Forests and biodiversity			
Forest area (% of land area)	3.0	16.8	25.0
Deforestation (average annual %, 1990–2005)	0.0	–0.1	0.1
Nationally protected area (% of land area)	..	5.6	11.0
Animal species, total known	181		
Animal species, threatened	55		
Higher plant species, total known	583		
Higher plant species, threatened	..		
GEF benefits index for biodiversity (0–100, median is 1.5)	1.4		
Energy			
GDP per unit of energy use (2005 PPP $/kg oil equivalent)	..	4.8	3.9
Energy use per capita (kg oil equivalent)	..	468	1,019
Energy from biomass products and waste (% of total)	..	30.4	15.2
Electric power consumption per capita (kWh)	..	453	1,269
Electricity generated using fossil fuel (% of total)	..	78.3	79.0
Electricity generated by hydropower (% of total)	..	17.4	16.3
Emissions and pollution			
CO_2 emissions per unit of GDP (kg/2005 PPP $)	0.6	0.5	0.8
CO_2 emissions per capita (metric tons)	2.4	1.1	2.8
CO_2 emissions growth (%, 1990–2005)	364.3	106.7	93.5
Particulate matter (urban-pop.-weighted avg., µg/cu. m)	32	78	67
Transport sector fuel consumption per capita (liters)	..	33	99
Water and sanitation			
Internal freshwater resources per capita (cu. m)	98	1,196	4,117
Freshwater withdrawal			
Total (% of internal resources)	..	51.7	8.7
Agriculture (% of total freshwater withdrawal)	..	89	80
Access to improved water source (% of total population)	83	87	88
Rural (% of rural population)	76	84	82
Urban (% of urban population)	98	94	96
Access to improved sanitation (% of total population)	59	33	55
Rural (% of rural population)	42	23	43
Urban (% of urban population)	100	57	71
Environment and health			
Acute resp. infection prevalence (% of children under five)	22.0		
Diarrhea prevalence (% of children under five)	7.9		
Under-five mortality rate (per 1,000 live births)	30	78	50
National accounting aggregates			
Gross savings (% of GNI)	..	36.2	41.7
Consumption of fixed capital (% of GNI)	11.9	9.5	10.7
Education expenditure (% of GNI)	6.5	3.0	2.6
Energy depletion (% of GNI)	0.0	2.7	6.6
Mineral depletion (% of GNI)	0.0	0.6	1.2
Net forest depletion (% of GNI)	0.0	0.9	0.2
CO_2 damage (% of GNI)	0.6	1.0	1.2
Particulate emission damage (% of GNI)	0.3	0.8	1.1
Adjusted net savings (% of GNI)	..	23.9	23.5

Mali

Population (millions)	12	Land area (1,000 sq. km)	**1,220**	GDP ($ billions)	**6.9**

	Country data	Sub-Saharan Africa group	Low-income group
GNI per capita, *World Bank Atlas* method ($)	500	951	574
Urban population (% of total)	32	36	32
Urban population growth (average annual %, 1990–2007)	4.6	4.0	3.7
Population growth (average annual %, 1990–2007)	2.8	2.6	2.4
Agriculture			
Agricultural land (% of land area)	32	44	39
Agricultural productivity (value added per worker, 2000 $)	244	287	330
Food production index (1999–2001 = 100)	117	109	112
Population density, rural (people/sq. km of arable land)	168	351	603
Forests and biodiversity			
Forest area (% of land area)	10.3	26.5	24.7
Deforestation (average annual %, 1990–2005)	0.7	0.6	0.7
Nationally protected area (% of land area)	2.1	11.3	10.8
Animal species, total known	758		
Animal species, threatened	19		
Higher plant species, total known	1,741		
Higher plant species, threatened	6		
GEF benefits index for biodiversity (0–100, median is 1.5)	1.5		
Energy			
GDP per unit of energy use (2005 PPP $/kg oil equivalent)	..	3.0	3.2
Energy use per capita (kg oil equivalent)	..	670	478
Energy from biomass products and waste (% of total)	..	56.3	53.8
Electric power consumption per capita (kWh)	..	531	309
Electricity generated using fossil fuel (% of total)	..	65.6	48.4
Electricity generated by hydropower (% of total)	..	18.0	38.8
Emissions and pollution			
CO_2 emissions per unit of GDP (kg/2005 PPP $)	0.05	0.49	0.39
CO_2 emissions per capita (metric tons)	0.05	0.85	0.58
CO_2 emissions growth (%, 1990–2005)	33.9	40.1	39.3
Particulate matter (urban-pop.-weighted avg., µg/cu. m)	152	53	69
Transport sector fuel consumption per capita (liters)	..	64	41
Water and sanitation			
Internal freshwater resources per capita (cu. m)	4,865	4,824	4,619
Freshwater withdrawal			
Total (% of internal resources)	10.9	3.2	9.4
Agriculture (% of total freshwater withdrawal)	90	87	90
Access to improved water source (% of total population)	60	58	68
Rural (% of rural population)	48	46	60
Urban (% of urban population)	86	81	84
Access to improved sanitation (% of total population)	45	31	39
Rural (% of rural population)	39	24	33
Urban (% of urban population)	59	42	54
Environment and health			
Acute resp. infection prevalence (% of children under five)	10.0		
Diarrhea prevalence (% of children under five)	18.6		
Under-five mortality rate (per 1,000 live births)	196	146	126
National accounting aggregates			
Gross savings (% of GNI)	13.6	17.4	25.4
Consumption of fixed capital (% of GNI)	9.0	11.1	9.3
Education expenditure (% of GNI)	3.6	3.6	2.6
Energy depletion (% of GNI)	0.0	11.7	9.8
Mineral depletion (% of GNI)	0.0	1.5	0.9
Net forest depletion (% of GNI)	0.0	0.5	0.8
CO_2 damage (% of GNI)	0.1	0.7	0.7
Particulate emission damage (% of GNI)	1.6	0.4	0.7
Adjusted net savings (% of GNI)	6.5	−5.0	5.8

Malta

| Population (thousands) **409** | Land area (sq. km) | **320** | GDP ($ billions) | **7.4** |

	Country data	High-income group
GNI per capita, *World Bank Atlas* method ($)	16,680	37,572
Urban population (% of total)	94	78
Urban population growth (average annual %, 1990–2007)	1.0	1.0
Population growth (average annual %, 1990–2007)	0.8	0.7
Agriculture		
Agricultural land (% of land area)	31	38
Agricultural productivity (value added per worker, 2000 $)	..	27,680
Food production index (1999–2001 = 100)	96	102
Population density, rural (people/sq. km of arable land)	287	323
Forests and biodiversity		
Forest area (% of land area)	0.9	28.8
Deforestation (average annual %, 1990–2005)	..	-0.1
Nationally protected area (% of land area)	14.1	11.8
Animal species, total known	391	
Animal species, threatened	22	
Higher plant species, total known	914	
Higher plant species, threatened	3	
GEF benefits index for biodiversity (0–100, median is 1.5)	0.0	
Energy		
GDP per unit of energy use (2005 PPP $/kg oil equivalent)	9.9	6.3
Energy use per capita (kg oil equivalent)	2,153	5,416
Energy from biomass products and waste (% of total)	0.0	3.4
Electric power consumption per capita (kWh)	4,970	9,675
Electricity generated using fossil fuel (% of total)	100.0	62.0
Electricity generated by hydropower (% of total)	0.0	11.4
Emissions and pollution		
CO_2 emissions per unit of GDP (kg/2005 PPP $)	0.3	0.4
CO_2 emissions per capita (metric tons)	6.3	12.6
CO_2 emissions growth (%, 1990–2005)	14.3	19.1
Particulate matter (urban-pop.-weighted avg., μg/cu. m)	..	26
Transport sector fuel consumption per capita (liters)	489	1,159
Water and sanitation		
Internal freshwater resources per capita (cu. m)	123	9,313
Freshwater withdrawal		
Total (% of internal resources)	100.0	10.4
Agriculture (% of total freshwater withdrawal)	20	43
Access to improved water source (% of total population)	100	100
Rural (% of rural population)	100	98
Urban (% of urban population)	100	100
Access to improved sanitation (% of total population)	..	100
Rural (% of rural population)	..	99
Urban (% of urban population)	100	100
Environment and health		
Acute resp. infection prevalence (% of children under five)	..	
Diarrhea prevalence (% of children under five)	..	
Under-five mortality rate (per 1,000 live births)	5	7
National accounting aggregates		
Gross savings (% of GNI)	..	20.6
Consumption of fixed capital (% of GNI)	14.0	14.5
Education expenditure (% of GNI)	4.6	4.6
Energy depletion (% of GNI)	0.0	1.5
Mineral depletion (% of GNI)	0.0	0.2
Net forest depletion (% of GNI)	..	0.0
CO_2 damage (% of GNI)	0.2	0.3
Particulate emission damage (% of GNI)	..	0.3
Adjusted net savings (% of GNI)	..	8.5

Marshall Islands

Population (thousands)	58	Land area (sq. km)	180	GDP ($ millions)	149

	Country data	East Asia & Pacific group	Lower middle-income group
GNI per capita, *World Bank Atlas* method ($)	3,240	2,182	1,905
Urban population (% of total)	71	43	42
Urban population growth (average annual %, 1990–2007)	1.9	3.5	2.9
Population growth (average annual %, 1990–2007)	1.4	1.1	1.3
Agriculture			
Agricultural land (% of land area)	78	51	47
Agricultural productivity (value added per worker, 2000 $)	..	458	532
Food production index (1999–2001 = 100)	93	120	116
Population density, rural (people/sq. km of arable land)	837	547	511
Forests and biodiversity			
Forest area (% of land area)	..	28.4	25.0
Deforestation (average annual %, 1990–2005)	..	-0.1	0.1
Nationally protected area (% of land area)	..	14.0	11.0
Animal species, total known	61		
Animal species, threatened	85		
Higher plant species, total known	100		
Higher plant species, threatened	..		
GEF benefits index for biodiversity (0–100, median is 1.5)	1.3		
Energy			
GDP per unit of energy use (2005 PPP $/kg oil equivalent)	..	3.4	3.9
Energy use per capita (kg oil equivalent)	..	1,258	1,019
Energy from biomass products and waste (% of total)	..	14.7	15.2
Electric power consumption per capita (kWh)	..	1,669	1,269
Electricity generated using fossil fuel (% of total)	..	82.0	79.0
Electricity generated by hydropower (% of total)	..	15.0	16.3
Emissions and pollution			
CO_2 emissions per unit of GDP (kg/2005 PPP $)	..	0.9	0.8
CO_2 emissions per capita (metric tons)	1.5	3.6	2.8
CO_2 emissions growth (%, 1990–2005)	76.9	123.4	93.5
Particulate matter (urban-pop.-weighted avg., µg/cu. m)	..	69	67
Transport sector fuel consumption per capita (liters)	..	106	99
Water and sanitation			
Internal freshwater resources per capita (cu. m)	..	4,948	4,117
Freshwater withdrawal			
Total (% of internal resources)	..	10.2	8.7
Agriculture (% of total freshwater withdrawal)	..	74	80
Access to improved water source (% of total population)	..	87	88
Rural (% of rural population)	..	81	82
Urban (% of urban population)	..	96	96
Access to improved sanitation (% of total population)	..	66	55
Rural (% of rural population)	..	59	43
Urban (% of urban population)	..	75	71
Environment and health			
Acute resp. infection prevalence (% of children under five)	..		
Diarrhea prevalence (% of children under five)	..		
Under-five mortality rate (per 1,000 live births)	54	27	50
National accounting aggregates			
Gross savings (% of GNI)	..	48.0	41.7
Consumption of fixed capital (% of GNI)	8.8	10.7	10.7
Education expenditure (% of GNI)	6.6	2.1	2.6
Energy depletion (% of GNI)	0.0	4.9	6.6
Mineral depletion (% of GNI)	0.0	1.3	1.2
Net forest depletion (% of GNI)	..	0.0	0.2
CO_2 damage (% of GNI)	..	1.3	1.2
Particulate emission damage (% of GNI)	..	1.3	1.1
Adjusted net savings (% of GNI)	..	30.6	23.5

Mauritania

| | Population (millions) | **3.1** | Land area (1,000 sq. km) | **1,030.7** | GDP ($ billions) | **2.6** |

	Country data	Sub-Saharan Africa group	Low-income group
GNI per capita, *World Bank Atlas* method ($)	840	951	574
Urban population (% of total)	41	36	32
Urban population growth (average annual %, 1990–2007)	2.9	4.0	3.7
Population growth (average annual %, 1990–2007)	2.8	2.6	2.4
Agriculture			
Agricultural land (% of land area)	39	44	39
Agricultural productivity (value added per worker, 2000 $)	356	287	330
Food production index (1999–2001 = 100)	105	109	112
Population density, rural (people/sq. km of arable land)	353	351	603
Forests and biodiversity			
Forest area (% of land area)	0.3	26.5	24.7
Deforestation (average annual %, 1990–2005)	2.9	0.6	0.7
Nationally protected area (% of land area)	..	11.3	10.8
Animal species, total known	615		
Animal species, threatened	49		
Higher plant species, total known	1,100		
Higher plant species, threatened	..		
GEF benefits index for biodiversity (0–100, median is 1.5)	1.3		
Energy			
GDP per unit of energy use (2005 PPP $/kg oil equivalent)	..	3.0	3.2
Energy use per capita (kg oil equivalent)	..	670	478
Energy from biomass products and waste (% of total)	..	56.3	53.8
Electric power consumption per capita (kWh)	..	531	309
Electricity generated using fossil fuel (% of total)	..	65.6	48.4
Electricity generated by hydropower (% of total)	..	18.0	38.8
Emissions and pollution			
CO_2 emissions per unit of GDP (kg/2005 PPP $)	0.3	0.5	0.4
CO_2 emissions per capita (metric tons)	0.6	0.8	0.6
CO_2 emissions growth (%, 1990–2005)	-38.1	40.1	39.3
Particulate matter (urban-pop.-weighted avg., µg/cu. m)	86	53	69
Transport sector fuel consumption per capita (liters)	..	64	41
Water and sanitation			
Internal freshwater resources per capita (cu. m)	128	4,824	4,619
Freshwater withdrawal			
Total (% of internal resources)	425.0	3.2	9.4
Agriculture (% of total freshwater withdrawal)	88	87	90
Access to improved water source (% of total population)	60	58	68
Rural (% of rural population)	54	46	60
Urban (% of urban population)	70	81	84
Access to improved sanitation (% of total population)	24	31	39
Rural (% of rural population)	10	24	33
Urban (% of urban population)	44	42	54
Environment and health			
Acute resp. infection prevalence (% of children under five)	10.0		
Diarrhea prevalence (% of children under five)	18.3		
Under-five mortality rate (per 1,000 live births)	119	146	126
National accounting aggregates			
Gross savings (% of GNI)	28.0	17.4	25.4
Consumption of fixed capital (% of GNI)	8.9	11.1	9.3
Education expenditure (% of GNI)	2.8	3.6	2.6
Energy depletion (% of GNI)	0.0	11.7	9.8
Mineral depletion (% of GNI)	17.0	1.5	0.9
Net forest depletion (% of GNI)	0.5	0.5	0.8
CO_2 damage (% of GNI)	0.8	0.7	0.7
Particulate emission damage (% of GNI)	2.3	0.4	0.7
Adjusted net savings (% of GNI)	1.2	-5.0	5.8

Mauritius

	Country data	Sub-Saharan Africa group	Upper middle-income group
Population (millions) **1.3** Land area (1,000 sq. km) **2.0** GDP ($ billions) **6.8**			

	Country data	Sub-Saharan Africa group	Upper middle-income group
GNI per capita, *World Bank Atlas* method ($)	5,580	951	7,107
Urban population (% of total)	42	36	75
Urban population growth (average annual %, 1990–2007)	0.8	4.0	1.4
Population growth (average annual %, 1990–2007)	1.0	2.6	0.9
Agriculture			
Agricultural land (% of land area)	56	44	31
Agricultural productivity (value added per worker, 2000 $)	5,338	287	2,947
Food production index (1999–2001 = 100)	106	109	113
Population density, rural (people/sq. km of arable land)	717	351	110
Forests and biodiversity			
Forest area (% of land area)	18.2	26.5	39.3
Deforestation (average annual %, 1990–2005)	0.4	0.6	0.2
Nationally protected area (% of land area)	3.3	11.3	10.3
Animal species, total known	151		
Animal species, threatened	131		
Higher plant species, total known	750		
Higher plant species, threatened	88		
GEF benefits index for biodiversity (0–100, median is 1.5)	3.3		
Energy			
GDP per unit of energy use (2005 PPP $/kg oil equivalent)	..	3.0	4.8
Energy use per capita (kg oil equivalent)	..	670	2,300
Energy from biomass products and waste (% of total)	..	56.3	7.0
Electric power consumption per capita (kWh)	..	531	3,242
Electricity generated using fossil fuel (% of total)	..	65.6	62.8
Electricity generated by hydropower (% of total)	..	18.0	27.6
Emissions and pollution			
CO_2 emissions per unit of GDP (kg/2005 PPP $)	0.3	0.5	0.5
CO_2 emissions per capita (metric tons)	2.7	0.8	5.5
CO_2 emissions growth (%, 1990–2005)	133.1	40.1	-8.3
Particulate matter (urban-pop.-weighted avg., µg/cu. m)	18	53	30
Transport sector fuel consumption per capita (liters)	..	64	332
Water and sanitation			
Internal freshwater resources per capita (cu. m)	2,182	4,824	16,993
Freshwater withdrawal			
Total (% of internal resources)	26.4	3.2	13.8
Agriculture (% of total freshwater withdrawal)	68	87	57
Access to improved water source (% of total population)	100	58	95
Rural (% of rural population)	100	46	83
Urban (% of urban population)	100	81	98
Access to improved sanitation (% of total population)	94	31	83
Rural (% of rural population)	94	24	64
Urban (% of urban population)	95	42	89
Environment and health			
Acute resp. infection prevalence (% of children under five)	..		
Diarrhea prevalence (% of children under five)	..		
Under-five mortality rate (per 1,000 live births)	15	146	24
National accounting aggregates			
Gross savings (% of GNI)	19.7	17.4	23.2
Consumption of fixed capital (% of GNI)	11.8	11.1	12.8
Education expenditure (% of GNI)	3.4	3.6	4.4
Energy depletion (% of GNI)	0.0	11.7	7.6
Mineral depletion (% of GNI)	0.0	1.5	1.3
Net forest depletion (% of GNI)	0.0	0.5	0.0
CO_2 damage (% of GNI)	0.4	0.7	0.6
Particulate emission damage (% of GNI)	..	0.4	0.4
Adjusted net savings (% of GNI)	10.9	-5.0	4.9

Mayotte

| Population (thousands) **186** | Land area (sq. km) | **374** GDP ($ millions) | .. |

	Country data	Sub-Saharan Africa group	Upper middle-income group
GNI per capita, *World Bank Atlas* method ($)	..	951	7,107
Urban population (% of total)	..	36	75
Urban population growth (average annual %, 1990–2007)	..	4.0	1.4
Population growth (average annual %, 1990–2007)	..	2.6	0.9
Agriculture			
Agricultural land (% of land area)	53	44	31
Agricultural productivity (value added per worker, 2000 $)	..	287	2,947
Food production index (1999–2001 = 100)	..	109	113
Population density, rural (people/sq. km of arable land)	..	351	110
Forests and biodiversity			
Forest area (% of land area)	14.7	26.5	39.3
Deforestation (average annual %, 1990–2005)	1.2	0.6	0.2
Nationally protected area (% of land area)	..	11.3	10.3
Animal species, total known	..		
Animal species, threatened	68		
Higher plant species, total known	..		
Higher plant species, threatened	0		
GEF benefits index for biodiversity (0–100, median is 1.5)	0.3		
Energy			
GDP per unit of energy use (2005 PPP $/kg oil equivalent)	..	3.0	4.8
Energy use per capita (kg oil equivalent)	..	670	2,300
Energy from biomass products and waste (% of total)	..	56.3	7.0
Electric power consumption per capita (kWh)	..	531	3,242
Electricity generated using fossil fuel (% of total)	..	65.6	62.8
Electricity generated by hydropower (% of total)	..	18.0	27.6
Emissions and pollution			
CO_2 emissions per unit of GDP (kg/2005 PPP $)	..	0.5	0.5
CO_2 emissions per capita (metric tons)	..	0.8	5.5
CO_2 emissions growth (%, 1990–2005)	..	40.1	-8.3
Particulate matter (urban-pop.-weighted avg., µg/cu. m)	..	53	30
Transport sector fuel consumption per capita (liters)	..	64	332
Water and sanitation			
Internal freshwater resources per capita (cu. m)	..	4,824	16,993
Freshwater withdrawal			
Total (% of internal resources)	..	3.2	13.8
Agriculture (% of total freshwater withdrawal)	..	87	57
Access to improved water source (% of total population)	..	58	95
Rural (% of rural population)	..	46	83
Urban (% of urban population)	..	81	98
Access to improved sanitation (% of total population)	..	31	83
Rural (% of rural population)	..	24	64
Urban (% of urban population)	..	42	89
Environment and health			
Acute resp. infection prevalence (% of children under five)	..		
Diarrhea prevalence (% of children under five)	..		
Under-five mortality rate (per 1,000 live births)	..	146	24
National accounting aggregates			
Gross savings (% of GNI)	..	17.4	23.2
Consumption of fixed capital (% of GNI)	..	11.1	12.8
Education expenditure (% of GNI)	..	3.6	4.4
Energy depletion (% of GNI)	..	11.7	7.6
Mineral depletion (% of GNI)	..	1.5	1.3
Net forest depletion (% of GNI)	..	0.5	0.0
CO_2 damage (% of GNI)	..	0.7	0.6
Particulate emission damage (% of GNI)	..	0.4	0.4
Adjusted net savings (% of GNI)	..	-5.0	4.9

Mexico

Population (millions)	**105**	Land area (1,000 sq. km)	**1,944**	GDP ($ billions)	**1,022.8**

	Country data	Latin America & Caribbean group	Upper middle-income group
GNI per capita, *World Bank Atlas* method ($)	9,400	5,801	7,107
Urban population (% of total)	77	78	75
Urban population growth (average annual %, 1990–2007)	1.8	2.1	1.4
Population growth (average annual %, 1990–2007)	1.4	1.5	0.9
Agriculture			
Agricultural land (% of land area)	55	36	31
Agricultural productivity (value added per worker, 2000 $)	2,821	3,158	2,947
Food production index (1999–2001 = 100)	110	117	113
Population density, rural (people/sq. km of arable land)	98	232	110
Forests and biodiversity			
Forest area (% of land area)	33.0	45.4	39.3
Deforestation (average annual %, 1990–2005)	0.5	0.5	0.2
Nationally protected area (% of land area)	5.3	16.7	10.3
Animal species, total known	1,570		
Animal species, threatened	636		
Higher plant species, total known	26,071		
Higher plant species, threatened	261		
GEF benefits index for biodiversity (0–100, median is 1.5)	68.7		
Energy			
GDP per unit of energy use (2005 PPP $/kg oil equivalent)	7.7	7.3	4.8
Energy use per capita (kg oil equivalent)	1,702	1,240	2,300
Energy from biomass products and waste (% of total)	4.6	15.9	7.0
Electric power consumption per capita (kWh)	2,003	1,808	3,242
Electricity generated using fossil fuel (% of total)	79.8	37.0	62.8
Electricity generated by hydropower (% of total)	12.2	57.3	27.6
Emissions and pollution			
CO_2 emissions per unit of GDP (kg/2005 PPP $)	0.3	0.3	0.5
CO_2 emissions per capita (metric tons)	4.1	2.5	5.5
CO_2 emissions growth (%, 1990–2005)	12.3	33.4	-8.3
Particulate matter (urban-pop.-weighted avg., µg/cu. m)	36	35	30
Transport sector fuel consumption per capita (liters)	486	295	332
Water and sanitation			
Internal freshwater resources per capita (cu. m)	3,885	23,965	16,993
Freshwater withdrawal			
Total (% of internal resources)	19.1	2.0	13.8
Agriculture (% of total freshwater withdrawal)	77	71	57
Access to improved water source (% of total population)	95	91	95
Rural (% of rural population)	85	73	83
Urban (% of urban population)	98	97	98
Access to improved sanitation (% of total population)	81	78	83
Rural (% of rural population)	48	51	64
Urban (% of urban population)	91	86	89
Environment and health			
Acute resp. infection prevalence (% of children under five)	..		
Diarrhea prevalence (% of children under five)	9.7		
Under-five mortality rate (per 1,000 live births)	35	26	24
National accounting aggregates			
Gross savings (% of GNI)	25.7	22.9	23.2
Consumption of fixed capital (% of GNI)	12.9	12.6	12.8
Education expenditure (% of GNI)	5.5	4.5	4.4
Energy depletion (% of GNI)	6.9	5.4	7.6
Mineral depletion (% of GNI)	0.4	1.9	1.3
Net forest depletion (% of GNI)	0.0	0.0	0.0
CO_2 damage (% of GNI)	0.4	0.3	0.6
Particulate emission damage (% of GNI)	0.4	0.4	0.4
Adjusted net savings (% of GNI)	10.3	6.7	4.9

Micronesia, Fed. Sts.

Population (thousands) **111** Land area (sq. km) **700** GDP ($ millions) **236**

	Country data	East Asia & Pacific group	Lower middle-income group
GNI per capita, *World Bank Atlas* method ($)	2,280	2,182	1,905
Urban population (% of total)	22	43	42
Urban population growth (average annual %, 1990–2007)	0.0	3.5	2.9
Population growth (average annual %, 1990–2007)	0.8	1.1	1.3
Agriculture			
Agricultural land (% of land area)	44	51	47
Agricultural productivity (value added per worker, 2000 $)	..	458	532
Food production index (1999–2001 = 100)	100	120	116
Population density, rural (people/sq. km of arable land)	2,851	547	511
Forests and biodiversity			
Forest area (% of land area)	90.6	28.4	25.0
Deforestation (average annual %, 1990–2005)	0.0	–0.1	0.1
Nationally protected area (% of land area)	7.3	14.0	11.0
Animal species, total known	105		
Animal species, threatened	139		
Higher plant species, total known	1,194		
Higher plant species, threatened	5		
GEF benefits index for biodiversity (0–100, median is 1.5)	2.6		
Energy			
GDP per unit of energy use (2005 PPP $/kg oil equivalent)	..	3.4	3.9
Energy use per capita (kg oil equivalent)	..	1,258	1,019
Energy from biomass products and waste (% of total)	..	14.7	15.2
Electric power consumption per capita (kWh)	..	1,669	1,269
Electricity generated using fossil fuel (% of total)	..	82.0	79.0
Electricity generated by hydropower (% of total)	..	15.0	16.3
Emissions and pollution			
CO_2 emissions per unit of GDP (kg/2005 PPP $)	..	0.9	0.8
CO_2 emissions per capita (metric tons)	..	3.6	2.8
CO_2 emissions growth (%, 1990–2005)	..	123.4	93.5
Particulate matter (urban-pop.-weighted avg., µg/cu. m)	..	69	67
Transport sector fuel consumption per capita (liters)	..	106	99
Water and sanitation			
Internal freshwater resources per capita (cu. m)	..	4,948	4,117
Freshwater withdrawal			
Total (% of internal resources)	..	10.2	8.7
Agriculture (% of total freshwater withdrawal)	..	74	80
Access to improved water source (% of total population)	94	87	88
Rural (% of rural population)	94	81	82
Urban (% of urban population)	95	96	96
Access to improved sanitation (% of total population)	25	66	55
Rural (% of rural population)	14	59	43
Urban (% of urban population)	61	75	71
Environment and health			
Acute resp. infection prevalence (% of children under five)	..		
Diarrhea prevalence (% of children under five)	..		
Under-five mortality rate (per 1,000 live births)	40	27	50
National accounting aggregates			
Gross savings (% of GNI)	..	48.0	41.7
Consumption of fixed capital (% of GNI)	9.8	10.7	10.7
Education expenditure (% of GNI)	..	2.1	2.6
Energy depletion (% of GNI)	0.0	4.9	6.6
Mineral depletion (% of GNI)	0.0	1.3	1.2
Net forest depletion (% of GNI)	..	0.0	0.2
CO_2 damage (% of GNI)	..	1.3	1.2
Particulate emission damage (% of GNI)	..	1.3	1.1
Adjusted net savings (% of GNI)	..	30.6	23.5

Moldova

| Population (millions) | **3.8** | Land area (1,000 sq. km) | **32.9** | GDP ($ billions) | **4.4** |

	Country data	Europe & Central Asia group	Lower middle-income group
GNI per capita, *World Bank Atlas* method ($)	1,210	6,052	1,905
Urban population (% of total)	42	64	42
Urban population growth (average annual %, 1990-2007)	-1.5	0.2	2.9
Population growth (average annual %, 1990-2007)	-0.8	0.1	1.3
Agriculture			
Agricultural land (% of land area)	77	28	47
Agricultural productivity (value added per worker, 2000 $)	891	2,228	532
Food production index (1999-2001 = 100)	119	110	116
Population density, rural (people/sq. km of arable land)	120	129	511
Forests and biodiversity			
Forest area (% of land area)	10.0	38.3	25.0
Deforestation (average annual %, 1990-2005)	-0.2	0.0	0.1
Nationally protected area (% of land area)	1.4	6.1	11.0
Animal species, total known	253		
Animal species, threatened	27		
Higher plant species, total known	1,752		
Higher plant species, threatened	0		
GEF benefits index for biodiversity (0-100, median is 1.5)	0.0		
Energy			
GDP per unit of energy use (2005 PPP $/kg oil equivalent)	2.6	3.5	3.9
Energy use per capita (kg oil equivalent)	884	2,930	1,019
Energy from biomass products and waste (% of total)	2.2	2.2	15.2
Electric power consumption per capita (kWh)	1,516	3,835	1,269
Electricity generated using fossil fuel (% of total)	97.5	67.7	79.0
Electricity generated by hydropower (% of total)	2.0	17.4	16.3
Emissions and pollution			
CO_2 emissions per unit of GDP (kg/2005 PPP $)	0.9	0.7	0.8
CO_2 emissions per capita (metric tons)	2.1	7.0	2.8
CO_2 emissions growth (%, 1990-2005)	-66.2	-29.3	93.5
Particulate matter (urban-pop.-weighted avg., µg/cu. m)	36	27	67
Transport sector fuel consumption per capita (liters)	78	255	99
Water and sanitation			
Internal freshwater resources per capita (cu. m)	263	11,806	4,117
Freshwater withdrawal			
Total (% of internal resources)	231.0	7.2	8.7
Agriculture (% of total freshwater withdrawal)	33	60	80
Access to improved water source (% of total population)	90	95	88
Rural (% of rural population)	85	88	82
Urban (% of urban population)	96	99	96
Access to improved sanitation (% of total population)	79	89	55
Rural (% of rural population)	73	79	43
Urban (% of urban population)	85	94	71
Environment and health			
Acute resp. infection prevalence (% of children under five)	7.0		
Diarrhea prevalence (% of children under five)	7.4		
Under-five mortality rate (per 1,000 live births)	18	23	50
National accounting aggregates			
Gross savings (% of GNI)	20.4	24.0	41.7
Consumption of fixed capital (% of GNI)	8.8	12.8	10.7
Education expenditure (% of GNI)	6.6	4.0	2.6
Energy depletion (% of GNI)	0.0	9.8	6.6
Mineral depletion (% of GNI)	0.0	0.7	1.2
Net forest depletion (% of GNI)	0.1	0.0	0.2
CO_2 damage (% of GNI)	1.4	1.0	1.2
Particulate emission damage (% of GNI)	0.6	0.5	1.1
Adjusted net savings (% of GNI)	16.0	3.2	23.5

Monaco

Population (thousands) **33**	Land area (sq. km) **2**	GDP ($ millions) ..

	Country data	High-income group
GNI per capita, *World Bank Atlas* method ($)	..	37,572
Urban population (% of total)	100	78
Urban population growth (average annual %, 1990–2007)	..	1.0
Population growth (average annual %, 1990–2007)	..	0.7
Agriculture		
Agricultural land (% of land area)	..	38
Agricultural productivity (value added per worker, 2000 $)	..	27,680
Food production index (1999–2001 = 100)	..	102
Population density, rural (people/sq. km of arable land)	..	323
Forests and biodiversity		
Forest area (% of land area)	..	28.8
Deforestation (average annual %, 1990–2005)	..	−0.1
Nationally protected area (% of land area)	..	11.8
Animal species, total known	16	
Animal species, threatened	14	
Higher plant species, total known	..	
Higher plant species, threatened	0	
GEF benefits index for biodiversity (0–100, median is 1.5)	0.0	
Energy		
GDP per unit of energy use (2005 PPP $/kg oil equivalent)	..	6.3
Energy use per capita (kg oil equivalent)	..	5,416
Energy from biomass products and waste (% of total)	..	3.4
Electric power consumption per capita (kWh)	..	9,675
Electricity generated using fossil fuel (% of total)	..	62.0
Electricity generated by hydropower (% of total)	..	11.4
Emissions and pollution		
CO_2 emissions per unit of GDP (kg/2005 PPP $)	..	0.4
CO_2 emissions per capita (metric tons)	..	12.6
CO_2 emissions growth (%, 1990–2005)	..	19.1
Particulate matter (urban-pop.-weighted avg., µg/cu. m)	..	26
Transport sector fuel consumption per capita (liters)	..	1,159
Water and sanitation		
Internal freshwater resources per capita (cu. m)	..	9,313
Freshwater withdrawal		
Total (% of internal resources)	..	10.4
Agriculture (% of total freshwater withdrawal)	..	43
Access to improved water source (% of total population)	..	100
Rural (% of rural population)	..	98
Urban (% of urban population)	100	100
Access to improved sanitation (% of total population)	..	100
Rural (% of rural population)	..	99
Urban (% of urban population)	100	100
Environment and health		
Acute resp. infection prevalence (% of children under five)	..	
Diarrhea prevalence (% of children under five)	..	
Under-five mortality rate (per 1,000 live births)	4	7
National accounting aggregates		
Gross savings (% of GNI)	..	20.6
Consumption of fixed capital (% of GNI)	..	14.5
Education expenditure (% of GNI)	..	4.6
Energy depletion (% of GNI)	..	1.5
Mineral depletion (% of GNI)	..	0.2
Net forest depletion (% of GNI)	..	0.0
CO_2 damage (% of GNI)	..	0.3
Particulate emission damage (% of GNI)	..	0.3
Adjusted net savings (% of GNI)	..	8.5

Mongolia

	Country data	East Asia & Pacific group	Lower middle-income group
Population (millions) **2.6** Land area (1,000 sq. km) **1,566.5** GDP ($ billions) **3.9**			

	Country data	East Asia & Pacific group	Lower middle-income group
GNI per capita, *World Bank Atlas* method ($)	1,290	2,182	1,905
Urban population (% of total)	57	43	42
Urban population growth (average annual %, 1990–2007)	1.3	3.5	2.9
Population growth (average annual %, 1990–2007)	1.3	1.1	1.3
Agriculture			
Agricultural land (% of land area)	83	51	47
Agricultural productivity (value added per worker, 2000 $)	1,030	458	532
Food production index (1999–2001 = 100)	74	120	116
Population density, rural (people/sq. km of arable land)	95	547	511
Forests and biodiversity			
Forest area (% of land area)	6.5	28.4	25.0
Deforestation (average annual %, 1990–2005)	0.8	–0.1	0.1
Nationally protected area (% of land area)	13.9	14.0	11.0
Animal species, total known	527		
Animal species, threatened	36		
Higher plant species, total known	2,823		
Higher plant species, threatened	0		
GEF benefits index for biodiversity (0–100, median is 1.5)	4.2		
Energy			
GDP per unit of energy use (2005 PPP $/kg oil equivalent)	2.6	3.4	3.9
Energy use per capita (kg oil equivalent)	1,080	1,258	1,019
Energy from biomass products and waste (% of total)	3.8	14.7	15.2
Electric power consumption per capita (kWh)	1,298	1,669	1,269
Electricity generated using fossil fuel (% of total)	100.0	82.0	79.0
Electricity generated by hydropower (% of total)	0.0	15.0	16.3
Emissions and pollution			
CO_2 emissions per unit of GDP (kg/2005 PPP $)	1.3	0.9	0.8
CO_2 emissions per capita (metric tons)	3.4	3.6	2.8
CO_2 emissions growth (%, 1990–2005)	–12.0	123.4	93.5
Particulate matter (urban-pop.-weighted avg., µg/cu. m)	110	69	67
Transport sector fuel consumption per capita (liters)	166	106	99
Water and sanitation			
Internal freshwater resources per capita (cu. m)	13,341	4,948	4,117
Freshwater withdrawal			
Total (% of internal resources)	1.3	10.2	8.7
Agriculture (% of total freshwater withdrawal)	52	74	80
Access to improved water source (% of total population)	72	87	88
Rural (% of rural population)	48	81	82
Urban (% of urban population)	90	96	96
Access to improved sanitation (% of total population)	50	66	55
Rural (% of rural population)	31	59	43
Urban (% of urban population)	64	75	71
Environment and health			
Acute resp. infection prevalence (% of children under five)	2.0		
Diarrhea prevalence (% of children under five)	8.0		
Under-five mortality rate (per 1,000 live births)	43	27	50
National accounting aggregates			
Gross savings (% of GNI)	42.5	48.0	41.7
Consumption of fixed capital (% of GNI)	10.3	10.7	10.7
Education expenditure (% of GNI)	4.6	2.1	2.6
Energy depletion (% of GNI)	2.5	4.9	6.6
Mineral depletion (% of GNI)	14.0	1.3	1.2
Net forest depletion (% of GNI)	0.0	0.0	0.2
CO_2 damage (% of GNI)	2.2	1.3	1.2
Particulate emission damage (% of GNI)	2.0	1.3	1.1
Adjusted net savings (% of GNI)	16.3	30.6	23.5

Montenegro

Population (thousands) **599**   Land area (1,000 sq. km)   **14**   GDP ($ billions)   **3.5**

	Country data	Europe & Central Asia group	Upper middle-income group
GNI per capita, *World Bank Atlas* method ($)	5,270	6,052	7,107
Urban population (% of total)	61	64	75
Urban population growth (average annual %, 1990–2007)	1.5	0.2	1.4
Population growth (average annual %, 1990–2007)	0.1	0.1	0.9

Agriculture
Agricultural land (% of land area)	..	28	31
Agricultural productivity (value added per worker, 2000 $)	..	2,228	2,947
Food production index (1999–2001 = 100)	..	110	113
Population density, rural (people/sq. km of arable land)	..	129	110

Forests and biodiversity
Forest area (% of land area)	..	38.3	39.3
Deforestation (average annual %, 1990–2005)	..	0.0	0.2
Nationally protected area (% of land area)	..	6.1	10.3
Animal species, total known	..		
Animal species, threatened	52		
Higher plant species, total known	..		
Higher plant species, threatened	0		
GEF benefits index for biodiversity (0–100, median is 1.5)	0.0		

Energy
GDP per unit of energy use (2005 PPP $/kg oil equivalent)	..	3.5	4.8
Energy use per capita (kg oil equivalent)	..	2,930	2,300
Energy from biomass products and waste (% of total)	..	2.2	7.0
Electric power consumption per capita (kWh)	..	3,835	3,242
Electricity generated using fossil fuel (% of total)	..	67.7	62.8
Electricity generated by hydropower (% of total)	..	17.4	27.6

Emissions and pollution
CO_2 emissions per unit of GDP (kg/2005 PPP $)	..	0.7	0.5
CO_2 emissions per capita (metric tons)	..	7.0	5.5
CO_2 emissions growth (%, 1990–2005)	..	−29.3	−8.3
Particulate matter (urban-pop.-weighted avg., µg/cu. m)	..	27	30
Transport sector fuel consumption per capita (liters)	..	255	332

Water and sanitation
Internal freshwater resources per capita (cu. m)	..	11,806	16,993
Freshwater withdrawal			
Total (% of internal resources)	..	7.2	13.8
Agriculture (% of total freshwater withdrawal)	..	60	57
Access to improved water source (% of total population)	98	95	95
Rural (% of rural population)	96	88	83
Urban (% of urban population)	100	99	98
Access to improved sanitation (% of total population)	91	89	83
Rural (% of rural population)	86	79	64
Urban (% of urban population)	96	94	89

Environment and health
Acute resp. infection prevalence (% of children under five)	..		
Diarrhea prevalence (% of children under five)	..		
Under-five mortality rate (per 1,000 live births)	10	23	24

National accounting aggregates
Gross savings (% of GNI)	..	24.0	23.2
Consumption of fixed capital (% of GNI)	..	12.8	12.8
Education expenditure (% of GNI)	..	4.0	4.4
Energy depletion (% of GNI)	..	9.8	7.6
Mineral depletion (% of GNI)	..	0.7	1.3
Net forest depletion (% of GNI)	..	0.0	0.0
CO_2 damage (% of GNI)	..	1.0	0.6
Particulate emission damage (% of GNI)	..	0.5	0.4
Adjusted net savings (% of GNI)	..	3.2	4.9

Morocco

Population (millions)	**31**	Land area (1,000 sq. km)	**446**	GDP ($ billions)	**75.1**

	Country data	Middle East & N. Africa group	Lower middle-income group
GNI per capita, *World Bank Atlas* method ($)	2,290	2,820	1,905
Urban population (% of total)	56	57	42
Urban population growth (average annual %, 1990–2007)	2.3	2.6	2.9
Population growth (average annual %, 1990–2007)	1.4	2.0	1.3
Agriculture			
Agricultural land (% of land area)	68	22	47
Agricultural productivity (value added per worker, 2000 $)	1,623	2,313	532
Food production index (1999–2001 = 100)	117	116	116
Population density, rural (people/sq. km of arable land)	160	665	511
Forests and biodiversity			
Forest area (% of land area)	9.8	2.4	25.0
Deforestation (average annual %, 1990–2005)	–0.1	–0.4	0.1
Nationally protected area (% of land area)	1.1	3.6	11.0
Animal species, total known	559		
Animal species, threatened	80		
Higher plant species, total known	3,675		
Higher plant species, threatened	2		
GEF benefits index for biodiversity (0–100, median is 1.5)	3.5		
Energy			
GDP per unit of energy use (2005 PPP $/kg oil equivalent)	8.3	5.0	3.9
Energy use per capita (kg oil equivalent)	458	1,254	1,019
Energy from biomass products and waste (% of total)	3.2	1.2	15.2
Electric power consumption per capita (kWh)	685	1,418	1,269
Electricity generated using fossil fuel (% of total)	92.3	91.1	79.0
Electricity generated by hydropower (% of total)	6.9	7.4	16.3
Emissions and pollution			
CO_2 emissions per unit of GDP (kg/2005 PPP $)	0.4	0.6	0.8
CO_2 emissions per capita (metric tons)	1.6	3.7	2.8
CO_2 emissions growth (%, 1990–2005)	104.4	96.8	93.5
Particulate matter (urban-pop.-weighted avg., µg/cu. m)	21	72	67
Transport sector fuel consumption per capita (liters)	23	277	99
Water and sanitation			
Internal freshwater resources per capita (cu. m)	940	728	4,117
Freshwater withdrawal			
Total (% of internal resources)	43.4	122.3	8.7
Agriculture (% of total freshwater withdrawal)	87	86	80
Access to improved water source (% of total population)	83	89	88
Rural (% of rural population)	58	81	82
Urban (% of urban population)	100	95	96
Access to improved sanitation (% of total population)	72	77	55
Rural (% of rural population)	54	62	43
Urban (% of urban population)	85	88	71
Environment and health			
Acute resp. infection prevalence (% of children under five)	12.0		
Diarrhea prevalence (% of children under five)	10.4		
Under-five mortality rate (per 1,000 live births)	34	38	50
National accounting aggregates			
Gross savings (% of GNI)	32.8	33.3	41.7
Consumption of fixed capital (% of GNI)	10.9	11.3	10.7
Education expenditure (% of GNI)	5.2	4.7	2.6
Energy depletion (% of GNI)	0.0	21.3	6.6
Mineral depletion (% of GNI)	1.0	0.4	1.2
Net forest depletion (% of GNI)	0.0	0.0	0.2
CO_2 damage (% of GNI)	0.5	1.0	1.2
Particulate emission damage (% of GNI)	0.1	0.6	1.1
Adjusted net savings (% of GNI)	25.6	3.4	23.5

Mozambique

Population (millions)	21	Land area (1,000 sq. km)	786	GDP ($ billions)	7.8

	Country data	Sub-Saharan Africa group	Low-income group
GNI per capita, *World Bank Atlas* method ($)	330	951	574
Urban population (% of total)	36	36	32
Urban population growth (average annual %, 1990–2007)	5.8	4.0	3.7
Population growth (average annual %, 1990–2007)	2.7	2.6	2.4
Agriculture			
Agricultural land (% of land area)	62	44	39
Agricultural productivity (value added per worker, 2000 $)	154	287	330
Food production index (1999–2001 = 100)	107	109	112
Population density, rural (people/sq. km of arable land)	306	351	603
Forests and biodiversity			
Forest area (% of land area)	24.5	26.5	24.7
Deforestation (average annual %, 1990–2005)	0.3	0.6	0.7
Nationally protected area (% of land area)	5.8	11.3	10.8
Animal species, total known	913		
Animal species, threatened	143		
Higher plant species, total known	5,692		
Higher plant species, threatened	46		
GEF benefits index for biodiversity (0–100, median is 1.5)	7.2		
Energy			
GDP per unit of energy use (2005 PPP $/kg oil equivalent)	1.7	3.0	3.2
Energy use per capita (kg oil equivalent)	420	670	478
Energy from biomass products and waste (% of total)	81.6	56.3	53.8
Electric power consumption per capita (kWh)	461	531	309
Electricity generated using fossil fuel (% of total)	0.1	65.6	48.4
Electricity generated by hydropower (% of total)	99.9	18.0	38.8
Emissions and pollution			
CO_2 emissions per unit of GDP (kg/2005 PPP $)	0.1	0.5	0.4
CO_2 emissions per capita (metric tons)	0.09	0.85	0.58
CO_2 emissions growth (%, 1990–2005)	88.6	40.1	39.3
Particulate matter (urban-pop.-weighted avg., µg/cu. m)	28	53	69
Transport sector fuel consumption per capita (liters)	20	64	41
Water and sanitation			
Internal freshwater resources per capita (cu. m)	4,693	4,824	4,619
Freshwater withdrawal			
Total (% of internal resources)	0.6	3.2	9.4
Agriculture (% of total freshwater withdrawal)	87	87	90
Access to improved water source (% of total population)	42	58	68
Rural (% of rural population)	26	46	60
Urban (% of urban population)	71	81	84
Access to improved sanitation (% of total population)	31	31	39
Rural (% of rural population)	19	24	33
Urban (% of urban population)	53	42	54
Environment and health			
Acute resp. infection prevalence (% of children under five)	10.0		
Diarrhea prevalence (% of children under five)	20.7		
Under-five mortality rate (per 1,000 live births)	168	146	126
National accounting aggregates			
Gross savings (% of GNI)	3.1	17.4	25.4
Consumption of fixed capital (% of GNI)	8.9	11.1	9.3
Education expenditure (% of GNI)	3.8	3.6	2.6
Energy depletion (% of GNI)	7.1	11.7	9.8
Mineral depletion (% of GNI)	0.0	1.5	0.9
Net forest depletion (% of GNI)	0.6	0.5	0.8
CO_2 damage (% of GNI)	0.2	0.7	0.7
Particulate emission damage (% of GNI)	0.2	0.4	0.7
Adjusted net savings (% of GNI)	−10.2	−5.0	5.8

Myanmar

| | Population (millions) | **49** | Land area (1,000 sq. km) | **658** | GDP ($ billions) | .. |

	Country data	East Asia & Pacific group	Low-income group
GNI per capita, *World Bank Atlas* method ($)	..	2,182	574
Urban population (% of total)	32	43	32
Urban population growth (average annual %, 1990–2007)	2.6	3.5	3.7
Population growth (average annual %, 1990–2007)	1.1	1.1	2.4
Agriculture			
Agricultural land (% of land area)	17	51	39
Agricultural productivity (value added per worker, 2000 $)	..	458	330
Food production index (1999–2001 = 100)	124	120	112
Population density, rural (people/sq. km of arable land)	331	547	603
Forests and biodiversity			
Forest area (% of land area)	49.0	28.4	24.7
Deforestation (average annual %, 1990–2005)	1.3	–0.1	0.7
Nationally protected area (% of land area)	5.4	14.0	10.8
Animal species, total known	1,335		
Animal species, threatened	189		
Higher plant species, total known	7,000		
Higher plant species, threatened	38		
GEF benefits index for biodiversity (0–100, median is 1.5)	10.0		
Energy			
GDP per unit of energy use (2005 PPP $/kg oil equivalent)	2.9	3.4	3.2
Energy use per capita (kg oil equivalent)	295	1,258	478
Energy from biomass products and waste (% of total)	72.1	14.7	53.8
Electric power consumption per capita (kWh)	93	1,669	309
Electricity generated using fossil fuel (% of total)	46.1	82.0	48.4
Electricity generated by hydropower (% of total)	53.9	15.0	38.8
Emissions and pollution			
CO_2 emissions per unit of GDP (kg/2005 PPP $)	0.3	0.9	0.4
CO_2 emissions per capita (metric tons)	0.2	3.6	0.6
CO_2 emissions growth (%, 1990–2005)	165.3	123.4	39.3
Particulate matter (urban-pop.-weighted avg., µg/cu. m)	58	69	69
Transport sector fuel consumption per capita (liters)	28	106	41
Water and sanitation			
Internal freshwater resources per capita (cu. m)	18,051	4,948	4,619
Freshwater withdrawal			
Total (% of internal resources)	3.8	10.2	9.4
Agriculture (% of total freshwater withdrawal)	98	74	90
Access to improved water source (% of total population)	80	87	68
Rural (% of rural population)	80	81	60
Urban (% of urban population)	80	96	84
Access to improved sanitation (% of total population)	82	66	39
Rural (% of rural population)	81	59	33
Urban (% of urban population)	85	75	54
Environment and health			
Acute resp. infection prevalence (% of children under five)	2.0		
Diarrhea prevalence (% of children under five)	..		
Under-five mortality rate (per 1,000 live births)	103	27	126
National accounting aggregates			
Gross savings (% of GNI)	..	48.0	25.4
Consumption of fixed capital (% of GNI)	..	10.7	9.3
Education expenditure (% of GNI)	..	2.1	2.6
Energy depletion (% of GNI)	..	4.9	9.8
Mineral depletion (% of GNI)	..	1.3	0.9
Net forest depletion (% of GNI)	..	0.0	0.8
CO_2 damage (% of GNI)	..	1.3	0.7
Particulate emission damage (% of GNI)	..	1.3	0.7
Adjusted net savings (% of GNI)	..	30.6	5.8

Namibia

	Country data	Sub-Saharan Africa group	Lower middle-income group
Population (millions) **2.1** Land area (1,000 sq. km) **823.3** GDP ($ billions) **7.0**			

	Country data	Sub-Saharan Africa group	Lower middle-income group
GNI per capita, *World Bank Atlas* method ($)	3,450	951	1,905
Urban population (% of total)	36	36	42
Urban population growth (average annual %, 1990–2007)	3.8	4.0	2.9
Population growth (average annual %, 1990–2007)	2.3	2.6	1.3
Agriculture			
Agricultural land (% of land area)	47	44	47
Agricultural productivity (value added per worker, 2000 $)	1,134	287	532
Food production index (1999–2001 = 100)	135	109	116
Population density, rural (people/sq. km of arable land)	161	351	511
Forests and biodiversity			
Forest area (% of land area)	9.3	26.5	25.0
Deforestation (average annual %, 1990–2005)	0.9	0.6	0.1
Nationally protected area (% of land area)	5.2	11.3	11.0
Animal species, total known	811		
Animal species, threatened	58		
Higher plant species, total known	3,174		
Higher plant species, threatened	24		
GEF benefits index for biodiversity (0–100, median is 1.5)	5.2		
Energy			
GDP per unit of energy use (2005 PPP $/kg oil equivalent)	6.5	3.0	3.9
Energy use per capita (kg oil equivalent)	721	670	1,019
Energy from biomass products and waste (% of total)	12.7	56.3	15.2
Electric power consumption per capita (kWh)	1,546	531	1,269
Electricity generated using fossil fuel (% of total)	5.9	65.6	79.0
Electricity generated by hydropower (% of total)	94.1	18.0	16.3
Emissions and pollution			
CO_2 emissions per unit of GDP (kg/2005 PPP $)	0.3	0.5	0.8
CO_2 emissions per capita (metric tons)	1.3	0.8	2.8
CO_2 emissions growth (%, 1990–2005)	34,750.0	40.1	93.5
Particulate matter (urban-pop.-weighted avg., µg/cu. m)	47	53	67
Transport sector fuel consumption per capita (liters)	297	64	99
Water and sanitation			
Internal freshwater resources per capita (cu. m)	2,961	4,824	4,117
Freshwater withdrawal			
Total (% of internal resources)	4.9	3.2	8.7
Agriculture (% of total freshwater withdrawal)	71	87	80
Access to improved water source (% of total population)	93	58	88
Rural (% of rural population)	90	46	82
Urban (% of urban population)	99	81	96
Access to improved sanitation (% of total population)	35	31	55
Rural (% of rural population)	18	24	43
Urban (% of urban population)	66	42	71
Environment and health			
Acute resp. infection prevalence (% of children under five)	18.0		
Diarrhea prevalence (% of children under five)	20.6		
Under-five mortality rate (per 1,000 live births)	68	146	50
National accounting aggregates			
Gross savings (% of GNI)	40.3	17.4	41.7
Consumption of fixed capital (% of GNI)	11.3	11.1	10.7
Education expenditure (% of GNI)	7.3	3.6	2.6
Energy depletion (% of GNI)	0.0	11.7	6.6
Mineral depletion (% of GNI)	4.2	1.5	1.2
Net forest depletion (% of GNI)	0.0	0.5	0.2
CO_2 damage (% of GNI)	0.3	0.7	1.2
Particulate emission damage (% of GNI)	0.1	0.4	1.1
Adjusted net savings (% of GNI)	31.7	-5.0	23.5

Nepal

Population (millions)	**28**	Land area (1,000 sq. km)	**143**	GDP ($ billions)	**10.3**

	Country data	South Asia group	Low-income group
GNI per capita, *World Bank Atlas* method ($)	350	880	574
Urban population (% of total)	17	29	32
Urban population growth (average annual %, 1990–2007)	6.0	2.7	3.7
Population growth (average annual %, 1990–2007)	2.3	1.8	2.4
Agriculture			
Agricultural land (% of land area)	30	55	39
Agricultural productivity (value added per worker, 2000 $)	210	417	330
Food production index (1999–2001 = 100)	114	107	112
Population density, rural (people/sq. km of arable land)	968	617	603
Forests and biodiversity			
Forest area (% of land area)	25.4	16.8	24.7
Deforestation (average annual %, 1990–2005)	1.9	-0.1	0.7
Nationally protected area (% of land area)	16.0	5.6	10.8
Animal species, total known	..		
Animal species, threatened	74		
Higher plant species, total known	6,973		
Higher plant species, threatened	7		
GEF benefits index for biodiversity (0–100, median is 1.5)	2.1		
Energy			
GDP per unit of energy use (2005 PPP $/kg oil equivalent)	2.9	4.8	3.2
Energy use per capita (kg oil equivalent)	340	468	478
Energy from biomass products and waste (% of total)	86.2	30.4	53.8
Electric power consumption per capita (kWh)	80	453	309
Electricity generated using fossil fuel (% of total)	0.4	78.3	48.4
Electricity generated by hydropower (% of total)	99.6	17.4	38.8
Emissions and pollution			
CO_2 emissions per unit of GDP (kg/2005 PPP $)	0.1	0.5	0.4
CO_2 emissions per capita (metric tons)	0.1	1.1	0.6
CO_2 emissions growth (%, 1990–2005)	395.9	106.7	39.3
Particulate matter (urban-pop.-weighted avg., µg/cu. m)	34	78	69
Transport sector fuel consumption per capita (liters)	11	33	41
Water and sanitation			
Internal freshwater resources per capita (cu. m)	7,051	1,196	4,619
Freshwater withdrawal			
Total (% of internal resources)	5.1	51.7	9.4
Agriculture (% of total freshwater withdrawal)	96	89	90
Access to improved water source (% of total population)	89	87	68
Rural (% of rural population)	88	84	60
Urban (% of urban population)	94	94	84
Access to improved sanitation (% of total population)	27	33	39
Rural (% of rural population)	24	23	33
Urban (% of urban population)	45	57	54
Environment and health			
Acute resp. infection prevalence (% of children under five)	23.0		
Diarrhea prevalence (% of children under five)	27.5		
Under-five mortality rate (per 1,000 live births)	55	78	126
National accounting aggregates			
Gross savings (% of GNI)	28.2	36.2	25.4
Consumption of fixed capital (% of GNI)	8.0	9.5	9.3
Education expenditure (% of GNI)	2.4	3.0	2.6
Energy depletion (% of GNI)	0.0	2.7	9.8
Mineral depletion (% of GNI)	0.0	0.6	0.9
Net forest depletion (% of GNI)	4.4	0.9	0.8
CO_2 damage (% of GNI)	0.2	1.0	0.7
Particulate emission damage (% of GNI)	0.1	0.8	0.7
Adjusted net savings (% of GNI)	17.9	23.9	5.8

Netherlands

Population (millions)	**16**	Land area (1,000 sq. km)	**34**	GDP ($ billions)	**765.8**

	Country data	High-income group
GNI per capita, *World Bank Atlas* method ($)	45,650	37,572
Urban population (% of total)	81	78
Urban population growth (average annual %, 1990–2007)	1.5	1.0
Population growth (average annual %, 1990–2007)	0.5	0.7
Agriculture		
Agricultural land (% of land area)	57	38
Agricultural productivity (value added per worker, 2000 $)	44,232	27,680
Food production index (1999–2001 = 100)	93	102
Population density, rural (people/sq. km of arable land)	356	323
Forests and biodiversity		
Forest area (% of land area)	10.8	28.8
Deforestation (average annual %, 1990–2005)	-0.4	-0.1
Nationally protected area (% of land area)	12.7	11.8
Animal species, total known	539	
Animal species, threatened	23	
Higher plant species, total known	1,221	
Higher plant species, threatened	0	
GEF benefits index for biodiversity (0–100, median is 1.5)	0.2	
Energy		
GDP per unit of energy use (2005 PPP $/kg oil equivalent)	7.3	6.3
Energy use per capita (kg oil equivalent)	4,901	5,416
Energy from biomass products and waste (% of total)	3.3	3.4
Electric power consumption per capita (kWh)	7,055	9,675
Electricity generated using fossil fuel (% of total)	86.7	62.0
Electricity generated by hydropower (% of total)	0.1	11.4
Emissions and pollution		
CO_2 emissions per unit of GDP (kg/2005 PPP $)	0.2	0.4
CO_2 emissions per capita (metric tons)	7.7	12.6
CO_2 emissions growth (%, 1990–2005)	-10.0	19.1
Particulate matter (urban-pop.-weighted avg., µg/cu. m)	34	26
Transport sector fuel consumption per capita (liters)	792	1,159
Water and sanitation		
Internal freshwater resources per capita (cu. m)	672	9,313
Freshwater withdrawal		
Total (% of internal resources)	72.2	10.4
Agriculture (% of total freshwater withdrawal)	34	43
Access to improved water source (% of total population)	100	100
Rural (% of rural population)	100	98
Urban (% of urban population)	100	100
Access to improved sanitation (% of total population)	100	100
Rural (% of rural population)	100	99
Urban (% of urban population)	100	100
Environment and health		
Acute resp. infection prevalence (% of children under five)	..	
Diarrhea prevalence (% of children under five)	..	
Under-five mortality rate (per 1,000 live births)	5	7
National accounting aggregates		
Gross savings (% of GNI)	27.6	20.6
Consumption of fixed capital (% of GNI)	14.6	14.5
Education expenditure (% of GNI)	4.8	4.6
Energy depletion (% of GNI)	1.4	1.5
Mineral depletion (% of GNI)	0.0	0.2
Net forest depletion (% of GNI)	0.0	0.0
CO_2 damage (% of GNI)	0.1	0.3
Particulate emission damage (% of GNI)	0.6	0.3
Adjusted net savings (% of GNI)	15.6	8.5

Netherlands Antilles

Population (thousands) **191** Land area (sq. km) **800** GDP ($ millions) ..

	Country data	High-income group
GNI per capita, *World Bank Atlas* method ($)	..	37,572
Urban population (% of total)	92	78
Urban population growth (average annual %, 1990–2007)	0.5	1.0
Population growth (average annual %, 1990–2007)	0.0	0.7
Agriculture		
Agricultural land (% of land area)	10	38
Agricultural productivity (value added per worker, 2000 $)	..	27,680
Food production index (1999–2001 = 100)	107	102
Population density, rural (people/sq. km of arable land)	189	323
Forests and biodiversity		
Forest area (% of land area)	1.5	28.8
Deforestation (average annual %, 1990–2005)	0.0	-0.1
Nationally protected area (% of land area)	0.3	11.8
Animal species, total known	300	
Animal species, threatened	37	
Higher plant species, total known	..	
Higher plant species, threatened	2	
GEF benefits index for biodiversity (0–100, median is 1.5)	0.2	
Energy		
GDP per unit of energy use (2005 PPP $/kg oil equivalent)	..	6.3
Energy use per capita (kg oil equivalent)	9,161	5,416
Energy from biomass products and waste (% of total)	0.0	3.4
Electric power consumption per capita (kWh)	5,656	9,675
Electricity generated using fossil fuel (% of total)	100.0	62.0
Electricity generated by hydropower (% of total)	0.0	11.4
Emissions and pollution		
CO_2 emissions per unit of GDP (kg/2005 PPP $)	..	0.4
CO_2 emissions per capita (metric tons)	20.9	12.6
CO_2 emissions growth (%, 1990–2005)	223.8	19.1
Particulate matter (urban-pop.-weighted avg., µg/cu. m)	30	26
Transport sector fuel consumption per capita (liters)	2,916	1,159
Water and sanitation		
Internal freshwater resources per capita (cu. m)	..	9,313
Freshwater withdrawal		
Total (% of internal resources)	..	10.4
Agriculture (% of total freshwater withdrawal)	..	43
Access to improved water source (% of total population)	..	100
Rural (% of rural population)	..	98
Urban (% of urban population)	..	100
Access to improved sanitation (% of total population)	..	100
Rural (% of rural population)	..	99
Urban (% of urban population)	..	100
Environment and health		
Acute resp. infection prevalence (% of children under five)	..	
Diarrhea prevalence (% of children under five)	..	
Under-five mortality rate (per 1,000 live births)	..	7
National accounting aggregates		
Gross savings (% of GNI)	..	20.6
Consumption of fixed capital (% of GNI)	..	14.5
Education expenditure (% of GNI)	..	4.6
Energy depletion (% of GNI)	..	1.5
Mineral depletion (% of GNI)	..	0.2
Net forest depletion (% of GNI)	..	0.0
CO_2 damage (% of GNI)	..	0.3
Particulate emission damage (% of GNI)	..	0.3
Adjusted net savings (% of GNI)	..	8.5

New Caledonia

Population (thousands) **242**	Land area (1,000 sq. km) **18**	GDP ($ billions) **2.7**

	Country data	High-income group
GNI per capita, *World Bank Atlas* method ($)	14,020	37,572
Urban population (% of total)	64	78
Urban population growth (average annual %, 1990–2007)	2.6	1.0
Population growth (average annual %, 1990–2007)	2.2	0.7
Agriculture		
Agricultural land (% of land area)	14	38
Agricultural productivity (value added per worker, 2000 $)	..	27,680
Food production index (1999–2001 = 100)	103	102
Population density, rural (people/sq. km of arable land)	1,418	323
Forests and biodiversity		
Forest area (% of land area)	39.2	28.8
Deforestation (average annual %, 1990–2005)	0.0	−0.1
Nationally protected area (% of land area)	7.1	11.8
Animal species, total known	178	
Animal species, threatened	137	
Higher plant species, total known	3,250	
Higher plant species, threatened	218	
GEF benefits index for biodiversity (0–100, median is 1.5)	8.5	
Energy		
GDP per unit of energy use (2005 PPP $/kg oil equivalent)	..	6.3
Energy use per capita (kg oil equivalent)	..	5,416
Energy from biomass products and waste (% of total)	..	3.4
Electric power consumption per capita (kWh)	..	9,675
Electricity generated using fossil fuel (% of total)	..	62.0
Electricity generated by hydropower (% of total)	..	11.4
Emissions and pollution		
CO_2 emissions per unit of GDP (kg/2005 PPP $)	..	0.4
CO_2 emissions per capita (metric tons)	11.3	12.6
CO_2 emissions growth (%, 1990–2005)	63.6	19.1
Particulate matter (urban-pop.-weighted avg., µg/cu. m)	69	26
Transport sector fuel consumption per capita (liters)	..	1,159
Water and sanitation		
Internal freshwater resources per capita (cu. m)	..	9,313
Freshwater withdrawal		
Total (% of internal resources)	..	10.4
Agriculture (% of total freshwater withdrawal)	..	43
Access to improved water source (% of total population)	..	100
Rural (% of rural population)	..	98
Urban (% of urban population)	..	100
Access to improved sanitation (% of total population)	..	100
Rural (% of rural population)	..	99
Urban (% of urban population)	..	100
Environment and health		
Acute resp. infection prevalence (% of children under five)	..	
Diarrhea prevalence (% of children under five)	..	
Under-five mortality rate (per 1,000 live births)	..	7
National accounting aggregates		
Gross savings (% of GNI)	..	20.6
Consumption of fixed capital (% of GNI)	..	14.5
Education expenditure (% of GNI)	..	4.6
Energy depletion (% of GNI)	..	1.5
Mineral depletion (% of GNI)	..	0.2
Net forest depletion (% of GNI)	..	0.0
CO_2 damage (% of GNI)	..	0.3
Particulate emission damage (% of GNI)	..	0.3
Adjusted net savings (% of GNI)	..	8.5

New Zealand

Population (millions)	**4.2**	Land area (1,000 sq. km)	**267.7**	GDP ($ billions)	**135.7**

	Country data	High-income group
GNI per capita, *World Bank Atlas* method ($)	27,080	37,572
Urban population (% of total)	86	78
Urban population growth (average annual %, 1990–2007)	1.3	1.0
Population growth (average annual %, 1990–2007)	1.2	0.7
Agriculture		
Agricultural land (% of land area)	65	38
Agricultural productivity (value added per worker, 2000 $)	28,271	27,680
Food production index (1999–2001 = 100)	116	102
Population density, rural (people/sq. km of arable land)	38	323
Forests and biodiversity		
Forest area (% of land area)	31.0	28.8
Deforestation (average annual %, 1990–2005)	–0.5	–0.1
Nationally protected area (% of land area)	24.2	11.8
Animal species, total known	424	
Animal species, threatened	122	
Higher plant species, total known	2,382	
Higher plant species, threatened	21	
GEF benefits index for biodiversity (0–100, median is 1.5)	20.2	
Energy		
GDP per unit of energy use (2005 PPP $/kg oil equivalent)	5.9	6.3
Energy use per capita (kg oil equivalent)	4,192	5,416
Energy from biomass products and waste (% of total)	6.0	3.4
Electric power consumption per capita (kWh)	9,646	9,675
Electricity generated using fossil fuel (% of total)	35.2	62.0
Electricity generated by hydropower (% of total)	53.9	11.4
Emissions and pollution		
CO_2 emissions per unit of GDP (kg/2005 PPP $)	0.3	0.4
CO_2 emissions per capita (metric tons)	7.2	12.6
CO_2 emissions growth (%, 1990–2005)	33.4	19.1
Particulate matter (urban-pop.-weighted avg., µg/cu. m)	14	26
Transport sector fuel consumption per capita (liters)	1,196	1,159
Water and sanitation		
Internal freshwater resources per capita (cu. m)	77,336	9,313
Freshwater withdrawal		
Total (% of internal resources)	0.6	10.4
Agriculture (% of total freshwater withdrawal)	42	43
Access to improved water source (% of total population)	..	100
Rural (% of rural population)	..	98
Urban (% of urban population)	100	100
Access to improved sanitation (% of total population)	..	100
Rural (% of rural population)	..	99
Urban (% of urban population)	..	100
Environment and health		
Acute resp. infection prevalence (% of children under five)	..	
Diarrhea prevalence (% of children under five)	..	
Under-five mortality rate (per 1,000 live births)	6	7
National accounting aggregates		
Gross savings (% of GNI)	..	20.6
Consumption of fixed capital (% of GNI)	15.5	14.5
Education expenditure (% of GNI)	6.7	4.6
Energy depletion (% of GNI)	1.3	1.5
Mineral depletion (% of GNI)	0.2	0.2
Net forest depletion (% of GNI)	0.0	0.0
CO_2 damage (% of GNI)	0.2	0.3
Particulate emission damage (% of GNI)	0.0	0.3
Adjusted net savings (% of GNI)	..	8.5

Nicaragua

	Population (millions)	5.6	Land area (1,000 sq. km)	121.4	GDP ($ billions)	5.7

	Country data	Latin America & Caribbean group	Lower middle-income group
GNI per capita, *World Bank Atlas* method ($)	990	5,801	1,905
Urban population (% of total)	56	78	42
Urban population growth (average annual %, 1990–2007)	2.2	2.1	2.9
Population growth (average annual %, 1990–2007)	1.8	1.5	1.3
Agriculture			
Agricultural land (% of land area)	44	36	47
Agricultural productivity (value added per worker, 2000 $)	2,172	3,158	532
Food production index (1999–2001 = 100)	128	117	116
Population density, rural (people/sq. km of arable land)	125	232	511
Forests and biodiversity			
Forest area (% of land area)	42.7	45.4	25.0
Deforestation (average annual %, 1990–2005)	1.5	0.5	0.1
Nationally protected area (% of land area)	17.6	16.7	11.0
Animal species, total known	813		
Animal species, threatened	72		
Higher plant species, total known	7,590		
Higher plant species, threatened	39		
GEF benefits index for biodiversity (0–100, median is 1.5)	3.3		
Energy			
GDP per unit of energy use (2005 PPP $/kg oil equivalent)	3.8	7.3	3.9
Energy use per capita (kg oil equivalent)	624	1,240	1,019
Energy from biomass products and waste (% of total)	52.2	15.9	15.2
Electric power consumption per capita (kWh)	426	1,808	1,269
Electricity generated using fossil fuel (% of total)	72.2	37.0	79.0
Electricity generated by hydropower (% of total)	12.5	57.3	16.3
Emissions and pollution			
CO_2 emissions per unit of GDP (kg/2005 PPP $)	0.3	0.3	0.8
CO_2 emissions per capita (metric tons)	0.7	2.5	2.8
CO_2 emissions growth (%, 1990–2005)	47.9	33.4	93.5
Particulate matter (urban-pop.-weighted avg., µg/cu. m)	28	35	67
Transport sector fuel consumption per capita (liters)	100	295	99
Water and sanitation			
Internal freshwater resources per capita (cu. m)	33,854	23,965	4,117
Freshwater withdrawal			
Total (% of internal resources)	0.7	2.0	8.7
Agriculture (% of total freshwater withdrawal)	83	71	80
Access to improved water source (% of total population)	79	91	88
Rural (% of rural population)	63	73	82
Urban (% of urban population)	90	97	96
Access to improved sanitation (% of total population)	48	78	55
Rural (% of rural population)	34	51	43
Urban (% of urban population)	57	86	71
Environment and health			
Acute resp. infection prevalence (% of children under five)	31.0		
Diarrhea prevalence (% of children under five)	14.0		
Under-five mortality rate (per 1,000 live births)	35	26	50
National accounting aggregates			
Gross savings (% of GNI)	14.6	22.9	41.7
Consumption of fixed capital (% of GNI)	9.7	12.6	10.7
Education expenditure (% of GNI)	3.0	4.5	2.6
Energy depletion (% of GNI)	0.0	5.4	6.6
Mineral depletion (% of GNI)	0.7	1.9	1.2
Net forest depletion (% of GNI)	0.0	0.0	0.2
CO_2 damage (% of GNI)	0.6	0.3	1.2
Particulate emission damage (% of GNI)	0.1	0.4	1.1
Adjusted net savings (% of GNI)	6.5	6.7	23.5

Niger

Population (millions)	**14**	Land area (1,000 sq. km)	**1,267**	GDP ($ billions)	**4.2**

	Country data	Sub-Saharan Africa group	Low-income group
GNI per capita, *World Bank Atlas* method ($)	280	951	574
Urban population (% of total)	16	36	32
Urban population growth (average annual %, 1990–2007)	3.9	4.0	3.7
Population growth (average annual %, 1990–2007)	3.5	2.6	2.4

Agriculture

Agricultural land (% of land area)	30	44	39
Agricultural productivity (value added per worker, 2000 $)	157	287	330
Food production index (1999–2001 = 100)	102	109	112
Population density, rural (people/sq. km of arable land)	77	351	603

Forests and biodiversity

Forest area (% of land area)	1.0	26.5	24.7
Deforestation (average annual %, 1990–2005)	2.8	0.6	0.7
Nationally protected area (% of land area)	6.6	11.3	10.8
Animal species, total known	616		
Animal species, threatened	19		
Higher plant species, total known	1,460		
Higher plant species, threatened	2		
GEF benefits index for biodiversity (0–100, median is 1.5)	0.9		

Energy

GDP per unit of energy use (2005 PPP $/kg oil equivalent)	..	3.0	3.2
Energy use per capita (kg oil equivalent)	..	670	478
Energy from biomass products and waste (% of total)	..	56.3	53.8
Electric power consumption per capita (kWh)	..	531	309
Electricity generated using fossil fuel (% of total)	..	65.6	48.4
Electricity generated by hydropower (% of total)	..	18.0	38.8

Emissions and pollution

CO_2 emissions per unit of GDP (kg/2005 PPP $)	0.1	0.5	0.4
CO_2 emissions per capita (metric tons)	0.08	0.85	0.58
CO_2 emissions growth (%, 1990–2005)	1.0	40.1	39.3
Particulate matter (urban-pop.-weighted avg., µg/cu. m)	132	53	69
Transport sector fuel consumption per capita (liters)	..	64	41

Water and sanitation

Internal freshwater resources per capita (cu. m)	247	4,824	4,619
Freshwater withdrawal			
Total (% of internal resources)	62.3	3.2	9.4
Agriculture (% of total freshwater withdrawal)	95	87	90
Access to improved water source (% of total population)	42	58	68
Rural (% of rural population)	32	46	60
Urban (% of urban population)	91	81	84
Access to improved sanitation (% of total population)	7	31	39
Rural (% of rural population)	3	24	33
Urban (% of urban population)	27	42	54

Environment and health

Acute resp. infection prevalence (% of children under five)	12.0		
Diarrhea prevalence (% of children under five)	40.0		
Under-five mortality rate (per 1,000 live births)	176	146	126

National accounting aggregates

Gross savings (% of GNI)	..	17.4	25.4
Consumption of fixed capital (% of GNI)	7.7	11.1	9.3
Education expenditure (% of GNI)	2.6	3.6	2.6
Energy depletion (% of GNI)	0.0	11.7	9.8
Mineral depletion (% of GNI)	0.0	1.5	0.9
Net forest depletion (% of GNI)	2.4	0.5	0.8
CO_2 damage (% of GNI)	0.2	0.7	0.7
Particulate emission damage (% of GNI)	0.9	0.4	0.7
Adjusted net savings (% of GNI)	..	–5.0	5.8

Nigeria

Population (millions)	**148**	Land area (1,000 sq. km)	**911**	GDP ($ billions)	**165.5**

	Country data	Sub-Saharan Africa group	Low-income group
GNI per capita, *World Bank Atlas* method ($)	920	951	574
Urban population (% of total)	48	36	32
Urban population growth (average annual %, 1990–2007)	4.4	4.0	3.7
Population growth (average annual %, 1990–2007)	2.6	2.6	2.4
Agriculture			
Agricultural land (% of land area)	81	44	39
Agricultural productivity (value added per worker, 2000 $)	..	287	330
Food production index (1999–2001 = 100)	106	109	112
Population density, rural (people/sq. km of arable land)	238	351	603
Forests and biodiversity			
Forest area (% of land area)	12.2	26.5	24.7
Deforestation (average annual %, 1990–2005)	2.9	0.6	0.7
Nationally protected area (% of land area)	6.2	11.3	10.8
Animal species, total known	1,189		
Animal species, threatened	80		
Higher plant species, total known	4,715		
Higher plant species, threatened	171		
GEF benefits index for biodiversity (0–100, median is 1.5)	6.0		
Energy			
GDP per unit of energy use (2005 PPP $/kg oil equivalent)	2.5	3.0	3.2
Energy use per capita (kg oil equivalent)	726	670	478
Energy from biomass products and waste (% of total)	79.6	56.3	53.8
Electric power consumption per capita (kWh)	116	531	309
Electricity generated using fossil fuel (% of total)	66.6	65.6	48.4
Electricity generated by hydropower (% of total)	33.4	18.0	38.8
Emissions and pollution			
CO_2 emissions per unit of GDP (kg/2005 PPP $)	0.5	0.5	0.4
CO_2 emissions per capita (metric tons)	0.8	0.8	0.6
CO_2 emissions growth (%, 1990–2005)	152.1	40.1	39.3
Particulate matter (urban-pop.-weighted avg., µg/cu. m)	45	53	69
Transport sector fuel consumption per capita (liters)	60	64	41
Water and sanitation			
Internal freshwater resources per capita (cu. m)	1,493	4,824	4,619
Freshwater withdrawal			
Total (% of internal resources)	3.6	3.2	9.4
Agriculture (% of total freshwater withdrawal)	69	87	90
Access to improved water source (% of total population)	47	58	68
Rural (% of rural population)	30	46	60
Urban (% of urban population)	65	81	84
Access to improved sanitation (% of total population)	30	31	39
Rural (% of rural population)	25	24	33
Urban (% of urban population)	35	42	54
Environment and health			
Acute resp. infection prevalence (% of children under five)	10.0		
Diarrhea prevalence (% of children under five)	15.3		
Under-five mortality rate (per 1,000 live births)	189	146	126
National accounting aggregates			
Gross savings (% of GNI)	..	17.4	25.4
Consumption of fixed capital (% of GNI)	10.8	11.1	9.3
Education expenditure (% of GNI)	0.9	3.6	2.6
Energy depletion (% of GNI)	25.2	11.7	9.8
Mineral depletion (% of GNI)	0.0	1.5	0.9
Net forest depletion (% of GNI)	0.1	0.5	0.8
CO_2 damage (% of GNI)	0.7	0.7	0.7
Particulate emission damage (% of GNI)	0.5	0.4	0.7
Adjusted net savings (% of GNI)	..	-5.0	5.8

Northern Mariana Islands

Population (thousands) **84** Land area (sq. km) **180** GDP ($ millions) ..

	Country data	High-income group
GNI per capita, *World Bank Atlas* method ($)	..	37,572
Urban population (% of total)	91	78
Urban population growth (average annual %, 1990–2007)	..	1.0
Population growth (average annual %, 1990–2007)	..	0.7
Agriculture		
Agricultural land (% of land area)	7	38
Agricultural productivity (value added per worker, 2000 $)	..	27,680
Food production index (1999–2001 = 100)	..	102
Population density, rural (people/sq. km of arable land)	739	323
Forests and biodiversity		
Forest area (% of land area)	72.4	28.8
Deforestation (average annual %, 1990–2005)	0.4	–0.1
Nationally protected area (% of land area)	..	11.8
Animal species, total known	99	
Animal species, threatened	80	
Higher plant species, total known	..	
Higher plant species, threatened	5	
GEF benefits index for biodiversity (0–100, median is 1.5)	2.2	
Energy		
GDP per unit of energy use (2005 PPP $/kg oil equivalent)	..	6.3
Energy use per capita (kg oil equivalent)	..	5,416
Energy from biomass products and waste (% of total)	..	3.4
Electric power consumption per capita (kWh)	..	9,675
Electricity generated using fossil fuel (% of total)	..	62.0
Electricity generated by hydropower (% of total)	..	11.4
Emissions and pollution		
CO_2 emissions per unit of GDP (kg/2005 PPP $)	..	0.4
CO_2 emissions per capita (metric tons)	..	12.6
CO_2 emissions growth (%, 1990–2005)	..	19.1
Particulate matter (urban-pop.-weighted avg., µg/cu. m)	..	26
Transport sector fuel consumption per capita (liters)	..	1,159
Water and sanitation		
Internal freshwater resources per capita (cu. m)	..	9,313
Freshwater withdrawal		
Total (% of internal resources)	..	10.4
Agriculture (% of total freshwater withdrawal)	..	43
Access to improved water source (% of total population)	98	100
Rural (% of rural population)	97	98
Urban (% of urban population)	98	100
Access to improved sanitation (% of total population)	94	100
Rural (% of rural population)	96	99
Urban (% of urban population)	94	100
Environment and health		
Acute resp. infection prevalence (% of children under five)	..	
Diarrhea prevalence (% of children under five)	..	
Under-five mortality rate (per 1,000 live births)	..	7
National accounting aggregates		
Gross savings (% of GNI)	..	20.6
Consumption of fixed capital (% of GNI)	..	14.5
Education expenditure (% of GNI)	..	4.6
Energy depletion (% of GNI)	..	1.5
Mineral depletion (% of GNI)	..	0.2
Net forest depletion (% of GNI)	..	0.0
CO_2 damage (% of GNI)	..	0.3
Particulate emission damage (% of GNI)	..	0.3
Adjusted net savings (% of GNI)	..	8.5

Norway

	Country data	High-income group
Population (millions) **4.7** Land area (1,000 sq. km) **304.3** GDP ($ billions) **388.4**		

	Country data	High-income group
GNI per capita, *World Bank Atlas* method ($)	77,370	37,572
Urban population (% of total)	77	78
Urban population growth (average annual %, 1990–2007)	1.0	1.0
Population growth (average annual %, 1990–2007)	0.6	0.7
Agriculture		
Agricultural land (% of land area)	3	38
Agricultural productivity (value added per worker, 2000 $)	38,218	27,680
Food production index (1999–2001 = 100)	101	102
Population density, rural (people/sq. km of arable land)	121	323
Forests and biodiversity		
Forest area (% of land area)	30.8	28.8
Deforestation (average annual %, 1990–2005)	-0.2	-0.1
Nationally protected area (% of land area)	5.1	11.8
Animal species, total known	525	
Animal species, threatened	32	
Higher plant species, total known	1,715	
Higher plant species, threatened	2	
GEF benefits index for biodiversity (0–100, median is 1.5)	1.3	
Energy		
GDP per unit of energy use (2005 PPP $/kg oil equivalent)	8.6	6.3
Energy use per capita (kg oil equivalent)	5,598	5,416
Energy from biomass products and waste (% of total)	5.1	3.4
Electric power consumption per capita (kWh)	24,296	9,675
Electricity generated using fossil fuel (% of total)	0.5	62.0
Electricity generated by hydropower (% of total)	98.5	11.4
Emissions and pollution		
CO_2 emissions per unit of GDP (kg/2005 PPP $)	0.2	0.4
CO_2 emissions per capita (metric tons)	11.4	12.6
CO_2 emissions growth (%, 1990–2005)	74.7	19.1
Particulate matter (urban-pop.-weighted avg., µg/cu. m)	15	26
Transport sector fuel consumption per capita (liters)	1,023	1,159
Water and sanitation		
Internal freshwater resources per capita (cu. m)	81,119	9,313
Freshwater withdrawal		
Total (% of internal resources)	0.6	10.4
Agriculture (% of total freshwater withdrawal)	11	43
Access to improved water source (% of total population)	100	100
Rural (% of rural population)	100	98
Urban (% of urban population)	100	100
Access to improved sanitation (% of total population)	..	100
Rural (% of rural population)	..	99
Urban (% of urban population)	..	100
Environment and health		
Acute resp. infection prevalence (% of children under five)	..	
Diarrhea prevalence (% of children under five)	..	
Under-five mortality rate (per 1,000 live births)	4	7
National accounting aggregates		
Gross savings (% of GNI)	38.3	20.6
Consumption of fixed capital (% of GNI)	15.7	14.5
Education expenditure (% of GNI)	6.5	4.6
Energy depletion (% of GNI)	13.4	1.5
Mineral depletion (% of GNI)	0.0	0.2
Net forest depletion (% of GNI)	0.0	0.0
CO_2 damage (% of GNI)	0.2	0.3
Particulate emission damage (% of GNI)	0.0	0.3
Adjusted net savings (% of GNI)	15.5	8.5

Oman

| Population (millions) | **2.6** | Land area (1,000 sq. km) | **309.5** | GDP ($ billions) | **35.7** |

	Country data	High-income group
GNI per capita, *World Bank Atlas* method ($)	12,860	37,572
Urban population (% of total)	72	78
Urban population growth (average annual %, 1990-2007)	2.5	1.0
Population growth (average annual %, 1990-2007)	2.0	0.7
Agriculture		
Agricultural land (% of land area)	6	38
Agricultural productivity (value added per worker, 2000 $)	1,350	27,680
Food production index (1999-2001 = 100)	97	102
Population density, rural (people/sq. km of arable land)	1,152	323
Forests and biodiversity		
Forest area (% of land area)	0.0	28.8
Deforestation (average annual %, 1990-2005)	0.0	-0.1
Nationally protected area (% of land area)	0.1	11.8
Animal species, total known	557	
Animal species, threatened	68	
Higher plant species, total known	1,204	
Higher plant species, threatened	6	
GEF benefits index for biodiversity (0-100, median is 1.5)	3.7	
Energy		
GDP per unit of energy use (2005 PPP $/kg oil equivalent)	3.6	6.3
Energy use per capita (kg oil equivalent)	6,057	5,416
Energy from biomass products and waste (% of total)	0.0	3.4
Electric power consumption per capita (kWh)	4,456	9,675
Electricity generated using fossil fuel (% of total)	100.0	62.0
Electricity generated by hydropower (% of total)	0.0	11.4
Emissions and pollution		
CO_2 emissions per unit of GDP (kg/2005 PPP $)	0.6	0.4
CO_2 emissions per capita (metric tons)	12.5	12.6
CO_2 emissions growth (%, 1990-2005)	206.3	19.1
Particulate matter (urban-pop.-weighted avg., µg/cu. m)	108	26
Transport sector fuel consumption per capita (liters)	608	1,159
Water and sanitation		
Internal freshwater resources per capita (cu. m)	539	9,313
Freshwater withdrawal		
Total (% of internal resources)	94.4	10.4
Agriculture (% of total freshwater withdrawal)	88	43
Access to improved water source (% of total population)	..	100
Rural (% of rural population)	..	98
Urban (% of urban population)	..	100
Access to improved sanitation (% of total population)	..	100
Rural (% of rural population)	..	99
Urban (% of urban population)	97	100
Environment and health		
Acute resp. infection prevalence (% of children under five)	6.2	
Diarrhea prevalence (% of children under five)	6.7	
Under-five mortality rate (per 1,000 live births)	12	7
National accounting aggregates		
Gross savings (% of GNI)	..	20.6
Consumption of fixed capital (% of GNI)	..	14.5
Education expenditure (% of GNI)	3.9	4.6
Energy depletion (% of GNI)	..	1.5
Mineral depletion (% of GNI)	..	0.2
Net forest depletion (% of GNI)	0.0	0.0
CO_2 damage (% of GNI)	..	0.3
Particulate emission damage (% of GNI)	1.4	0.3
Adjusted net savings (% of GNI)	..	8.5

Pakistan

| Population (millions) | **162** | Land area (1,000 sq. km) | **771** | GDP ($ billions) | **142.9** |

	Country data	South Asia group	Low-income group
GNI per capita, *World Bank Atlas* method ($)	860	880	574
Urban population (% of total)	36	29	32
Urban population growth (average annual %, 1990–2007)	3.3	2.7	3.7
Population growth (average annual %, 1990–2007)	2.4	1.8	2.4
Agriculture			
Agricultural land (% of land area)	35	55	39
Agricultural productivity (value added per worker, 2000 $)	717	417	330
Food production index (1999–2001 = 100)	113	107	112
Population density, rural (people/sq. km of arable land)	477	617	603
Forests and biodiversity			
Forest area (% of land area)	2.5	16.8	24.7
Deforestation (average annual %, 1990–2005)	1.9	-0.1	0.7
Nationally protected area (% of land area)	8.5	5.6	10.8
Animal species, total known	820		
Animal species, threatened	97		
Higher plant species, total known	4,950		
Higher plant species, threatened	2		
GEF benefits index for biodiversity (0–100, median is 1.5)	4.9		
Energy			
GDP per unit of energy use (2005 PPP $/kg oil equivalent)	4.6	4.8	3.2
Energy use per capita (kg oil equivalent)	499	468	478
Energy from biomass products and waste (% of total)	34.9	30.4	53.8
Electric power consumption per capita (kWh)	480	453	309
Electricity generated using fossil fuel (% of total)	65.2	78.3	48.4
Electricity generated by hydropower (% of total)	32.5	17.4	38.8
Emissions and pollution			
CO_2 emissions per unit of GDP (kg/2005 PPP $)	0.4	0.5	0.4
CO_2 emissions per capita (metric tons)	0.9	1.1	0.6
CO_2 emissions growth (%, 1990–2005)	97.4	106.7	39.3
Particulate matter (urban-pop.-weighted avg., µg/cu. m)	120	78	69
Transport sector fuel consumption per capita (liters)	55	33	41
Water and sanitation			
Internal freshwater resources per capita (cu. m)	339	1,196	4,619
Freshwater withdrawal			
Total (% of internal resources)	308.0	51.7	9.4
Agriculture (% of total freshwater withdrawal)	96	89	90
Access to improved water source (% of total population)	90	87	68
Rural (% of rural population)	87	84	60
Urban (% of urban population)	95	94	84
Access to improved sanitation (% of total population)	58	33	39
Rural (% of rural population)	40	23	33
Urban (% of urban population)	90	57	54
Environment and health			
Acute resp. infection prevalence (% of children under five)	24.0		
Diarrhea prevalence (% of children under five)	26.0		
Under-five mortality rate (per 1,000 live births)	90	78	126
National accounting aggregates			
Gross savings (% of GNI)	24.5	36.2	25.4
Consumption of fixed capital (% of GNI)	9.1	9.5	9.3
Education expenditure (% of GNI)	2.1	3.0	2.6
Energy depletion (% of GNI)	3.3	2.7	9.8
Mineral depletion (% of GNI)	0.0	0.6	0.9
Net forest depletion (% of GNI)	0.9	0.9	0.8
CO_2 damage (% of GNI)	0.7	1.0	0.7
Particulate emission damage (% of GNI)	1.5	0.8	0.7
Adjusted net savings (% of GNI)	11.0	23.9	5.8

Palau

	Country data	East Asia & Pacific group	Upper middle-income group
Population (thousands) **20** Land area (sq. km)		**460** GDP ($ millions)	**164**

	Country data	East Asia & Pacific group	Upper middle-income group
GNI per capita, *World Bank Atlas* method ($)	8,270	2,182	7,107
Urban population (% of total)	79	43	75
Urban population growth (average annual %, 1990–2007)	..	3.5	1.4
Population growth (average annual %, 1990–2007)	1.7	1.1	0.9
Agriculture			
Agricultural land (% of land area)	20	51	31
Agricultural productivity (value added per worker, 2000 $)	..	458	2,947
Food production index (1999–2001 = 100)	..	120	113
Population density, rural (people/sq. km of arable land)	114	547	110
Forests and biodiversity			
Forest area (% of land area)	87.6	28.4	39.3
Deforestation (average annual %, 1990–2005)	-0.3	-0.1	0.2
Nationally protected area (% of land area)	0.0	14.0	10.3
Animal species, total known	120		
Animal species, threatened	122		
Higher plant species, total known	..		
Higher plant species, threatened	4		
GEF benefits index for biodiversity (0–100, median is 1.5)	1.2		
Energy			
GDP per unit of energy use (2005 PPP $/kg oil equivalent)	..	3.4	4.8
Energy use per capita (kg oil equivalent)	..	1,258	2,300
Energy from biomass products and waste (% of total)	..	14.7	7.0
Electric power consumption per capita (kWh)	..	1,669	3,242
Electricity generated using fossil fuel (% of total)	..	82.0	62.8
Electricity generated by hydropower (% of total)	..	15.0	27.6
Emissions and pollution			
CO_2 emissions per unit of GDP (kg/2005 PPP $)	..	0.9	0.5
CO_2 emissions per capita (metric tons)	5.7	3.6	5.5
CO_2 emissions growth (%, 1990–2005)	..	123.4	-8.3
Particulate matter (urban-pop.-weighted avg., µg/cu. m)	..	69	30
Transport sector fuel consumption per capita (liters)	..	106	332
Water and sanitation			
Internal freshwater resources per capita (cu. m)	..	4,948	16,993
Freshwater withdrawal			
Total (% of internal resources)	..	10.2	13.8
Agriculture (% of total freshwater withdrawal)	..	74	57
Access to improved water source (% of total population)	89	87	95
Rural (% of rural population)	94	81	83
Urban (% of urban population)	79	96	98
Access to improved sanitation (% of total population)	67	66	83
Rural (% of rural population)	52	59	64
Urban (% of urban population)	96	75	89
Environment and health			
Acute resp. infection prevalence (% of children under five)	..		
Diarrhea prevalence (% of children under five)	..		
Under-five mortality rate (per 1,000 live births)	10	27	24
National accounting aggregates			
Gross savings (% of GNI)	..	48.0	23.2
Consumption of fixed capital (% of GNI)	12.3	10.7	12.8
Education expenditure (% of GNI)	..	2.1	4.4
Energy depletion (% of GNI)	0.0	4.9	7.6
Mineral depletion (% of GNI)	0.0	1.3	1.3
Net forest depletion (% of GNI)	..	0.0	0.0
CO_2 damage (% of GNI)	1.1	1.3	0.6
Particulate emission damage (% of GNI)	..	1.3	0.4
Adjusted net savings (% of GNI)	..	30.6	4.9

Panama

Population (millions)	**3.3**	Land area (1,000 sq. km)	**74.4**	GDP ($ billions)	**19.5**

	Country data	Latin America & Caribbean group	Upper middle-income group
GNI per capita, *World Bank Atlas* method ($)	5,500	5,801	7,107
Urban population (% of total)	72	78	75
Urban population growth (average annual %, 1990–2007)	3.7	2.1	1.4
Population growth (average annual %, 1990–2007)	1.9	1.5	0.9
Agriculture			
Agricultural land (% of land area)	30	36	31
Agricultural productivity (value added per worker, 2000 $)	4,004	3,158	2,947
Food production index (1999–2001 = 100)	105	117	113
Population density, rural (people/sq. km of arable land)	172	232	110
Forests and biodiversity			
Forest area (% of land area)	57.7	45.4	39.3
Deforestation (average annual %, 1990–2005)	0.1	0.5	0.2
Nationally protected area (% of land area)	10.2	16.7	10.3
Animal species, total known	1,145		
Animal species, threatened	126		
Higher plant species, total known	9,915		
Higher plant species, threatened	194		
GEF benefits index for biodiversity (0–100, median is 1.5)	10.9		
Energy			
GDP per unit of energy use (2005 PPP $/kg oil equivalent)	11.6	7.3	4.8
Energy use per capita (kg oil equivalent)	845	1,240	2,300
Energy from biomass products and waste (% of total)	17.4	15.9	7.0
Electric power consumption per capita (kWh)	1,506	1,808	3,242
Electricity generated using fossil fuel (% of total)	38.9	37.0	62.8
Electricity generated by hydropower (% of total)	59.8	57.3	27.6
Emissions and pollution			
CO_2 emissions per unit of GDP (kg/2005 PPP $)	0.2	0.3	0.5
CO_2 emissions per capita (metric tons)	1.8	2.5	5.5
CO_2 emissions growth (%, 1990–2005)	88.1	33.4	-8.3
Particulate matter (urban-pop.-weighted avg., µg/cu. m)	35	35	30
Transport sector fuel consumption per capita (liters)	293	295	332
Water and sanitation			
Internal freshwater resources per capita (cu. m)	44,130	23,965	16,993
Freshwater withdrawal			
Total (% of internal resources)	0.6	2.0	13.8
Agriculture (% of total freshwater withdrawal)	28	71	57
Access to improved water source (% of total population)	92	91	95
Rural (% of rural population)	81	73	83
Urban (% of urban population)	96	97	98
Access to improved sanitation (% of total population)	74	78	83
Rural (% of rural population)	63	51	64
Urban (% of urban population)	78	86	89
Environment and health			
Acute resp. infection prevalence (% of children under five)	..		
Diarrhea prevalence (% of children under five)	12.6		
Under-five mortality rate (per 1,000 live births)	23	26	24
National accounting aggregates			
Gross savings (% of GNI)	24.7	22.9	23.2
Consumption of fixed capital (% of GNI)	12.9	12.6	12.8
Education expenditure (% of GNI)	4.4	4.5	4.4
Energy depletion (% of GNI)	0.0	5.4	7.6
Mineral depletion (% of GNI)	0.0	1.9	1.3
Net forest depletion (% of GNI)	0.0	0.0	0.0
CO_2 damage (% of GNI)	0.3	0.3	0.6
Particulate emission damage (% of GNI)	0.2	0.4	0.4
Adjusted net savings (% of GNI)	15.7	6.7	4.9

Papua New Guinea

| | Population (millions) | **6.3** | Land area (1,000 sq. km) | **452.9** | GDP ($ billions) | **6.3** |

	Country data	East Asia & Pacific group	Low-income group
GNI per capita, *World Bank Atlas* method ($)	850	2,182	574
Urban population (% of total)	13	43	32
Urban population growth (average annual %, 1990–2007)	1.5	3.5	3.7
Population growth (average annual %, 1990–2007)	2.5	1.1	2.4
Agriculture			
Agricultural land (% of land area)	2	51	39
Agricultural productivity (value added per worker, 2000 $)	601	458	330
Food production index (1999–2001 = 100)	110	120	112
Population density, rural (people/sq. km of arable land)	2,210	547	603
Forests and biodiversity			
Forest area (% of land area)	65.0	28.4	24.7
Deforestation (average annual %, 1990–2005)	0.5	–0.1	0.7
Nationally protected area (% of land area)	8.0	14.0	10.8
Animal species, total known	980		
Animal species, threatened	304		
Higher plant species, total known	11,544		
Higher plant species, threatened	142		
GEF benefits index for biodiversity (0–100, median is 1.5)	25.4		
Energy			
GDP per unit of energy use (2005 PPP $/kg oil equivalent)	..	3.4	3.2
Energy use per capita (kg oil equivalent)	..	1,258	478
Energy from biomass products and waste (% of total)	..	14.7	53.8
Electric power consumption per capita (kWh)	..	1,669	309
Electricity generated using fossil fuel (% of total)	..	82.0	48.4
Electricity generated by hydropower (% of total)	..	15.0	38.8
Emissions and pollution			
CO_2 emissions per unit of GDP (kg/2005 PPP $)	0.4	0.9	0.4
CO_2 emissions per capita (metric tons)	0.7	3.6	0.6
CO_2 emissions growth (%, 1990–2005)	82.7	123.4	39.3
Particulate matter (urban-pop.-weighted avg., µg/cu. m)	21	69	69
Transport sector fuel consumption per capita (liters)	..	106	41
Water and sanitation			
Internal freshwater resources per capita (cu. m)	126,658	4,948	4,619
Freshwater withdrawal			
Total (% of internal resources)	0.0	10.2	9.4
Agriculture (% of total freshwater withdrawal)	1	74	90
Access to improved water source (% of total population)	40	87	68
Rural (% of rural population)	32	81	60
Urban (% of urban population)	88	96	84
Access to improved sanitation (% of total population)	45	66	39
Rural (% of rural population)	41	59	33
Urban (% of urban population)	67	75	54
Environment and health			
Acute resp. infection prevalence (% of children under five)	13.0		
Diarrhea prevalence (% of children under five)	16.5		
Under-five mortality rate (per 1,000 live births)	65	27	126
National accounting aggregates			
Gross savings (% of GNI)	39.2	48.0	25.4
Consumption of fixed capital (% of GNI)	10.6	10.7	9.3
Education expenditure (% of GNI)	..	2.1	2.6
Energy depletion (% of GNI)	18.0	4.9	9.8
Mineral depletion (% of GNI)	30.0	1.3	0.9
Net forest depletion (% of GNI)	0.0	0.0	0.8
CO_2 damage (% of GNI)	0.4	1.3	0.7
Particulate emission damage (% of GNI)	0.0	1.3	0.7
Adjusted net savings (% of GNI)	..	30.6	5.8

Paraguay

	Population (millions)	**6.1**	Land area (1,000 sq. km)	**397.3**	GDP ($ billions)	**12.2**

	Country data	Latin America & Caribbean group	Lower middle-income group
GNI per capita, *World Bank Atlas* method ($)	1,710	5,801	1,905
Urban population (% of total)	60	78	42
Urban population growth (average annual %, 1990–2007)	3.4	2.1	2.9
Population growth (average annual %, 1990–2007)	2.2	1.5	1.3
Agriculture			
Agricultural land (% of land area)	61	36	47
Agricultural productivity (value added per worker, 2000 $)	2,047	3,158	532
Food production index (1999–2001 = 100)	114	117	116
Population density, rural (people/sq. km of arable land)	58	232	511
Forests and biodiversity			
Forest area (% of land area)	46.5	45.4	25.0
Deforestation (average annual %, 1990–2005)	0.9	0.5	0.1
Nationally protected area (% of land area)	5.9	16.7	11.0
Animal species, total known	864		
Animal species, threatened	37		
Higher plant species, total known	7,851		
Higher plant species, threatened	10		
GEF benefits index for biodiversity (0–100, median is 1.5)	2.8		
Energy			
GDP per unit of energy use (2005 PPP $/kg oil equivalent)	6.0	7.3	3.9
Energy use per capita (kg oil equivalent)	660	1,240	1,019
Energy from biomass products and waste (% of total)	52.0	15.9	15.2
Electric power consumption per capita (kWh)	900	1,808	1,269
Electricity generated using fossil fuel (% of total)	0.0	37.0	79.0
Electricity generated by hydropower (% of total)	100.0	57.3	16.3
Emissions and pollution			
CO_2 emissions per unit of GDP (kg/2005 PPP $)	0.2	0.3	0.8
CO_2 emissions per capita (metric tons)	0.7	2.5	2.8
CO_2 emissions growth (%, 1990–2005)	71.5	33.4	93.5
Particulate matter (urban-pop.-weighted avg., μg/cu. m)	77	35	67
Transport sector fuel consumption per capita (liters)	197	295	99
Water and sanitation			
Internal freshwater resources per capita (cu. m)	15,358	23,965	4,117
Freshwater withdrawal			
Total (% of internal resources)	0.5	2.0	8.7
Agriculture (% of total freshwater withdrawal)	71	71	80
Access to improved water source (% of total population)	77	91	88
Rural (% of rural population)	52	73	82
Urban (% of urban population)	94	97	96
Access to improved sanitation (% of total population)	70	78	55
Rural (% of rural population)	42	51	43
Urban (% of urban population)	89	86	71
Environment and health			
Acute resp. infection prevalence (% of children under five)	17.0		
Diarrhea prevalence (% of children under five)	16.1		
Under-five mortality rate (per 1,000 live births)	29	26	50
National accounting aggregates			
Gross savings (% of GNI)	19.6	22.9	41.7
Consumption of fixed capital (% of GNI)	10.3	12.6	10.7
Education expenditure (% of GNI)	3.9	4.5	2.6
Energy depletion (% of GNI)	0.0	5.4	6.6
Mineral depletion (% of GNI)	0.0	1.9	1.2
Net forest depletion (% of GNI)	0.0	0.0	0.2
CO_2 damage (% of GNI)	0.3	0.3	1.2
Particulate emission damage (% of GNI)	0.7	0.4	1.1
Adjusted net savings (% of GNI)	12.3	6.7	23.5

Peru

Population (millions)	**28**	Land area (1,000 sq. km)	**1,280**	GDP ($ billions)	**107.3**

	Country data	Latin America & Caribbean group	Lower middle-income group
GNI per capita, *World Bank Atlas* method ($)	3,410	5,801	1,905
Urban population (% of total)	71	78	42
Urban population growth (average annual %, 1990–2007)	1.7	2.1	2.9
Population growth (average annual %, 1990–2007)	1.5	1.5	1.3
Agriculture			
Agricultural land (% of land area)	17	36	47
Agricultural productivity (value added per worker, 2000 $)	1,526	3,158	532
Food production index (1999–2001 = 100)	115	117	116
Population density, rural (people/sq. km of arable land)	213	232	511
Forests and biodiversity			
Forest area (% of land area)	53.7	45.4	25.0
Deforestation (average annual %, 1990–2005)	0.1	0.5	0.1
Nationally protected area (% of land area)	13.7	16.7	11.0
Animal species, total known	2,222		
Animal species, threatened	261		
Higher plant species, total known	17,144		
Higher plant species, threatened	275		
GEF benefits index for biodiversity (0–100, median is 1.5)	33.4		
Energy			
GDP per unit of energy use (2005 PPP $/kg oil equivalent)	14.0	7.3	3.9
Energy use per capita (kg oil equivalent)	491	1,240	1,019
Energy from biomass products and waste (% of total)	17.4	15.9	15.2
Electric power consumption per capita (kWh)	899	1,808	1,269
Electricity generated using fossil fuel (% of total)	20.8	37.0	79.0
Electricity generated by hydropower (% of total)	78.5	57.3	16.3
Emissions and pollution			
CO_2 emissions per unit of GDP (kg/2005 PPP $)	0.2	0.3	0.8
CO_2 emissions per capita (metric tons)	1.4	2.5	2.8
CO_2 emissions growth (%, 1990–2005)	76.0	33.4	93.5
Particulate matter (urban-pop.-weighted avg., µg/cu. m)	54	35	67
Transport sector fuel consumption per capita (liters)	135	295	99
Water and sanitation			
Internal freshwater resources per capita (cu. m)	57,925	23,965	4,117
Freshwater withdrawal			
Total (% of internal resources)	1.2	2.0	8.7
Agriculture (% of total freshwater withdrawal)	82	71	80
Access to improved water source (% of total population)	84	91	88
Rural (% of rural population)	63	73	82
Urban (% of urban population)	92	97	96
Access to improved sanitation (% of total population)	72	78	55
Rural (% of rural population)	36	51	43
Urban (% of urban population)	85	86	71
Environment and health			
Acute resp. infection prevalence (% of children under five)	17.3		
Diarrhea prevalence (% of children under five)	15.4		
Under-five mortality rate (per 1,000 live births)	20	26	50
National accounting aggregates			
Gross savings (% of GNI)	25.7	22.9	41.7
Consumption of fixed capital (% of GNI)	12.4	12.6	10.7
Education expenditure (% of GNI)	2.6	4.5	2.6
Energy depletion (% of GNI)	1.5	5.4	6.6
Mineral depletion (% of GNI)	10.5	1.9	1.2
Net forest depletion (% of GNI)	0.0	0.0	0.2
CO_2 damage (% of GNI)	0.3	0.3	1.2
Particulate emission damage (% of GNI)	0.6	0.4	1.1
Adjusted net savings (% of GNI)	3.1	6.7	23.5

Philippines

| | Population (millions) | **88** | Land area (1,000 sq. km) | **298** | GDP ($ billions) | **144.1** |

	Country data	East Asia & Pacific group	Lower middle-income group
GNI per capita, *World Bank Atlas* method ($)	1,620	2,182	1,905
Urban population (% of total)	64	43	42
Urban population growth (average annual %, 1990–2007)	3.7	3.5	2.9
Population growth (average annual %, 1990–2007)	2.1	1.1	1.3
Agriculture			
Agricultural land (% of land area)	41	51	47
Agricultural productivity (value added per worker, 2000 $)	1,097	458	532
Food production index (1999–2001 = 100)	114	120	116
Population density, rural (people/sq. km of arable land)	553	547	511
Forests and biodiversity			
Forest area (% of land area)	24.0	28.4	25.0
Deforestation (average annual %, 1990–2005)	2.6	–0.1	0.1
Nationally protected area (% of land area)	10.1	14.0	11.0
Animal species, total known	812		
Animal species, threatened	425		
Higher plant species, total known	8,931		
Higher plant species, threatened	216		
GEF benefits index for biodiversity (0–100, median is 1.5)	32.3		
Energy			
GDP per unit of energy use (2005 PPP $/kg oil equivalent)	6.1	3.4	3.9
Energy use per capita (kg oil equivalent)	498	1,258	1,019
Energy from biomass products and waste (% of total)	26.1	14.7	15.2
Electric power consumption per capita (kWh)	578	1,669	1,269
Electricity generated using fossil fuel (% of total)	64.0	82.0	79.0
Electricity generated by hydropower (% of total)	17.5	15.0	16.3
Emissions and pollution			
CO_2 emissions per unit of GDP (kg/2005 PPP $)	0.3	0.9	0.8
CO_2 emissions per capita (metric tons)	0.9	3.6	2.8
CO_2 emissions growth (%, 1990–2005)	70.7	123.4	93.5
Particulate matter (urban-pop.-weighted avg., µg/cu. m)	23	69	67
Transport sector fuel consumption per capita (liters)	89	106	99
Water and sanitation			
Internal freshwater resources per capita (cu. m)	5,450	4,948	4,117
Freshwater withdrawal			
Total (% of internal resources)	6.0	10.2	8.7
Agriculture (% of total freshwater withdrawal)	74	74	80
Access to improved water source (% of total population)	93	87	88
Rural (% of rural population)	88	81	82
Urban (% of urban population)	96	96	96
Access to improved sanitation (% of total population)	78	66	55
Rural (% of rural population)	72	59	43
Urban (% of urban population)	81	75	71
Environment and health			
Acute resp. infection prevalence (% of children under five)	10.0		
Diarrhea prevalence (% of children under five)	7.4		
Under-five mortality rate (per 1,000 live births)	28	27	50
National accounting aggregates			
Gross savings (% of GNI)	31.6	48.0	41.7
Consumption of fixed capital (% of GNI)	9.3	10.7	10.7
Education expenditure (% of GNI)	2.2	2.1	2.6
Energy depletion (% of GNI)	0.4	4.9	6.6
Mineral depletion (% of GNI)	1.6	1.3	1.2
Net forest depletion (% of GNI)	0.1	0.0	0.2
CO_2 damage (% of GNI)	0.5	1.3	1.2
Particulate emission damage (% of GNI)	0.2	1.3	1.1
Adjusted net savings (% of GNI)	21.7	30.6	23.5

Poland

	Country data	Europe & Central Asia group	Upper middle-income group
Population (millions) **38** Land area (1,000 sq. km) **306** GDP ($ billions) **422.1**			
GNI per capita, *World Bank Atlas* method ($)	9,850	6,052	7,107
Urban population (% of total)	61	64	75
Urban population growth (average annual %, 1990–2007)	0.0	0.2	1.4
Population growth (average annual %, 1990–2007)	0.0	0.1	0.9
Agriculture			
Agricultural land (% of land area)	52	28	31
Agricultural productivity (value added per worker, 2000 $)	2,260	2,228	2,947
Food production index (1999–2001 = 100)	95	110	113
Population density, rural (people/sq. km of arable land)	121	129	110
Forests and biodiversity			
Forest area (% of land area)	30.0	38.3	39.3
Deforestation (average annual %, 1990–2005)	–0.2	0.0	0.2
Nationally protected area (% of land area)	24.6	6.1	10.3
Animal species, total known	534		
Animal species, threatened	33		
Higher plant species, total known	2,450		
Higher plant species, threatened	4		
GEF benefits index for biodiversity (0–100, median is 1.5)	0.5		
Energy			
GDP per unit of energy use (2005 PPP $/kg oil equivalent)	5.7	3.5	4.8
Energy use per capita (kg oil equivalent)	2,562	2,930	2,300
Energy from biomass products and waste (% of total)	5.5	2.2	7.0
Electric power consumption per capita (kWh)	3,585	3,835	3,242
Electricity generated using fossil fuel (% of total)	97.1	67.7	62.8
Electricity generated by hydropower (% of total)	1.3	17.4	27.6
Emissions and pollution			
CO_2 emissions per unit of GDP (kg/2005 PPP $)	0.6	0.7	0.5
CO_2 emissions per capita (metric tons)	7.9	7.0	5.5
CO_2 emissions growth (%, 1990–2005)	–13.0	–29.3	–8.3
Particulate matter (urban-pop.-weighted avg., µg/cu. m)	37	27	30
Transport sector fuel consumption per capita (liters)	323	255	332
Water and sanitation			
Internal freshwater resources per capita (cu. m)	1,406	11,806	16,993
Freshwater withdrawal			
Total (% of internal resources)	30.2	7.2	13.8
Agriculture (% of total freshwater withdrawal)	8	60	57
Access to improved water source (% of total population)	..	95	95
Rural (% of rural population)	..	88	83
Urban (% of urban population)	100	99	98
Access to improved sanitation (% of total population)	..	89	83
Rural (% of rural population)	..	79	64
Urban (% of urban population)	..	94	89
Environment and health			
Acute resp. infection prevalence (% of children under five)	..		
Diarrhea prevalence (% of children under five)	..		
Under-five mortality rate (per 1,000 live births)	7	23	24
National accounting aggregates			
Gross savings (% of GNI)	22.0	24.0	23.2
Consumption of fixed capital (% of GNI)	13.3	12.8	12.8
Education expenditure (% of GNI)	5.3	4.0	4.4
Energy depletion (% of GNI)	0.9	9.8	7.6
Mineral depletion (% of GNI)	0.5	0.7	1.3
Net forest depletion (% of GNI)	0.1	0.0	0.0
CO_2 damage (% of GNI)	0.7	1.0	0.6
Particulate emission damage (% of GNI)	0.4	0.5	0.4
Adjusted net savings (% of GNI)	11.5	3.2	4.9

Portugal

| Population (millions) | **11** | Land area (1,000 sq. km) | **92** | GDP ($ billions) | **222.8** |

	Country data	High-income group
GNI per capita, *World Bank Atlas* method ($)	18,950	37,572
Urban population (% of total)	59	78
Urban population growth (average annual %, 1990–2007)	1.6	1.0
Population growth (average annual %, 1990–2007)	0.4	0.7
Agriculture		
Agricultural land (% of land area)	40	38
Agricultural productivity (value added per worker, 2000 $)	6,279	27,680
Food production index (1999–2001 = 100)	99	102
Population density, rural (people/sq. km of arable land)	354	323
Forests and biodiversity		
Forest area (% of land area)	41.3	28.8
Deforestation (average annual %, 1990–2005)	–1.3	–0.1
Nationally protected area (% of land area)	5.0	11.8
Animal species, total known	606	
Animal species, threatened	143	
Higher plant species, total known	5,050	
Higher plant species, threatened	16	
GEF benefits index for biodiversity (0–100, median is 1.5)	5.5	
Energy		
GDP per unit of energy use (2005 PPP $/kg oil equivalent)	8.7	6.3
Energy use per capita (kg oil equivalent)	2,402	5,416
Energy from biomass products and waste (% of total)	11.9	3.4
Electric power consumption per capita (kWh)	4,799	9,675
Electricity generated using fossil fuel (% of total)	67.0	62.0
Electricity generated by hydropower (% of total)	22.6	11.4
Emissions and pollution		
CO_2 emissions per unit of GDP (kg/2005 PPP $)	0.3	0.4
CO_2 emissions per capita (metric tons)	5.9	12.6
CO_2 emissions growth (%, 1990–2005)	47.3	19.1
Particulate matter (urban-pop.-weighted avg., µg/cu. m)	23	26
Transport sector fuel consumption per capita (liters)	659	1,159
Water and sanitation		
Internal freshwater resources per capita (cu. m)	3,582	9,313
Freshwater withdrawal		
Total (% of internal resources)	29.6	10.4
Agriculture (% of total freshwater withdrawal)	78	43
Access to improved water source (% of total population)	99	100
Rural (% of rural population)	100	98
Urban (% of urban population)	99	100
Access to improved sanitation (% of total population)	99	100
Rural (% of rural population)	98	99
Urban (% of urban population)	99	100
Environment and health		
Acute resp. infection prevalence (% of children under five)	..	
Diarrhea prevalence (% of children under five)	..	
Under-five mortality rate (per 1,000 live births)	4	7
National accounting aggregates		
Gross savings (% of GNI)	12.6	20.6
Consumption of fixed capital (% of GNI)	14.4	14.5
Education expenditure (% of GNI)	5.4	4.6
Energy depletion (% of GNI)	0.0	1.5
Mineral depletion (% of GNI)	0.1	0.2
Net forest depletion (% of GNI)	0.0	0.0
CO_2 damage (% of GNI)	0.2	0.3
Particulate emission damage (% of GNI)	0.3	0.3
Adjusted net savings (% of GNI)	3.0	8.5

Puerto Rico

Population (millions)	**3.9**	Land area (1,000 sq. km)	**8.9**	GDP ($ billions)	**67.9**

	Country data	High-income group
GNI per capita, *World Bank Atlas* method ($)	10,950	37,572
Urban population (% of total)	98	78
Urban population growth (average annual %, 1990–2007)	2.4	1.0
Population growth (average annual %, 1990–2007)	0.6	0.7
Agriculture		
Agricultural land (% of land area)	25	38
Agricultural productivity (value added per worker, 2000 $)	..	27,680
Food production index (1999–2001 = 100)	98	102
Population density, rural (people/sq. km of arable land)	132	323
Forests and biodiversity		
Forest area (% of land area)	46.0	28.8
Deforestation (average annual %, 1990–2005)	–0.1	–0.1
Nationally protected area (% of land area)	3.3	11.8
Animal species, total known	348	
Animal species, threatened	48	
Higher plant species, total known	2,493	
Higher plant species, threatened	53	
GEF benefits index for biodiversity (0–100, median is 1.5)	4.0	
Energy		
GDP per unit of energy use (2005 PPP $/kg oil equivalent)	..	6.3
Energy use per capita (kg oil equivalent)	..	5,416
Energy from biomass products and waste (% of total)	..	3.4
Electric power consumption per capita (kWh)	..	9,675
Electricity generated using fossil fuel (% of total)	..	62.0
Electricity generated by hydropower (% of total)	..	11.4
Emissions and pollution		
CO_2 emissions per unit of GDP (kg/2005 PPP $)	..	0.4
CO_2 emissions per capita (metric tons)	..	12.6
CO_2 emissions growth (%, 1990–2005)	..	19.1
Particulate matter (urban-pop.-weighted avg., µg/cu. m)	21	26
Transport sector fuel consumption per capita (liters)	..	1,159
Water and sanitation		
Internal freshwater resources per capita (cu. m)	1,801	9,313
Freshwater withdrawal		
Total (% of internal resources)	..	10.4
Agriculture (% of total freshwater withdrawal)	..	43
Access to improved water source (% of total population)	..	100
Rural (% of rural population)	..	98
Urban (% of urban population)	..	100
Access to improved sanitation (% of total population)	..	100
Rural (% of rural population)	..	99
Urban (% of urban population)	..	100
Environment and health		
Acute resp. infection prevalence (% of children under five)	..	
Diarrhea prevalence (% of children under five)	..	
Under-five mortality rate (per 1,000 live births)	..	7
National accounting aggregates		
Gross savings (% of GNI)	..	20.6
Consumption of fixed capital (% of GNI)	..	14.5
Education expenditure (% of GNI)	..	4.6
Energy depletion (% of GNI)	..	1.5
Mineral depletion (% of GNI)	..	0.2
Net forest depletion (% of GNI)	..	0.0
CO_2 damage (% of GNI)	..	0.3
Particulate emission damage (% of GNI)	..	0.3
Adjusted net savings (% of GNI)	..	8.5

Qatar

| Population (thousands) **836** | Land area (1,000 sq. km) | **11** | GDP ($ billions) | **52.7** |

	Country data	High-income group
GNI per capita, *World Bank Atlas* method ($)	..	37,572
Urban population (% of total)	96	78
Urban population growth (average annual %, 1990–2007)	3.6	1.0
Population growth (average annual %, 1990–2007)	3.4	0.7
Agriculture		
Agricultural land (% of land area)	6	38
Agricultural productivity (value added per worker, 2000 $)	..	27,680
Food production index (1999–2001 = 100)	108	102
Population density, rural (people/sq. km of arable land)	203	323
Forests and biodiversity		
Forest area (% of land area)	..	28.8
Deforestation (average annual %, 1990–2005)	..	−0.1
Nationally protected area (% of land area)	0.0	11.8
Animal species, total known	159	
Animal species, threatened	27	
Higher plant species, total known	355	
Higher plant species, threatened	..	
GEF benefits index for biodiversity (0–100, median is 1.5)	0.1	
Energy		
GDP per unit of energy use (2005 PPP $/kg oil equivalent)	3.5	6.3
Energy use per capita (kg oil equivalent)	22,057	5,416
Energy from biomass products and waste (% of total)	0.0	3.4
Electric power consumption per capita (kWh)	17,181	9,675
Electricity generated using fossil fuel (% of total)	100.0	62.0
Electricity generated by hydropower (% of total)	0.0	11.4
Emissions and pollution		
CO_2 emissions per unit of GDP (kg/2005 PPP $)	0.9	0.4
CO_2 emissions per capita (metric tons)	62.6	12.6
CO_2 emissions growth (%, 1990–2005)	308.9	19.1
Particulate matter (urban-pop.-weighted avg., µg/cu. m)	51	26
Transport sector fuel consumption per capita (liters)	2,558	1,159
Water and sanitation		
Internal freshwater resources per capita (cu. m)	61	9,313
Freshwater withdrawal		
Total (% of internal resources)	870.6	10.4
Agriculture (% of total freshwater withdrawal)	59	43
Access to improved water source (% of total population)	100	100
Rural (% of rural population)	100	98
Urban (% of urban population)	100	100
Access to improved sanitation (% of total population)	100	100
Rural (% of rural population)	100	99
Urban (% of urban population)	100	100
Environment and health		
Acute resp. infection prevalence (% of children under five)	7.8	
Diarrhea prevalence (% of children under five)	8.8	
Under-five mortality rate (per 1,000 live births)	15	7
National accounting aggregates		
Gross savings (% of GNI)	..	20.6
Consumption of fixed capital (% of GNI)	..	14.5
Education expenditure (% of GNI)	..	4.6
Energy depletion (% of GNI)	..	1.5
Mineral depletion (% of GNI)	..	0.2
Net forest depletion (% of GNI)	..	0.0
CO_2 damage (% of GNI)	..	0.3
Particulate emission damage (% of GNI)	..	0.3
Adjusted net savings (% of GNI)	..	8.5

Romania

Population (millions)	**22**	Land area (1,000 sq. km)	**230**	GDP ($ billions)	**166.0**

	Country data	Europe & Central Asia group	Upper middle-income group
GNI per capita, *World Bank Atlas* method ($)	6,390	6,052	7,107
Urban population (% of total)	54	64	75
Urban population growth (average annual %, 1990–2007)	–0.3	0.2	1.4
Population growth (average annual %, 1990–2007)	–0.4	0.1	0.9
Agriculture			
Agricultural land (% of land area)	63	28	31
Agricultural productivity (value added per worker, 2000 $)	5,294	2,228	2,947
Food production index (1999–2001 = 100)	110	110	113
Population density, rural (people/sq. km of arable land)	108	129	110
Forests and biodiversity			
Forest area (% of land area)	27.7	38.3	39.3
Deforestation (average annual %, 1990–2005)	0.0	0.0	0.2
Nationally protected area (% of land area)	2.2	6.1	10.3
Animal species, total known	466		
Animal species, threatened	59		
Higher plant species, total known	3,400		
Higher plant species, threatened	1		
GEF benefits index for biodiversity (0–100, median is 1.5)	0.7		
Energy			
GDP per unit of energy use (2005 PPP $/kg oil equivalent)	5.4	3.5	4.8
Energy use per capita (kg oil equivalent)	1,860	2,930	2,300
Energy from biomass products and waste (% of total)	8.1	2.2	7.0
Electric power consumption per capita (kWh)	2,402	3,835	3,242
Electricity generated using fossil fuel (% of total)	61.7	67.7	62.8
Electricity generated by hydropower (% of total)	29.3	17.4	27.6
Emissions and pollution			
CO_2 emissions per unit of GDP (kg/2005 PPP $)	0.4	0.7	0.5
CO_2 emissions per capita (metric tons)	4.1	7.0	5.5
CO_2 emissions growth (%, 1990–2005)	–42.6	–29.3	–8.3
Particulate matter (urban-pop.-weighted avg., µg/cu. m)	14	27	30
Transport sector fuel consumption per capita (liters)	216	255	332
Water and sanitation			
Internal freshwater resources per capita (cu. m)	1,963	11,806	16,993
Freshwater withdrawal			
Total (% of internal resources)	54.8	7.2	13.8
Agriculture (% of total freshwater withdrawal)	57	60	57
Access to improved water source (% of total population)	88	95	95
Rural (% of rural population)	76	88	83
Urban (% of urban population)	99	99	98
Access to improved sanitation (% of total population)	72	89	83
Rural (% of rural population)	54	79	64
Urban (% of urban population)	88	94	89
Environment and health			
Acute resp. infection prevalence (% of children under five)	..		
Diarrhea prevalence (% of children under five)	..		
Under-five mortality rate (per 1,000 live births)	15	23	24
National accounting aggregates			
Gross savings (% of GNI)	21.1	24.0	23.2
Consumption of fixed capital (% of GNI)	12.4	12.8	12.8
Education expenditure (% of GNI)	3.4	4.0	4.4
Energy depletion (% of GNI)	2.1	9.8	7.6
Mineral depletion (% of GNI)	0.1	0.7	1.3
Net forest depletion (% of GNI)	0.0	0.0	0.0
CO_2 damage (% of GNI)	0.5	1.0	0.6
Particulate emission damage (% of GNI)	0.0	0.5	0.4
Adjusted net savings (% of GNI)	9.3	3.2	4.9

Russian Federation

Population (millions)	**142**	Land area (1,000 sq. km)	**16,381**	GDP ($ billions)	**1,290.1**

	Country data	Europe & Central Asia group	Upper middle-income group
GNI per capita, *World Bank Atlas* method ($)	7,530	6,052	7,107
Urban population (% of total)	73	64	75
Urban population growth (average annual %, 1990–2007)	–0.3	0.2	1.4
Population growth (average annual %, 1990–2007)	–0.3	0.1	0.9
Agriculture			
Agricultural land (% of land area)	13	28	31
Agricultural productivity (value added per worker, 2000 $)	2,629	2,228	2,947
Food production index (1999–2001 = 100)	113	110	113
Population density, rural (people/sq. km of arable land)	32	129	110
Forests and biodiversity			
Forest area (% of land area)	49.4	38.3	39.3
Deforestation (average annual %, 1990–2005)	0.0	0.0	0.2
Nationally protected area (% of land area)	6.8	6.1	10.3
Animal species, total known	941		
Animal species, threatened	151		
Higher plant species, total known	11,400		
Higher plant species, threatened	7		
GEF benefits index for biodiversity (0–100, median is 1.5)	34.1		
Energy			
GDP per unit of energy use (2005 PPP $/kg oil equivalent)	2.7	3.5	4.8
Energy use per capita (kg oil equivalent)	4,745	2,930	2,300
Energy from biomass products and waste (% of total)	1.1	2.2	7.0
Electric power consumption per capita (kWh)	6,122	3,835	3,242
Electricity generated using fossil fuel (% of total)	66.4	67.7	62.8
Electricity generated by hydropower (% of total)	17.4	17.4	27.6
Emissions and pollution			
CO_2 emissions per unit of GDP (kg/2005 PPP $)	0.9	0.7	0.5
CO_2 emissions per capita (metric tons)	10.5	7.0	5.5
CO_2 emissions growth (%, 1990–2005)	–33.5	–29.3	–8.3
Particulate matter (urban-pop.-weighted avg., µg/cu. m)	18	27	30
Transport sector fuel consumption per capita (liters)	349	255	332
Water and sanitation			
Internal freshwater resources per capita (cu. m)	30,350	11,806	16,993
Freshwater withdrawal			
Total (% of internal resources)	1.8	7.2	13.8
Agriculture (% of total freshwater withdrawal)	18	60	57
Access to improved water source (% of total population)	97	95	95
Rural (% of rural population)	88	88	83
Urban (% of urban population)	100	99	98
Access to improved sanitation (% of total population)	87	89	83
Rural (% of rural population)	70	79	64
Urban (% of urban population)	93	94	89
Environment and health			
Acute resp. infection prevalence (% of children under five)	..		
Diarrhea prevalence (% of children under five)	..		
Under-five mortality rate (per 1,000 live births)	15	23	24
National accounting aggregates			
Gross savings (% of GNI)	31.3	24.0	23.2
Consumption of fixed capital (% of GNI)	12.9	12.8	12.8
Education expenditure (% of GNI)	3.5	4.0	4.4
Energy depletion (% of GNI)	17.9	9.8	7.6
Mineral depletion (% of GNI)	1.3	0.7	1.3
Net forest depletion (% of GNI)	0.0	0.0	0.0
CO_2 damage (% of GNI)	1.1	1.0	0.6
Particulate emission damage (% of GNI)	0.2	0.5	0.4
Adjusted net savings (% of GNI)	1.4	3.2	4.9

Rwanda

	Country data	Sub-Saharan Africa group	Low-income group
Population (millions) **9.7**	Land area (1,000 sq. km) **24.7**	GDP ($ billions)	**3.3**

	Country data	Sub-Saharan Africa group	Low-income group
GNI per capita, *World Bank Atlas* method ($)	320	951	574
Urban population (% of total)	18	36	32
Urban population growth (average annual %, 1990–2007)	8.8	4.0	3.7
Population growth (average annual %, 1990–2007)	1.7	2.6	2.4
Agriculture			
Agricultural land (% of land area)	79	44	39
Agricultural productivity (value added per worker, 2000 $)	184	287	330
Food production index (1999–2001 = 100)	121	109	112
Population density, rural (people/sq. km of arable land)	635	351	603
Forests and biodiversity			
Forest area (% of land area)	19.5	26.5	24.7
Deforestation (average annual %, 1990–2005)	-2.8	0.6	0.7
Nationally protected area (% of land area)	8.1	11.3	10.8
Animal species, total known	871		
Animal species, threatened	49		
Higher plant species, total known	2,288		
Higher plant species, threatened	3		
GEF benefits index for biodiversity (0–100, median is 1.5)	0.9		
Energy			
GDP per unit of energy use (2005 PPP $/kg oil equivalent)	..	3.0	3.2
Energy use per capita (kg oil equivalent)	..	670	478
Energy from biomass products and waste (% of total)	..	56.3	53.8
Electric power consumption per capita (kWh)	..	531	309
Electricity generated using fossil fuel (% of total)	..	65.6	48.4
Electricity generated by hydropower (% of total)	..	18.0	38.8
Emissions and pollution			
CO_2 emissions per unit of GDP (kg/2005 PPP $)	0.08	0.49	0.39
CO_2 emissions per capita (metric tons)	0.07	0.85	0.58
CO_2 emissions growth (%, 1990–2005)	14.6	40.1	39.3
Particulate matter (urban-pop.-weighted avg., µg/cu. m)	26	53	69
Transport sector fuel consumption per capita (liters)	..	64	41
Water and sanitation			
Internal freshwater resources per capita (cu. m)	976	4,824	4,619
Freshwater withdrawal			
Total (% of internal resources)	1.6	3.2	9.4
Agriculture (% of total freshwater withdrawal)	68	87	90
Access to improved water source (% of total population)	65	58	68
Rural (% of rural population)	61	46	60
Urban (% of urban population)	82	81	84
Access to improved sanitation (% of total population)	23	31	39
Rural (% of rural population)	20	24	33
Urban (% of urban population)	34	42	54
Environment and health			
Acute resp. infection prevalence (% of children under five)	17.1		
Diarrhea prevalence (% of children under five)	14.1		
Under-five mortality rate (per 1,000 live births)	181	146	126
National accounting aggregates			
Gross savings (% of GNI)	16.2	17.4	25.4
Consumption of fixed capital (% of GNI)	8.0	11.1	9.3
Education expenditure (% of GNI)	4.6	3.6	2.6
Energy depletion (% of GNI)	0.0	11.7	9.8
Mineral depletion (% of GNI)	0.0	1.5	0.9
Net forest depletion (% of GNI)	3.6	0.5	0.8
CO_2 damage (% of GNI)	0.2	0.7	0.7
Particulate emission damage (% of GNI)	0.1	0.4	0.7
Adjusted net savings (% of GNI)	9.0	-5.0	5.8

Samoa

	Country data	East Asia & Pacific group	Lower middle-income group
Population (thousands) **181** Land area (1,000 sq. km) **3** GDP ($ millions) **525**			

	Country data	East Asia & Pacific group	Lower middle-income group
GNI per capita, *World Bank Atlas* method ($)	2,700	2,182	1,905
Urban population (% of total)	23	43	42
Urban population growth (average annual %, 1990–2007)	1.1	3.5	2.9
Population growth (average annual %, 1990–2007)	0.7	1.1	1.3
Agriculture			
Agricultural land (% of land area)	33	51	47
Agricultural productivity (value added per worker, 2000 $)	1,768	458	532
Food production index (1999–2001 = 100)	103	120	116
Population density, rural (people/sq. km of arable land)	463	547	511
Forests and biodiversity			
Forest area (% of land area)	60.4	28.4	25.0
Deforestation (average annual %, 1990–2005)	-1.8	-0.1	0.1
Nationally protected area (% of land area)	2.0	14.0	11.0
Animal species, total known	55		
Animal species, threatened	71		
Higher plant species, total known	..		
Higher plant species, threatened	2		
GEF benefits index for biodiversity (0–100, median is 1.5)	1.6		
Energy			
GDP per unit of energy use (2005 PPP $/kg oil equivalent)	..	3.4	3.9
Energy use per capita (kg oil equivalent)	..	1,258	1,019
Energy from biomass products and waste (% of total)	..	14.7	15.2
Electric power consumption per capita (kWh)	..	1,669	1,269
Electricity generated using fossil fuel (% of total)	..	82.0	79.0
Electricity generated by hydropower (% of total)	..	15.0	16.3
Emissions and pollution			
CO_2 emissions per unit of GDP (kg/2005 PPP $)	0.2	0.9	0.8
CO_2 emissions per capita (metric tons)	0.8	3.6	2.8
CO_2 emissions growth (%, 1990–2005)	20.6	123.4	93.5
Particulate matter (urban-pop.-weighted avg., µg/cu. m)	..	69	67
Transport sector fuel consumption per capita (liters)	..	106	99
Water and sanitation			
Internal freshwater resources per capita (cu. m)	..	4,948	4,117
Freshwater withdrawal			
Total (% of internal resources)	..	10.2	8.7
Agriculture (% of total freshwater withdrawal)	..	74	80
Access to improved water source (% of total population)	88	87	88
Rural (% of rural population)	87	81	82
Urban (% of urban population)	90	96	96
Access to improved sanitation (% of total population)	100	66	55
Rural (% of rural population)	100	59	43
Urban (% of urban population)	100	75	71
Environment and health			
Acute resp. infection prevalence (% of children under five)	..		
Diarrhea prevalence (% of children under five)	..		
Under-five mortality rate (per 1,000 live births)	27	27	50
National accounting aggregates			
Gross savings (% of GNI)	..	48.0	41.7
Consumption of fixed capital (% of GNI)	11.3	10.7	10.7
Education expenditure (% of GNI)	4.0	2.1	2.6
Energy depletion (% of GNI)	0.0	4.9	6.6
Mineral depletion (% of GNI)	0.0	1.3	1.2
Net forest depletion (% of GNI)	0.8	0.0	0.2
CO_2 damage (% of GNI)	0.2	1.3	1.2
Particulate emission damage (% of GNI)	..	1.3	1.1
Adjusted net savings (% of GNI)	..	30.6	23.5

San Marino

Population (thousands)	**31**	Land area (sq. km)	**60**	GDP ($ billions)	**1.7**

	Country data	High-income group
GNI per capita, *World Bank Atlas* method ($)	46,770	37,572
Urban population (% of total)	94	78
Urban population growth (average annual %, 1990–2007)	..	1.0
Population growth (average annual %, 1990–2007)	..	0.7
Agriculture		
Agricultural land (% of land area)	17	38
Agricultural productivity (value added per worker, 2000 $)	..	27,680
Food production index (1999–2001 = 100)	..	102
Population density, rural (people/sq. km of arable land)	176	323
Forests and biodiversity		
Forest area (% of land area)	1.7	28.8
Deforestation (average annual %, 1990–2005)	..	-0.1
Nationally protected area (% of land area)	..	11.8
Animal species, total known	9	
Animal species, threatened	1	
Higher plant species, total known	..	
Higher plant species, threatened	0	
GEF benefits index for biodiversity (0–100, median is 1.5)	0.0	
Energy		
GDP per unit of energy use (2005 PPP $/kg oil equivalent)	..	6.3
Energy use per capita (kg oil equivalent)	..	5,416
Energy from biomass products and waste (% of total)	..	3.4
Electric power consumption per capita (kWh)	..	9,675
Electricity generated using fossil fuel (% of total)	..	62.0
Electricity generated by hydropower (% of total)	..	11.4
Emissions and pollution		
CO_2 emissions per unit of GDP (kg/2005 PPP $)	..	0.4
CO_2 emissions per capita (metric tons)	..	12.6
CO_2 emissions growth (%, 1990–2005)	..	19.1
Particulate matter (urban-pop.-weighted avg., µg/cu. m)	9	26
Transport sector fuel consumption per capita (liters)	..	1,159
Water and sanitation		
Internal freshwater resources per capita (cu. m)	..	9,313
Freshwater withdrawal		
Total (% of internal resources)	..	10.4
Agriculture (% of total freshwater withdrawal)	..	43
Access to improved water source (% of total population)	..	100
Rural (% of rural population)	..	98
Urban (% of urban population)	..	100
Access to improved sanitation (% of total population)	..	100
Rural (% of rural population)	..	99
Urban (% of urban population)	..	100
Environment and health		
Acute resp. infection prevalence (% of children under five)	..	
Diarrhea prevalence (% of children under five)	..	
Under-five mortality rate (per 1,000 live births)	4	7
National accounting aggregates		
Gross savings (% of GNI)	..	20.6
Consumption of fixed capital (% of GNI)	17.3	14.5
Education expenditure (% of GNI)	..	4.6
Energy depletion (% of GNI)	0.0	1.5
Mineral depletion (% of GNI)	0.0	0.2
Net forest depletion (% of GNI)	..	0.0
CO_2 damage (% of GNI)	..	0.3
Particulate emission damage (% of GNI)	..	0.3
Adjusted net savings (% of GNI)	..	8.5

São Tomé and Principe

Population (thousands) **158**   Land area (1,000 sq. km) **1**   GDP ($ millions) **145**

	Country data	Sub-Saharan Africa group	Low-income group
GNI per capita, *World Bank Atlas* method ($)	870	951	574
Urban population (% of total)	60	36	32
Urban population growth (average annual %, 1990–2007)	3.7	4.0	3.7
Population growth (average annual %, 1990–2007)	1.8	2.6	2.4
Agriculture			
Agricultural land (% of land area)	59	44	39
Agricultural productivity (value added per worker, 2000 $)	..	287	330
Food production index (1999–2001 = 100)	109	109	112
Population density, rural (people/sq. km of arable land)	711	351	603
Forests and biodiversity			
Forest area (% of land area)	28.5	26.5	24.7
Deforestation (average annual %, 1990–2005)	0.0	0.6	0.7
Nationally protected area (% of land area)	..	11.3	10.8
Animal species, total known	126		
Animal species, threatened	31		
Higher plant species, total known	895		
Higher plant species, threatened	35		
GEF benefits index for biodiversity (0–100, median is 1.5)	2.7		
Energy			
GDP per unit of energy use (2005 PPP $/kg oil equivalent)	..	3.0	3.2
Energy use per capita (kg oil equivalent)	..	670	478
Energy from biomass products and waste (% of total)	..	56.3	53.8
Electric power consumption per capita (kWh)	..	531	309
Electricity generated using fossil fuel (% of total)	..	65.6	48.4
Electricity generated by hydropower (% of total)	..	18.0	38.8
Emissions and pollution			
CO_2 emissions per unit of GDP (kg/2005 PPP $)	0.5	0.5	0.4
CO_2 emissions per capita (metric tons)	0.7	0.8	0.6
CO_2 emissions growth (%, 1990–2005)	55.6	40.1	39.3
Particulate matter (urban-pop.-weighted avg., µg/cu. m)	39	53	69
Transport sector fuel consumption per capita (liters)	..	64	41
Water and sanitation			
Internal freshwater resources per capita (cu. m)	13,796	4,824	4,619
Freshwater withdrawal			
Total (% of internal resources)	..	3.2	9.4
Agriculture (% of total freshwater withdrawal)	..	87	90
Access to improved water source (% of total population)	86	58	68
Rural (% of rural population)	83	46	60
Urban (% of urban population)	88	81	84
Access to improved sanitation (% of total population)	24	31	39
Rural (% of rural population)	18	24	33
Urban (% of urban population)	29	42	54
Environment and health			
Acute resp. infection prevalence (% of children under five)	5.0		
Diarrhea prevalence (% of children under five)	..		
Under-five mortality rate (per 1,000 live births)	99	146	126
National accounting aggregates			
Gross savings (% of GNI)	..	17.4	25.4
Consumption of fixed capital (% of GNI)	9.4	11.1	9.3
Education expenditure (% of GNI)	..	3.6	2.6
Energy depletion (% of GNI)	0.0	11.7	9.8
Mineral depletion (% of GNI)	0.0	1.5	0.9
Net forest depletion (% of GNI)	0.0	0.5	0.8
CO_2 damage (% of GNI)	0.6	0.7	0.7
Particulate emission damage (% of GNI)	0.1	0.4	0.7
Adjusted net savings (% of GNI)	..	−5.0	5.8

Saudi Arabia

Population (millions)	**24**	Land area (1,000 sq. km)	**2,000**	GDP ($ billions)	**381.7**

	Country data	High-income group
GNI per capita, *World Bank Atlas* method ($)	15,470	37,572
Urban population (% of total)	83	78
Urban population growth (average annual %, 1990–2007)	2.7	1.0
Population growth (average annual %, 1990–2007)	2.3	0.7
Agriculture		
Agricultural land (% of land area)	81	38
Agricultural productivity (value added per worker, 2000 $)	16,651	27,680
Food production index (1999–2001 = 100)	112	102
Population density, rural (people/sq. km of arable land)	123	323
Forests and biodiversity		
Forest area (% of land area)	1.4	28.8
Deforestation (average annual %, 1990–2005)	0.0	-0.1
Nationally protected area (% of land area)	38.1	11.8
Animal species, total known	527	
Animal species, threatened	94	
Higher plant species, total known	2,028	
Higher plant species, threatened	3	
GEF benefits index for biodiversity (0–100, median is 1.5)	3.2	
Energy		
GDP per unit of energy use (2005 PPP $/kg oil equivalent)	3.5	6.3
Energy use per capita (kg oil equivalent)	6,170	5,416
Energy from biomass products and waste (% of total)	0.0	3.4
Electric power consumption per capita (kWh)	7,080	9,675
Electricity generated using fossil fuel (% of total)	100.0	62.0
Electricity generated by hydropower (% of total)	0.0	11.4
Emissions and pollution		
CO_2 emissions per unit of GDP (kg/2005 PPP $)	0.8	0.4
CO_2 emissions per capita (metric tons)	16.5	12.6
CO_2 emissions growth (%, 1990–2005)	93.0	19.1
Particulate matter (urban-pop.-weighted avg., µg/cu. m)	113	26
Transport sector fuel consumption per capita (liters)	1,262	1,159
Water and sanitation		
Internal freshwater resources per capita (cu. m)	99	9,313
Freshwater withdrawal		
Total (% of internal resources)	986.1	10.4
Agriculture (% of total freshwater withdrawal)	88	43
Access to improved water source (% of total population)	96	100
Rural (% of rural population)	..	98
Urban (% of urban population)	97	100
Access to improved sanitation (% of total population)	99	100
Rural (% of rural population)	..	99
Urban (% of urban population)	100	100
Environment and health		
Acute resp. infection prevalence (% of children under five)	8.8	
Diarrhea prevalence (% of children under five)	9.1	
Under-five mortality rate (per 1,000 live births)	25	7
National accounting aggregates		
Gross savings (% of GNI)	..	20.6
Consumption of fixed capital (% of GNI)	13.4	14.5
Education expenditure (% of GNI)	7.2	4.6
Energy depletion (% of GNI)	42.1	1.5
Mineral depletion (% of GNI)	0.0	0.2
Net forest depletion (% of GNI)	0.0	0.0
CO_2 damage (% of GNI)	0.7	0.3
Particulate emission damage (% of GNI)	1.4	0.3
Adjusted net savings (% of GNI)	..	8.5

Senegal

Population (millions)	12	Land area (1,000 sq. km)	193	GDP ($ billions)	11.2

	Country data	Sub-Saharan Africa group	Low-income group
GNI per capita, *World Bank Atlas* method ($)	830	951	574
Urban population (% of total)	42	36	32
Urban population growth (average annual %, 1990–2007)	3.1	4.0	3.7
Population growth (average annual %, 1990–2007)	2.7	2.6	2.4
Agriculture			
Agricultural land (% of land area)	43	44	39
Agricultural productivity (value added per worker, 2000 $)	227	287	330
Food production index (1999–2001 = 100)	100	109	112
Population density, rural (people/sq. km of arable land)	270	351	603
Forests and biodiversity			
Forest area (% of land area)	45.0	26.5	24.7
Deforestation (average annual %, 1990–2005)	0.5	0.6	0.7
Nationally protected area (% of land area)	11.2	11.3	10.8
Animal species, total known	803		
Animal species, threatened	57		
Higher plant species, total known	2,086		
Higher plant species, threatened	7		
GEF benefits index for biodiversity (0–100, median is 1.5)	1.0		
Energy			
GDP per unit of energy use (2005 PPP $/kg oil equivalent)	6.2	3.0	3.2
Energy use per capita (kg oil equivalent)	250	670	478
Energy from biomass products and waste (% of total)	39.6	56.3	53.8
Electric power consumption per capita (kWh)	150	531	309
Electricity generated using fossil fuel (% of total)	87.0	65.6	48.4
Electricity generated by hydropower (% of total)	9.6	18.0	38.8
Emissions and pollution			
CO_2 emissions per unit of GDP (kg/2005 PPP $)	0.3	0.5	0.4
CO_2 emissions per capita (metric tons)	0.4	0.8	0.6
CO_2 emissions growth (%, 1990–2005)	61.9	40.1	39.3
Particulate matter (urban-pop.-weighted avg., µg/cu. m)	95	53	69
Transport sector fuel consumption per capita (liters)	47	64	41
Water and sanitation			
Internal freshwater resources per capita (cu. m)	2,079	4,824	4,619
Freshwater withdrawal			
Total (% of internal resources)	8.6	3.2	9.4
Agriculture (% of total freshwater withdrawal)	93	87	90
Access to improved water source (% of total population)	77	58	68
Rural (% of rural population)	65	46	60
Urban (% of urban population)	93	81	84
Access to improved sanitation (% of total population)	28	31	39
Rural (% of rural population)	9	24	33
Urban (% of urban population)	54	42	54
Environment and health			
Acute resp. infection prevalence (% of children under five)	7.0		
Diarrhea prevalence (% of children under five)	15.1		
Under-five mortality rate (per 1,000 live births)	114	146	126
National accounting aggregates			
Gross savings (% of GNI)	21.8	17.4	25.4
Consumption of fixed capital (% of GNI)	9.4	11.1	9.3
Education expenditure (% of GNI)	4.5	3.6	2.6
Energy depletion (% of GNI)	0.0	11.7	9.8
Mineral depletion (% of GNI)	0.1	1.5	0.9
Net forest depletion (% of GNI)	0.0	0.5	0.8
CO_2 damage (% of GNI)	0.3	0.7	0.7
Particulate emission damage (% of GNI)	1.2	0.4	0.7
Adjusted net savings (% of GNI)	15.2	-5.0	5.8

Serbia

Population (millions)	7.4	Land area (1,000 sq. km)	88.4	GDP ($ billions)	40.1

	Country data	Europe & Central Asia group	Upper middle-income group
GNI per capita, *World Bank Atlas* method ($)	4,540	6,052	7,107
Urban population (% of total)	52	64	75
Urban population growth (average annual %, 1990–2007)	0.0	0.2	1.4
Population growth (average annual %, 1990–2007)	-0.2	0.1	0.9

Agriculture

Agricultural land (% of land area)	..	28	31
Agricultural productivity (value added per worker, 2000 $)	..	2,228	2,947
Food production index (1999–2001 = 100)	..	110	113
Population density, rural (people/sq. km of arable land)	103	129	110

Forests and biodiversity

Forest area (% of land area)	..	38.3	39.3
Deforestation (average annual %, 1990–2005)	..	0.0	0.2
Nationally protected area (% of land area)	..	6.1	10.3
Animal species, total known	..		
Animal species, threatened	42		
Higher plant species, total known	..		
Higher plant species, threatened	1		
GEF benefits index for biodiversity (0–100, median is 1.5)	0.2		

Energy

GDP per unit of energy use (2005 PPP $/kg oil equivalent)	4.1	3.5	4.8
Energy use per capita (kg oil equivalent)	2,303	2,930	2,300
Energy from biomass products and waste (% of total)	4.7	2.2	7.0
Electric power consumption per capita (kWh)	4,040	3,835	3,242
Electricity generated using fossil fuel (% of total)	69.9	67.7	62.8
Electricity generated by hydropower (% of total)	30.1	17.4	27.6

Emissions and pollution

CO_2 emissions per unit of GDP (kg/2005 PPP $)	..	0.7	0.5
CO_2 emissions per capita (metric tons)	..	7.0	5.5
CO_2 emissions growth (%, 1990–2005)	..	-29.3	-8.3
Particulate matter (urban-pop.-weighted avg., µg/cu. m)	..	27	30
Transport sector fuel consumption per capita (liters)	363	255	332

Water and sanitation

Internal freshwater resources per capita (cu. m)	..	11,806	16,993
Freshwater withdrawal			
Total (% of internal resources)	..	7.2	13.8
Agriculture (% of total freshwater withdrawal)	..	60	57
Access to improved water source (% of total population)	99	95	95
Rural (% of rural population)	98	88	83
Urban (% of urban population)	99	99	98
Access to improved sanitation (% of total population)	92	89	83
Rural (% of rural population)	88	79	64
Urban (% of urban population)	96	94	89

Environment and health

Acute resp. infection prevalence (% of children under five)	..		
Diarrhea prevalence (% of children under five)	..		
Under-five mortality rate (per 1,000 live births)	8	23	24

National accounting aggregates

Gross savings (% of GNI)	..	24.0	23.2
Consumption of fixed capital (% of GNI)	..	12.8	12.8
Education expenditure (% of GNI)	..	4.0	4.4
Energy depletion (% of GNI)	..	9.8	7.6
Mineral depletion (% of GNI)	..	0.7	1.3
Net forest depletion (% of GNI)	..	0.0	0.0
CO_2 damage (% of GNI)	..	1.0	0.6
Particulate emission damage (% of GNI)	..	0.5	0.4
Adjusted net savings (% of GNI)	..	3.2	4.9

Seychelles

| | Population (thousands) 85 | Land area (sq. km) | 460 | GDP ($ millions) | 728 |

	Country data	Sub-Saharan Africa group	Upper middle-income group
GNI per capita, *World Bank Atlas* method ($)	8,960	951	7,107
Urban population (% of total)	54	36	75
Urban population growth (average annual %, 1990–2007)	1.7	4.0	1.4
Population growth (average annual %, 1990–2007)	1.1	2.6	0.9
Agriculture			
Agricultural land (% of land area)	13	44	31
Agricultural productivity (value added per worker, 2000 $)	433	287	2,947
Food production index (1999–2001 = 100)	..	109	113
Population density, rural (people/sq. km of arable land)	3,905	351	110
Forests and biodiversity			
Forest area (% of land area)	87.0	26.5	39.3
Deforestation (average annual %, 1990–2005)	0.0	0.6	0.2
Nationally protected area (% of land area)	8.3	11.3	10.3
Animal species, total known	263		
Animal species, threatened	110		
Higher plant species, total known	250		
Higher plant species, threatened	45		
GEF benefits index for biodiversity (0–100, median is 1.5)	3.5		
Energy			
GDP per unit of energy use (2005 PPP $/kg oil equivalent)	..	3.0	4.8
Energy use per capita (kg oil equivalent)	..	670	2,300
Energy from biomass products and waste (% of total)	..	56.3	7.0
Electric power consumption per capita (kWh)	..	531	3,242
Electricity generated using fossil fuel (% of total)	..	65.6	62.8
Electricity generated by hydropower (% of total)	..	18.0	27.6
Emissions and pollution			
CO_2 emissions per unit of GDP (kg/2005 PPP $)	0.5	0.5	0.5
CO_2 emissions per capita (metric tons)	7.0	0.8	5.5
CO_2 emissions growth (%, 1990–2005)	409.7	40.1	–8.3
Particulate matter (urban-pop.-weighted avg., µg/cu. m)	..	53	30
Transport sector fuel consumption per capita (liters)	..	64	332
Water and sanitation			
Internal freshwater resources per capita (cu. m)	..	4,824	16,993
Freshwater withdrawal			
Total (% of internal resources)	..	3.2	13.8
Agriculture (% of total freshwater withdrawal)	7	87	57
Access to improved water source (% of total population)	..	58	95
Rural (% of rural population)	..	46	83
Urban (% of urban population)	100	81	98
Access to improved sanitation (% of total population)	..	31	83
Rural (% of rural population)	100	24	64
Urban (% of urban population)	..	42	89
Environment and health			
Acute resp. infection prevalence (% of children under five)	..		
Diarrhea prevalence (% of children under five)	..		
Under-five mortality rate (per 1,000 live births)	13	146	24
National accounting aggregates			
Gross savings (% of GNI)	–0.3	17.4	23.2
Consumption of fixed capital (% of GNI)	13.3	11.1	12.8
Education expenditure (% of GNI)	5.8	3.6	4.4
Energy depletion (% of GNI)	0.0	11.7	7.6
Mineral depletion (% of GNI)	0.0	1.5	1.3
Net forest depletion (% of GNI)	0.0	0.5	0.0
CO_2 damage (% of GNI)	0.6	0.7	0.6
Particulate emission damage (% of GNI)	..	0.4	0.4
Adjusted net savings (% of GNI)	–8.4	–5.0	4.9

Sierra Leone

| | Population (millions) | 5.8 | Land area (1,000 sq. km) | 71.6 | GDP ($ billions) | 1.7 |

	Country data	Sub-Saharan Africa group	Low-income group
GNI per capita, *World Bank Atlas* method ($)	260	951	574
Urban population (% of total)	37	36	32
Urban population growth (average annual %, 1990–2007)	2.9	4.0	3.7
Population growth (average annual %, 1990–2007)	2.1	2.6	2.4
Agriculture			
Agricultural land (% of land area)	40	44	39
Agricultural productivity (value added per worker, 2000 $)	..	287	330
Food production index (1999–2001 = 100)	114	109	112
Population density, rural (people/sq. km of arable land)	588	351	603
Forests and biodiversity			
Forest area (% of land area)	38.5	26.5	24.7
Deforestation (average annual %, 1990–2005)	0.7	0.6	0.7
Nationally protected area (% of land area)	4.1	11.3	10.8
Animal species, total known	823		
Animal species, threatened	47		
Higher plant species, total known	2,090		
Higher plant species, threatened	47		
GEF benefits index for biodiversity (0–100, median is 1.5)	1.3		
Energy			
GDP per unit of energy use (2005 PPP $/kg oil equivalent)	..	3.0	3.2
Energy use per capita (kg oil equivalent)	..	670	478
Energy from biomass products and waste (% of total)	..	56.3	53.8
Electric power consumption per capita (kWh)	..	531	309
Electricity generated using fossil fuel (% of total)	..	65.6	48.4
Electricity generated by hydropower (% of total)	..	18.0	38.8
Emissions and pollution			
CO_2 emissions per unit of GDP (kg/2005 PPP $)	0.3	0.5	0.4
CO_2 emissions per capita (metric tons)	0.2	0.8	0.6
CO_2 emissions growth (%, 1990–2005)	181.3	40.1	39.3
Particulate matter (urban-pop.-weighted avg., µg/cu. m)	50	53	69
Transport sector fuel consumption per capita (liters)	..	64	41
Water and sanitation			
Internal freshwater resources per capita (cu. m)	27,358	4,824	4,619
Freshwater withdrawal			
Total (% of internal resources)	0.2	3.2	9.4
Agriculture (% of total freshwater withdrawal)	92	87	90
Access to improved water source (% of total population)	53	58	68
Rural (% of rural population)	32	46	60
Urban (% of urban population)	83	81	84
Access to improved sanitation (% of total population)	11	31	39
Rural (% of rural population)	5	24	33
Urban (% of urban population)	20	42	54
Environment and health			
Acute resp. infection prevalence (% of children under five)	9.0		
Diarrhea prevalence (% of children under five)	25.3		
Under-five mortality rate (per 1,000 live births)	262	146	126
National accounting aggregates			
Gross savings (% of GNI)	9.8	17.4	25.4
Consumption of fixed capital (% of GNI)	7.9	11.1	9.3
Education expenditure (% of GNI)	3.9	3.6	2.6
Energy depletion (% of GNI)	0.0	11.7	9.8
Mineral depletion (% of GNI)	0.9	1.5	0.9
Net forest depletion (% of GNI)	1.6	0.5	0.8
CO_2 damage (% of GNI)	0.4	0.7	0.7
Particulate emission damage (% of GNI)	0.9	0.4	0.7
Adjusted net savings (% of GNI)	2.1	–5.0	5.8

Singapore

Population (millions)	**4.6**	Land area (1,000 sq. km)	**0.7**	GDP ($ billions)	**161.3**

	Country data	High-income group
GNI per capita, *World Bank Atlas* method ($)	32,340	37,572
Urban population (% of total)	100	78
Urban population growth (average annual %, 1990–2007)	2.4	1.0
Population growth (average annual %, 1990–2007)	2.4	0.7
Agriculture		
Agricultural land (% of land area)	1	38
Agricultural productivity (value added per worker, 2000 $)	46,408	27,680
Food production index (1999–2001 = 100)	116	102
Population density, rural (people/sq. km of arable land)	0	323
Forests and biodiversity		
Forest area (% of land area)	3.3	28.8
Deforestation (average annual %, 1990–2005)	0.0	-0.1
Nationally protected area (% of land area)	4.2	11.8
Animal species, total known	473	
Animal species, threatened	213	
Higher plant species, total known	2,282	
Higher plant species, threatened	54	
GEF benefits index for biodiversity (0–100, median is 1.5)	0.1	
Energy		
GDP per unit of energy use (2005 PPP $/kg oil equivalent)	6.5	6.3
Energy use per capita (kg oil equivalent)	6,968	5,416
Energy from biomass products and waste (% of total)	0.0	3.4
Electric power consumption per capita (kWh)	8,520	9,675
Electricity generated using fossil fuel (% of total)	100.0	62.0
Electricity generated by hydropower (% of total)	0.0	11.4
Emissions and pollution		
CO_2 emissions per unit of GDP (kg/2005 PPP $)	0.3	0.4
CO_2 emissions per capita (metric tons)	13.2	12.6
CO_2 emissions growth (%, 1990–2005)	34.2	19.1
Particulate matter (urban-pop.-weighted avg., µg/cu. m)	41	26
Transport sector fuel consumption per capita (liters)	580	1,159
Water and sanitation		
Internal freshwater resources per capita (cu. m)	131	9,313
Freshwater withdrawal		
Total (% of internal resources)	..	10.4
Agriculture (% of total freshwater withdrawal)	..	43
Access to improved water source (% of total population)	100	100
Rural (% of rural population)	..	98
Urban (% of urban population)	100	100
Access to improved sanitation (% of total population)	100	100
Rural (% of rural population)	..	99
Urban (% of urban population)	100	100
Environment and health		
Acute resp. infection prevalence (% of children under five)	..	
Diarrhea prevalence (% of children under five)	..	
Under-five mortality rate (per 1,000 live births)	3	7
National accounting aggregates		
Gross savings (% of GNI)	..	20.6
Consumption of fixed capital (% of GNI)	15.1	14.5
Education expenditure (% of GNI)	2.7	4.6
Energy depletion (% of GNI)	0.0	1.5
Mineral depletion (% of GNI)	0.0	0.2
Net forest depletion (% of GNI)	0.0	0.0
CO_2 damage (% of GNI)	0.3	0.3
Particulate emission damage (% of GNI)	0.9	0.3
Adjusted net savings (% of GNI)	..	8.5

Slovak Republic

Population (millions) **5.4** Land area (1,000 sq. km) **48.1** GDP ($ billions) **75.0**

	Country data	High-income group
GNI per capita, *World Bank Atlas* method ($)	11,720	37,572
Urban population (% of total)	56	78
Urban population growth (average annual %, 1990–2007)	0.1	1.0
Population growth (average annual %, 1990–2007)	0.1	0.7
Agriculture		
Agricultural land (% of land area)	40	38
Agricultural productivity (value added per worker, 2000 $)	5,848	27,680
Food production index (1999–2001 = 100)	106	102
Population density, rural (people/sq. km of arable land)	170	323
Forests and biodiversity		
Forest area (% of land area)	40.1	28.8
Deforestation (average annual %, 1990–2005)	0.0	–0.1
Nationally protected area (% of land area)	20.0	11.8
Animal species, total known	419	
Animal species, threatened	37	
Higher plant species, total known	3,124	
Higher plant species, threatened	2	
GEF benefits index for biodiversity (0–100, median is 1.5)	0.1	
Energy		
GDP per unit of energy use (2005 PPP $/kg oil equivalent)	5.1	6.3
Energy use per capita (kg oil equivalent)	3,465	5,416
Energy from biomass products and waste (% of total)	2.6	3.4
Electric power consumption per capita (kWh)	5,136	9,675
Electricity generated using fossil fuel (% of total)	26.8	62.0
Electricity generated by hydropower (% of total)	14.1	11.4
Emissions and pollution		
CO_2 emissions per unit of GDP (kg/2005 PPP $)	0.4	0.4
CO_2 emissions per capita (metric tons)	6.8	12.6
CO_2 emissions growth (%, 1990–2005)	-28.8	19.1
Particulate matter (urban-pop.-weighted avg., µg/cu. m)	15	26
Transport sector fuel consumption per capita (liters)	359	1,159
Water and sanitation		
Internal freshwater resources per capita (cu. m)	2,334	9,313
Freshwater withdrawal		
Total (% of internal resources)	..	10.4
Agriculture (% of total freshwater withdrawal)	..	43
Access to improved water source (% of total population)	100	100
Rural (% of rural population)	100	98
Urban (% of urban population)	100	100
Access to improved sanitation (% of total population)	100	100
Rural (% of rural population)	99	99
Urban (% of urban population)	100	100
Environment and health		
Acute resp. infection prevalence (% of children under five)	..	
Diarrhea prevalence (% of children under five)	..	
Under-five mortality rate (per 1,000 live births)	8	7
National accounting aggregates		
Gross savings (% of GNI)	24.0	20.6
Consumption of fixed capital (% of GNI)	13.8	14.5
Education expenditure (% of GNI)	3.8	4.6
Energy depletion (% of GNI)	0.1	1.5
Mineral depletion (% of GNI)	0.0	0.2
Net forest depletion (% of GNI)	0.4	0.0
CO_2 damage (% of GNI)	0.5	0.3
Particulate emission damage (% of GNI)	0.0	0.3
Adjusted net savings (% of GNI)	13.1	8.5

Slovenia

Population (millions)	**2.0**	Land area (1,000 sq. km)	**20.1**	GDP ($ billions)	**47.2**

	Country data	High-income group
GNI per capita, *World Bank Atlas* method ($)	21,510	37,572
Urban population (% of total)	49	78
Urban population growth (average annual %, 1990–2007)	–0.1	1.0
Population growth (average annual %, 1990–2007)	0.1	0.7
Agriculture		
Agricultural land (% of land area)	25	38
Agricultural productivity (value added per worker, 2000 $)	47,995	27,680
Food production index (1999–2001 = 100)	107	102
Population density, rural (people/sq. km of arable land)	574	323
Forests and biodiversity		
Forest area (% of land area)	62.8	28.8
Deforestation (average annual %, 1990–2005)	–0.4	–0.1
Nationally protected area (% of land area)	6.7	11.8
Animal species, total known	437	
Animal species, threatened	77	
Higher plant species, total known	3,200	
Higher plant species, threatened	..	
GEF benefits index for biodiversity (0–100, median is 1.5)	0.2	
Energy		
GDP per unit of energy use (2005 PPP $/kg oil equivalent)	6.8	6.3
Energy use per capita (kg oil equivalent)	3,618	5,416
Energy from biomass products and waste (% of total)	6.5	3.4
Electric power consumption per capita (kWh)	7,124	9,675
Electricity generated using fossil fuel (% of total)	38.8	62.0
Electricity generated by hydropower (% of total)	23.8	11.4
Emissions and pollution		
CO_2 emissions per unit of GDP (kg/2005 PPP $)	0.3	0.4
CO_2 emissions per capita (metric tons)	7.4	12.6
CO_2 emissions growth (%, 1990–2005)	–17.6	19.1
Particulate matter (urban-pop.-weighted avg., µg/cu. m)	30	26
Transport sector fuel consumption per capita (liters)	858	1,159
Water and sanitation		
Internal freshwater resources per capita (cu. m)	9,251	9,313
Freshwater withdrawal		
Total (% of internal resources)	..	10.4
Agriculture (% of total freshwater withdrawal)	..	43
Access to improved water source (% of total population)	..	100
Rural (% of rural population)	..	98
Urban (% of urban population)	..	100
Access to improved sanitation (% of total population)	..	100
Rural (% of rural population)	..	99
Urban (% of urban population)	..	100
Environment and health		
Acute resp. infection prevalence (% of children under five)	..	
Diarrhea prevalence (% of children under five)	..	
Under-five mortality rate (per 1,000 live births)	4	7
National accounting aggregates		
Gross savings (% of GNI)	28.0	20.6
Consumption of fixed capital (% of GNI)	14.2	14.5
Education expenditure (% of GNI)	5.5	4.6
Energy depletion (% of GNI)	0.1	1.5
Mineral depletion (% of GNI)	0.0	0.2
Net forest depletion (% of GNI)	0.2	0.0
CO_2 damage (% of GNI)	0.3	0.3
Particulate emission damage (% of GNI)	0.2	0.3
Adjusted net savings (% of GNI)	18.4	8.5

Solomon Islands

Population (thousands) **495**   Land area (1,000 sq. km)   **28**   GDP ($ millions)   **388**

	Country data	East Asia & Pacific group	Low-income group
GNI per capita, *World Bank Atlas* method ($)	750	2,182	574
Urban population (% of total)	18	43	32
Urban population growth (average annual %, 1990–2007)	4.2	3.5	3.7
Population growth (average annual %, 1990–2007)	2.7	1.1	2.4
Agriculture			
Agricultural land (% of land area)	3	51	39
Agricultural productivity (value added per worker, 2000 $)	613	458	330
Food production index (1999–2001 = 100)	119	120	112
Population density, rural (people/sq. km of arable land)	2,178	547	603
Forests and biodiversity			
Forest area (% of land area)	77.6	28.4	24.7
Deforestation (average annual %, 1990–2005)	1.6	-0.1	0.7
Nationally protected area (% of land area)	0.7	14.0	10.8
Animal species, total known	320		
Animal species, threatened	195		
Higher plant species, total known	3,172		
Higher plant species, threatened	16		
GEF benefits index for biodiversity (0–100, median is 1.5)	4.4		
Energy			
GDP per unit of energy use (2005 PPP $/kg oil equivalent)	..	3.4	3.2
Energy use per capita (kg oil equivalent)	..	1,258	478
Energy from biomass products and waste (% of total)	..	14.7	53.8
Electric power consumption per capita (kWh)	..	1,669	309
Electricity generated using fossil fuel (% of total)	..	82.0	48.4
Electricity generated by hydropower (% of total)	..	15.0	38.8
Emissions and pollution			
CO_2 emissions per unit of GDP (kg/2005 PPP $)	0.3	0.9	0.4
CO_2 emissions per capita (metric tons)	0.4	3.6	0.6
CO_2 emissions growth (%, 1990–2005)	9.1	123.4	39.3
Particulate matter (urban-pop.-weighted avg., µg/cu. m)	37	69	69
Transport sector fuel consumption per capita (liters)	..	106	41
Water and sanitation			
Internal freshwater resources per capita (cu. m)	90,237	4,948	4,619
Freshwater withdrawal			
Total (% of internal resources)	..	10.2	9.4
Agriculture (% of total freshwater withdrawal)	..	74	90
Access to improved water source (% of total population)	70	87	68
Rural (% of rural population)	65	81	60
Urban (% of urban population)	94	96	84
Access to improved sanitation (% of total population)	32	66	39
Rural (% of rural population)	18	59	33
Urban (% of urban population)	98	75	54
Environment and health			
Acute resp. infection prevalence (% of children under five)	..		
Diarrhea prevalence (% of children under five)	..		
Under-five mortality rate (per 1,000 live births)	70	27	126
National accounting aggregates			
Gross savings (% of GNI)	..	48.0	25.4
Consumption of fixed capital (% of GNI)	9.2	10.7	9.3
Education expenditure (% of GNI)	3.8	2.1	2.6
Energy depletion (% of GNI)	0.0	4.9	9.8
Mineral depletion (% of GNI)	0.0	1.3	0.9
Net forest depletion (% of GNI)	13.0	0.0	0.8
CO_2 damage (% of GNI)	0.4	1.3	0.7
Particulate emission damage (% of GNI)	0.2	1.3	0.7
Adjusted net savings (% of GNI)	..	30.6	5.8

Somalia

	Country data	Sub-Saharan Africa group	Low-income group
Population (millions) **8.7** Land area (1,000 sq. km) **627.3** GDP ($ billions) **..**			

	Country data	Sub-Saharan Africa group	Low-income group
GNI per capita, *World Bank Atlas* method ($)	..	951	574
Urban population (% of total)	36	36	32
Urban population growth (average annual %, 1990–2007)	2.7	4.0	3.7
Population growth (average annual %, 1990–2007)	1.5	2.6	2.4
Agriculture			
Agricultural land (% of land area)	71	44	39
Agricultural productivity (value added per worker, 2000 $)	..	287	330
Food production index (1999–2001 = 100)	106	109	112
Population density, rural (people/sq. km of arable land)	393	351	603
Forests and biodiversity			
Forest area (% of land area)	11.4	26.5	24.7
Deforestation (average annual %, 1990–2005)	1.0	0.6	0.7
Nationally protected area (% of land area)	0.3	11.3	10.8
Animal species, total known	824		
Animal species, threatened	106		
Higher plant species, total known	3,028		
Higher plant species, threatened	17		
GEF benefits index for biodiversity (0–100, median is 1.5)	6.1		
Energy			
GDP per unit of energy use (2005 PPP $/kg oil equivalent)	..	3.0	3.2
Energy use per capita (kg oil equivalent)	..	670	478
Energy from biomass products and waste (% of total)	..	56.3	53.8
Electric power consumption per capita (kWh)	..	531	309
Electricity generated using fossil fuel (% of total)	..	65.6	48.4
Electricity generated by hydropower (% of total)	..	18.0	38.8
Emissions and pollution			
CO_2 emissions per unit of GDP (kg/2005 PPP $)	..	0.5	0.4
CO_2 emissions per capita (metric tons)	0.07	0.85	0.58
CO_2 emissions growth (%, 1990–2005)	3,120.0	40.1	39.3
Particulate matter (urban-pop.-weighted avg., µg/cu. m)	31	53	69
Transport sector fuel consumption per capita (liters)	..	64	41
Water and sanitation			
Internal freshwater resources per capita (cu. m)	690	4,824	4,619
Freshwater withdrawal			
Total (% of internal resources)	55.0	3.2	9.4
Agriculture (% of total freshwater withdrawal)	99	87	90
Access to improved water source (% of total population)	29	58	68
Rural (% of rural population)	10	46	60
Urban (% of urban population)	63	81	84
Access to improved sanitation (% of total population)	23	31	39
Rural (% of rural population)	7	24	33
Urban (% of urban population)	51	42	54
Environment and health			
Acute resp. infection prevalence (% of children under five)	..		
Diarrhea prevalence (% of children under five)	23.4		
Under-five mortality rate (per 1,000 live births)	142	146	126
National accounting aggregates			
Gross savings (% of GNI)	..	17.4	25.4
Consumption of fixed capital (% of GNI)	..	11.1	9.3
Education expenditure (% of GNI)	..	3.6	2.6
Energy depletion (% of GNI)	..	11.7	9.8
Mineral depletion (% of GNI)	..	1.5	0.9
Net forest depletion (% of GNI)	..	0.5	0.8
CO_2 damage (% of GNI)	..	0.7	0.7
Particulate emission damage (% of GNI)	..	0.4	0.7
Adjusted net savings (% of GNI)	..	-5.0	5.8

South Africa

Population (millions)	48	Land area (1,000 sq. km)	1,214	GDP ($ billions)	283.0

	Country data	Sub-Saharan Africa group	Upper middle-income group
GNI per capita, *World Bank Atlas* method ($)	5,720	951	7,107
Urban population (% of total)	60	36	75
Urban population growth (average annual %, 1990–2007)	2.7	4.0	1.4
Population growth (average annual %, 1990–2007)	1.8	2.6	0.9
Agriculture			
Agricultural land (% of land area)	82	44	31
Agricultural productivity (value added per worker, 2000 $)	2,670	287	2,947
Food production index (1999–2001 = 100)	111	109	113
Population density, rural (people/sq. km of arable land)	129	351	110
Forests and biodiversity			
Forest area (% of land area)	7.6	26.5	39.3
Deforestation (average annual %, 1990–2005)	0.0	0.6	0.2
Nationally protected area (% of land area)	6.1	11.3	10.3
Animal species, total known	1,149		
Animal species, threatened	324		
Higher plant species, total known	23,420		
Higher plant species, threatened	74		
GEF benefits index for biodiversity (0–100, median is 1.5)	20.7		
Energy			
GDP per unit of energy use (2005 PPP $/kg oil equivalent)	3.2	3.0	4.8
Energy use per capita (kg oil equivalent)	2,739	670	2,300
Energy from biomass products and waste (% of total)	10.5	56.3	7.0
Electric power consumption per capita (kWh)	4,810	531	3,242
Electricity generated using fossil fuel (% of total)	93.5	65.6	62.8
Electricity generated by hydropower (% of total)	1.5	18.0	27.6
Emissions and pollution			
CO_2 emissions per unit of GDP (kg/2005 PPP $)	1.0	0.5	0.5
CO_2 emissions per capita (metric tons)	8.7	0.8	5.5
CO_2 emissions growth (%, 1990–2005)	23.2	40.1	−8.3
Particulate matter (urban-pop.-weighted avg., µg/cu. m)	21	53	30
Transport sector fuel consumption per capita (liters)	334	64	332
Water and sanitation			
Internal freshwater resources per capita (cu. m)	936	4,824	16,993
Freshwater withdrawal			
Total (% of internal resources)	27.9	3.2	13.8
Agriculture (% of total freshwater withdrawal)	63	87	57
Access to improved water source (% of total population)	93	58	95
Rural (% of rural population)	82	46	83
Urban (% of urban population)	100	81	98
Access to improved sanitation (% of total population)	59	31	83
Rural (% of rural population)	49	24	64
Urban (% of urban population)	66	42	89
Environment and health			
Acute resp. infection prevalence (% of children under five)	19.0		
Diarrhea prevalence (% of children under five)	13.2		
Under-five mortality rate (per 1,000 live births)	59	146	24
National accounting aggregates			
Gross savings (% of GNI)	14.5	17.4	23.2
Consumption of fixed capital (% of GNI)	12.4	11.1	12.8
Education expenditure (% of GNI)	5.3	3.6	4.4
Energy depletion (% of GNI)	3.1	11.7	7.6
Mineral depletion (% of GNI)	2.2	1.5	1.3
Net forest depletion (% of GNI)	0.2	0.5	0.0
CO_2 damage (% of GNI)	1.3	0.7	0.6
Particulate emission damage (% of GNI)	0.1	0.4	0.4
Adjusted net savings (% of GNI)	0.4	−5.0	4.9

Population (millions)	**45**	Land area (1,000 sq. km)	**499**	GDP ($ billions)	**1,436.9**

	Country data	High-income group
GNI per capita, *World Bank Atlas* method ($)	29,290	37,572
Urban population (% of total)	77	78
Urban population growth (average annual %, 1990–2007)	1.0	1.0
Population growth (average annual %, 1990–2007)	0.9	0.7
Agriculture		
Agricultural land (% of land area)	58	38
Agricultural productivity (value added per worker, 2000 $)	18,054	27,680
Food production index (1999–2001 = 100)	96	102
Population density, rural (people/sq. km of arable land)	74	323
Forests and biodiversity		
Forest area (% of land area)	35.9	28.8
Deforestation (average annual %, 1990–2005)	-1.9	-0.1
Nationally protected area (% of land area)	8.3	11.8
Animal species, total known	647	
Animal species, threatened	169	
Higher plant species, total known	5,050	
Higher plant species, threatened	49	
GEF benefits index for biodiversity (0–100, median is 1.5)	6.8	
Energy		
GDP per unit of energy use (2005 PPP $/kg oil equivalent)	8.5	6.3
Energy use per capita (kg oil equivalent)	3,277	5,416
Energy from biomass products and waste (% of total)	3.6	3.4
Electric power consumption per capita (kWh)	6,206	9,675
Electricity generated using fossil fuel (% of total)	61.0	62.0
Electricity generated by hydropower (% of total)	8.5	11.4
Emissions and pollution		
CO_2 emissions per unit of GDP (kg/2005 PPP $)	0.3	0.4
CO_2 emissions per capita (metric tons)	7.9	12.6
CO_2 emissions growth (%, 1990–2005)	62.2	19.1
Particulate matter (urban-pop.-weighted avg., µg/cu. m)	32	26
Transport sector fuel consumption per capita (liters)	893	1,159
Water and sanitation		
Internal freshwater resources per capita (cu. m)	2,478	9,313
Freshwater withdrawal		
Total (% of internal resources)	32.0	10.4
Agriculture (% of total freshwater withdrawal)	68	43
Access to improved water source (% of total population)	100	100
Rural (% of rural population)	100	98
Urban (% of urban population)	100	100
Access to improved sanitation (% of total population)	100	100
Rural (% of rural population)	100	99
Urban (% of urban population)	100	100
Environment and health		
Acute resp. infection prevalence (% of children under five)	..	
Diarrhea prevalence (% of children under five)	..	
Under-five mortality rate (per 1,000 live births)	4	7
National accounting aggregates		
Gross savings (% of GNI)	21.9	20.6
Consumption of fixed capital (% of GNI)	14.8	14.5
Education expenditure (% of GNI)	3.9	4.6
Energy depletion (% of GNI)	0.0	1.5
Mineral depletion (% of GNI)	0.0	0.2
Net forest depletion (% of GNI)	0.0	0.0
CO_2 damage (% of GNI)	0.2	0.3
Particulate emission damage (% of GNI)	0.4	0.3
Adjusted net savings (% of GNI)	10.4	8.5

Sri Lanka

Population (millions)	**20**	Land area (1,000 sq. km)	**65** GDP ($ billions) **32.3**

	Country data	South Asia group	Lower middle- income group
GNI per capita, *World Bank Atlas* method ($)	1,540	880	1,905
Urban population (% of total)	15	29	42
Urban population growth (average annual %, 1990–2007)	0.2	2.7	2.9
Population growth (average annual %, 1990–2007)	0.9	1.8	1.3
Agriculture			
Agricultural land (% of land area)	36	55	47
Agricultural productivity (value added per worker, 2000 $)	705	417	532
Food production index (1999–2001 = 100)	107	107	116
Population density, rural (people/sq. km of arable land)	1,823	617	511
Forests and biodiversity			
Forest area (% of land area)	29.9	16.8	25.0
Deforestation (average annual %, 1990–2005)	1.3	−0.1	0.1
Nationally protected area (% of land area)	17.5	5.6	11.0
Animal species, total known	504		
Animal species, threatened	254		
Higher plant species, total known	3,314		
Higher plant species, threatened	280		
GEF benefits index for biodiversity (0–100, median is 1.5)	7.9		
Energy			
GDP per unit of energy use (2005 PPP $/kg oil equivalent)	8.0	4.8	3.9
Energy use per capita (kg oil equivalent)	472	468	1,019
Energy from biomass products and waste (% of total)	54.3	30.4	15.2
Electric power consumption per capita (kWh)	400	453	1,269
Electricity generated using fossil fuel (% of total)	50.6	78.3	79.0
Electricity generated by hydropower (% of total)	49.4	17.4	16.3
Emissions and pollution			
CO_2 emissions per unit of GDP (kg/2005 PPP $)	0.2	0.5	0.8
CO_2 emissions per capita (metric tons)	0.6	1.1	2.8
CO_2 emissions growth (%, 1990–2005)	193.1	106.7	93.5
Particulate matter (urban-pop.-weighted avg., µg/cu. m)	82	78	67
Transport sector fuel consumption per capita (liters)	90	33	99
Water and sanitation			
Internal freshwater resources per capita (cu. m)	2,499	1,196	4,117
Freshwater withdrawal			
Total (% of internal resources)	25.2	51.7	8.7
Agriculture (% of total freshwater withdrawal)	95	89	80
Access to improved water source (% of total population)	82	87	88
Rural (% of rural population)	79	84	82
Urban (% of urban population)	98	94	96
Access to improved sanitation (% of total population)	86	33	55
Rural (% of rural population)	86	23	43
Urban (% of urban population)	89	57	71
Environment and health			
Acute resp. infection prevalence (% of children under five)	..		
Diarrhea prevalence (% of children under five)	5.0		
Under-five mortality rate (per 1,000 live births)	21	78	50
National accounting aggregates			
Gross savings (% of GNI)	23.3	36.2	41.7
Consumption of fixed capital (% of GNI)	10.3	9.5	10.7
Education expenditure (% of GNI)	2.6	3.0	2.6
Energy depletion (% of GNI)	0.0	2.7	6.6
Mineral depletion (% of GNI)	0.0	0.6	1.2
Net forest depletion (% of GNI)	0.6	0.9	0.2
CO_2 damage (% of GNI)	0.3	1.0	1.2
Particulate emission damage (% of GNI)	0.3	0.8	1.1
Adjusted net savings (% of GNI)	14.3	23.9	23.5

St. Kitts and Nevis

Population (thousands) **49**	Land area (sq. km) **260**	GDP ($ millions) **527**

	Country data	Latin America & Caribbean group	Upper middle-income group
GNI per capita, *World Bank Atlas* method ($)	9,990	5,801	7,107
Urban population (% of total)	32	78	75
Urban population growth (average annual %, 1990–2007)	0.5	2.1	1.4
Population growth (average annual %, 1990–2007)	0.9	1.5	0.9
Agriculture			
Agricultural land (% of land area)	38	36	31
Agricultural productivity (value added per worker, 2000 $)	2,228	3,158	2,947
Food production index (1999–2001 = 100)	60	117	113
Population density, rural (people/sq. km of arable land)	465	232	110
Forests and biodiversity			
Forest area (% of land area)	20.4	45.4	39.3
Deforestation (average annual %, 1990–2005)	0.0	0.5	0.2
Nationally protected area (% of land area)	0.0	16.7	10.3
Animal species, total known	139		
Animal species, threatened	33		
Higher plant species, total known	659		
Higher plant species, threatened	2		
GEF benefits index for biodiversity (0–100, median is 1.5)	0.1		
Energy			
GDP per unit of energy use (2005 PPP $/kg oil equivalent)	..	7.3	4.8
Energy use per capita (kg oil equivalent)	..	1,240	2,300
Energy from biomass products and waste (% of total)	..	15.9	7.0
Electric power consumption per capita (kWh)	..	1,808	3,242
Electricity generated using fossil fuel (% of total)	..	37.0	62.8
Electricity generated by hydropower (% of total)	..	57.3	27.6
Emissions and pollution			
CO_2 emissions per unit of GDP (kg/2005 PPP $)	0.2	0.3	0.5
CO_2 emissions per capita (metric tons)	2.8	2.5	5.5
CO_2 emissions growth (%, 1990–2005)	105.6	33.4	-8.3
Particulate matter (urban-pop.-weighted avg., μg/cu. m)	15	35	30
Transport sector fuel consumption per capita (liters)	..	295	332
Water and sanitation			
Internal freshwater resources per capita (cu. m)	492	23,965	16,993
Freshwater withdrawal			
Total (% of internal resources)	..	2.0	13.8
Agriculture (% of total freshwater withdrawal)	..	71	57
Access to improved water source (% of total population)	99	91	95
Rural (% of rural population)	99	73	83
Urban (% of urban population)	99	97	98
Access to improved sanitation (% of total population)	96	78	83
Rural (% of rural population)	96	51	64
Urban (% of urban population)	96	86	89
Environment and health			
Acute resp. infection prevalence (% of children under five)	..		
Diarrhea prevalence (% of children under five)	..		
Under-five mortality rate (per 1,000 live births)	18	26	24
National accounting aggregates			
Gross savings (% of GNI)	..	22.9	23.2
Consumption of fixed capital (% of GNI)	13.6	12.6	12.8
Education expenditure (% of GNI)	4.1	4.5	4.4
Energy depletion (% of GNI)	0.0	5.4	7.6
Mineral depletion (% of GNI)	0.0	1.9	1.3
Net forest depletion (% of GNI)		0.0	0.0
CO_2 damage (% of GNI)	0.2	0.3	0.6
Particulate emission damage (% of GNI)	..	0.4	0.4
Adjusted net savings (% of GNI)	..	6.7	4.9

St. Lucia

Population (thousands) **168** Land area (sq. km) **610** GDP ($ millions) **980**

	Country data	Latin America & Caribbean group	Upper middle-income group
GNI per capita, *World Bank Atlas* method ($)	5,520	5,801	7,107
Urban population (% of total)	28	78	75
Urban population growth (average annual %, 1990–2007)	1.0	2.1	1.4
Population growth (average annual %, 1990–2007)	1.3	1.5	0.9
Agriculture			
Agricultural land (% of land area)	33	36	31
Agricultural productivity (value added per worker, 2000 $)	1,246	3,158	2,947
Food production index (1999–2001 = 100)	74	117	113
Population density, rural (people/sq. km of arable land)	2,983	232	110
Forests and biodiversity			
Forest area (% of land area)	27.9	45.4	39.3
Deforestation (average annual %, 1990–2005)	0.0	0.5	0.2
Nationally protected area (% of land area)	15.4	16.7	10.3
Animal species, total known	175		
Animal species, threatened	38		
Higher plant species, total known	1,028		
Higher plant species, threatened	6		
GEF benefits index for biodiversity (0–100, median is 1.5)	1.4		
Energy			
GDP per unit of energy use (2005 PPP $/kg oil equivalent)	..	7.3	4.8
Energy use per capita (kg oil equivalent)	..	1,240	2,300
Energy from biomass products and waste (% of total)	..	15.9	7.0
Electric power consumption per capita (kWh)	..	1,808	3,242
Electricity generated using fossil fuel (% of total)	..	37.0	62.8
Electricity generated by hydropower (% of total)	..	57.3	27.6
Emissions and pollution			
CO_2 emissions per unit of GDP (kg/2005 PPP $)	0.3	0.3	0.5
CO_2 emissions per capita (metric tons)	2.2	2.5	5.5
CO_2 emissions growth (%, 1990–2005)	129.5	33.4	-8.3
Particulate matter (urban-pop.-weighted avg., µg/cu. m)	31	35	30
Transport sector fuel consumption per capita (liters)	..	295	332
Water and sanitation			
Internal freshwater resources per capita (cu. m)	..	23,965	16,993
Freshwater withdrawal			
Total (% of internal resources)	..	2.0	13.8
Agriculture (% of total freshwater withdrawal)	..	71	57
Access to improved water source (% of total population)	98	91	95
Rural (% of rural population)	98	73	83
Urban (% of urban population)	98	97	98
Access to improved sanitation (% of total population)	..	78	83
Rural (% of rural population)	..	51	64
Urban (% of urban population)	..	86	89
Environment and health			
Acute resp. infection prevalence (% of children under five)	..		
Diarrhea prevalence (% of children under five)	..		
Under-five mortality rate (per 1,000 live births)	18	26	24
National accounting aggregates			
Gross savings (% of GNI)	..	22.9	23.2
Consumption of fixed capital (% of GNI)	12.7	12.6	12.8
Education expenditure (% of GNI)	5.0	4.5	4.4
Energy depletion (% of GNI)	0.0	5.4	7.6
Mineral depletion (% of GNI)	0.0	1.9	1.3
Net forest depletion (% of GNI)	0.0	0.0	0.0
CO_2 damage (% of GNI)	0.3	0.3	0.6
Particulate emission damage (% of GNI)	0.2	0.4	0.4
Adjusted net savings (% of GNI)	..	6.7	4.9

St. Vincent & Grenadines

Population (thousands) **120** Land area (sq. km) **390** GDP ($ millions) **553**

	Country data	Latin America & Caribbean group	Upper middle-income group
GNI per capita, *World Bank Atlas* method ($)	4,210	5,801	7,107
Urban population (% of total)	47	78	75
Urban population growth (average annual %, 1990–2007)	1.4	2.1	1.4
Population growth (average annual %, 1990–2007)	0.6	1.5	0.9
Agriculture			
Agricultural land (% of land area)	26	36	31
Agricultural productivity (value added per worker, 2000 $)	2,215	3,158	2,947
Food production index (1999–2001 = 100)	111	117	113
Population density, rural (people/sq. km of arable land)	1,289	232	110
Forests and biodiversity			
Forest area (% of land area)	27.4	45.4	39.3
Deforestation (average annual %, 1990–2005)	-1.3	0.5	0.2
Nationally protected area (% of land area)	11.3	16.7	10.3
Animal species, total known	185		
Animal species, threatened	34		
Higher plant species, total known	1,166		
Higher plant species, threatened	4		
GEF benefits index for biodiversity (0–100, median is 1.5)	1.0		
Energy			
GDP per unit of energy use (2005 PPP $/kg oil equivalent)	..	7.3	4.8
Energy use per capita (kg oil equivalent)	..	1,240	2,300
Energy from biomass products and waste (% of total)	..	15.9	7.0
Electric power consumption per capita (kWh)	..	1,808	3,242
Electricity generated using fossil fuel (% of total)	..	37.0	62.8
Electricity generated by hydropower (% of total)	..	57.3	27.6
Emissions and pollution			
CO_2 emissions per unit of GDP (kg/2005 PPP $)	0.2	0.3	0.5
CO_2 emissions per capita (metric tons)	1.6	2.5	5.5
CO_2 emissions growth (%, 1990–2005)	136.4	33.4	-8.3
Particulate matter (urban-pop.-weighted avg., μg/cu. m)	28	35	30
Transport sector fuel consumption per capita (liters)	..	295	332
Water and sanitation			
Internal freshwater resources per capita (cu. m)	..	23,965	16,993
Freshwater withdrawal			
Total (% of internal resources)	..	2.0	13.8
Agriculture (% of total freshwater withdrawal)	..	71	57
Access to improved water source (% of total population)	..	91	95
Rural (% of rural population)	..	73	83
Urban (% of urban population)	..	97	98
Access to improved sanitation (% of total population)	..	78	83
Rural (% of rural population)	96	51	64
Urban (% of urban population)	..	86	89
Environment and health			
Acute resp. infection prevalence (% of children under five)	..		
Diarrhea prevalence (% of children under five)	..		
Under-five mortality rate (per 1,000 live births)	19	26	24
National accounting aggregates			
Gross savings (% of GNI)	..	22.9	23.2
Consumption of fixed capital (% of GNI)	12.5	12.6	12.8
Education expenditure (% of GNI)	5.8	4.5	4.4
Energy depletion (% of GNI)	0.0	5.4	7.6
Mineral depletion (% of GNI)	0.0	1.9	1.3
Net forest depletion (% of GNI)	0.0	0.0	0.0
CO_2 damage (% of GNI)	0.3	0.3	0.6
Particulate emission damage (% of GNI)	0.1	0.4	0.4
Adjusted net savings (% of GNI)	..	6.7	4.9

Sudan

	Country data	Sub-Saharan Africa group	Lower middle-income group
Population (millions) **39** Land area (1,000 sq. km) **2,376** GDP ($ billions) **46.2**			

	Country data	Sub-Saharan Africa group	Lower middle-income group
GNI per capita, *World Bank Atlas* method ($)	950	951	1,905
Urban population (% of total)	43	36	42
Urban population growth (average annual %, 1990–2007)	5.1	4.0	2.9
Population growth (average annual %, 1990–2007)	2.3	2.6	1.3
Agriculture			
Agricultural land (% of land area)	58	44	47
Agricultural productivity (value added per worker, 2000 $)	661	287	532
Food production index (1999–2001 = 100)	116	109	116
Population density, rural (people/sq. km of arable land)	112	351	511
Forests and biodiversity			
Forest area (% of land area)	28.4	26.5	25.0
Deforestation (average annual %, 1990–2005)	0.8	0.6	0.1
Nationally protected area (% of land area)	4.8	11.3	11.0
Animal species, total known	1,254		
Animal species, threatened	88		
Higher plant species, total known	3,137		
Higher plant species, threatened	17		
GEF benefits index for biodiversity (0–100, median is 1.5)	5.1		
Energy			
GDP per unit of energy use (2005 PPP $/kg oil equivalent)	3.9	3.0	3.9
Energy use per capita (kg oil equivalent)	470	670	1,019
Energy from biomass products and waste (% of total)	77.5	56.3	15.2
Electric power consumption per capita (kWh)	95	531	1,269
Electricity generated using fossil fuel (% of total)	67.5	65.6	79.0
Electricity generated by hydropower (% of total)	32.5	18.0	16.3
Emissions and pollution			
CO_2 emissions per unit of GDP (kg/2005 PPP $)	0.2	0.5	0.8
CO_2 emissions per capita (metric tons)	0.3	0.8	2.8
CO_2 emissions growth (%, 1990–2005)	97.3	40.1	93.5
Particulate matter (urban-pop.-weighted avg., µg/cu. m)	165	53	67
Transport sector fuel consumption per capita (liters)	65	64	99
Water and sanitation			
Internal freshwater resources per capita (cu. m)	778	4,824	4,117
Freshwater withdrawal			
Total (% of internal resources)	124.4	3.2	8.7
Agriculture (% of total freshwater withdrawal)	97	87	80
Access to improved water source (% of total population)	70	58	88
Rural (% of rural population)	64	46	82
Urban (% of urban population)	78	81	96
Access to improved sanitation (% of total population)	35	31	55
Rural (% of rural population)	24	24	43
Urban (% of urban population)	50	42	71
Environment and health			
Acute resp. infection prevalence (% of children under five)	5.0		
Diarrhea prevalence (% of children under five)	29.4		
Under-five mortality rate (per 1,000 live births)	109	146	50
National accounting aggregates			
Gross savings (% of GNI)	13.2	17.4	41.7
Consumption of fixed capital (% of GNI)	10.8	11.1	10.7
Education expenditure (% of GNI)	0.9	3.6	2.6
Energy depletion (% of GNI)	15.7	11.7	6.6
Mineral depletion (% of GNI)	0.1	1.5	1.2
Net forest depletion (% of GNI)	0.0	0.5	0.2
CO_2 damage (% of GNI)	0.2	0.7	1.2
Particulate emission damage (% of GNI)	0.4	0.4	1.1
Adjusted net savings (% of GNI)	-13.2	-5.0	23.5

Suriname

	Country data	Latin America & Caribbean group	Upper middle-income group
Population (thousands) **458** Land area (1,000 sq. km) **156** GDP ($ billions) **2.2**			

	Country data	Latin America & Caribbean group	Upper middle-income group
GNI per capita, *World Bank Atlas* method ($)	4,730	5,801	7,107
Urban population (% of total)	75	78	75
Urban population growth (average annual %, 1990–2007)	1.3	2.1	1.4
Population growth (average annual %, 1990–2007)	0.8	1.5	0.9
Agriculture			
Agricultural land (% of land area)	1	36	31
Agricultural productivity (value added per worker, 2000 $)	3,166	3,158	2,947
Food production index (1999–2001 = 100)	107	117	113
Population density, rural (people/sq. km of arable land)	197	232	110
Forests and biodiversity			
Forest area (% of land area)	94.7	45.4	39.3
Deforestation (average annual %, 1990–2005)	0.0	0.5	0.2
Nationally protected area (% of land area)	11.8	16.7	10.3
Animal species, total known	877		
Animal species, threatened	33		
Higher plant species, total known	5,018		
Higher plant species, threatened	26		
GEF benefits index for biodiversity (0–100, median is 1.5)	2.7		
Energy			
GDP per unit of energy use (2005 PPP $/kg oil equivalent)	..	7.3	4.8
Energy use per capita (kg oil equivalent)	..	1,240	2,300
Energy from biomass products and waste (% of total)	..	15.9	7.0
Electric power consumption per capita (kWh)	..	1,808	3,242
Electricity generated using fossil fuel (% of total)	..	37.0	62.8
Electricity generated by hydropower (% of total)	..	57.3	27.6
Emissions and pollution			
CO_2 emissions per unit of GDP (kg/2005 PPP $)	0.8	0.3	0.5
CO_2 emissions per capita (metric tons)	5.2	2.5	5.5
CO_2 emissions growth (%, 1990–2005)	31.2	33.4	-8.3
Particulate matter (urban-pop.-weighted avg., µg/cu. m)	28	35	30
Transport sector fuel consumption per capita (liters)	..	295	332
Water and sanitation			
Internal freshwater resources per capita (cu. m)	192,272	23,965	16,993
Freshwater withdrawal			
Total (% of internal resources)	0.8	2.0	13.8
Agriculture (% of total freshwater withdrawal)	93	71	57
Access to improved water source (% of total population)	92	91	95
Rural (% of rural population)	79	73	83
Urban (% of urban population)	97	97	98
Access to improved sanitation (% of total population)	82	78	83
Rural (% of rural population)	60	51	64
Urban (% of urban population)	89	86	89
Environment and health			
Acute resp. infection prevalence (% of children under five)	4.0		
Diarrhea prevalence (% of children under five)	14.8		
Under-five mortality rate (per 1,000 live births)	29	26	24
National accounting aggregates			
Gross savings (% of GNI)	..	22.9	23.2
Consumption of fixed capital (% of GNI)	12.0	12.6	12.8
Education expenditure (% of GNI)	..	4.5	4.4
Energy depletion (% of GNI)	0.0	5.4	7.6
Mineral depletion (% of GNI)	2.7	1.9	1.3
Net forest depletion (% of GNI)	0.0	0.0	0.0
CO_2 damage (% of GNI)	0.9	0.3	0.6
Particulate emission damage (% of GNI)	0.4	0.4	0.4
Adjusted net savings (% of GNI)	..	6.7	4.9

Swaziland

| | Population (millions) | 1.1 | Land area (1,000 sq. km) | 17.2 | GDP ($ billions) | 2.9 |

	Country data	Sub-Saharan Africa group	Lower middle-income group
GNI per capita, *World Bank Atlas* method ($)	2,560	951	1,905
Urban population (% of total)	25	36	42
Urban population growth (average annual %, 1990–2007)	2.8	4.0	2.9
Population growth (average annual %, 1990–2007)	2.3	2.6	1.3
Agriculture			
Agricultural land (% of land area)	81	44	47
Agricultural productivity (value added per worker, 2000 $)	1,376	287	532
Food production index (1999–2001 = 100)	105	109	116
Population density, rural (people/sq. km of arable land)	482	351	511
Forests and biodiversity			
Forest area (% of land area)	31.5	26.5	25.0
Deforestation (average annual %, 1990–2005)	-0.9	0.6	0.1
Nationally protected area (% of land area)	3.1	11.3	11.0
Animal species, total known	614		
Animal species, threatened	14		
Higher plant species, total known	2,715		
Higher plant species, threatened	11		
GEF benefits index for biodiversity (0–100, median is 1.5)	0.1		
Energy			
GDP per unit of energy use (2005 PPP $/kg oil equivalent)	..	3.0	3.9
Energy use per capita (kg oil equivalent)	..	670	1,019
Energy from biomass products and waste (% of total)	..	56.3	15.2
Electric power consumption per capita (kWh)	..	531	1,269
Electricity generated using fossil fuel (% of total)	..	65.6	79.0
Electricity generated by hydropower (% of total)	..	18.0	16.3
Emissions and pollution			
CO_2 emissions per unit of GDP (kg/2005 PPP $)	0.2	0.5	0.8
CO_2 emissions per capita (metric tons)	0.8	0.8	2.8
CO_2 emissions growth (%, 1990–2005)	125.0	40.1	93.5
Particulate matter (urban-pop.-weighted avg., µg/cu. m)	33	53	67
Transport sector fuel consumption per capita (liters)	..	64	99
Water and sanitation			
Internal freshwater resources per capita (cu. m)	2,300	4,824	4,117
Freshwater withdrawal			
Total (% of internal resources)	39.5	3.2	8.7
Agriculture (% of total freshwater withdrawal)	97	87	80
Access to improved water source (% of total population)	60	58	88
Rural (% of rural population)	51	46	82
Urban (% of urban population)	87	81	96
Access to improved sanitation (% of total population)	50	31	55
Rural (% of rural population)	46	24	43
Urban (% of urban population)	64	42	71
Environment and health			
Acute resp. infection prevalence (% of children under five)	10.0		
Diarrhea prevalence (% of children under five)	..		
Under-five mortality rate (per 1,000 live births)	91	146	50
National accounting aggregates			
Gross savings (% of GNI)	19.8	17.4	41.7
Consumption of fixed capital (% of GNI)	10.6	11.1	10.7
Education expenditure (% of GNI)	6.4	3.6	2.6
Energy depletion (% of GNI)	0.0	11.7	6.6
Mineral depletion (% of GNI)	0.0	1.5	1.2
Net forest depletion (% of GNI)	0.0	0.5	0.2
CO_2 damage (% of GNI)	0.3	0.7	1.2
Particulate emission damage (% of GNI)	0.1	0.4	1.1
Adjusted net savings (% of GNI)	15.2	-5.0	23.5

Sweden

| | Population (millions) | **9.1** | Land area (1,000 sq. km) | **410.3** | GDP ($ billions) | **454.3** |

	Country data	High-income group
GNI per capita, *World Bank Atlas* method ($)	47,870	37,572
Urban population (% of total)	84	78
Urban population growth (average annual %, 1990–2007)	0.5	1.0
Population growth (average annual %, 1990–2007)	0.4	0.7
Agriculture		
Agricultural land (% of land area)	8	38
Agricultural productivity (value added per worker, 2000 $)	36,162	27,680
Food production index (1999–2001 = 100)	99	102
Population density, rural (people/sq. km of arable land)	52	323
Forests and biodiversity		
Forest area (% of land area)	67.1	28.8
Deforestation (average annual %, 1990–2005)	0.0	-0.1
Nationally protected area (% of land area)	10.3	11.8
Animal species, total known	542	
Animal species, threatened	29	
Higher plant species, total known	1,750	
Higher plant species, threatened	3	
GEF benefits index for biodiversity (0–100, median is 1.5)	0.3	
Energy		
GDP per unit of energy use (2005 PPP $/kg oil equivalent)	5.9	6.3
Energy use per capita (kg oil equivalent)	5,650	5,416
Energy from biomass products and waste (% of total)	18.4	3.4
Electric power consumption per capita (kWh)	15,231	9,675
Electricity generated using fossil fuel (% of total)	2.6	62.0
Electricity generated by hydropower (% of total)	43.1	11.4
Emissions and pollution		
CO_2 emissions per unit of GDP (kg/2005 PPP $)	0.2	0.4
CO_2 emissions per capita (metric tons)	5.4	12.6
CO_2 emissions growth (%, 1990–2005)	-1.9	19.1
Particulate matter (urban-pop.-weighted avg., µg/cu. m)	12	26
Transport sector fuel consumption per capita (liters)	899	1,159
Water and sanitation		
Internal freshwater resources per capita (cu. m)	18,692	9,313
Freshwater withdrawal		
Total (% of internal resources)	1.7	10.4
Agriculture (% of total freshwater withdrawal)	9	43
Access to improved water source (% of total population)	100	100
Rural (% of rural population)	100	98
Urban (% of urban population)	100	100
Access to improved sanitation (% of total population)	100	100
Rural (% of rural population)	100	99
Urban (% of urban population)	100	100
Environment and health		
Acute resp. infection prevalence (% of children under five)	..	
Diarrhea prevalence (% of children under five)	..	
Under-five mortality rate (per 1,000 live births)	3	7
National accounting aggregates		
Gross savings (% of GNI)	27.5	20.6
Consumption of fixed capital (% of GNI)	14.7	14.5
Education expenditure (% of GNI)	7.2	4.6
Energy depletion (% of GNI)	0.0	1.5
Mineral depletion (% of GNI)	0.3	0.2
Net forest depletion (% of GNI)	0.0	0.0
CO_2 damage (% of GNI)	0.1	0.3
Particulate emission damage (% of GNI)	..	0.3
Adjusted net savings (% of GNI)	19.6	8.5

Switzerland

Population (millions)	**7.6** Land area (1,000 sq. km)	**40.0** GDP ($ billions) **424.4**

	Country data	High-income group
GNI per capita, *World Bank Atlas* method ($)	60,820	37,572
Urban population (% of total)	73	78
Urban population growth (average annual %, 1990–2007)	0.7	1.0
Population growth (average annual %, 1990–2007)	0.7	0.7
Agriculture		
Agricultural land (% of land area)	38	38
Agricultural productivity (value added per worker, 2000 $)	24,526	27,680
Food production index (1999–2001 = 100)	100	102
Population density, rural (people/sq. km of arable land)	484	323
Forests and biodiversity		
Forest area (% of land area)	30.5	28.8
Deforestation (average annual %, 1990–2005)	-0.4	-0.1
Nationally protected area (% of land area)	29.5	11.8
Animal species, total known	475	
Animal species, threatened	45	
Higher plant species, total known	3,030	
Higher plant species, threatened	3	
GEF benefits index for biodiversity (0–100, median is 1.5)	0.2	
Energy		
GDP per unit of energy use (2005 PPP $/kg oil equivalent)	9.7	6.3
Energy use per capita (kg oil equivalent)	3,770	5,416
Energy from biomass products and waste (% of total)	7.2	3.4
Electric power consumption per capita (kWh)	8,360	9,675
Electricity generated using fossil fuel (% of total)	1.6	62.0
Electricity generated by hydropower (% of total)	49.8	11.4
Emissions and pollution		
CO_2 emissions per unit of GDP (kg/2005 PPP $)	0.2	0.4
CO_2 emissions per capita (metric tons)	5.5	12.6
CO_2 emissions growth (%, 1990–2005)	-3.6	19.1
Particulate matter (urban-pop.-weighted avg., µg/cu. m)	26	26
Transport sector fuel consumption per capita (liters)	839	1,159
Water and sanitation		
Internal freshwater resources per capita (cu. m)	5,351	9,313
Freshwater withdrawal		
Total (% of internal resources)	6.4	10.4
Agriculture (% of total freshwater withdrawal)	2	43
Access to improved water source (% of total population)	100	100
Rural (% of rural population)	100	98
Urban (% of urban population)	100	100
Access to improved sanitation (% of total population)	100	100
Rural (% of rural population)	100	99
Urban (% of urban population)	100	100
Environment and health		
Acute resp. infection prevalence (% of children under five)	..	
Diarrhea prevalence (% of children under five)	..	
Under-five mortality rate (per 1,000 live births)	5	7
National accounting aggregates		
Gross savings (% of GNI)	..	20.6
Consumption of fixed capital (% of GNI)	13.9	14.5
Education expenditure (% of GNI)	4.8	4.6
Energy depletion (% of GNI)	0.0	1.5
Mineral depletion (% of GNI)	0.0	0.2
Net forest depletion (% of GNI)	0.0	0.0
CO_2 damage (% of GNI)	0.1	0.3
Particulate emission damage (% of GNI)	0.2	0.3
Adjusted net savings (% of GNI)	..	8.5

Syrian Arab Republic

Population (millions)	20	Land area (1,000 sq. km)	**184**	GDP ($ billions)	**37.7**

	Country data	Middle East & N. Africa group	Lower middle-income group
GNI per capita, *World Bank Atlas* method ($)	1,780	2,820	1,905
Urban population (% of total)	54	57	42
Urban population growth (average annual %, 1990–2007)	3.2	2.6	2.9
Population growth (average annual %, 1990–2007)	2.6	2.0	1.3
Agriculture			
Agricultural land (% of land area)	76	22	47
Agricultural productivity (value added per worker, 2000 $)	3,382	2,313	532
Food production index (1999–2001 = 100)	120	116	116
Population density, rural (people/sq. km of arable land)	181	665	511
Forests and biodiversity			
Forest area (% of land area)	2.5	2.4	25.0
Deforestation (average annual %, 1990–2005)	-1.4	-0.4	0.1
Nationally protected area (% of land area)	0.7	3.6	11.0
Animal species, total known	432		
Animal species, threatened	68		
Higher plant species, total known	3,000		
Higher plant species, threatened	0		
GEF benefits index for biodiversity (0–100, median is 1.5)	0.9		
Energy			
GDP per unit of energy use (2005 PPP $/kg oil equivalent)	4.2	5.0	3.9
Energy use per capita (kg oil equivalent)	975	1,254	1,019
Energy from biomass products and waste (% of total)	0.0	1.2	15.2
Electric power consumption per capita (kWh)	1,466	1,418	1,269
Electricity generated using fossil fuel (% of total)	89.3	91.1	79.0
Electricity generated by hydropower (% of total)	10.7	7.4	16.3
Emissions and pollution			
CO_2 emissions per unit of GDP (kg/2005 PPP $)	0.9	0.6	0.8
CO_2 emissions per capita (metric tons)	3.6	3.7	2.8
CO_2 emissions growth (%, 1990–2005)	90.9	96.8	93.5
Particulate matter (urban-pop.-weighted avg., µg/cu. m)	75	72	67
Transport sector fuel consumption per capita (liters)	264	277	99
Water and sanitation			
Internal freshwater resources per capita (cu. m)	352	728	4,117
Freshwater withdrawal			
Total (% of internal resources)	238.4	122.3	8.7
Agriculture (% of total freshwater withdrawal)	88	86	80
Access to improved water source (% of total population)	89	89	88
Rural (% of rural population)	83	81	82
Urban (% of urban population)	95	95	96
Access to improved sanitation (% of total population)	92	77	55
Rural (% of rural population)	88	62	43
Urban (% of urban population)	96	88	71
Environment and health			
Acute resp. infection prevalence (% of children under five)	18.0		
Diarrhea prevalence (% of children under five)	8.6		
Under-five mortality rate (per 1,000 live births)	17	38	50
National accounting aggregates			
Gross savings (% of GNI)	19.7	33.3	41.7
Consumption of fixed capital (% of GNI)	10.6	11.3	10.7
Education expenditure (% of GNI)	2.6	4.7	2.6
Energy depletion (% of GNI)	19.2	21.3	6.6
Mineral depletion (% of GNI)	0.0	0.4	1.2
Net forest depletion (% of GNI)	0.0	0.0	0.2
CO_2 damage (% of GNI)	1.3	1.0	1.2
Particulate emission damage (% of GNI)	0.9	0.6	1.1
Adjusted net savings (% of GNI)	-9.7	3.4	23.5

Tajikistan

Population (millions)	**6.7**	Land area (1,000 sq. km)	**140.0**	GDP ($ billions)	**3.7**

	Country data	Europe & Central Asia group	Low-income group
GNI per capita, *World Bank Atlas* method ($)	460	6,052	574
Urban population (% of total)	26	64	32
Urban population growth (average annual %, 1990–2007)	0.3	0.2	3.7
Population growth (average annual %, 1990–2007)	1.4	0.1	2.4
Agriculture			
Agricultural land (% of land area)	30	28	39
Agricultural productivity (value added per worker, 2000 $)	426	2,228	330
Food production index (1999–2001 = 100)	158	110	112
Population density, rural (people/sq. km of arable land)	518	129	603
Forests and biodiversity			
Forest area (% of land area)	2.9	38.3	24.7
Deforestation (average annual %, 1990–2005)	0.0	0.0	0.7
Nationally protected area (% of land area)	14.0	6.1	10.8
Animal species, total known	427		
Animal species, threatened	28		
Higher plant species, total known	5,000		
Higher plant species, threatened	14		
GEF benefits index for biodiversity (0–100, median is 1.5)	0.7		
Energy			
GDP per unit of energy use (2005 PPP $/kg oil equivalent)	2.8	3.5	3.2
Energy use per capita (kg oil equivalent)	548	2,930	478
Energy from biomass products and waste (% of total)	0.0	2.2	53.8
Electric power consumption per capita (kWh)	2,241	3,835	309
Electricity generated using fossil fuel (% of total)	2.3	67.7	48.4
Electricity generated by hydropower (% of total)	97.7	17.4	38.8
Emissions and pollution			
CO_2 emissions per unit of GDP (kg/2005 PPP $)	0.5	0.7	0.4
CO_2 emissions per capita (metric tons)	0.8	7.0	0.6
CO_2 emissions growth (%, 1990–2005)	–77.8	–29.3	39.3
Particulate matter (urban-pop.-weighted avg., µg/cu. m)	50	27	69
Transport sector fuel consumption per capita (liters)	226	255	41
Water and sanitation			
Internal freshwater resources per capita (cu. m)	9,837	11,806	4,619
Freshwater withdrawal			
Total (% of internal resources)	18.0	7.2	9.4
Agriculture (% of total freshwater withdrawal)	92	60	90
Access to improved water source (% of total population)	67	95	68
Rural (% of rural population)	58	88	60
Urban (% of urban population)	93	99	84
Access to improved sanitation (% of total population)	92	89	39
Rural (% of rural population)	91	79	33
Urban (% of urban population)	95	94	54
Environment and health			
Acute resp. infection prevalence (% of children under five)	1.0		
Diarrhea prevalence (% of children under five)	20.8		
Under-five mortality rate (per 1,000 live births)	67	23	126
National accounting aggregates			
Gross savings (% of GNI)	13.9	24.0	25.4
Consumption of fixed capital (% of GNI)	8.9	12.8	9.3
Education expenditure (% of GNI)	3.2	4.0	2.6
Energy depletion (% of GNI)	0.3	9.8	9.8
Mineral depletion (% of GNI)	0.0	0.7	0.9
Net forest depletion (% of GNI)	0.0	0.0	0.8
CO_2 damage (% of GNI)	1.3	1.0	0.7
Particulate emission damage (% of GNI)	0.4	0.5	0.7
Adjusted net savings (% of GNI)	6.3	3.2	5.8

Tanzania

	Population (millions)	**40**	Land area (1,000 sq. km)	**886**	GDP ($ billions)	**16.2**

	Country data	Sub-Saharan Africa group	Low-income group
GNI per capita, *World Bank Atlas* method ($)	410	951	574
Urban population (% of total)	25	36	32
Urban population growth (average annual %, 1990–2007)	4.4	4.0	3.7
Population growth (average annual %, 1990–2007)	2.7	2.6	2.4
Agriculture			
Agricultural land (% of land area)	39	44	39
Agricultural productivity (value added per worker, 2000 $)	306	287	330
Food production index (1999–2001 = 100)	109	109	112
Population density, rural (people/sq. km of arable land)	317	351	603
Forests and biodiversity			
Forest area (% of land area)	39.8	26.5	24.7
Deforestation (average annual %, 1990–2005)	1.1	0.6	0.7
Nationally protected area (% of land area)	38.7	11.3	10.8
Animal species, total known	1,431		
Animal species, threatened	349		
Higher plant species, total known	10,008		
Higher plant species, threatened	240		
GEF benefits index for biodiversity (0–100, median is 1.5)	14.8		
Energy			
GDP per unit of energy use (2005 PPP $/kg oil equivalent)	2.1	3.0	3.2
Energy use per capita (kg oil equivalent)	527	670	478
Energy from biomass products and waste (% of total)	91.0	56.3	53.8
Electric power consumption per capita (kWh)	59	531	309
Electricity generated using fossil fuel (% of total)	48.3	65.6	48.4
Electricity generated by hydropower (% of total)	51.7	18.0	38.8
Emissions and pollution			
CO_2 emissions per unit of GDP (kg/2005 PPP $)	0.1	0.5	0.4
CO_2 emissions per capita (metric tons)	0.1	0.8	0.6
CO_2 emissions growth (%, 1990–2005)	100.2	40.1	39.3
Particulate matter (urban-pop.-weighted avg., µg/cu. m)	25	53	69
Transport sector fuel consumption per capita (liters)	27	64	41
Water and sanitation			
Internal freshwater resources per capita (cu. m)	2,078	4,824	4,619
Freshwater withdrawal			
Total (% of internal resources)	6.2	3.2	9.4
Agriculture (% of total freshwater withdrawal)	89	87	90
Access to improved water source (% of total population)	55	58	68
Rural (% of rural population)	46	46	60
Urban (% of urban population)	81	81	84
Access to improved sanitation (% of total population)	33	31	39
Rural (% of rural population)	34	24	33
Urban (% of urban population)	31	42	54
Environment and health			
Acute resp. infection prevalence (% of children under five)	8.1		
Diarrhea prevalence (% of children under five)	12.6		
Under-five mortality rate (per 1,000 live births)	116	146	126
National accounting aggregates			
Gross savings (% of GNI)	..	17.4	25.4
Consumption of fixed capital (% of GNI)	8.2	11.1	9.3
Education expenditure (% of GNI)	2.4	3.6	2.6
Energy depletion (% of GNI)	0.5	11.7	9.8
Mineral depletion (% of GNI)	5.6	1.5	0.9
Net forest depletion (% of GNI)	0.0	0.5	0.8
CO_2 damage (% of GNI)	0.2	0.7	0.7
Particulate emission damage (% of GNI)	0.1	0.4	0.7
Adjusted net savings (% of GNI)	..	-5.0	5.8

Thailand

| Population (millions) | **64** | Land area (1,000 sq. km) | **511** | GDP ($ billions) | **245.4** |

	Country data	East Asia & Pacific group	Lower middle-income group
GNI per capita, *World Bank Atlas* method ($)	3,400	2,182	1,905
Urban population (% of total)	33	43	42
Urban population growth (average annual %, 1990–2007)	1.6	3.5	2.9
Population growth (average annual %, 1990–2007)	1.0	1.1	1.3
Agriculture			
Agricultural land (% of land area)	36	51	47
Agricultural productivity (value added per worker, 2000 $)	615	458	532
Food production index (1999–2001 = 100)	103	120	116
Population density, rural (people/sq. km of arable land)	300	547	511
Forests and biodiversity			
Forest area (% of land area)	28.4	28.4	25.0
Deforestation (average annual %, 1990–2005)	0.6	–0.1	0.1
Nationally protected area (% of land area)	19.9	14.0	11.0
Animal species, total known	1,271		
Animal species, threatened	357		
Higher plant species, total known	11,625		
Higher plant species, threatened	86		
GEF benefits index for biodiversity (0–100, median is 1.5)	8.0		
Energy			
GDP per unit of energy use (2005 PPP $/kg oil equivalent)	4.5	3.4	3.9
Energy use per capita (kg oil equivalent)	1,630	1,258	1,019
Energy from biomass products and waste (% of total)	16.6	14.7	15.2
Electric power consumption per capita (kWh)	2,080	1,669	1,269
Electricity generated using fossil fuel (% of total)	91.9	82.0	79.0
Electricity generated by hydropower (% of total)	5.9	15.0	16.3
Emissions and pollution			
CO_2 emissions per unit of GDP (kg/2005 PPP $)	0.6	0.9	0.8
CO_2 emissions per capita (metric tons)	4.3	3.6	2.8
CO_2 emissions growth (%, 1990–2005)	182.9	123.4	93.5
Particulate matter (urban-pop.-weighted avg., µg/cu. m)	71	69	67
Transport sector fuel consumption per capita (liters)	314	106	99
Water and sanitation			
Internal freshwater resources per capita (cu. m)	3,290	4,948	4,117
Freshwater withdrawal			
Total (% of internal resources)	41.5	10.2	8.7
Agriculture (% of total freshwater withdrawal)	95	74	80
Access to improved water source (% of total population)	98	87	88
Rural (% of rural population)	97	81	82
Urban (% of urban population)	99	96	96
Access to improved sanitation (% of total population)	96	66	55
Rural (% of rural population)	96	59	43
Urban (% of urban population)	95	75	71
Environment and health			
Acute resp. infection prevalence (% of children under five)	..		
Diarrhea prevalence (% of children under five)	..		
Under-five mortality rate (per 1,000 live births)	7	27	50
National accounting aggregates			
Gross savings (% of GNI)	34.0	48.0	41.7
Consumption of fixed capital (% of GNI)	11.8	10.7	10.7
Education expenditure (% of GNI)	4.8	2.1	2.6
Energy depletion (% of GNI)	4.1	4.9	6.6
Mineral depletion (% of GNI)	0.0	1.3	1.2
Net forest depletion (% of GNI)	0.2	0.0	0.2
CO_2 damage (% of GNI)	0.9	1.3	1.2
Particulate emission damage (% of GNI)	0.4	1.3	1.1
Adjusted net savings (% of GNI)	21.4	30.6	23.5

Timor-Leste

| | Population (millions) | **1.1** | Land area (1,000 sq. km) | **14.9** | GDP ($ billions) | **395** |

	Country data	East Asia & Pacific group	Lower middle-income group
GNI per capita, *World Bank Atlas* method ($)	1,510	2,182	1,905
Urban population (% of total)	27	43	42
Urban population growth (average annual %, 1990–2007)	3.6	3.5	2.9
Population growth (average annual %, 1990–2007)	2.1	1.1	1.3
Agriculture			
Agricultural land (% of land area)	23	51	47
Agricultural productivity (value added per worker, 2000 $)	..	458	532
Food production index (1999–2001 = 100)	114	120	116
Population density, rural (people/sq. km of arable land)	591	547	511
Forests and biodiversity			
Forest area (% of land area)	53.7	28.4	25.0
Deforestation (average annual %, 1990–2005)	1.3	–0.1	0.1
Nationally protected area (% of land area)	6.3	14.0	11.0
Animal species, total known	..		
Animal species, threatened	15		
Higher plant species, total known	..		
Higher plant species, threatened	0		
GEF benefits index for biodiversity (0–100, median is 1.5)	0.6		
Energy			
GDP per unit of energy use (2005 PPP $/kg oil equivalent)	..	3.4	3.9
Energy use per capita (kg oil equivalent)	..	1,258	1,019
Energy from biomass products and waste (% of total)	..	14.7	15.2
Electric power consumption per capita (kWh)	..	1,669	1,269
Electricity generated using fossil fuel (% of total)	..	82.0	79.0
Electricity generated by hydropower (% of total)	..	15.0	16.3
Emissions and pollution			
CO_2 emissions per unit of GDP (kg/2005 PPP $)	0.2	0.9	0.8
CO_2 emissions per capita (metric tons)	0.2	3.6	2.8
CO_2 emissions growth (%, 1990–2005)	123.4	123.4	93.5
Particulate matter (urban-pop.-weighted avg., µg/cu. m)	..	69	67
Transport sector fuel consumption per capita (liters)	..	106	99
Water and sanitation			
Internal freshwater resources per capita (cu. m)	..	4,948	4,117
Freshwater withdrawal			
Total (% of internal resources)	..	10.2	8.7
Agriculture (% of total freshwater withdrawal)	..	74	80
Access to improved water source (% of total population)	62	87	88
Rural (% of rural population)	56	81	82
Urban (% of urban population)	77	96	96
Access to improved sanitation (% of total population)	41	66	55
Rural (% of rural population)	32	59	43
Urban (% of urban population)	64	75	71
Environment and health			
Acute resp. infection prevalence (% of children under five)	14.0		
Diarrhea prevalence (% of children under five)	..		
Under-five mortality rate (per 1,000 live births)	97	27	50
National accounting aggregates			
Gross savings (% of GNI)	..	48.0	41.7
Consumption of fixed capital (% of GNI)	1.9	10.7	10.7
Education expenditure (% of GNI)	..	2.1	2.6
Energy depletion (% of GNI)	0.0	4.9	6.6
Mineral depletion (% of GNI)	0.0	1.3	1.2
Net forest depletion (% of GNI)	..	0.0	0.2
CO_2 damage (% of GNI)	0.1	1.3	1.2
Particulate emission damage (% of GNI)	..	1.3	1.1
Adjusted net savings (% of GNI)	..	30.6	23.5

Togo

Population (millions)	**6.6**	Land area (1,000 sq. km)	**54.4**	GDP ($ billions)	**2.5**

	Country data	Sub-Saharan Africa group	Low-income group
GNI per capita, *World Bank Atlas* method ($)	360	951	574
Urban population (% of total)	41	36	32
Urban population growth (average annual %, 1990–2007)	4.8	4.0	3.7
Population growth (average annual %, 1990–2007)	3.0	2.6	2.4
Agriculture			
Agricultural land (% of land area)	67	44	39
Agricultural productivity (value added per worker, 2000 $)	353	287	330
Food production index (1999–2001 = 100)	112	109	112
Population density, rural (people/sq. km of arable land)	151	351	603
Forests and biodiversity			
Forest area (% of land area)	7.1	26.5	24.7
Deforestation (average annual %, 1990–2005)	3.8	0.6	0.7
Nationally protected area (% of land area)	11.1	11.3	10.8
Animal species, total known	740		
Animal species, threatened	34		
Higher plant species, total known	3,085		
Higher plant species, threatened	10		
GEF benefits index for biodiversity (0–100, median is 1.5)	0.3		
Energy			
GDP per unit of energy use (2005 PPP $/kg oil equivalent)	2.0	3.0	3.2
Energy use per capita (kg oil equivalent)	375	670	478
Energy from biomass products and waste (% of total)	84.5	56.3	53.8
Electric power consumption per capita (kWh)	97	531	309
Electricity generated using fossil fuel (% of total)	57.5	65.6	48.4
Electricity generated by hydropower (% of total)	41.2	18.0	38.8
Emissions and pollution			
CO_2 emissions per unit of GDP (kg/2005 PPP $)	0.3	0.5	0.4
CO_2 emissions per capita (metric tons)	0.2	0.8	0.6
CO_2 emissions growth (%, 1990–2005)	79.0	40.1	39.3
Particulate matter (urban-pop.-weighted avg., µg/cu. m)	35	53	69
Transport sector fuel consumption per capita (liters)	34	64	41
Water and sanitation			
Internal freshwater resources per capita (cu. m)	1,748	4,824	4,619
Freshwater withdrawal			
Total (% of internal resources)	1.5	3.2	9.4
Agriculture (% of total freshwater withdrawal)	45	87	90
Access to improved water source (% of total population)	59	58	68
Rural (% of rural population)	40	46	60
Urban (% of urban population)	86	81	84
Access to improved sanitation (% of total population)	12	31	39
Rural (% of rural population)	3	24	33
Urban (% of urban population)	24	42	54
Environment and health			
Acute resp. infection prevalence (% of children under five)	9.0		
Diarrhea prevalence (% of children under five)	31.1		
Under-five mortality rate (per 1,000 live births)	100	146	126
National accounting aggregates			
Gross savings (% of GNI)	..	17.4	25.4
Consumption of fixed capital (% of GNI)	8.3	11.1	9.3
Education expenditure (% of GNI)	2.5	3.6	2.6
Energy depletion (% of GNI)	0.0	11.7	9.8
Mineral depletion (% of GNI)	0.6	1.5	0.9
Net forest depletion (% of GNI)	2.6	0.5	0.8
CO_2 damage (% of GNI)	0.6	0.7	0.7
Particulate emission damage (% of GNI)	0.2	0.4	0.7
Adjusted net savings (% of GNI)	..	-5.0	5.8

Tonga

	Country data	East Asia & Pacific group	Lower middle-income group
Population (thousands) **102** Land area (sq. km)	**720**	GDP ($ millions)	**253**

	Country data	East Asia & Pacific group	Lower middle-income group
GNI per capita, *World Bank Atlas* method ($)	2,480	2,182	1,905
Urban population (% of total)	25	43	42
Urban population growth (average annual %, 1990–2007)	0.9	3.5	2.9
Population growth (average annual %, 1990–2007)	0.5	1.1	1.3
Agriculture			
Agricultural land (% of land area)	42	51	47
Agricultural productivity (value added per worker, 2000 $)	3,340	458	532
Food production index (1999–2001 = 100)	103	120	116
Population density, rural (people/sq. km of arable land)	514	547	511
Forests and biodiversity			
Forest area (% of land area)	5.0	28.4	25.0
Deforestation (average annual %, 1990–2005)	0.0	–0.1	0.1
Nationally protected area (% of land area)	8.6	14.0	11.0
Animal species, total known	51		
Animal species, threatened	52		
Higher plant species, total known	463		
Higher plant species, threatened	4		
GEF benefits index for biodiversity (0–100, median is 1.5)	1.0		
Energy			
GDP per unit of energy use (2005 PPP $/kg oil equivalent)	..	3.4	3.9
Energy use per capita (kg oil equivalent)	..	1,258	1,019
Energy from biomass products and waste (% of total)	..	14.7	15.2
Electric power consumption per capita (kWh)	..	1,669	1,269
Electricity generated using fossil fuel (% of total)	..	82.0	79.0
Electricity generated by hydropower (% of total)	..	15.0	16.3
Emissions and pollution			
CO_2 emissions per unit of GDP (kg/2005 PPP $)	0.3	0.9	0.8
CO_2 emissions per capita (metric tons)	1.2	3.6	2.8
CO_2 emissions growth (%, 1990–2005)	52.4	123.4	93.5
Particulate matter (urban-pop.-weighted avg., µg/cu. m)	..	69	67
Transport sector fuel consumption per capita (liters)	..	106	99
Water and sanitation			
Internal freshwater resources per capita (cu. m)	..	4,948	4,117
Freshwater withdrawal			
Total (% of internal resources)	..	10.2	8.7
Agriculture (% of total freshwater withdrawal)	..	74	80
Access to improved water source (% of total population)	100	87	88
Rural (% of rural population)	100	81	82
Urban (% of urban population)	100	96	96
Access to improved sanitation (% of total population)	96	66	55
Rural (% of rural population)	96	59	43
Urban (% of urban population)	98	75	71
Environment and health			
Acute resp. infection prevalence (% of children under five)	..		
Diarrhea prevalence (% of children under five)	..		
Under-five mortality rate (per 1,000 live births)	23	27	50
National accounting aggregates			
Gross savings (% of GNI)	5.4	48.0	41.7
Consumption of fixed capital (% of GNI)	10.4	10.7	10.7
Education expenditure (% of GNI)	3.8	2.1	2.6
Energy depletion (% of GNI)	0.0	4.9	6.6
Mineral depletion (% of GNI)	0.0	1.3	1.2
Net forest depletion (% of GNI)	0.0	0.0	0.2
CO_2 damage (% of GNI)	0.3	1.3	1.2
Particulate emission damage (% of GNI)	..	1.3	1.1
Adjusted net savings (% of GNI)	–1.6	30.6	23.5

Trinidad and Tobago

Population (millions)	**1.3**	Land area (1,000 sq. km)	**5.1**	GDP ($ billions)	**20.9**

	Country data	High-income group
GNI per capita, *World Bank Atlas* method ($)	14,480	37,572
Urban population (% of total)	13	78
Urban population growth (average annual %, 1990–2007)	2.9	1.0
Population growth (average annual %, 1990–2007)	0.5	0.7
Agriculture		
Agricultural land (% of land area)	26	38
Agricultural productivity (value added per worker, 2000 $)	1,408	27,680
Food production index (1999–2001 = 100)	114	102
Population density, rural (people/sq. km of arable land)	1,550	323
Forests and biodiversity		
Forest area (% of land area)	44.1	28.8
Deforestation (average annual %, 1990–2005)	0.3	-0.1
Nationally protected area (% of land area)	4.7	11.8
Animal species, total known	551	
Animal species, threatened	47	
Higher plant species, total known	2,259	
Higher plant species, threatened	1	
GEF benefits index for biodiversity (0–100, median is 1.5)	2.2	
Energy		
GDP per unit of energy use (2005 PPP $/kg oil equivalent)	2.0	6.3
Energy use per capita (kg oil equivalent)	10,768	5,416
Energy from biomass products and waste (% of total)	0.2	3.4
Electric power consumption per capita (kWh)	5,006	9,675
Electricity generated using fossil fuel (% of total)	99.6	62.0
Electricity generated by hydropower (% of total)	0.0	11.4
Emissions and pollution		
CO_2 emissions per unit of GDP (kg/2005 PPP $)	1.3	0.4
CO_2 emissions per capita (metric tons)	24.7	12.6
CO_2 emissions growth (%, 1990–2005)	93.1	19.1
Particulate matter (urban-pop.-weighted avg., µg/cu. m)	101	26
Transport sector fuel consumption per capita (liters)	607	1,159
Water and sanitation		
Internal freshwater resources per capita (cu. m)	2,881	9,313
Freshwater withdrawal		
Total (% of internal resources)	8.1	10.4
Agriculture (% of total freshwater withdrawal)	6	43
Access to improved water source (% of total population)	94	100
Rural (% of rural population)	93	98
Urban (% of urban population)	97	100
Access to improved sanitation (% of total population)	92	100
Rural (% of rural population)	92	99
Urban (% of urban population)	92	100
Environment and health		
Acute resp. infection prevalence (% of children under five)	3.0	
Diarrhea prevalence (% of children under five)	..	
Under-five mortality rate (per 1,000 live births)	35	7
National accounting aggregates		
Gross savings (% of GNI)	31.0	20.6
Consumption of fixed capital (% of GNI)	14.0	14.5
Education expenditure (% of GNI)	4.0	4.6
Energy depletion (% of GNI)	41.9	1.5
Mineral depletion (% of GNI)	0.0	0.2
Net forest depletion (% of GNI)	0.0	0.0
CO_2 damage (% of GNI)	1.6	0.3
Particulate emission damage (% of GNI)	0.3	0.3
Adjusted net savings (% of GNI)	-22.8	8.5

Tunisia

	Country data	Middle East & N. Africa group	Lower middle-income group
Population (millions)	**10**	Land area (1,000 sq. km)	**155**	GDP ($ billions)	**35.0**

	Country data	Middle East & N. Africa group	Lower middle-income group
GNI per capita, *World Bank Atlas* method ($)	3,210	2,820	1,905
Urban population (% of total)	66	57	42
Urban population growth (average annual %, 1990–2007)	2.1	2.6	2.9
Population growth (average annual %, 1990–2007)	1.3	2.0	1.3
Agriculture			
Agricultural land (% of land area)	63	22	47
Agricultural productivity (value added per worker, 2000 $)	2,630	2,313	532
Food production index (1999–2001 = 100)	109	116	116
Population density, rural (people/sq. km of arable land)	128	665	511
Forests and biodiversity			
Forest area (% of land area)	6.8	2.4	25.0
Deforestation (average annual %, 1990–2005)	-3.4	-0.4	0.1
Nationally protected area (% of land area)	1.5	3.6	11.0
Animal species, total known	438		
Animal species, threatened	54		
Higher plant species, total known	2,196		
Higher plant species, threatened	0		
GEF benefits index for biodiversity (0–100, median is 1.5)	0.5		
Energy			
GDP per unit of energy use (2005 PPP $/kg oil equivalent)	7.8	5.0	3.9
Energy use per capita (kg oil equivalent)	863	1,254	1,019
Energy from biomass products and waste (% of total)	13.3	1.2	15.2
Electric power consumption per capita (kWh)	1,221	1,418	1,269
Electricity generated using fossil fuel (% of total)	99.1	91.1	79.0
Electricity generated by hydropower (% of total)	0.7	7.4	16.3
Emissions and pollution			
CO_2 emissions per unit of GDP (kg/2005 PPP $)	0.3	0.6	0.8
CO_2 emissions per capita (metric tons)	2.2	3.7	2.8
CO_2 emissions growth (%, 1990–2005)	65.7	96.8	93.5
Particulate matter (urban-pop.-weighted avg., µg/cu. m)	30	72	67
Transport sector fuel consumption per capita (liters)	165	277	99
Water and sanitation			
Internal freshwater resources per capita (cu. m)	410	728	4,117
Freshwater withdrawal			
Total (% of internal resources)	62.9	122.3	8.7
Agriculture (% of total freshwater withdrawal)	82	86	80
Access to improved water source (% of total population)	94	89	88
Rural (% of rural population)	84	81	82
Urban (% of urban population)	99	95	96
Access to improved sanitation (% of total population)	85	77	55
Rural (% of rural population)	64	62	43
Urban (% of urban population)	96	88	71
Environment and health			
Acute resp. infection prevalence (% of children under five)	9.0		
Diarrhea prevalence (% of children under five)	5.8		
Under-five mortality rate (per 1,000 live births)	21	38	50
National accounting aggregates			
Gross savings (% of GNI)	23.9	33.3	41.7
Consumption of fixed capital (% of GNI)	11.8	11.3	10.7
Education expenditure (% of GNI)	6.7	4.7	2.6
Energy depletion (% of GNI)	4.6	21.3	6.6
Mineral depletion (% of GNI)	0.6	0.4	1.2
Net forest depletion (% of GNI)	0.1	0.0	0.2
CO_2 damage (% of GNI)	0.6	1.0	1.2
Particulate emission damage (% of GNI)	0.2	0.6	1.1
Adjusted net savings (% of GNI)	12.5	3.4	23.5

Turkey

| Population (millions) | **74** | Land area (1,000 sq. km) | **770** | GDP ($ billions) | **655.9** |

	Country data	Europe & Central Asia group	Upper middle-income group
GNI per capita, *World Bank Atlas* method ($)	8,030	6,052	7,107
Urban population (% of total)	68	64	75
Urban population growth (average annual %, 1990–2007)	2.4	0.2	1.4
Population growth (average annual %, 1990–2007)	1.6	0.1	0.9
Agriculture			
Agricultural land (% of land area)	54	28	31
Agricultural productivity (value added per worker, 2000 $)	1,946	2,228	2,947
Food production index (1999–2001 = 100)	107	110	113
Population density, rural (people/sq. km of arable land)	99	129	110
Forests and biodiversity			
Forest area (% of land area)	13.2	38.3	39.3
Deforestation (average annual %, 1990–2005)	-0.3	0.0	0.2
Nationally protected area (% of land area)	1.6	6.1	10.3
Animal species, total known	581		
Animal species, threatened	128		
Higher plant species, total known	8,650		
Higher plant species, threatened	3		
GEF benefits index for biodiversity (0–100, median is 1.5)	6.2		
Energy			
GDP per unit of energy use (2005 PPP $/kg oil equivalent)	8.9	3.5	4.8
Energy use per capita (kg oil equivalent)	1,288	2,930	2,300
Energy from biomass products and waste (% of total)	5.5	2.2	7.0
Electric power consumption per capita (kWh)	2,053	3,835	3,242
Electricity generated using fossil fuel (% of total)	74.7	67.7	62.8
Electricity generated by hydropower (% of total)	25.1	17.4	27.6
Emissions and pollution			
CO_2 emissions per unit of GDP (kg/2005 PPP $)	0.3	0.7	0.5
CO_2 emissions per capita (metric tons)	3.4	7.0	5.5
CO_2 emissions growth (%, 1990–2005)	75.2	-29.3	-8.3
Particulate matter (urban-pop.-weighted avg., µg/cu. m)	40	27	30
Transport sector fuel consumption per capita (liters)	176	255	332
Water and sanitation			
Internal freshwater resources per capita (cu. m)	3,072	11,806	16,993
Freshwater withdrawal			
Total (% of internal resources)	17.7	7.2	13.8
Agriculture (% of total freshwater withdrawal)	74	60	57
Access to improved water source (% of total population)	97	95	95
Rural (% of rural population)	95	88	83
Urban (% of urban population)	98	99	98
Access to improved sanitation (% of total population)	88	89	83
Rural (% of rural population)	72	79	64
Urban (% of urban population)	96	94	89
Environment and health			
Acute resp. infection prevalence (% of children under five)	29.0		
Diarrhea prevalence (% of children under five)	29.7		
Under-five mortality rate (per 1,000 live births)	23	23	24
National accounting aggregates			
Gross savings (% of GNI)	16.0	24.0	23.2
Consumption of fixed capital (% of GNI)	12.7	12.8	12.8
Education expenditure (% of GNI)	3.7	4.0	4.4
Energy depletion (% of GNI)	0.2	9.8	7.6
Mineral depletion (% of GNI)	0.1	0.7	1.3
Net forest depletion (% of GNI)	0.0	0.0	0.0
CO_2 damage (% of GNI)	0.3	1.0	0.6
Particulate emission damage (% of GNI)	1.1	0.5	0.4
Adjusted net savings (% of GNI)	5.3	3.2	4.9

Turkmenistan

	Country data	Europe & Central Asia group	Lower middle-income group
Population (millions) **5.0** Land area (1,000 sq. km) **469.9** GDP ($ billions) **12.9**			

	Country data	Europe & Central Asia group	Lower middle-income group
GNI per capita, *World Bank Atlas* method ($)	650	6,052	1,905
Urban population (% of total)	48	64	42
Urban population growth (average annual %, 1990–2007)	2.2	0.2	2.9
Population growth (average annual %, 1990–2007)	1.8	0.1	1.3
Agriculture			
Agricultural land (% of land area)	70	28	47
Agricultural productivity (value added per worker, 2000 $)	..	2,228	532
Food production index (1999–2001 = 100)	144	110	116
Population density, rural (people/sq. km of arable land)	111	129	511
Forests and biodiversity			
Forest area (% of land area)	8.8	38.3	25.0
Deforestation (average annual %, 1990–2005)	0.0	0.0	0.1
Nationally protected area (% of land area)	2.7	6.1	11.0
Animal species, total known	421		
Animal species, threatened	42		
Higher plant species, total known	..		
Higher plant species, threatened	3		
GEF benefits index for biodiversity (0–100, median is 1.5)	1.8		
Energy			
GDP per unit of energy use (2005 PPP $/kg oil equivalent)	1.4	3.5	3.9
Energy use per capita (kg oil equivalent)	3,524	2,930	1,019
Energy from biomass products and waste (% of total)	0.0	2.2	15.2
Electric power consumption per capita (kWh)	2,123	3,835	1,269
Electricity generated using fossil fuel (% of total)	100.0	67.7	79.0
Electricity generated by hydropower (% of total)	0.0	17.4	16.3
Emissions and pollution			
CO_2 emissions per unit of GDP (kg/2005 PPP $)	1.8	0.7	0.8
CO_2 emissions per capita (metric tons)	8.6	7.0	2.8
CO_2 emissions growth (%, 1990–2005)	29.9	-29.3	93.5
Particulate matter (urban-pop.-weighted avg., µg/cu. m)	55	27	67
Transport sector fuel consumption per capita (liters)	217	255	99
Water and sanitation			
Internal freshwater resources per capita (cu. m)	274	11,806	4,117
Freshwater withdrawal			
Total (% of internal resources)	1,812.5	7.2	8.7
Agriculture (% of total freshwater withdrawal)	98	60	80
Access to improved water source (% of total population)	..	95	88
Rural (% of rural population)	..	88	82
Urban (% of urban population)	..	99	96
Access to improved sanitation (% of total population)	..	89	55
Rural (% of rural population)	..	79	43
Urban (% of urban population)	..	94	71
Environment and health			
Acute resp. infection prevalence (% of children under five)	1.0		
Diarrhea prevalence (% of children under five)	3.2		
Under-five mortality rate (per 1,000 live births)	50	23	50
National accounting aggregates			
Gross savings (% of GNI)	..	24.0	41.7
Consumption of fixed capital (% of GNI)	11.1	12.8	10.7
Education expenditure (% of GNI)	..	4.0	2.6
Energy depletion (% of GNI)	92.6	9.8	6.6
Mineral depletion (% of GNI)	0.0	0.7	1.2
Net forest depletion (% of GNI)	..	0.0	0.2
CO_2 damage (% of GNI)	2.5	1.0	1.2
Particulate emission damage (% of GNI)	1.0	0.5	1.1
Adjusted net savings (% of GNI)	..	3.2	23.5

Uganda

| | Population (millions) | **31** | Land area (1,000 sq. km) | **197** | GDP ($ billions) | **11.8** |

	Country data	Sub-Saharan Africa group	Low-income group
GNI per capita, *World Bank Atlas* method ($)	370	951	574
Urban population (% of total)	13	36	32
Urban population growth (average annual %, 1990–2007)	4.1	4.0	3.7
Population growth (average annual %, 1990–2007)	3.2	2.6	2.4
Agriculture			
Agricultural land (% of land area)	64	44	39
Agricultural productivity (value added per worker, 2000 $)	179	287	330
Food production index (1999–2001 = 100)	109	109	112
Population density, rural (people/sq. km of arable land)	469	351	603
Forests and biodiversity			
Forest area (% of land area)	18.4	26.5	24.7
Deforestation (average annual %, 1990–2005)	2.0	0.6	0.7
Nationally protected area (% of land area)	31.9	11.3	10.8
Animal species, total known	1,375		
Animal species, threatened	121		
Higher plant species, total known	4,900		
Higher plant species, threatened	38		
GEF benefits index for biodiversity (0–100, median is 1.5)	2.8		
Energy			
GDP per unit of energy use (2005 PPP $/kg oil equivalent)	..	3.0	3.2
Energy use per capita (kg oil equivalent)	..	670	478
Energy from biomass products and waste (% of total)	..	56.3	53.8
Electric power consumption per capita (kWh)	..	531	309
Electricity generated using fossil fuel (% of total)	..	65.6	48.4
Electricity generated by hydropower (% of total)	..	18.0	38.8
Emissions and pollution			
CO_2 emissions per unit of GDP (kg/2005 PPP $)	0.09	0.49	0.39
CO_2 emissions per capita (metric tons)	0.08	0.85	0.58
CO_2 emissions growth (%, 1990–2005)	183.8	40.1	39.3
Particulate matter (urban-pop.-weighted avg., µg/cu. m)	12	53	69
Transport sector fuel consumption per capita (liters)	..	64	41
Water and sanitation			
Internal freshwater resources per capita (cu. m)	1,261	4,824	4,619
Freshwater withdrawal			
Total (% of internal resources)	..	3.2	9.4
Agriculture (% of total freshwater withdrawal)	..	87	90
Access to improved water source (% of total population)	64	58	68
Rural (% of rural population)	60	46	60
Urban (% of urban population)	90	81	84
Access to improved sanitation (% of total population)	33	31	39
Rural (% of rural population)	34	24	33
Urban (% of urban population)	29	42	54
Environment and health			
Acute resp. infection prevalence (% of children under five)	22.0		
Diarrhea prevalence (% of children under five)	19.6		
Under-five mortality rate (per 1,000 live births)	130	146	126
National accounting aggregates			
Gross savings (% of GNI)	14.0	17.4	25.4
Consumption of fixed capital (% of GNI)	8.3	11.1	9.3
Education expenditure (% of GNI)	4.0	3.6	2.6
Energy depletion (% of GNI)	0.0	11.7	9.8
Mineral depletion (% of GNI)	0.0	1.5	0.9
Net forest depletion (% of GNI)	4.6	0.5	0.8
CO_2 damage (% of GNI)	0.1	0.7	0.7
Particulate emission damage (% of GNI)	..	0.4	0.7
Adjusted net savings (% of GNI)	4.9	-5.0	5.8

Ukraine

| | Population (millions) | 47 | Land area (1,000 sq. km) | 579 | GDP ($ billions) | 141.2 |

	Country data	Europe & Central Asia group	Lower middle-income group
GNI per capita, *World Bank Atlas* method ($)	2,560	6,052	1,905
Urban population (% of total)	68	64	42
Urban population growth (average annual %, 1990-2007)	-0.5	0.2	2.9
Population growth (average annual %, 1990-2007)	-0.6	0.1	1.3
Agriculture			
Agricultural land (% of land area)	71	28	47
Agricultural productivity (value added per worker, 2000 $)	1,872	2,228	532
Food production index (1999-2001 = 100)	118	110	116
Population density, rural (people/sq. km of arable land)	47	129	511
Forests and biodiversity			
Forest area (% of land area)	16.5	38.3	25.0
Deforestation (average annual %, 1990-2005)	-0.2	0.0	0.1
Nationally protected area (% of land area)	3.3	6.1	11.0
Animal species, total known	445		
Animal species, threatened	59		
Higher plant species, total known	5,100		
Higher plant species, threatened	1		
GEF benefits index for biodiversity (0-100, median is 1.5)	0.5		
Energy			
GDP per unit of energy use (2005 PPP $/kg oil equivalent)	2.1	3.5	3.9
Energy use per capita (kg oil equivalent)	2,937	2,930	1,019
Energy from biomass products and waste (% of total)	0.4	2.2	15.2
Electric power consumption per capita (kWh)	3,400	3,835	1,269
Electricity generated using fossil fuel (% of total)	46.6	67.7	79.0
Electricity generated by hydropower (% of total)	6.7	17.4	16.3
Emissions and pollution			
CO_2 emissions per unit of GDP (kg/2005 PPP $)	1.2	0.7	0.8
CO_2 emissions per capita (metric tons)	6.9	7.0	2.8
CO_2 emissions growth (%, 1990-2005)	-52.2	-29.3	93.5
Particulate matter (urban-pop.-weighted avg., µg/cu. m)	21	27	67
Transport sector fuel consumption per capita (liters)	189	255	99
Water and sanitation			
Internal freshwater resources per capita (cu. m)	1,142	11,806	4,117
Freshwater withdrawal			
Total (% of internal resources)	70.7	7.2	8.7
Agriculture (% of total freshwater withdrawal)	52	60	80
Access to improved water source (% of total population)	97	95	88
Rural (% of rural population)	97	88	82
Urban (% of urban population)	97	99	96
Access to improved sanitation (% of total population)	93	89	55
Rural (% of rural population)	83	79	43
Urban (% of urban population)	97	94	71
Environment and health			
Acute resp. infection prevalence (% of children under five)	..		
Diarrhea prevalence (% of children under five)	..		
Under-five mortality rate (per 1,000 live births)	24	23	50
National accounting aggregates			
Gross savings (% of GNI)	23.1	24.0	41.7
Consumption of fixed capital (% of GNI)	11.2	12.8	10.7
Education expenditure (% of GNI)	4.4	4.0	2.6
Energy depletion (% of GNI)	3.0	9.8	6.6
Mineral depletion (% of GNI)	0.0	0.7	1.2
Net forest depletion (% of GNI)	0.0	0.0	0.2
CO_2 damage (% of GNI)	2.2	1.0	1.2
Particulate emission damage (% of GNI)	0.3	0.5	1.1
Adjusted net savings (% of GNI)	10.7	3.2	23.5

United Arab Emirates

Population (millions)	**4.4**	Land area (1,000 sq. km)	**83.6**	GDP ($ billions)	**163.3**

	Country data	High-income group
GNI per capita, *World Bank Atlas* method ($)	26,270	37,572
Urban population (% of total)	78	78
Urban population growth (average annual %, 1990–2007)	4.9	1.0
Population growth (average annual %, 1990–2007)	5.0	0.7
Agriculture		
Agricultural land (% of land area)	7	38
Agricultural productivity (value added per worker, 2000 $)	27,487	27,680
Food production index (1999–2001 = 100)	66	102
Population density, rural (people/sq. km of arable land)	1,430	323
Forests and biodiversity		
Forest area (% of land area)	3.7	28.8
Deforestation (average annual %, 1990–2005)	-1.6	-0.1
Nationally protected area (% of land area)	0.2	11.8
Animal species, total known	298	
Animal species, threatened	42	
Higher plant species, total known	..	
Higher plant species, threatened	..	
GEF benefits index for biodiversity (0–100, median is 1.5)	0.2	
Energy		
GDP per unit of energy use (2005 PPP $/kg oil equivalent)	4.7	6.3
Energy use per capita (kg oil equivalent)	11,036	5,416
Energy from biomass products and waste (% of total)	0.0	3.4
Electric power consumption per capita (kWh)	14,567	9,675
Electricity generated using fossil fuel (% of total)	100.0	62.0
Electricity generated by hydropower (% of total)	0.0	11.4
Emissions and pollution		
CO_2 emissions per unit of GDP (kg/2005 PPP $)	0.6	0.4
CO_2 emissions per capita (metric tons)	30.1	12.6
CO_2 emissions growth (%, 1990–2005)	126.3	19.1
Particulate matter (urban-pop.-weighted avg., µg/cu. m)	127	26
Transport sector fuel consumption per capita (liters)	2,044	1,159
Water and sanitation		
Internal freshwater resources per capita (cu. m)	34	9,313
Freshwater withdrawal		
Total (% of internal resources)	2,665.3	10.4
Agriculture (% of total freshwater withdrawal)	83	43
Access to improved water source (% of total population)	100	100
Rural (% of rural population)	100	98
Urban (% of urban population)	100	100
Access to improved sanitation (% of total population)	97	100
Rural (% of rural population)	95	99
Urban (% of urban population)	98	100
Environment and health		
Acute resp. infection prevalence (% of children under five)	6.2	
Diarrhea prevalence (% of children under five)	8.8	
Under-five mortality rate (per 1,000 live births)	8	7
National accounting aggregates		
Gross savings (% of GNI)	..	20.6
Consumption of fixed capital (% of GNI)	..	14.5
Education expenditure (% of GNI)	..	4.6
Energy depletion (% of GNI)	..	1.5
Mineral depletion (% of GNI)	..	0.2
Net forest depletion (% of GNI)	..	0.0
CO_2 damage (% of GNI)	..	0.3
Particulate emission damage (% of GNI)	..	0.3
Adjusted net savings (% of GNI)	..	8.5

United Kingdom

Population (millions)	**61**	Land area (1,000 sq. km)	**242**	GDP ($ billions)	**2,772.0**

	Country data	High-income group
GNI per capita, *World Bank Atlas* method ($)	40,660	37,572
Urban population (% of total)	90	78
Urban population growth (average annual %, 1990–2007)	0.5	1.0
Population growth (average annual %, 1990–2007)	0.4	0.7
Agriculture		
Agricultural land (% of land area)	70	38
Agricultural productivity (value added per worker, 2000 $)	27,701	27,680
Food production index (1999–2001 = 100)	98	102
Population density, rural (people/sq. km of arable land)	108	323
Forests and biodiversity		
Forest area (% of land area)	11.8	28.8
Deforestation (average annual %, 1990–2005)	-0.6	-0.1
Nationally protected area (% of land area)	19.6	11.8
Animal species, total known	660	
Animal species, threatened	51	
Higher plant species, total known	1,623	
Higher plant species, threatened	14	
GEF benefits index for biodiversity (0–100, median is 1.5)	3.5	
Energy		
GDP per unit of energy use (2005 PPP $/kg oil equivalent)	8.6	6.3
Energy use per capita (kg oil equivalent)	3,814	5,416
Energy from biomass products and waste (% of total)	1.7	3.4
Electric power consumption per capita (kWh)	6,185	9,675
Electricity generated using fossil fuel (% of total)	75.6	62.0
Electricity generated by hydropower (% of total)	1.2	11.4
Emissions and pollution		
CO_2 emissions per unit of GDP (kg/2005 PPP $)	0.3	0.4
CO_2 emissions per capita (metric tons)	9.1	12.6
CO_2 emissions growth (%, 1990–2005)	-4.0	19.1
Particulate matter (urban-pop.-weighted avg., µg/cu. m)	15	26
Transport sector fuel consumption per capita (liters)	779	1,159
Water and sanitation		
Internal freshwater resources per capita (cu. m)	2,377	9,313
Freshwater withdrawal		
Total (% of internal resources)	6.6	10.4
Agriculture (% of total freshwater withdrawal)	3	43
Access to improved water source (% of total population)	100	100
Rural (% of rural population)	100	98
Urban (% of urban population)	100	100
Access to improved sanitation (% of total population)	..	100
Rural (% of rural population)	..	99
Urban (% of urban population)	..	100
Environment and health		
Acute resp. infection prevalence (% of children under five)	..	
Diarrhea prevalence (% of children under five)	..	
Under-five mortality rate (per 1,000 live births)	6	7
National accounting aggregates		
Gross savings (% of GNI)	15.7	20.6
Consumption of fixed capital (% of GNI)	14.7	14.5
Education expenditure (% of GNI)	5.0	4.6
Energy depletion (% of GNI)	1.5	1.5
Mineral depletion (% of GNI)	0.0	0.2
Net forest depletion (% of GNI)	0.0	0.0
CO_2 damage (% of GNI)	0.2	0.3
Particulate emission damage (% of GNI)	0.0	0.3
Adjusted net savings (% of GNI)	4.3	8.5

United States

Population (millions) **302** Land area (1,000 sq. km) **9,162** GDP ($ billions) **13,751.4**

	Country data	High-income group
GNI per capita, *World Bank Atlas* method ($)	46,040	37,572
Urban population (% of total)	81	78
Urban population growth (average annual %, 1990–2007)	1.6	1.0
Population growth (average annual %, 1990–2007)	1.1	0.7
Agriculture		
Agricultural land (% of land area)	45	38
Agricultural productivity (value added per worker, 2000 $)	47,463	27,680
Food production index (1999–2001 = 100)	105	102
Population density, rural (people/sq. km of arable land)	33	323
Forests and biodiversity		
Forest area (% of land area)	33.1	28.8
Deforestation (average annual %, 1990–2005)	-0.1	-0.1
Nationally protected area (% of land area)	15.1	11.8
Animal species, total known	1,356	
Animal species, threatened	948	
Higher plant species, total known	19,473	
Higher plant species, threatened	244	
GEF benefits index for biodiversity (0–100, median is 1.5)	94.2	
Energy		
GDP per unit of energy use (2005 PPP $/kg oil equivalent)	5.5	6.3
Energy use per capita (kg oil equivalent)	7,768	5,416
Energy from biomass products and waste (% of total)	3.4	3.4
Electric power consumption per capita (kWh)	13,564	9,675
Electricity generated using fossil fuel (% of total)	71.3	62.0
Electricity generated by hydropower (% of total)	6.8	11.4
Emissions and pollution		
CO_2 emissions per unit of GDP (kg/2005 PPP $)	0.5	0.4
CO_2 emissions per capita (metric tons)	19.5	12.6
CO_2 emissions growth (%, 1990–2005)	20.4	19.1
Particulate matter (urban-pop.-weighted avg., µg/cu. m)	21	26
Transport sector fuel consumption per capita (liters)	2,016	1,159
Water and sanitation		
Internal freshwater resources per capita (cu. m)	9,283	9,313
Freshwater withdrawal		
Total (% of internal resources)	17.1	10.4
Agriculture (% of total freshwater withdrawal)	41	43
Access to improved water source (% of total population)	99	100
Rural (% of rural population)	94	98
Urban (% of urban population)	100	100
Access to improved sanitation (% of total population)	100	100
Rural (% of rural population)	99	99
Urban (% of urban population)	100	100
Environment and health		
Acute resp. infection prevalence (% of children under five)	..	
Diarrhea prevalence (% of children under five)	..	
Under-five mortality rate (per 1,000 live births)	8	7
National accounting aggregates		
Gross savings (% of GNI)	14.0	20.6
Consumption of fixed capital (% of GNI)	14.8	14.5
Education expenditure (% of GNI)	4.8	4.6
Energy depletion (% of GNI)	1.2	1.5
Mineral depletion (% of GNI)	0.1	0.2
Net forest depletion (% of GNI)	0.0	0.0
CO_2 damage (% of GNI)	0.3	0.3
Particulate emission damage (% of GNI)	0.3	0.3
Adjusted net savings (% of GNI)	2.0	8.5

Uruguay

Population (millions)	**3.3**	Land area (1,000 sq. km)	**175.0**	GDP ($ billions)	**23.1**

	Country data	Latin America & Caribbean group	Upper middle-income group
GNI per capita, *World Bank Atlas* method ($)	6,390	5,801	7,107
Urban population (% of total)	92	78	75
Urban population growth (average annual %, 1990–2007)	0.6	2.1	1.4
Population growth (average annual %, 1990–2007)	0.4	1.5	0.9
Agriculture			
Agricultural land (% of land area)	85	36	31
Agricultural productivity (value added per worker, 2000 $)	8,482	3,158	2,947
Food production index (1999–2001 = 100)	..	117	113
Population density, rural (people/sq. km of arable land)	19	232	110
Forests and biodiversity			
Forest area (% of land area)	8.6	45.4	39.3
Deforestation (average annual %, 1990–2005)	-3.5	0.5	0.2
Nationally protected area (% of land area)	0.3	16.7	10.3
Animal species, total known	532		
Animal species, threatened	71		
Higher plant species, total known	2,278		
Higher plant species, threatened	1		
GEF benefits index for biodiversity (0–100, median is 1.5)	1.2		
Energy			
GDP per unit of energy use (2005 PPP $/kg oil equivalent)	10.3	7.3	4.8
Energy use per capita (kg oil equivalent)	962	1,240	2,300
Energy from biomass products and waste (% of total)	14.9	15.9	7.0
Electric power consumption per capita (kWh)	2,042	1,808	3,242
Electricity generated using fossil fuel (% of total)	35.2	37.0	62.8
Electricity generated by hydropower (% of total)	64.0	57.3	27.6
Emissions and pollution			
CO_2 emissions per unit of GDP (kg/2005 PPP $)	0.2	0.3	0.5
CO_2 emissions per capita (metric tons)	1.7	2.5	5.5
CO_2 emissions growth (%, 1990–2005)	42.2	33.4	-8.3
Particulate matter (urban-pop.-weighted avg., µg/cu. m)	175	35	30
Transport sector fuel consumption per capita (liters)	258	295	332
Water and sanitation			
Internal freshwater resources per capita (cu. m)	17,750	23,965	16,993
Freshwater withdrawal			
Total (% of internal resources)	5.3	2.0	13.8
Agriculture (% of total freshwater withdrawal)	96	71	57
Access to improved water source (% of total population)	100	91	95
Rural (% of rural population)	100	73	83
Urban (% of urban population)	100	97	98
Access to improved sanitation (% of total population)	100	78	83
Rural (% of rural population)	99	51	64
Urban (% of urban population)	100	86	89
Environment and health			
Acute resp. infection prevalence (% of children under five)	..		
Diarrhea prevalence (% of children under five)	..		
Under-five mortality rate (per 1,000 live births)	14	26	24
National accounting aggregates			
Gross savings (% of GNI)	13.4	22.9	23.2
Consumption of fixed capital (% of GNI)	12.5	12.6	12.8
Education expenditure (% of GNI)	2.6	4.5	4.4
Energy depletion (% of GNI)	0.0	5.4	7.6
Mineral depletion (% of GNI)	0.0	1.9	1.3
Net forest depletion (% of GNI)	0.3	0.0	0.0
CO_2 damage (% of GNI)	0.2	0.3	0.6
Particulate emission damage (% of GNI)	1.9	0.4	0.4
Adjusted net savings (% of GNI)	1.2	6.7	4.9

Uzbekistan

	Population (millions)	27	Land area (1,000 sq. km)	425	GDP ($ billions)	22.3

	Country data	Europe & Central Asia group	Low-income group
GNI per capita, *World Bank Atlas* method ($)	730	6,052	574
Urban population (% of total)	37	64	32
Urban population growth (average annual %, 1990–2007)	1.1	0.2	3.7
Population growth (average annual %, 1990–2007)	1.6	0.1	2.4
Agriculture			
Agricultural land (% of land area)	66	28	39
Agricultural productivity (value added per worker, 2000 $)	1,927	2,228	330
Food production index (1999–2001 = 100)	119	110	112
Population density, rural (people/sq. km of arable land)	352	129	603
Forests and biodiversity			
Forest area (% of land area)	7.7	38.3	24.7
Deforestation (average annual %, 1990–2005)	-0.5	0.0	0.7
Nationally protected area (% of land area)	2.0	6.1	10.8
Animal species, total known	434		
Animal species, threatened	37		
Higher plant species, total known	4,800		
Higher plant species, threatened	15		
GEF benefits index for biodiversity (0–100, median is 1.5)	1.1		
Energy			
GDP per unit of energy use (2005 PPP $/kg oil equivalent)	1.2	3.5	3.2
Energy use per capita (kg oil equivalent)	1,829	2,930	478
Energy from biomass products and waste (% of total)	0.0	2.2	53.8
Electric power consumption per capita (kWh)	1,694	3,835	309
Electricity generated using fossil fuel (% of total)	87.2	67.7	48.4
Electricity generated by hydropower (% of total)	12.8	17.4	38.8
Emissions and pollution			
CO_2 emissions per unit of GDP (kg/2005 PPP $)	2.1	0.7	0.4
CO_2 emissions per capita (metric tons)	4.3	7.0	0.6
CO_2 emissions growth (%, 1990–2005)	-10.3	-29.3	39.3
Particulate matter (urban-pop.-weighted avg., µg/cu. m)	55	27	69
Transport sector fuel consumption per capita (liters)	68	255	41
Water and sanitation			
Internal freshwater resources per capita (cu. m)	608	11,806	4,619
Freshwater withdrawal			
Total (% of internal resources)	357.0	7.2	9.4
Agriculture (% of total freshwater withdrawal)	93	60	90
Access to improved water source (% of total population)	88	95	68
Rural (% of rural population)	82	88	60
Urban (% of urban population)	98	99	84
Access to improved sanitation (% of total population)	96	89	39
Rural (% of rural population)	95	79	33
Urban (% of urban population)	97	94	54
Environment and health			
Acute resp. infection prevalence (% of children under five)	0.0		
Diarrhea prevalence (% of children under five)	5.3		
Under-five mortality rate (per 1,000 live births)	41	23	126
National accounting aggregates			
Gross savings (% of GNI)	38.6	24.0	25.4
Consumption of fixed capital (% of GNI)	9.2	12.8	9.3
Education expenditure (% of GNI)	9.4	4.0	2.6
Energy depletion (% of GNI)	38.5	9.8	9.8
Mineral depletion (% of GNI)	0.0	0.7	0.9
Net forest depletion (% of GNI)	0.0	0.0	0.8
CO_2 damage (% of GNI)	5.8	1.0	0.7
Particulate emission damage (% of GNI)	0.7	0.5	0.7
Adjusted net savings (% of GNI)	-6.2	3.2	5.8

Vanuatu

	Country data	East Asia & Pacific group	Lower middle-income group
Population (thousands) **226**	Land area (1,000 sq. km)	**12**	GDP ($ millions) **452**

	Country data	East Asia & Pacific group	Lower middle-income group
GNI per capita, *World Bank Atlas* method ($)	1,840	2,182	1,905
Urban population (% of total)	24	43	42
Urban population growth (average annual %, 1990–2007)	4.0	3.5	2.9
Population growth (average annual %, 1990–2007)	2.4	1.1	1.3
Agriculture			
Agricultural land (% of land area)	12	51	47
Agricultural productivity (value added per worker, 2000 $)	1,219	458	532
Food production index (1999–2001 = 100)	110	120	116
Population density, rural (people/sq. km of arable land)	824	547	511
Forests and biodiversity			
Forest area (% of land area)	36.1	28.4	25.0
Deforestation (average annual %, 1990–2005)	0.0	–0.1	0.1
Nationally protected area (% of land area)	0.7	14.0	11.0
Animal species, total known	130		
Animal species, threatened	108		
Higher plant species, total known	870		
Higher plant species, threatened	10		
GEF benefits index for biodiversity (0–100, median is 1.5)	2.1		
Energy			
GDP per unit of energy use (2005 PPP $/kg oil equivalent)	..	3.4	3.9
Energy use per capita (kg oil equivalent)	..	1,258	1,019
Energy from biomass products and waste (% of total)	..	14.7	15.2
Electric power consumption per capita (kWh)	..	1,669	1,269
Electricity generated using fossil fuel (% of total)	..	82.0	79.0
Electricity generated by hydropower (% of total)	..	15.0	16.3
Emissions and pollution			
CO_2 emissions per unit of GDP (kg/2005 PPP $)	0.1	0.9	0.8
CO_2 emissions per capita (metric tons)	0.4	3.6	2.8
CO_2 emissions growth (%, 1990–2005)	33.3	123.4	93.5
Particulate matter (urban-pop.-weighted avg., µg/cu. m)	18	69	67
Transport sector fuel consumption per capita (liters)	..	106	99
Water and sanitation			
Internal freshwater resources per capita (cu. m)	..	4,948	4,117
Freshwater withdrawal			
Total (% of internal resources)	..	10.2	8.7
Agriculture (% of total freshwater withdrawal)	..	74	80
Access to improved water source (% of total population)	..	87	88
Rural (% of rural population)	..	81	82
Urban (% of urban population)	..	96	96
Access to improved sanitation (% of total population)	..	66	55
Rural (% of rural population)	..	59	43
Urban (% of urban population)	..	75	71
Environment and health			
Acute resp. infection prevalence (% of children under five)	..		
Diarrhea prevalence (% of children under five)	..		
Under-five mortality rate (per 1,000 live births)	34	27	50
National accounting aggregates			
Gross savings (% of GNI)	..	48.0	41.7
Consumption of fixed capital (% of GNI)	11.2	10.7	10.7
Education expenditure (% of GNI)	5.9	2.1	2.6
Energy depletion (% of GNI)	0.0	4.9	6.6
Mineral depletion (% of GNI)	0.0	1.3	1.2
Net forest depletion (% of GNI)	0.0	0.0	0.2
CO_2 damage (% of GNI)	0.2	1.3	1.2
Particulate emission damage (% of GNI)	..	1.3	1.1
Adjusted net savings (% of GNI)	..	30.6	23.5

Venezuela, RB

	Country data	Latin America & Caribbean group	Upper middle-income group
Population (millions) **27** Land area (1,000 sq. km) **882** GDP ($ billions) **228.1**			

	Country data	Latin America & Caribbean group	Upper middle-income group
GNI per capita, *World Bank Atlas* method ($)	7,550	5,801	7,107
Urban population (% of total)	93	78	75
Urban population growth (average annual %, 1990–2007)	2.5	2.1	1.4
Population growth (average annual %, 1990–2007)	1.9	1.5	0.9
Agriculture			
Agricultural land (% of land area)	25	36	31
Agricultural productivity (value added per worker, 2000 $)	6,916	3,158	2,947
Food production index (1999–2001 = 100)	95	117	113
Population density, rural (people/sq. km of arable land)	77	232	110
Forests and biodiversity			
Forest area (% of land area)	54.1	45.4	39.3
Deforestation (average annual %, 1990–2005)	0.6	0.5	0.2
Nationally protected area (% of land area)	72.3	16.7	10.3
Animal species, total known	1,745		
Animal species, threatened	190		
Higher plant species, total known	21,073		
Higher plant species, threatened	69		
GEF benefits index for biodiversity (0–100, median is 1.5)	25.3		
Energy			
GDP per unit of energy use (2005 PPP $/kg oil equivalent)	4.7	7.3	4.8
Energy use per capita (kg oil equivalent)	2,302	1,240	2,300
Energy from biomass products and waste (% of total)	0.9	15.9	7.0
Electric power consumption per capita (kWh)	3,174	1,808	3,242
Electricity generated using fossil fuel (% of total)	28.0	37.0	62.8
Electricity generated by hydropower (% of total)	72.0	57.3	27.6
Emissions and pollution			
CO_2 emissions per unit of GDP (kg/2005 PPP $)	0.6	0.3	0.5
CO_2 emissions per capita (metric tons)	5.6	2.5	5.5
CO_2 emissions growth (%, 1990–2005)	26.2	33.4	-8.3
Particulate matter (urban-pop.-weighted avg., µg/cu. m)	11	35	30
Transport sector fuel consumption per capita (liters)	609	295	332
Water and sanitation			
Internal freshwater resources per capita (cu. m)	26,287	23,965	16,993
Freshwater withdrawal			
Total (% of internal resources)	1.2	2.0	13.8
Agriculture (% of total freshwater withdrawal)	47	71	57
Access to improved water source (% of total population)	..	91	95
Rural (% of rural population)	..	73	83
Urban (% of urban population)	..	97	98
Access to improved sanitation (% of total population)	..	78	83
Rural (% of rural population)	..	51	64
Urban (% of urban population)	..	86	89
Environment and health			
Acute resp. infection prevalence (% of children under five)	9.0		
Diarrhea prevalence (% of children under five)	..		
Under-five mortality rate (per 1,000 live births)	19	26	24
National accounting aggregates			
Gross savings (% of GNI)	34.8	22.9	23.2
Consumption of fixed capital (% of GNI)	12.3	12.6	12.8
Education expenditure (% of GNI)	3.4	4.5	4.4
Energy depletion (% of GNI)	18.7	5.4	7.6
Mineral depletion (% of GNI)	0.7	1.9	1.3
Net forest depletion (% of GNI)	0.0	0.0	0.0
CO_2 damage (% of GNI)	0.7	0.3	0.6
Particulate emission damage (% of GNI)	0.0	0.4	0.4
Adjusted net savings (% of GNI)	5.9	6.7	4.9

Vietnam

	Population (millions)	**85**	Land area (1,000 sq. km)	**310**	GDP ($ billions)	**68.6**

	Country data	East Asia & Pacific group	Low-income group
GNI per capita, *World Bank Atlas* method ($)	770	2,182	574
Urban population (% of total)	27	43	32
Urban population growth (average annual %, 1990–2007)	3.2	3.5	3.7
Population growth (average annual %, 1990–2007)	1.5	1.1	2.4
Agriculture			
Agricultural land (% of land area)	31	51	39
Agricultural productivity (value added per worker, 2000 $)	313	458	330
Food production index (1999–2001 = 100)	125	120	112
Population density, rural (people/sq. km of arable land)	927	547	603
Forests and biodiversity			
Forest area (% of land area)	41.7	28.4	24.7
Deforestation (average annual %, 1990–2005)	-2.2	-0.1	0.7
Nationally protected area (% of land area)	5.2	14.0	10.8
Animal species, total known	1,116		
Animal species, threatened	261		
Higher plant species, total known	10,500		
Higher plant species, threatened	147		
GEF benefits index for biodiversity (0–100, median is 1.5)	12.1		
Energy			
GDP per unit of energy use (2005 PPP $/kg oil equivalent)	3.7	3.4	3.2
Energy use per capita (kg oil equivalent)	621	1,258	478
Energy from biomass products and waste (% of total)	46.4	14.7	53.8
Electric power consumption per capita (kWh)	598	1,669	309
Electricity generated using fossil fuel (% of total)	58.2	82.0	48.4
Electricity generated by hydropower (% of total)	41.8	15.0	38.8
Emissions and pollution			
CO_2 emissions per unit of GDP (kg/2005 PPP $)	0.6	0.9	0.4
CO_2 emissions per capita (metric tons)	1.2	3.6	0.6
CO_2 emissions growth (%, 1990–2005)	376.0	123.4	39.3
Particulate matter (urban-pop.-weighted avg., µg/cu. m)	55	69	69
Transport sector fuel consumption per capita (liters)	84	106	41
Water and sanitation			
Internal freshwater resources per capita (cu. m)	4,304	4,948	4,619
Freshwater withdrawal			
Total (% of internal resources)	19.5	10.2	9.4
Agriculture (% of total freshwater withdrawal)	68	74	90
Access to improved water source (% of total population)	92	87	68
Rural (% of rural population)	90	81	60
Urban (% of urban population)	98	96	84
Access to improved sanitation (% of total population)	65	66	39
Rural (% of rural population)	56	59	33
Urban (% of urban population)	88	75	54
Environment and health			
Acute resp. infection prevalence (% of children under five)	20.0		
Diarrhea prevalence (% of children under five)	11.3		
Under-five mortality rate (per 1,000 live births)	15	27	126
National accounting aggregates			
Gross savings (% of GNI)	35.5	48.0	25.4
Consumption of fixed capital (% of GNI)	9.4	10.7	9.3
Education expenditure (% of GNI)	2.8	2.1	2.6
Energy depletion (% of GNI)	11.6	4.9	9.8
Mineral depletion (% of GNI)	0.1	1.3	0.9
Net forest depletion (% of GNI)	0.4	0.0	0.8
CO_2 damage (% of GNI)	1.2	1.3	0.7
Particulate emission damage (% of GNI)	0.5	1.3	0.7
Adjusted net savings (% of GNI)	15.2	30.6	5.8

Virgin Islands (U.S.)

Population (thousands) **108**   Land area (sq. km)   **350** GDP ($ millions)   ..

	Country data	High-income group
GNI per capita, *World Bank Atlas* method ($)	..	37,572
Urban population (% of total)	95	78
Urban population growth (average annual %, 1990–2007)	0.7	1.0
Population growth (average annual %, 1990–2007)	0.2	0.7
Agriculture		
Agricultural land (% of land area)	17	38
Agricultural productivity (value added per worker, 2000 $)	..	27,680
Food production index (1999–2001 = 100)	99	102
Population density, rural (people/sq. km of arable land)	315	323
Forests and biodiversity		
Forest area (% of land area)	27.1	28.8
Deforestation (average annual %, 1990–2005)	1.2	-0.1
Nationally protected area (% of land area)	0.3	11.8
Animal species, total known	234	
Animal species, threatened	20	
Higher plant species, total known	..	
Higher plant species, threatened	11	
GEF benefits index for biodiversity (0–100, median is 1.5)	0.2	
Energy		
GDP per unit of energy use (2005 PPP $/kg oil equivalent)	..	6.3
Energy use per capita (kg oil equivalent)	..	5,416
Energy from biomass products and waste (% of total)	..	3.4
Electric power consumption per capita (kWh)	..	9,675
Electricity generated using fossil fuel (% of total)	..	62.0
Electricity generated by hydropower (% of total)	..	11.4
Emissions and pollution		
CO_2 emissions per unit of GDP (kg/2005 PPP $)	..	0.4
CO_2 emissions per capita (metric tons)	..	12.6
CO_2 emissions growth (%, 1990–2005)	..	19.1
Particulate matter (urban-pop.-weighted avg., µg/cu. m)	39	26
Transport sector fuel consumption per capita (liters)	..	1,159
Water and sanitation		
Internal freshwater resources per capita (cu. m)	..	9,313
Freshwater withdrawal		
Total (% of internal resources)	..	10.4
Agriculture (% of total freshwater withdrawal)	..	43
Access to improved water source (% of total population)	..	100
Rural (% of rural population)	..	98
Urban (% of urban population)	..	100
Access to improved sanitation (% of total population)	..	100
Rural (% of rural population)	..	99
Urban (% of urban population)	..	100
Environment and health		
Acute resp. infection prevalence (% of children under five)	..	
Diarrhea prevalence (% of children under five)	..	
Under-five mortality rate (per 1,000 live births)	..	7
National accounting aggregates		
Gross savings (% of GNI)	..	20.6
Consumption of fixed capital (% of GNI)	..	14.5
Education expenditure (% of GNI)	..	4.6
Energy depletion (% of GNI)	..	1.5
Mineral depletion (% of GNI)	..	0.2
Net forest depletion (% of GNI)	..	0.0
CO_2 damage (% of GNI)	..	0.3
Particulate emission damage (% of GNI)	..	0.3
Adjusted net savings (% of GNI)	..	8.5

West Bank and Gaza

| Population (millions) | **3.7** | Land area (1,000 sq. km) | **6.0** | GDP ($ billions) | **4.0** |

	Country data	Middle East & N. Africa group	Lower middle-income group
GNI per capita, *World Bank Atlas* method ($)	1,290	2,820	1,905
Urban population (% of total)	72	57	42
Urban population growth (average annual %, 1990–2007)	4.0	2.6	2.9
Population growth (average annual %, 1990–2007)	3.7	2.0	1.3
Agriculture			
Agricultural land (% of land area)	62	22	47
Agricultural productivity (value added per worker, 2000 $)	..	2,313	532
Food production index (1999–2001 = 100)	113	116	116
Population density, rural (people/sq. km of arable land)	919	665	511
Forests and biodiversity			
Forest area (% of land area)	1.5	2.4	25.0
Deforestation (average annual %, 1990–2005)	0.0	-0.4	0.1
Nationally protected area (% of land area)	..	3.6	11.0
Animal species, total known	..		
Animal species, threatened	17		
Higher plant species, total known	..		
Higher plant species, threatened	0		
GEF benefits index for biodiversity (0–100, median is 1.5)	..		
Energy			
GDP per unit of energy use (2005 PPP $/kg oil equivalent)	..	5.0	3.9
Energy use per capita (kg oil equivalent)	..	1,254	1,019
Energy from biomass products and waste (% of total)	..	1.2	15.2
Electric power consumption per capita (kWh)	..	1,418	1,269
Electricity generated using fossil fuel (% of total)	..	91.1	79.0
Electricity generated by hydropower (% of total)	..	7.4	16.3
Emissions and pollution			
CO_2 emissions per unit of GDP (kg/2005 PPP $)	..	0.6	0.8
CO_2 emissions per capita (metric tons)	..	3.7	2.8
CO_2 emissions growth (%, 1990–2005)	..	96.8	93.5
Particulate matter (urban-pop.-weighted avg., µg/cu. m)	..	72	67
Transport sector fuel consumption per capita (liters)	..	277	99
Water and sanitation			
Internal freshwater resources per capita (cu. m)	..	728	4,117
Freshwater withdrawal			
Total (% of internal resources)	..	122.3	8.7
Agriculture (% of total freshwater withdrawal)	..	86	80
Access to improved water source (% of total population)	89	89	88
Rural (% of rural population)	88	81	82
Urban (% of urban population)	90	95	96
Access to improved sanitation (% of total population)	80	77	55
Rural (% of rural population)	69	62	43
Urban (% of urban population)	84	88	71
Environment and health			
Acute resp. infection prevalence (% of children under five)	17.0		
Diarrhea prevalence (% of children under five)	..		
Under-five mortality rate (per 1,000 live births)	27	38	50
National accounting aggregates			
Gross savings (% of GNI)	..	33.3	41.7
Consumption of fixed capital (% of GNI)	..	11.3	10.7
Education expenditure (% of GNI)	..	4.7	2.6
Energy depletion (% of GNI)	..	21.3	6.6
Mineral depletion (% of GNI)	..	0.4	1.2
Net forest depletion (% of GNI)	..	0.0	0.2
CO_2 damage (% of GNI)	..	1.0	1.2
Particulate emission damage (% of GNI)	..	0.6	1.1
Adjusted net savings (% of GNI)	..	3.4	23.5

Yemen, Rep.

Population (millions)	22	Land area (1,000 sq. km)	528	GDP ($ billions)	22.5

	Country data	Middle East & N. Africa group	Low-income group
GNI per capita, *World Bank Atlas* method ($)	870	2,820	574
Urban population (% of total)	30	57	32
Urban population growth (average annual %, 1990–2007)	5.7	2.6	3.7
Population growth (average annual %, 1990–2007)	3.5	2.0	2.4
Agriculture			
Agricultural land (% of land area)	34	22	39
Agricultural productivity (value added per worker, 2000 $)	328	2,313	330
Food production index (1999–2001 = 100)	106	116	112
Population density, rural (people/sq. km of arable land)	990	665	603
Forests and biodiversity			
Forest area (% of land area)	1.0	2.4	24.7
Deforestation (average annual %, 1990–2005)	0.0	-0.4	0.7
Nationally protected area (% of land area)	0.0	3.6	10.8
Animal species, total known	459		
Animal species, threatened	107		
Higher plant species, total known	1,650		
Higher plant species, threatened	159		
GEF benefits index for biodiversity (0–100, median is 1.5)	3.2		
Energy			
GDP per unit of energy use (2005 PPP $/kg oil equivalent)	6.7	5.0	3.2
Energy use per capita (kg oil equivalent)	326	1,254	478
Energy from biomass products and waste (% of total)	1.1	1.2	53.8
Electric power consumption per capita (kWh)	190	1,418	309
Electricity generated using fossil fuel (% of total)	100.0	91.1	48.4
Electricity generated by hydropower (% of total)	0.0	7.4	38.8
Emissions and pollution			
CO_2 emissions per unit of GDP (kg/2005 PPP $)	0.4	0.6	0.4
CO_2 emissions per capita (metric tons)	1.0	3.7	0.6
CO_2 emissions growth (%, 1990–2005)	110.2	96.8	39.3
Particulate matter (urban-pop.-weighted avg., µg/cu. m)	..	72	69
Transport sector fuel consumption per capita (liters)	106	277	41
Water and sanitation			
Internal freshwater resources per capita (cu. m)	94	728	4,619
Freshwater withdrawal			
Total (% of internal resources)	161.9	122.3	9.4
Agriculture (% of total freshwater withdrawal)	90	86	90
Access to improved water source (% of total population)	66	89	68
Rural (% of rural population)	65	81	60
Urban (% of urban population)	68	95	84
Access to improved sanitation (% of total population)	46	77	39
Rural (% of rural population)	30	62	33
Urban (% of urban population)	88	88	54
Environment and health			
Acute resp. infection prevalence (% of children under five)	24.0		
Diarrhea prevalence (% of children under five)	27.5		
Under-five mortality rate (per 1,000 live births)	73	38	126
National accounting aggregates			
Gross savings (% of GNI)	..	33.3	25.4
Consumption of fixed capital (% of GNI)	10.1	11.3	9.3
Education expenditure (% of GNI)	..	4.7	2.6
Energy depletion (% of GNI)	22.5	21.3	9.8
Mineral depletion (% of GNI)	0.0	0.4	0.9
Net forest depletion (% of GNI)	0.0	0.0	0.8
CO_2 damage (% of GNI)	0.8	1.0	0.7
Particulate emission damage (% of GNI)	..	0.6	0.7
Adjusted net savings (% of GNI)	..	3.4	5.8

Zambia

Population (millions)	12	Land area (1,000 sq. km)	743	GDP ($ billions)	11.4

	Country data	Sub-Saharan Africa group	Low-income group
GNI per capita, *World Bank Atlas* method ($)	770	951	574
Urban population (% of total)	35	36	32
Urban population growth (average annual %, 1990–2007)	1.6	4.0	3.7
Population growth (average annual %, 1990–2007)	2.3	2.6	2.4
Agriculture			
Agricultural land (% of land area)	35	44	39
Agricultural productivity (value added per worker, 2000 $)	204	287	330
Food production index (1999–2001 = 100)	101	109	112
Population density, rural (people/sq. km of arable land)	142	351	603
Forests and biodiversity			
Forest area (% of land area)	57.1	26.5	24.7
Deforestation (average annual %, 1990–2005)	1.0	0.6	0.7
Nationally protected area (% of land area)	40.4	11.3	10.8
Animal species, total known	1,025		
Animal species, threatened	35		
Higher plant species, total known	4,747		
Higher plant species, threatened	8		
GEF benefits index for biodiversity (0–100, median is 1.5)	3.8		
Energy			
GDP per unit of energy use (2005 PPP $/kg oil equivalent)	2.0	3.0	3.2
Energy use per capita (kg oil equivalent)	625	670	478
Energy from biomass products and waste (% of total)	78.2	56.3	53.8
Electric power consumption per capita (kWh)	730	531	309
Electricity generated using fossil fuel (% of total)	0.6	65.6	48.4
Electricity generated by hydropower (% of total)	99.4	18.0	38.8
Emissions and pollution			
CO_2 emissions per unit of GDP (kg/2005 PPP $)	0.2	0.5	0.4
CO_2 emissions per capita (metric tons)	0.2	0.8	0.6
CO_2 emissions growth (%, 1990–2005)	-3.1	40.1	39.3
Particulate matter (urban-pop.-weighted avg., µg/cu. m)	40	53	69
Transport sector fuel consumption per capita (liters)	32	64	41
Water and sanitation			
Internal freshwater resources per capita (cu. m)	6,728	4,824	4,619
Freshwater withdrawal			
Total (% of internal resources)	2.2	3.2	9.4
Agriculture (% of total freshwater withdrawal)	76	87	90
Access to improved water source (% of total population)	58	58	68
Rural (% of rural population)	41	46	60
Urban (% of urban population)	90	81	84
Access to improved sanitation (% of total population)	52	31	39
Rural (% of rural population)	51	24	33
Urban (% of urban population)	55	42	54
Environment and health			
Acute resp. infection prevalence (% of children under five)	15.0		
Diarrhea prevalence (% of children under five)	21.2		
Under-five mortality rate (per 1,000 live births)	170	146	126
National accounting aggregates			
Gross savings (% of GNI)	26.2	17.4	25.4
Consumption of fixed capital (% of GNI)	10.7	11.1	9.3
Education expenditure (% of GNI)	2.1	3.6	2.6
Energy depletion (% of GNI)	0.1	11.7	9.8
Mineral depletion (% of GNI)	19.8	1.5	0.9
Net forest depletion (% of GNI)	0.0	0.5	0.8
CO_2 damage (% of GNI)	0.2	0.7	0.7
Particulate emission damage (% of GNI)	0.6	0.4	0.7
Adjusted net savings (% of GNI)	-3.0	-5.0	5.8

Zimbabwe

| | Population (millions) | **13** | Land area (1,000 sq. km) | **387** | GDP ($ billions) | **3.4** |

	Country data	Sub-Saharan Africa group	Low-income group
GNI per capita, *World Bank Atlas* method ($)	340	951	574
Urban population (% of total)	37	36	32
Urban population growth (average annual %, 1990–2007)	2.9	4.0	3.7
Population growth (average annual %, 1990–2007)	1.4	2.6	2.4
Agriculture			
Agricultural land (% of land area)	40	44	39
Agricultural productivity (value added per worker, 2000 $)	205	287	330
Food production index (1999–2001 = 100)	84	109	112
Population density, rural (people/sq. km of arable land)	261	351	603
Forests and biodiversity			
Forest area (% of land area)	45.3	26.5	24.7
Deforestation (average annual %, 1990–2005)	1.6	0.6	0.7
Nationally protected area (% of land area)	14.8	11.3	10.8
Animal species, total known	883		
Animal species, threatened	32		
Higher plant species, total known	4,440		
Higher plant species, threatened	17		
GEF benefits index for biodiversity (0–100, median is 1.5)	1.9		
Energy			
GDP per unit of energy use (2005 PPP $/kg oil equivalent)	..	3.0	3.2
Energy use per capita (kg oil equivalent)	724	670	478
Energy from biomass products and waste (% of total)	63.3	56.3	53.8
Electric power consumption per capita (kWh)	900	531	309
Electricity generated using fossil fuel (% of total)	43.2	65.6	48.4
Electricity generated by hydropower (% of total)	56.8	18.0	38.8
Emissions and pollution			
CO_2 emissions per unit of GDP (kg/2005 PPP $)	..	0.5	0.4
CO_2 emissions per capita (metric tons)	0.9	0.8	0.6
CO_2 emissions growth (%, 1990–2005)	–31.2	40.1	39.3
Particulate matter (urban-pop.-weighted avg., µg/cu. m)	27	53	69
Transport sector fuel consumption per capita (liters)	35	64	41
Water and sanitation			
Internal freshwater resources per capita (cu. m)	915	4,824	4,619
Freshwater withdrawal			
Total (% of internal resources)	34.3	3.2	9.4
Agriculture (% of total freshwater withdrawal)	79	87	90
Access to improved water source (% of total population)	81	58	68
Rural (% of rural population)	72	46	60
Urban (% of urban population)	98	81	84
Access to improved sanitation (% of total population)	46	31	39
Rural (% of rural population)	37	24	33
Urban (% of urban population)	63	42	54
Environment and health			
Acute resp. infection prevalence (% of children under five)	16.0		
Diarrhea prevalence (% of children under five)	13.9		
Under-five mortality rate (per 1,000 live births)	90	146	126
National accounting aggregates			
Gross savings (% of GNI)	..	17.4	25.4
Consumption of fixed capital (% of GNI)	..	11.1	9.3
Education expenditure (% of GNI)	..	3.6	2.6
Energy depletion (% of GNI)	..	11.7	9.8
Mineral depletion (% of GNI)	..	1.5	0.9
Net forest depletion (% of GNI)	..	0.5	0.8
CO_2 damage (% of GNI)	..	0.7	0.7
Particulate emission damage (% of GNI)	..	0.4	0.7
Adjusted net savings (% of GNI)	..	–5.0	5.8

Glossary

Access to improved sanitation is the percentage of population with adequate access to excreta disposal facilities (private or shared, but not public) that can effectively prevent human, animal, and insect contact with excreta. Improved facilities range from simple but protected pit latrines to flush toilets with a sewerage connection. To be effective, facilities must be correctly constructed and properly maintained. (World Health Organization; data are for 2006)

Access to improved water source is the percentage of the population with reasonable access to an adequate amount of water from an improved source, such as piped water into a dwelling, plot, or yard; public tap or standpipe; tubewell or borehole; protected dug well or spring; or rainwater collection. Unimproved sources include an unprotected dug well or spring, cart with small tank or drum, bottled water, and tanker trucks. Reasonable access to an adequate amount means the availability of at least 20 liters a person a day from a source within 1 kilometer of the dwelling. (World Health Organization; data are for 2006)

Acute respiratory infection prevalence is the percentage of children under age five with acute respiratory infection in the two weeks prior to the survey. (United Nations Children's Fund; data are for the most recent year available during 1998–2005)

Adjusted net savings equal gross savings minus consumption of fixed capital, plus education expenditures, minus energy depletion, mineral depletion, net forest depletion, and particulate emission and carbon dioxide damage. (World Bank; data are for 2007)

Agricultural land is arable land, land under permanent crops, and permanent pastures. Arable land includes land defined by the Food and Agriculture Organization of the United Nations as land under temporary crops (double-cropped areas are counted once), temporary meadows for mowing or for pasture, land under market or kitchen gardens, and land temporarily fallow. Land abandoned as a result of shifting cultivation is excluded. Land under permanent crops is land cultivated with crops that occupy the land for long periods and need not be replanted after each harvest, such as cocoa, coffee, and rubber. This category includes land under flowering shrubs, fruit trees, nut trees, and vines but excludes land under trees grown for wood or timber. Permanent pasture is land used for five or more years for forage, including natural and cultivated crops. (Food and Agriculture Organization; data are for 2005)

Agricultural productivity is the ratio of agricultural value added, measured in 2000 U.S. dollars, to the number of workers in agriculture. Agricultural productivity is measured by value added per unit of input. Agricultural value added includes that from forestry and fishing. Thus interpretations of land productivity should be made with caution. (See World Bank 2009 for details; data are for 2003–05)

Animal species, threatened, include the number of birds and mammal species classified by the World Conservation Union as endangered, vulnerable, rare, indeterminate, out of danger, or insufficiently known. (World Conservation Monitoring Centre and *World Conservation Union; data are for 2008)

Glossary

Animal species, total known, are mammals (excluding whales and porpoises) and birds included within a country's breeding or wintering ranges. (World Conservation Monitoring Centre and World Conservation Union; data are for 2004)

Carbon dioxide (CO_2) damage is estimated at $20 per ton of carbon (the unit damage in 1995 U.S. dollars) times the number of tons of carbon emitted. (World Bank estimates; data are for 2007)

Carbon dioxide (CO_2) emissions growth is the cumulative percentage change in emissions stemming from the burning of fossil fuels and the manufacture of cement. Emissions include carbon dioxide produced during consumption of solid, liquid, and gas fuels and gas flaring. (Carbon Dioxide Information Analysis Center; data are for 1990–2005)

Carbon dioxide (CO_2) emissions per capita are carbon dioxide emissions divided by midyear population. (Carbon Dioxide Information Analysis Center, World Bank, and United Nations; data are for 2005)

Carbon dioxide (CO_2) emissions per unit of GDP are carbon dioxide emissions in kilograms per unit of GDP in 2005 purchasing power parity (PPP) terms. PPP GDP is gross domestic product converted to international dollars using PPP rates. An international dollar has the same purchasing power over GDP that a U.S. dollar has in the United States. (Carbon Dioxide Information Analysis Center and World Bank; data are for 2005)

Consumption of fixed capital is the replacement value of capital used up in the process of production. (United Nations; data are extrapolated to 2006 from the most recent year available)

Deforestation is the permanent conversion of natural forest area to other uses, including shifting cultivation, permanent agriculture, ranching, settlements, and infrastructure development. Deforested areas do not include areas logged but intended for regeneration or areas degraded by fuelwood gathering, acid precipitation, or forest fires. Negative numbers indicate an increase in forest areas. (Food and Agriculture Organization; data are for 1990–2005)

Diarrhea prevalence is the percentage of children under age five who had diarrhea in the two weeks prior to the survey. (United Nations Children's Fund; data are for the most recent year available during 1998–2005)

Education expenditure is public current operating expenditures in education, including wages and salaries and excluding capital investments in buildings and equipment. (United Nations; data are extrapolated to 2007 from the most recent year available)

Electricity generated using fossil fuel is use of coal, oil, and gas as a percentage of total inputs to the generation of electricity. (International Energy Agency; data are for 2006)

Electricity generated by hydropower is use of hydropower as a percentage of total inputs to the generation of electricity. (International Energy Agency; data are for 2006)

Electric power consumption per capita is the production of power plants and combined heat and power plants, minus transmission, distribution, and transformation losses and own use by heat and power plants plus imports minus exports divided by midyear population. (International Energy Agency; data are for 2006)

Energy depletion is the ratio of the value of the stock of energy resources to the remaining reserve lifetime (capped at 25 years). It covers crude oil, natural gas, and coal. (See World Bank 2009 for details; estimates are based on sources and methods in Kunte and others 1998; data are for 2007.)

Energy from biomass products and waste is energy from solid biomass, liquid biomass, biogas, industrial waste, and municipal waste as a percentage of total energy use. (International Energy Agency; data are for 2006)

Energy use per capita refers to apparent consumption, which is equal to indigenous production plus imports and stock changes, minus exports and fuels supplied to ships and aircraft engaged in international transport. (International Energy Agency; data are for 2006)

Food production index indicates the relative level of net food production compared with the base period 1999–2001. It covers food crops that are considered edible and that contain nutrients. Coffee and tea are excluded because, although edible, they have no nutritive value (See the Food and Agriculture Organization's *Production Yearbook* for details; data are for 2005)

Forest area is land under natural or planted stands of trees, whether productive or not. (Food and Agriculture Organization; data are for 2005)

Freshwater withdrawal, agriculture, is withdrawals for irrigation and livestock production as a percentage of total freshwater withdrawal. (World Resources Institute; data are for various years; for details see *World Development Indicators 2009, Primary data documentation*.)

Freshwater withdrawal, total, is total water withdrawal, excluding evaporation losses from storage basins and including water from desalination plants in countries where they are a significant source. Withdrawals can exceed 100 percent of internal renewable resources because river flows from other countries are not included, because extraction from nonrenewable aquifers or desalination plants is considerable, or because there is significant water reuse. (Food and Agriculture Organization and World Resources Institute; data are for various years; for details see *World Development Indicators 2009, Primary data documentation*.)

GDP is gross domestic product and measures the total output of goods and services for final use occurring within the domestic territory of a given country, regardless of the allocation to domestic and foreign claims. GDP at purchaser values (market prices) is the sum of gross value added by all resident and nonresident producers in the economy plus any taxes and minus any subsidies not included in the value of the products. It is calculated without deductions for depreciation of fabricated assets or for depletion and degradation of natural resources. (World Bank, Organization for Economic Co-operation and Development, and United Nations; data are for 2007)

Glossary

GDP per unit of energy use is 2006 gross domestic product (GDP) in purchasing power parity (PPP) terms per kilogram of oil equivalent of energy use. PPP GDP is GDP converted to international dollars using PPP rates. An international dollar has the same purchasing power over GDP that a U.S. dollar has in the United States. (International Energy Agency and World Bank; data are for 2006)

GEF benefits index for biodiversity is a composite index of relative biodiversity potential for each country developed by the Global Environment Facility, based on the species represented in each country, their threat status, and the diversity of habitat types in each country. The index shown in the tables has been normalized so that values run from 0 (no biodiversity potential) to 100 (maximum biodiversity potential) (World Bank; estimates are for 2008)

GNI per capita is gross national income (GNI) divided by midyear population. GNI is gross domestic product plus net receipts of primary income (employee compensation and property income) from abroad. GNI per capita is in current U.S. dollars, converted using the *World Bank Atlas* method (see *World Development Indicators 2008, Statistical methods*). (World Bank, Organization for Economic Co-operation and Development, and United Nations; data are for 2007)

Gross savings are the difference between gross national income and public and private consumption plus net current transfers. (World Bank, Organization for Economic Co-operation and Development, and United Nations; data are for 2007)

Higher plant species, threatened, are the number of species classified by the World Conservation Union as endangered, vulnerable, rare, indeterminate, out of danger, or insufficiently known. (World Conservation Monitoring Centre and World Conservation Union; data are for 2008)

Higher plant species, total known, are native vascular plant species. (World Conservation Monitoring Centre and World Conservation Union; data are for 2004)

Internal freshwater resources per capita are internal renewable resources, which include flows of rivers and groundwater from rainfall in the country but excludes river flows from other countries, divided by midyear population. (Refers to data reported to the Food and Agriculture Organization as of 2007)

Land area is a country's total land area, excluding area under inland water bodies, national claims to continental shelf, and exclusive economic zones. In most cases the definition of inland water bodies includes major rivers and lakes. (Food and Agriculture Organization; data are for 2007)

Mineral depletion is the ratio of the value of the stock of mineral resources to the remaining reserve lifetime (capped at 25 years). It covers bauxite, copper, iron, lead, nickel, phosphate, tin, gold, silver, and zinc. (See World Bank 2009 for details; estimates are based on sources and methods in Kunte and others 1998; data are for 2007).

Nationally protected area is totally or partially protected areas of at least 1,000 hectares that are designated as national parks, natural monuments, nature reserves or wildlife sanctuaries; protected landscapes and seascapes; and scientific reserves. It includes World Conservation Union–protected area categories I–VI. (World Conservation Monitoring Centre; data are for the most recent year available)

Net forest depletion is the product of unit resource rents and the excess of roundwood harvest over natural growth. If growth exceeds harvest, this figure is zero. (Food and Agriculture Organization and World Bank estimates of natural growth; data are for 2007)

Particulate emission damage is calculated as the willingness to pay to reduce the risk of illness and death attributable to particulate emissions. (World Bank estimates; data are for 2006)

Particulate matter is fine suspended particulates of less than 10 microns in diameter that are capable of penetrating deep into the respiratory tract and causing damage. The indicator is the population-weighted average of all cities in the country with a population greater than 100,000. (World Bank estimates; data are for 2006)

Population includes all residents who are present regardless of legal status or citizenship except for refugees not permanently settled in the country of asylum, who are generally considered part of the population of their country of origin. (United Nations; data are midyear estimates for 2007)

Population density, rural, is rural population divided by arable land area. Rural population is estimated as the difference between the total population and urban population. (See *urban population*; data are for 2007)

Population growth is the exponential change in population for the period indicated. (United Nations; data are for 1990–2007)

Transport sector fuel consumption is the average volume of fuel consumed per capita in the transport sector (International Road Federation 2008; data are for 2006).

Under-five mortality rate is the probability that a newborn baby will die before reaching age five if subject to current age-specific mortality rates. (United Nations and United Nations Children's Fund; data are for 2005)

Urban population is the share of the midyear population living in areas defined as urban in each country (United Nations; data are for 2007)

Urban population growth is the exponential change in urban population for the period indicated. (United Nations; data are for 1990–2007)

References

CIESIN (Center for International Earth Science Information Network). 2007. "Low Elevation Coastal Zone (LECZ) Urban-Rural Estimates." Global Rural-Urban Mapping Project, Alpha Version. Columbia University, Socioeconomic Data and Applications Center, Palisades, N.Y. [http://sedac.ciesin.columbia.edu/gpw/lecz].

City Mayors. 2007. "The Largest Cities in the World by Land Area, Population and Density." City Mayors, London. [www.citymayors.com/statistics/largest-cities-area-125.html].

IEA (International Energy Agency). 2008. *World Energy Outlook 2008*. Paris: International Energy Agency.

IPCC (Intergovernmental Panel on Climate Change). 2007. *Climate Change 2007: The Physical Science Basis. Contribution of Working Group I to the Fourth Assessment Report of the Intergovernmental Panel on Climate Change.* Cambridge, U.K.: Cambridge University Press.

International Road Federation. 2008. *World Road Statistics 2008*. Geneva: International Road Federation.

Kenworthy, J., and F. Laube. 2001. The Millennium Cities Database for Sustainable Transport. CD-ROM database. International Union of Public Transport, Brussels, and Institute for Sustainability and Technology Policy, Murdoch University, Perth, Australia.

Kunte, Arundhati, Kirk Hamilton, John Dixon, and Michael Clemens. 1998. "Estimating National Wealth: Methodology and Results." Environmental Economics Series 57. World Bank, Environment Department, Washington, D.C.

World Bank. 2009. *World Development Indicators 2009*. Washington, D.C.: World Bank.